Vaughan **Williams**

About the author

Keith Alldritt was educated at Wolverhampton Grammar School and St Catharine's College, Cambridge. He has taught at universities in Europe and North America. His books include studies of Winston Churchill, Franklin Delano Roosevelt, George Orwell, W.B. Yeats, D.H. Lawrence and the music of T.S. Eliot's Four Quartets. He is a Fellow of the Royal Society of Literature.

Vaughan **Williams**
Composer, Radical, Patriot – a Biography

Keith Alldritt

ROBERT HALE

First published in 2015 by
Robert Hale, an imprint of
The Crowood Press Ltd,
Ramsbury, Marlborough
Wiltshire SN8 2HR

www.crowood.com

Paperback edition 2019

British Library Cataloguing-in-Publication Data
A catalogue record for this book is available from the
British Library.

ISBN 978 0 7198 3001 3

Typeset by Chapter One Book Production, Knebworth

Printed and bound in India by Parksons Graphics

For Janet
With love

CONTENTS

Preface   9
Acknowledgements   11

THE YOUNG VICTORIAN
One   Childhood and Schooldays   15
Two   Kensington   36
Three   Cambridge   45
Four   London, Love and Marriage 1895–7   61
Five   Berlin and After   80
Six   Barton Street, Westminster   91
Seven   Cheyne Walk, Chelsea   113

THE EDWARDIAN ACHIEVER
Eight   The First Two Symphonies 1910–14   135

THE SOLDIER AND EX-SERVICEMAN
Nine   World War One   161
Ten   In Lodgings   170
Eleven   A Career Re-established   184
Twelve   Pondering Apocalypse   196
Thirteen   White Gates   210

EMINENCE
Fourteen   The Gathering Storm   233
Fifteen   A Love Affair   243
Sixteen   A Threesome   274

Seventeen   In The Cold War   301
Eighteen   The Widower   314
Nineteen   10 Hanover Terrace   325

HAPPILY EVER AFTER
Twenty   Excursions   341
Twenty-One   The Final Year   357
Twenty-Two   In Memoriam   367

Endnotes   369
Select Bibliography   378
Index   379

Preface

This telling of the life of the composer Ralph Vaughan Williams is only glancingly musicological. Earlier books and articles in specialist magazines have discussed and analysed in detail his large number of compositions. This biography portrays the man in a much larger historical, social and political context.

In this respect it differs from the two indispensable biographies instigated by Vaughan Williams himself at the end of his life: that by his friend Michael Kennedy which offers an exhaustive account of the development of his music, and that by his widow Ursula, who supplied, as much as was feasible at the time of her writing in the 1960s, a detailed and illuminating account of his personal life. Vaughan Williams was a highly creative, productive composer whose life centred on his music. But he was also very much involved with the momentous events that took place in the world during his long lifetime. His art also reveals the influence of the economic depression that followed the First World War, in which he served, and the austerity and Cold War that lasted long after the end of the Second World War, in which he made every possible contribution to help his country's cause. He was unusual among composers in that he was an active campaigning member of a political movement.

From our present perspective it is also now appropriate, in a way that was not possible for previous biographers, to describe events in the composer's personal life and their impact on his music. Of central importance in his creative development was his first marriage, which lasted well over half a century. Also important, but hitherto less fully described, was the extra-marital affair into which he entered at the beginning of the last two decades of his life and the consequent second marriage that so vitalized the conclusion of his career. A great part of his output, including five of his nine symphonies, belongs to his last, highly eventful twenty years.

9

This was a period which also saw a widening of the range of Vaughan Williams's music. He had long disparaged the Modernist idiom and often mocked composers such as Stravinsky. But from the Piano Concerto and Symphony No. 4 onwards he became affected by this mode of expression, as he had experiences of being socially, politically and personally destabilized.

The title of this book salutes a familiar and, to a degree justified, image of Vaughan Williams. But the story this biography tells is also one of a more troubled life than the five words of the title might suggest. Vaughan Williams was a major artist. (The term 'genius' is appropriate.) And an important aspect of his art is its great range. It extends far beyond the spirituality of an English pastoral tradition and aligns him in terms of subject matter with writers such as Samuel Beckett and T.S. Eliot. His early music recalls the rural England of George Borrow, Thomas Hardy and A.E. Housman, whereas his later compositions, especially Symphony No. 6, derive from upheavals in his life and the life of his society and are, consequently, more in tune with the sensibilities of those two Modernist writers. One of Vaughan Williams's distinctions is that he musicalized a very long historical tract of English experiences and feeling.

This biography portrays a more troubled life than has previously been described. It shows times of intense happiness but also suffering, self-doubt and bleakness that have hitherto been understated. It also shows how another important aspect of Vaughan Williams's genius was his particular mode, in his life and in his art, of triumphing over them.

Acknowledgements

In writing this book I have been helped by a number of people. I am most grateful to the staff of the Music Division of the British Library for their assistance. Nicolas Bell provided skilful help with the illustrations and Christopher Scobie was expert in making available the countless Vaughan Williams items in the British Library. I must also thank the staff at the Surrey Performing Arts Library at Dorking where a large Vaughan Williams collection is kept.

Especial thanks are due to Hugh Cobbe and to the Vaughan Williams Trust for granting permission to reproduce written and visual materials.

In the early stages of the writing I benefited greatly from the enthusiasm and knowledge of Renee Stewart. Stephen Connock readily answered questions I put to him and Richard Thorpe offered some helpful insights. I have also been assisted by Margaret and Richard Eckersley, Frances Rhodes and John Pullinger. Claudia Towle gave professional help with the illustrations. I am very grateful to my editor, Lavinia Porter, for her patience and dedication.

But my greatest debt by far is to the dedicatee of this book, Janet Tennant. She has helped at every stage of the writing and has typed each of the drafts. I have also benefited greatly from her extensive and detailed research into the life and writings of Ursula Vaughan Williams. Generously, she has always been ready to share her knowledge with me. Her perceptions have greatly improved my understanding of Vaughan Williams. Her involvement has been very much that of a co-author.

All plate images supplied by the author.

THE YOUNG VICTORIAN

Chapter One

CHILDHOOD AND SCHOOLDAYS

The country vicarage in which Ralph Vaughan Williams was born on 12 October 1872 is a large and imposing one. It brings to mind the substantial residences of the well-to-do clergymen in the novels of Jane Austen. The birthplace stands in spacious grounds in the centre of the Cotswold village of Down Ampney, close to the parish church of All Saints which dates from the thirteenth century. This was the well-endowed living into which the composer's father, Arthur Vaughan Williams, had been inducted in the spring of 1868, not quite five years before Ralph was born.

The vicar came from a wealthy family that had done well – and very rapidly so – in the law in London. The family had obscure origins in South Wales. Ralph's great-grandfather had moved from Carmarthen to London at the end of the eighteenth century. Here he had built a career as a lawyer and became a sergeant-at-law, a member of an ancient order of advocates at the English Bar. He and his Staffordshire wife had seven children and his second son, Edward (the composer's grandfather), also went into the law. Edward was even more successful than his father. He was educated at Winchester College, then at Westminster School, entered Trinity College, Cambridge, as a scholar and, highly expert in jurisprudence, was soon called to the Bar. In 1826 Edward married well. His bride was Jane Margaret Bagot, a niece of the first Baron Bagot of Bagot's Bromley in Staffordshire. Through Grandma Jane, Ralph could trace his ancestry back to the Norman nobility which had accompanied William the Conqueror in the invasion of England in 1066.

15

The Bagot baronetcy continues to this day, the ancestral home of the family being at Blithfield Hall in Staffordshire. Over the generations the family has been active, though not at the very highest levels, in scholarship, politics and the church. A fourteenth-century Bagot is a character in Shakespeare's *Richard II*. He is a morally questionable figure who denounces his fellow nobleman, the Duke Aumerle, to the usurping King Henry IV. And he voices sentiments that would have grated on the democratic sensibilities of his descendant of some six centuries later. Of the common people, Shakespeare's Sir William Bagot observes:

> And that's the wavering commons; for their love
> Lies in their purses, and whoso empties them
> By so much fills their heart with deadly hate.[1]

After their marriage, Jane Bagot and Edward Vaughan Williams took up residence in a grand house at 24 Queen Anne's Gate, just to the south of Buckingham Palace. Ralph was to remember visiting them as a child. His grandfather became the very first Judge of Common Pleas and received a knighthood from Queen Victoria in 1847.

Sir Edward and Lady Jane Vaughan Williams decided to have an estate in the country. They chose to rent Tanhurst, a large mansion surrounded by many acres on the richly wooded slopes of Leith Hill in Surrey. Dating from the late eighteenth century, the house had been the home of a famous law reformer, Sir Samuel Romilly, during the Regency. It was a place for riding, shooting, planting, botanizing and all the pleasures of country life. Plenty to occupy the couple's family of six sons and daughters.

Two of the sons continued the family involvement in the law, Roland Vaughan Williams becoming a Lord Justice of Appeal. The second and third sons, Edward and Arthur, had careers in the church. Edward became rector of North Tedworth in Wiltshire, a living in the gift of Baron Kelk, a London businessman and property developer in the circle of his father Edward Vaughan Williams. And Arthur, the father of Ralph, was given the living of Down Ampney in Gloucestershire. Arthur, who had been an undergraduate at Christ Church in Oxford, took this position after serving briefly as curate in the poet George Herbert's parish of Bemerton, near Salisbury, then at Halsall near Ormskirk in Lancashire, and then at Alverstoke, another well-to-do parish on the coast in Hampshire.

There was a story, much repeated in the Vaughan Williams family that when Arthur's father was asked why he had selected Tanhurst to be the family's country house, he had given as his reason the fact that the Leith Hill area in Surrey was 'full of charming young heiresses'. There was clearly an element of truth in this seemingly light-hearted comment made by the head of a family marked recently by such rapid upward mobility. For indeed, if Sir Edward did have hopes of fortune-hunting in Surrey, his calculations proved to be extremely effective. The estate immediately adjacent to Tanhurst was Leith Hill Place, owned since 1847 by the extremely wealthy Wedgwood family. Their daughter Margaret would become the wife of the young Reverend Arthur Vaughan Williams.

∼∼∼

The history of the Wedgwood family was very much intertwined with that of another dynasty that came to prominence in the Industrial Revolution and its aftermath, the Darwins. And the wife of Josiah Wedgwood III who resided at Leith Hill Place at the time of the arrival of the Vaughan Williamses next door was Caroline Darwin, sister of the author of *On The Origin Of Species*.

The relationship between the Darwin and Wedgwood families dated back to well over a century before, to the 1760s, when Josiah Wedgwood, the great potter, industrialist, canal promoter and general entrepreneur, developed a very close friendship with Erasmus Darwin, physician, poet, philosopher, zoologist, naturalist and free thinker. These two greatly gifted men lived not far from each other in Staffordshire, Josiah in Burslem close to his successful pottery and Erasmus in the ancient cathedral city of Lichfield. The doctor had disturbed the quiet of the Close there by building a fine house (now the Darwin Museum) on the moat which surrounded the cathedral and which had been much fought over in the Civil War. In this house, to the discomfort of the local clergy, he had dissected corpses which he purchased from the hangman after executions at nearby No-Man's Heath. And here he had written his books which included the long poem *The Loves of the Plants* – considered very risqué at the time – and *Zoonomia*, which pre-figured the writings on evolution of his grandson Charles Darwin. Erasmus was a peripatetic doctor who travelled all over the Midlands to attend his patients. A memorable moment that profoundly consolidated his friendship with Josiah Wedgwood came when the potter was compelled to undergo the amputation of a septic leg. Darwin assisted at the procedure, which was conducted without anaesthetic.

Around the two friends there gathered other progressive people of that place and time. They formed something of a club which was to become known as the Lunar Society. This included, at different times, Richard Edgworth, father of the novelist Maria Edgworth, the industrialists Matthew Boulton and James Watt, and the chemist Joseph Priestley. An important connection in the American colonies was the philosopher Benjamin Franklin, whom Josiah had known well during the American's years in England. Another contact was the highly influential French philosopher Jean Jacques Rousseau, some of whose essays were first published in Lichfield and who botanized with Erasmus Darwin in rural Staffordshire. Meetings of the Lunar Society were sometimes hosted by the poetess Anna Seward, known as The Swan of Lichfield. She resided in the imposing Bishop's Palace in the Close and attempted to maintain a *salon* there in the grand French style. Unfortunately the tone could be lowered by the entry of that other citizen of Lichfield, the loud, lumbering and opinionated Tory, Dr Samuel Johnson. Portraits of some of the members of the Lunar Society have come down to us in pictures painted by the great artist of the day in that area of the Midlands, Joseph Wright of Derby.

Children of members of the Lunar Society became close. They shared their parents' belief in radical, even revolutionary, politics. In 1792, as the French Revolution proceeded on its erratic, violent course, Josiah's son Tom went to Paris with James Watt's son (whom he described as 'a furious democrat') to show solidarity with the revolutionaries in the celebrations of the third anniversary of the storming of the Bastille. Two years later the inter-family marriages began when Josiah's daughter Sukey and Erasmus's son Robert announced their engagement. The two fathers, close friends for some thirty years now, were utterly delighted. This was to be the first of several Darwin–Wedgwood marriages during the course of the nineteenth century, including that of Ralph's maternal grandparents Josiah Wedgwood III and Caroline Darwin.

By 1847 Josiah Wedgwood III had sold his considerable share of the large Wedgwood enterprise based in the Potteries of North Staffordshire and bought Leith Hill Place in Surrey in order to live the life of a country gentleman. The days of the Wedgwood family's heroic industrial achievement were over. Josiah Wedgwood III had become a *rentier*, living on his large investments. Ralph once conceded that he had been born with a small silver spoon in his mouth. The Wedgwood inheritance helped to pay for the spoon and to support him throughout his life and, most importantly, through those long years of his early adulthood when he had to struggle to establish himself as a musician and a composer.

Josiah Wedgwood III had three daughters: Sophy, Lucy and Margaret. Margaret, who was Ralph's mother, was to live to be ninety-five and was an important figure in Ralph's life until his mid-sixties, despite what one observer described as Margaret's 'deeply evangelical austerity against which Ralph revolted with passion. Margaret and her sisters were not considered beautiful girls.'[2]

∿

Ralph had very few memories of his life at the vicarage at Down Ampney. In February 1875, when he was some two and a half years old, his father died and Ralph's mother was compelled to give up the parsonage. She returned to her parents' forbidding looking mansion at Leith Hill Place with her three children: Ralph; Hervey, who was four years Ralph's senior and always very conscious of his status as the older brother; and their sister Meggie, who was just under two years older than Ralph. One of the Darwin relatives visited Leith Hill Place shortly after the widow's return home and reported in a letter that Margaret, wearing the mourning clothes customary at that time, 'looks very thin and speaks in a low voice as if she was weak, but was quite calm and joined in everything; she looks very pretty in her widow's cap. Hervey was playing about all the time and the other two came after. Little Ralph has regular features.'[3]

Leith Hill Place with its dozen or so servants was a household controlled by women. At its head was Caroline Wedgwood, Ralph's recently widowed maternal grandmother, an elder sister and first teacher of the author of *On The Origin Of Species*. Although Caroline had been seriously ill around the time her grandchildren had taken refuge at Leith Hill, she resolutely set about teaching Ralph to read. She used a book recommended by their ancestor, Erasmus Darwin, in his *Plan for the Conduct of Female Education in Boarding Schools*, a prospectus employed in the girls' school in Ashbourne in Derbyshire which Erasmus had set up to provide a home and an income for his two illegitimate daughters. Caroline also used the same book, *Cobwebs to Catch Flies* (first published in 1837, when Victoria became Queen) to teach her brother Charles Darwin to read. It was one of many links between Ralph and his distinguished ancestor.

Also living at the large, austere Surrey house was Ralph's Aunt Sophy, his mother's sister, who was never to marry. She was quick to see Ralph's strong musical bent and gave him his first music lessons. By the time he was six he had composed his first piano piece which, as he later remembered, was 'four bars long, called, heaven knows why, "The Robin's nest".[4] He went on to write more small pieces which were 'respectfully dedicated to Miss Sophy Wedgewood [sic]'.[5] Aunt Sophy maintained the Wedgwood tradition of strenuous frugality. Newspapers torn into neat squares furnished the lavatories at Leith Hill Place. Although the evangelical women who brought him up told him that the torn papers 'were not there to read', his early knowledge of crime, politics and society came from his surreptitious reading of them.[6]

Aunt Sophy was somewhat vague and beginning to show the eccentricities that would become more pronounced as she grew older. Visitors to Leith Hill Place found her rather sad and lethargic. When Charles Darwin and his wife Emma came to visit his sister's family, Emma commented in a letter, 'Poor Sophy strikes one anew every time one sees her as utterly dead and quite as much dead to mother and sisters as to the outsiders.'[7] Emma was also dismayed by the interior of the Wedgwood mansion. She 'felt the house with that long dark passage and no carpet so depressing and wondered how they would ever get thro' the winter. The children keep them alive'.[8] Ralph later confirmed that in that time, before the coming of electric light, the dark passageways in the big house were 'a place of terror'.[9] Years later the son of the gardener at Leith Hill Place recalled that 'Their mother was kind but rather severe. She never forgot to punish when she thought it necessary. The two forms of punishment being to bed immediately or to walk up and down the cold, rather dark passage between the kitchen and front hall with a pile of books on their heads.'[10]

Nevertheless Ralph seems to have been happy enough as a child. He and his sister Meggie were companionable, enjoyed taking care of their pet dog Coffee, and shared the many books which their nursery contained. These included works by Thackeray, Ruskin and Charles Lamb. There were also fairy stories in versions by Andrew Lang and the Brothers Grimm. In wintertime after nursery tea, their mother Margaret would read them adventure stories by Henty and Ballantyne and more serious works by Scott and Shakespeare. As very much a Christian woman, Mrs Vaughan Williams felt it necessary to omit certain words as she read. Ralph soon learned to steal silently into a position from which he could read over her shoulder and ponder on what had been expurgated. This introduction to Shakespeare began a literary passion that stayed with Ralph throughout his life.

In the nursery he had a toy theatre for which he wrote playlets and operas. The performers were a set of china dogs known as 'The Obligers'. The largest of them was called the Judge and represented the distant, somewhat intimidating figure of Judge Vaughan Williams, now the very wealthy representative of the paternal side of Ralph's family who lived in a grand house in Westminster. Along with the toy theatre presentations Ralph also performed piano duets with Hervey and Meggie. There were also antiquated books to hand in the house, 'funny old volumes containing choruses from *Messiah* and *Israel* which I loved and arias from *Don Giovanni* and the overture to *Figaro*, which we used to play *Andante Sostenuto!*'[11] When Ralph and Meggie first heard concert performances of these favourites of theirs they were taken aback by the speed at which they were played.

An important figure in the well-staffed household was Sarah Wager who was in charge of the nursery. She was deeply interested in politics. A keen radical and a passionate supporter of the radical wing of the Liberal Party, she was overjoyed when, in the same year Ralph had his eighth birthday, William Gladstone and his Liberal Party defeated Benjamin Disraeli and the Tories in the General Election. It seems likely that Ralph's Liberal views and his unceasing concern with the condition of his country derived at least in part from his childhood conversations with Sarah Wager. But Liberalism pervaded his family. His cousin Lady Diana Montgomery Massingberd recalled that in 1881 the two of them had sung together a campaign song which she had composed to support a Mr Davey, the Liberal candidate in Bournemouth and to denigrate a Mr Moss, his Conservative opponent. What she remembered of her elegant words ran:

Hold the fort for Davey's coming
Moss is in the sea;
Up to his neck in rhubarb pudding,
That's the place for he.

The lines were sung to the tune of the famous Victorian hymn, Sankey and Moody's 'Hold the Fort'. Nearly seventy years later, at one of their very last meetings, Ralph could still, Diana recalled, remember perfectly these words, and sing them.[12]

21

Sarah Wager may have been a strident radical but in some respects she was extremely conservative. She insisted on proper table manners, obedience and honesty. Perhaps this was one of the origins of that commitment to ethical conduct which everyone remarked on in Ralph in later years. A very early instance of this occurred when the family at Leith Hill went to visit the famous Charles Darwin and his wife at their house at Downe in Kent. After their return to Surrey Margaret received a letter from her uncle telling her 'of a trait in Ralph more than amusing – when I gave him his tip I said "don't mention it till after you are in the carriage". He presently afterwards said to me, "I suppose I ought to give it back to you for I have told Aunt Sophy". A proof of pleasure which he could not forbear to show and of honesty which he could not resist.'[13]

Another figure in the nursery was the French governess known as 'Mademoiselle' who introduced Ralph and his two siblings to the French language and, more entertainingly, to French songs, poems and literature. She and Sarah Wager did not get on. Secretly and confidentially they volunteered very serious criticisms of one another. Ralph liked them both very much, however. He especially enjoyed playing Bezique with Mademoiselle who participated in the game with emotions of operatic intensity. When about to lose she would cry out *Quel desespoir – que ferai je?*' And as defeat approached her shrieks of *'Mon Dieu! Mon Dieu!'* sounded out beyond the nursery. Ralph's devout mother was shocked at what she took to be blasphemy. She was even more shocked by the instances of blazing anger and discourtesy, which despite his characteristic kindliness, were to recur throughout Ralph's life. One occasion was remembered by the son of one of the Leith Hill servants. 'One morning Mr Ralph took his new boat to the pond, the wind being most favourable the boat made good headway all the morning. In the afternoon he asked my mother, who was the cook at L.H.P. and his nurse to go with him to sail his boat – but alas the wind had changed and the boat was becalmed. He turned round and said to mother: "Jonesy, it is because of your big ugly face". His nurse told Mrs Vaughan Williams and he had two afternoons in bed for this, one for saying it was mother's big ugly face and one for calling her Jonesy instead of giving her her name, Mrs Jones.'[14]

When he was six, Margaret Vaughan Williams decided that her younger son should have formal music lessons. These were given him by Mr Goodchild, who rode over to Leith Hill Place from the nearby village of Ockley. Ralph was taught sometimes with Meggie and sometimes with Vivian Bosanquet, who was from another of the wealthy families who had emigrated to this part of Surrey. The Bosanquets had paid, some years before, for the construction of the church at Coldharbour, which was Ralph's parish church.

A year or so later, when Ralph was seven, his mother suggested that he might take up another instrument. He remembered that he was walking with her through the streets of Eastbourne when in the window of a music shop they saw an advertisement for violin lessons. 'My mother said to me, "Would you like to learn the violin?" and I, without thinking, said "Yes". Accordingly, next day, a wizened old German called Cramer appeared on the scene and gave me my first violin lesson'.[15] It was to be Ralph's preferred instrument for the next few years; later, at his public school he took up the viola. Margaret Vaughan Williams also ensured that her son heard music performed. She took the children to the Three Choirs Festival where Ralph heard choral music for the first time. He also remembered going to concerts in the huge central transept at the Crystal Palace in south-east London, an important musical venue of late Victorian times. Perhaps such visits took place when he was taken to London to see his well-connected Vaughan Williams's relatives. Another important concert venue in the later years of Queen Victoria's reign was St James's Hall, which was close to Piccadilly Circus and had frontages on both Regent Street and Piccadilly. It could seat over two thousand and had very large Gothic windows. Ralph was taken there when he was ten. Amidst the large array of his souvenirs now kept at the British Library is the programme for a concert on 14 May 1883. This was the year that electric trams were first introduced in London. On that day, in St James's Hall with its green, horse-hair covered benches, the Bach Choir performed Mozart's Requiem Mass, Brahms's 'Song of the Fates' from Goethe's *Iphigenie* and the Credo from Cherubini's *Messe Solemnelle*.

Music was not Ralph's only enthusiasm as he prepared to go away to school. He had also become passionately interested in architecture. It seems probable that like many of his generation he was affected by the influence of the forceful writer John Ruskin, whose views on architecture (especially Gothic architecture) as a cultural and moral force had great currency at the time. Ralph developed a passion for visiting cathedrals, churches and castles. He was also avid for books about them. For his Christmas present in December 1883, after his first few months at his prep school, his mother catered to this enthusiasm by giving him a finely illustrated volume of *Pictorial Architecture of the British Isles*. When, many years later, he came to investigate the music of Tudor composers such as Thomas Tallis, he found that he had an understanding of the sound world of those who had written for the spaces created by chapels such as those of King's College, Cambridge, and that of Henry VII in Westminster Abbey.

The year before Ralph went off to prep school, Margaret Vaughan Williams and her sister Sophy took the three children on a holiday abroad that very much suited Ralph's fascination with medieval buildings. They went to Normandy. They stayed in Rouen where Ralph and Hervey climbed the tower of the cathedral. Ralph remembered the experience as both frightening and exciting. Even more memorable for him was their visit to Mont St Michel, the offshore island fortress near Avranches which is dominated by the grand medieval abbey and monastery. As he told a later biographer, 'he remembered his first sight of the grey and golden buildings rising beyond the salt marshes, the steep streets, the mazes of halls and chapels with a ghost of incense seeming to linger in the darkness, and the great wheel where the prisoners used to walk to wind the pulley ropes lifting loads of supplies up to the battlements. He did not go back there for seventy years but that first impression of romance never faded.'[16]

᭞

At the age of ten, in September 1883, Ralph was sent to his preparatory school, Rottingdean, named for the village in which it was then situated, close to Brighton in East Sussex. The origins of the school went back to the late eighteenth century when the vicar of Rottingdean at that time, Dr Thomas Hooker, founded a small educational establishment where boys could be boarded. The enterprise subsequently changed hands and in 1863 was taken over by Mr James Hewitt who was still headmaster when Ralph arrived. The second master was Mr Hewitt's brother William, and Miss Hewitt, their sister, was the school housekeeper.

Some five years after Ralph left, the school was reconstituted and renamed St Aubyns and continues as such today. But in Ralph's day it was known as Field House. The original building is a large white house on Rottingdean High Street. It has a semi-circular drive and steep steps up to the front door. Ralph slept in the dormitory room above the Masters' common room in a cottage across the road. He enjoyed being in Sussex. He recalled, 'Most of the boys thought the country around dull.

I thought it lovely and enjoyed our walks. The great bare hills impressed me by their grandeur. I have loved the Downs ever since.'[17] His sensitivity to landscape showed early in his life.

Ralph appears to have been happy during his three years at Field House though, by today's standards, the living conditions were rather harsh. Not long before his death Ralph recalled, and dictated, his memories of Rottingdean for inclusion in the biography that he had asked his second wife Ursula to write. He told her that 'the boys had a fairly hard life'.

> They got up at half past six for half an hour of preparation followed by practice of a musical instrument, which excused the players from prayers, before eight o'clock breakfast which consisted of tea, bread and butter with a small piece of cold beef. There were lessons all the morning, then luncheon – large and coarse joints and lots of stodgy pudding. The boys went to a shop nearby for kippers and chocolate with pink cream inside to supplement Miss Hewitt's housekeeping economies. Games and walks filled the afternoon, followed by tea and bread and butter at five, and after that preparation, punctuated by baths once a week. There were four tin hip baths filled by the school manservants, 'David and Solomon', so that four boys could scrub simultaneously and briskly before returning to prep. until bedtime at eight. The uniform was black suits, white shirts and stiff collars, which they did not change for games.[18]

Ralph's subsequent assessment of the teaching at Field House was that 'on the whole the general education was good'. 'We learned Latin and Greek. The mathematical teaching was far the best. Hewitt was a magnificent teacher.' Ralph added, 'I certainly got further in Latin [Public School Primer] and Greek [Farrar's Green Card] and Mathematics than I did for years later on, at Charterhouse.' Another Classics master at Rottingdean was the Reverend W. G. Riley, who long remembered Ralph's abilities in Latin and Greek. He was especially impressed by the young man's 'outstanding proficiency in irregular and defective Greek verbs.'

Ralph also made his first acquaintance with the German language at prep school. 'Towards the end of my time a visiting German master came in from Brighton once a week and any boy who wished could – I need hardly say – for an extra fee – attend his classes. The little German I now know I learned from him.'[19] Given Ralph's intense study of the German language and also its literature during the months he spent in Berlin later in life, this seems to be an exaggeration.

Ralph's love of English literature was also encouraged and catered for at Rottingdean. Again, the lively headmaster put memorable experiences Ralph's way. 'Jimmy Hewitt once took me to a performance by a well-known reciter called Brandrum who recited a bit of *Twelfth Night* which I loved, and later to another by Mr Ellaby, who, among other things, recited Coleridge's 'Ode to Mont Blanc' which has been among my favourite poems ever since. It may be worth noting that, on one of these occasions we came home cold and tired, and Jimmy insisted on my drinking some whisky and hot water. This did not lead to my downfall, so all is well.'[20] A Coleridge poem would resurface in Ralph's life nearly seventy years later when it supplied lines for one of the epigraphs introducing the different movements of the Seventh Symphony.

Ralph's literary education was also widened by 'a remarkable undermaster, Suttlery, who tried to add a little general culture to our rather meagre book learning. He used to read translations of the great speeches out of Greek plays, and I remember once his explaining the philosophy of the thirteenth chapter of 1 Corinthians.'

At Rottingdean the other boys were also an education, of course. There was politics, for instance. At home his mother and Sarah Wager had accustomed him to the Liberal, progressive politics that were the tradition in the Darwin–Wedgwood dynasty. As Ursula Vaughan Williams reports: 'Sarah had interested him in politics and from his earlier years he had shared her radical views. Now he met rabid conservatism, as well as class consciousness and snobbery which shocked him.'

And there was sex. The boys' information, he again told Ursula was 'Inaccurate and depressing'. He once asked the question, if it is so dangerous, why do they do it? 'Because it's awfully nice,' one of his friends answered.' This was just as intriguing as atheism which he also heard voiced for the first time at Rottingdean. In a letter written around 1947, Ralph's first wife, Adeline, reported that one of his fellow schoolboys had asked him 'to write incidental music to a play that he was working on, *The Rape of Lucretia*.' Ralph had written an opening drinking chorus but the play remained unfinished. 'His friend was quite innocent of the full meaning – R not quite.'[21]

Field House proved to be an excellent school for the fostering of Ralph's musical abilities. He recalled that 'I took my violin with me to a preparatory school at Rottingdean where I had lessons from a well-known fiddler in Ireland, in County Tipperary.'[22] William Michael Quirke had gone on to study in Leipzig and, so he claimed in his memoirs, to play the violin in orchestras conducted by Hans Richter and by Wagner himself. He also performed as a soloist in aristocratic circles throughout Europe and eventually in the then very fashionable resort of Brighton. Ralph remembered him as 'a fine player and a good teacher, but not a very cultivated musician'.[23] Under Quirke's teaching Ralph progressed to a level at which he was able to perform as a soloist in public. A fashionable violin piece often played in the 1880s was the *Cavatina* by Joseph Joachim Raff. Ralph later recalled: 'The climax of my career at Rottingdean was when I played Raff's *Cavatina* at a school concert. Fifty years later at The Three Choirs Festival, I was suddenly moved to seize W.H. Reed's violin and play through Raff's *Cavatina* by heart, double stops and all, while Reed vamped an accompaniment ... .' At Rottingdean Ralph also took piano lessons. He was taught by a visiting teacher, Mr C.T. West, from whom he also received what was, in terms of his musical development, a momentous gift. Ralph describes what happened: 'First he gave me the ordinary music teacher's rubbish, 'Petite Valse' and so on; but he had the insight to perceive that I should like something better, and he brought me a little book which I have always considered a great treasure – Novello's *Bach Album*'. At that stage in his life Ralph knew very little of Bach. 'Bach had never been part of the home curriculum – Handel, Mozart, Haydn and some early Beethoven was what we were fed on at home.' Ralph admitted: 'Of Bach I then knew nothing and I imagined vaguely that he was like Handel but not so good.' The itinerant music teacher's small present changed all that. The gift, in fact, constituted one of those moments of epiphany which punctuate Ralph's essay in autobiography. 'This Bach album was a revelation, something quite different from anything I knew, and Bach still remains for me in a niche by himself.'[24]

The second master at Field House, Mr William Hewitt, also helped with Ralph's musical development. There was a memorable occasion on which 'Billy took me to a Richter concert in Brighton. The programme consisted, I remember, of the Weber-Berlioz *Invitation a la Valse* which I was at that moment learning as a pianoforte piece, also the *Eroica Symphony*, which passed me by completely, the Prelude to *Lohengrin* which thrilled me and, even more, *The Ride of the Valkyries* on which theme I used to improvise to my friends at Rottingdean on the pianoforte, and called it *The Charge of the Light Brigade*.' Ralph's readiness to entertain his fellow pupils would occasionally get him into trouble. A family member reported that: 'He got into a scrape the other day for playing his violin after he had gone to bed which set the boys dancing in their shirts and the masters came in. However nothing very severe was awarded to him.'[25]

Ralph's fast developing musical skills were a considerable asset when it came to arranging school concerts. A programme survives for the Christmas concert at Rottingdean in 1886 when Ralph was fourteen. This 'Musical and Dramatic Entertainment' began with him playing a violin trio with two other boys and then playing solo a piece by Gounod. There followed something entirely different, a theatrical piece entitled 'Our Toys/A Fairy Vision in One Peep'. A musical play set in a Victorian nursery, it contained characters such as 'Our Lady Doll – Named by the Children "Lady Angelina de Montmorency"', and the doll who was 'The demon of Mischief who haunts every Nursery'. In this drama, the erstwhile violin soloist appeared as 'Our Wooden Soldier – Sole Survivor of a Boxful'. Seemingly Ralph's voice was breaking around this time; so he had to recite rather than sing his lines.

These included:

> For I am a wooden soldier bold
> And used to war's alarms.
> I've got a pair of wooden legs
> and little wooden arms ...

This Christmas celebration marked the end of Ralph's time at his preparatory school. The following month he began the next stage of his education when he entered what was, initially at least, the chilliest, most daunting phase of his life – public school.

〰

Ralph went to his public school, Charterhouse, in January 1887, the year of Queen Victoria's Golden Jubilee and of the very first Sherlock Holmes novel.

His elder brother Hervey had gone to the same school some five years earlier. There seems to have been sadness in the family at the end of Christmas as the brothers went off to school at the conclusion of the holidays. Their mother, aunts and sister arranged a special small meal of coffee and little cakes 'because the boys would miss their tea'. The afternoon was taken up by the journey through the countryside of western

Surrey to the old market town of Godalming which had recently become the location of the centuries-old school. The Leith Hill coachman drove the two boys along the then quiet country roads in the pony carriage, the boys' boxes piled up on the back.

For more than three hundred years Charterhouse had been in the centre of the City of London on a site just north of Smithfield Market. The Public Schools Act which went through Parliament in 1868 had required changes in the nine institutions identified by the legislation for the first time as 'public schools'. One consequence of the Act was that Charterhouse relocated to Surrey. The new buildings, designed by the eminent architect Philip Charles Hardwick, who was also responsible for that distinguished Victorian space, the great hall of Euston Station, were opened in 1872. That is to say, they were the same age as young Ralph himself and their red brick must have looked raw against the green countryside when he first arrived at the school.

His first term at Charterhouse, he told his wife Ursula, was not a happy one. Those early months of 1887 were very cold and dark. He was not gifted at or even interested in games, which were a very important part of public school life. He acquired the nickname 'Froddy', a word which does not appear in the Oxford dictionary. In a letter now in the British Library one of his school contemporaries, Nigel Davidson, suggests that the nickname indicating an unattractive appearance may have been inherited from his elder brother Hervey. Nigel Davidson remarks that 'It was quite inappropriate in the case of Ralph (V.W. Minor) who was a pleasant-looking boy.'

Ralph's grounding in Latin and Greek at Rottingdean held him in good stead at Charterhouse, and he did well enough scholastically. And there were memorable acquaintances to be made. One was Max Beerbohm, Ralph's exact contemporary. The 'Incomparable Max', as George Bernard Shaw was to call him, was, within a very few years of leaving school, a central figure in the very distinctive cultural decade of the 1890s in London. Ralph, a slow developer, had no part in that ferment. A brilliant caricaturist and writer, Max quickly became associated with the milieu that created the periodical *The Yellow Book* to which the illustrator Aubrey Beardsley, also an exact contemporary of Ralph and Max, contributed.

Ralph bumped into Max on his first day at Charterhouse as this very assured young man was emerging from the school library, nonchalantly reciting one of Edward Lear's alphabetical rhymes.

'I' was some ice
So white and so nice
Which no-body tasted
And so it was wasted

Charterhouse School Monitors' Register for Saturday 19 February 1888, contains a note that Ralph and Max were listed in the punishment book on the same day, Ralph for 'noisiness' and Max for 'silliness'. After his schooldays, Max remarked that he enjoyed 'having been at Charterhouse far more than being at'.

Ralph found Max entertaining but the two never became close at school. Some sixty years later they would find themselves neighbours and a friendship would develop. At Charterhouse a much more important fellow pupil for Ralph was an older boy, and one from his very large network of cousins, Stephen Massingberd. Later in life Stephen would have a career as a statistician and also as an army officer. A major in the Leicestershire Regiment he would be mentioned in despatches during the Great War of 1914–18. Stephen's family was from Gunby Hall in Lincolnshire to which, over his lifetime, Ralph would continue to return as a guest. Not long before his death, Ralph took Ursula to Gunby and he and Stephen's sister Diana recalled for her how more than sixty years before they had performed together 'Happy Day at Gunby', one of the 20-year-old Ralph's lost compositions.

When Ralph met Stephen Massingberd at Charterhouse, Stephen's great interest was music. And Stephen it was who introduced him to a figure in the world of music who was to be of major importance in Ralph's musical development, Hubert Parry. He long remembered first hearing of Parry:

> When I was still a schoolboy, I remember my cousin, Stephen Massingberd, coming in to the room full of that new book *Studies of Great Composers*. 'This man Parry', he said, 'declares that a composer must write music as his conscience demands.' This was quite a new idea to me, the loyalty of an artist to his art … and I think I can truly say that I have never been disloyal to it …

Other boys also shared and encouraged Ralph's emerging calling. H.C. Erskine, whom Ralph remembered as 'elegant', was also studying the organ and his playing of Bach's Prelude and 'St Anne' Fugue in E flat major greatly impressed him. N.G. Swainson, N.G. Scott and H.V. Hamilton, all of whom were to have careers in music, were serious students of the piano. In a letter of October 1889, Ralph wrote home reporting that Hamilton had stayed in his room from half past ten in the evening until three the following morning. They talked endlessly of music, Hamilton taking the view that: 'Mendellsohn [sic] is NOT a great composer, that though Beethoven is great he is old-fashioned. As to Handel, etc. they are quite out of date.'[26] Hamilton, however, had a burning enthusiasm that was to affect Ralph greatly: 'he has been to Bayreuth and is now a Wagnerite'. Hamilton's passion for music was infectious. 'Since H has been here I started a practising mania yesterday. I practised 2½ hours of piano besides counterpt.'[27]

Ralph remembered the music masters at Charterhouse with much gratitude. Especially important to him was a figure bearing a colourful nickname that alluded to his gait: 'Duck' Girdlestone. More than sixty years after leaving Charterhouse, Ralph recalled: 'One cannot write of Carthusian music without mentioning 'Duck' Girdlestone. He was an amateur musician and conducted weekly practices of the school orchestra. I was one of the two violas, the other being the famous Mr Stewart ['Stewfug'] whose chief business in life was to preside with complete inefficiency at 'extra school'; however, he was a good viola player and a great help in the orchestra. One of my first practical lessons in orchestration came from playing the viola part in the slow movement of Beethoven's first symphony, when I was excited to find that my repeated notes on the viola were enriched by a long holding note on Mr Becker's horn.' Ralph continues. 'Girdlestone also lives in my affectionate remembrance because in the winter months he used to invite some of us to his house on Sunday afternoons and there we played through many of the Italian Concerti Grossi from old band parts. The performances were pretty rough ['Duck' himself was an execrable violoncellist] but I learned much from the experience.'[28]

As Ralph continued in his Charterhouse career he became part of a musical set that included both masters and fellow pupils. An important member of this coterie was H.G. Robinson, the school organist, whom Ralph remembered as 'a sensitive musician and a kind-hearted man'. Max Beerbohm did a pen and ink caricature of him entitled 'Robinson Music Master'. Eight decades later the drawing was auctioned at Sothebys and brought in a considerable sum. It shows Robinson seated at the piano wearing a dark frock coat and pin-striped black trousers. He has a moustache, a bushy black beard and thinning hair. With right hand raised to pound the piano Robinson exclaims, so the caption says, 'I assure you, it's a gem'.

When Ralph went to Charterhouse there were just three houses; there are several more now. Initially Ralph was part of the headmaster's house, Saunderites. But late on in Ralph's schooldays H.G. Robinson created his own house, ever after to be Robinites. Ralph then had the unusual experience, for a Carthusian, of changing houses. He left the headmaster's house and transferred to that of his music mentor H.G. Robinson where he remained for his last four terms, becoming head of house.

It was a mark of the intellectual ambitiousness of Charterhouse in those years that it sustained a French debating society. A contributor to the school magazine of 1953 recalled Ralph speaking in a debate as the unlikely defender of physical education and compulsory games. Charterhouse had recently won the Ashburton Shield, the most prestigious trophy in the shooting year for schoolboys and competed for annually at Bisley. Ralph was remembered in the debate 'sturdily' asserting that '*si les exercices n'avient pas ete obligatoires deux fois par semaine, nous n'aurions probablement jamais conquis le bouclier d'Ashburton.*' But while commending the public school cult of muscularity, he was also taking up what was to be his lifelong political position, one left of centre. Years later he remembered, 'When I was a boy at school, I and another boy stood out as Radicals (as we were called then) against all the other boys.'[29]

Though usually somewhat withdrawn at school, Ralph was capable of bold initiatives. In an environment that was not especially receptive to serious music he decided to organize a concert. In this enterprise he was supported by his friend, the Wagnerian devotee H.V. Hamilton and by his cousin Stephen Massingberd and by Robinson. The programme contained some well-known works by Spohr and Sullivan, and also the first performance of one of Ralph's own compositions, a Pianoforte Trio in G. The concert could not take place without the permission of the headmaster, Dr William Haig Brown. He was a very daunting figure. A Carthusian of the generation prior to Ralph's, Lord Robert Baden-Powell, the hero of the siege of Mafeking and founder of the Scouting Movement (and a man not easily daunted) recalled Haig Brown as having a 'great reputation for sternness'. And Ralph admitted that 'in later life I should never have dared to make the request'. But make it the young man did, driven by ambition and by the same 'musical conscience' which Stephen Massingberd had found and admired in Hubert Parry. Ralph's calling was becoming a part of his character.

The concert was attended by some of the masters, their wives and a few of the boys. Ralph retained only a very vague memory of his Trio. He later wrote, 'All I remember about it was that the principal theme was distinctly reminiscent of Cesar Franck, a composer whose name I did not even know in those days, and whom I have learned to dislike cordially. I must have got the theme from one of the French or Belgian imitators of Franck whose salon music was popular in those days.' But at least one member of the audience was impressed by the Trio. James Noon, the mathematics master at Charterhouse, went up to him and said 'in that sepulchral voice which Carthusians of my day knew so well, "Very good Williams, you must go on."'

Ralph's spearheading of the introduction of classical music into the life of Charterhouse encouraged 'Duck' Girdlestone, who ran the Sunday evening entertainments, to devote four of these 'Etceteras' to the music of the four nations of Great Britain. Perhaps because of his surname and ancestry, Ralph was made responsible for a concert of Welsh music. He remembered it as 'my first introduction to the beautiful melodies of the Principality.'[30] There was also a concert organized by the daughters of the headmaster, the Misses Haig Brown. 'Two of them played the pianoforte,' recalled Ralph, 'and they invited six of us boys to join them in music for sixteen hands on four pianofortes. As I was one of the performers I never appreciated the full horror of the result.'[31]

During the school holidays Ralph worked hard at his music. He arranged to have an organ installed for him in the hall at Leith Hill Place. He practised on it every morning for an hour, before family breakfast was served at half past seven. A persistent problem for him was to find an organ-blower. Philips, the old butler, studiously avoided the hall before breakfast. So the maids, and sometimes the groom or the gardener, were summoned to assist the young master. Close to Leith Hill Place was 'Parkhurst', another grand residence which was the home of Colonel Wilfred Lewin, who had recently concluded a career as a District Officer in India. This figure from the British Raj was a great enthusiast for music. He and his wife and family enjoyed house music. They particularly liked playing Haydn's string quartets in which performances Ralph was a very welcome, regular and dedicated participant.

But there was more to the holidays than practising music. Ralph and his siblings enjoyed the usual pleasures of the upper classes. There was tennis, croquet and dances. At one of these Ralph overheard a man being asked 'Why don't you ask that pretty Mrs Vaughan Williams to dance?'[32] This compliment to his long-widowed mother touched him and stayed in his memory. However, she was never to marry again. School holidays also brought visits to London, which meant theatre which was always important to him, and more importantly still, concerts.

There were also trips abroad. In the summer of 1890 when Ralph was seventeen there was a family holiday in Germany. Together with his mother, Aunt Sophy, his brother Hervey and sister Meggie, Ralph went to Oberammergau for the Passion Play. He did not enjoy it at all, very much disliking the unconvincing beards on stage and the religious fervour of the occasion. The experience further estranged him from religion. At Charterhouse he had been confirmed into the Church of England and he went to church regularly 'so as not to upset the family'. But as his schooldays drew to an end he had become an agnostic and by the time he went to Cambridge his religious views were those of an atheist.

For Ralph much more enjoyable than Oberammergau was the time he and his family members spent in Munich during that German holiday. In Munich he heard Wagner's *Die Walküre* for the very first time. He later wrote of it as one of the half dozen major experiences of his life and, to an extent, a mystical experience.

> We found that *Die Walküre* was down for that evening. The opera, we were told, would start at seven so at six o'clock we sat down to have a meal. Hardly had we started when the waiter rushed in – he had made a mistake – on a Wagner *abend* the opera started at six. The rest decided for dinner but I, like the hero of a novel, 'left my food untasted' and rushed off to the opera. I arrived just in time to hear that wonderful passage for strings when Sieglinde offers Siegfried the cup. This was my first introduction to the later Wagner, but I experienced no surprise, but rather that strange certainty that I had heard it all before. There was a feeling of recognition, as of meeting an old friend, which comes to us all in the face of great artistic experiences. I had the same experience when I first heard an English folk song, when I first saw Michelangelo's *Day and Night*, when I suddenly came upon Stonehenge or had my first sight of New York City – the intuition that I had been there already.'[33]

Ralph left Charterhouse in July 1890. He was now in no doubt whatsoever that he wanted to pursue a career as a musician. Recently he had taken up the viola, an instrument he came to love more and more, and in preference to his first choice, the violin. He would have liked to become an orchestral player. But his family had serious doubts about this idea. His uncle, Roland Vaughan Williams, so well placed in London society, would surely have considered viola playing to be no career for a gentleman. Some relatives would have preferred him to remain a little longer at Charterhouse. At least one of them, while recognizing Ralph's passion for music and his profound commitment to it, vociferously questioned his actual musical abilities. His mother's cousin, Charles Darwin's daughter Henrietta, known in the family as Aunt Hetty and also known for 'her drastic common sense', wrote that Ralph 'has been playing all his life and for six months <u>hard</u>, and yet he can't play the simplest thing decently. They say it will simply break his heart if he is too bad to hope to make something of it.'[34] A more distant relative, Gwen Raverat, remembered hearing scraps of conversation about 'that foolish young man, Ralph Vaughan Williams, who <u>would</u> go on working at music when he was so hopelessly bad at it.'[35]

The course that was finally agreed on in the family was that Ralph should begin a musical career by studying to be an organist rather than an orchestral player. In the numerous churches throughout the country there were opportunities that would enable him to supplement his private income and to respect that work ethic that was so strong in the Wedgwood and Darwin traditions and, indeed, in Ralph himself. Some sixty years later, in a brief essay in autobiography, Ralph still felt some irritation at this decision reached by the family 'authorities'. He wrote, 'I believe I should have made quite a decent fiddler , but the authorities decided that if I was to take up music at all the violin was too 'doubtful' a career and I must seek safety on the organ stool, a trade for which I was entirely unsuited.'[36] But the family prevailed. And so in September 1890, just approaching his eighteenth birthday, at the beginning of a characterful decade in which Ralph, unlike Max Beerbohm, would not be very prominent, this late developer entered the Royal College of Music in London.

Chapter Two

KENSINGTON

When Ralph entered the Royal College of Music in September 1890, the institution was of very recent foundation. To Ralph's sceptical relatives it must have seemed a very new-fangled place. It had been established just seven years before by Sir George Grove, one of the great arts entrepreneurs of the Victorian age. An energetic and successful civil engineer, with a passionate enthusiasm for music, Sir George had organized concerts at that famous, impressively engineered structure of the time, the Crystal Palace. A great friend of Sir George was a leading composer of the day, Sir Arthur Sullivan. Great admirers of Schubert the two travelled together to Vienna where they unearthed several of the composer's manuscripts, including some from *Rosamunde*, that had been lost. George Grove joined the publishing house of Macmillan where, having first produced a primer of geography, he launched into his famous *Dictionary of Music and Musicians*. A modest volume to begin with, this turned into the multi-volume compendium that we know today.

Grove's friend Sullivan was busy with another historic project, his collaboration with the librettist W.S. Gilbert in the creation of popular operas. Consequently, his interest in the National School for Music, which he headed, was lukewarm and spasmodic. Sir George Grove decided to take over the failing institution and reorganize and revitalize it. With German models in mind, he created a new college with well-defined professional standards, teaching procedures and syllabus. He also spotted, and recruited to his new organization, two highly distinguished musicians, Charles Villiers Stanford and Hubert Parry. His new Royal

College of Music was housed in a brand new building immediately to the west of the Royal Albert Hall. Some years later when the College moved to other premises nearby, the building became the home, for some time, of the Royal College of Organists. It is now privately owned.

The college stood on the northern edge of that quarter of London sometimes referred to as Albertopolis. This is the near rectangle which runs north from Cromwell Road with Exhibition Road as its eastern limit and Queens Gate as the western. Just above its northern edge of Kensington Road, there stands in Kensington Gardens the Albert Memorial, which enshrines the seated statue of Queen Victoria's consort whose memory inspired the building of the several colleges within the rectangle.

A serious, professional dedication to the arts and sciences was something that the Prince Consort preached and promoted in this country. In Albertopolis, containing so many institutions dedicated to his example and memory, this commitment has been productive for well over a century and a half. Ralph was both a beneficiary and an enhancer of the tradition in this place. A great tract of his life from his earliest student days to his time as a teacher and an *eminence* was centred on the Royal College of Music in Albertopolis. It seems appropriate that he was born in the very same year in which the Albert Memorial was unveiled.

When Ralph first became a student at the age of seventeen, he did not live in London. It had been agreed in the family that he should commute from home. Usually he travelled by rail but occasionally he would walk all the way from Kensington to his Surrey home. One of the servants at the house remembered that 'While at the College of Music he would walk down from London and arrive at Leith Hill Place in time for breakfast. The first his mother knew of his arrival was the playing of the organ'.[1] But on most teaching days he took the train from Ockley, the little country station which was the one closest to Leith Hill Place, up to Waterloo. In those autumn days of 1890 the newspaper-sellers at the station would have been crying out the latest headlines to do with the Kitty O'Shea divorce case. Charles Stewart Parnell, the leader of the Irish Home Rule Party in the House of Commons, had been cited as the co-respondent in the divorce of one of his backbenchers, Captain Terence O'Shea. The discrediting of Parnell was to affect the Westminster government's chances of coming to terms with Irish demands for a parliament in Dublin. During the first fifty years of Ralph's life the status of Ireland would be a major issue in the political life of his country. It would be of special importance in the life of a good friend of later years, Arnold Bax.

Like most students in their freshman year Ralph made some new friends. A frequent companion on the train to and from Waterloo was the young Lady Evangeline Farrer of the family that lived at Abinger House, just a few miles away from Leith Hill Place. She also was a student at the Royal College. Some years later, together with her friend, Ralph's sister Meggie, she would be a co-founder of an important institution in the musical calendar of England, the Leith Hill Music Festival held at Dorking. Another new friend, and an important one in Ralph's musical development, was Richard Walthew, a fellow student who lived with his parents in Highbury, North London. This was then a still fast-developing middle-class and lower middle-class suburb, engulfing a small, ancient village. Ralph would go to Richard's family home and sometimes stay overnight there. Here he would meet people of a social class completely different to the moneyed Surrey gentry familiar to him and to Lady Evangeline. Ralph long remembered his musical debts to Richard. He wrote 'I learnt much from him. I used occasionally to go to his house in Highbury and play duets with him, or rather, he played and I stumbled behind him as best I could. In this way I learnt to know a lot of music including, I remember, Stanford's "Irish Symphony".'[2] Ralph was a student long before the coming of recorded music and he recalled that 'In those days before the gramophone and the wireless and the miniature score, the pianoforte duet was the only way, unless you were an orchestral player, of getting to know orchestral music. Through these duets with Richard Walthew one really got to hear it from the inside.'

Richard was down to earth about music. Ralph was especially grateful to him for challenging the snobbish, exclusive taste that he had at that time. He recalled that he 'had become a complete prig. Bach, Beethoven (ex-officio), Brahms and Wagner were the only composers worth considering....' But Richard, just like Wagner's friend, Friedrich Nietzsche, admired Bizet's *Carmen*. And he made up his mind to confront Ralph with it. 'One day, Walthew, who had a holy terror of anything high-falutin in art, insisted on taking me to hear *Carmen*.' So Ralph went along to the opera 'prepared to scoff, but Walthew won the day and I remained to pray.'[3] Another earthy challenge to Ralph's devotion to the great German symphonic tradition, which was the concomitant of German idealism in literature and philosophy, was his first hearing, at the same time, of Verdi's Requiem. This Italian music was a surprise and an education. 'At first I was properly shocked by the frank sentimentalism and sensationalism of the music. I remember being particularly horrified at the drop of a semitone on the word 'Dona'. Was not this the purest 'village organist'? But in a very few minutes the music possessed me. I realised that here was a composer who could do all the things which I, with my youthful pedantry, thought wrong, indeed would be unbearable in a lesser man; music which was sentimental, theatrical, occasionally even cheap, and yet an overpowering masterpiece.' Verdi was an early stage in Ralph's lifelong exploration of related notions that became crucially important in his time: the popular, the people and the folk.

In later years Richard Walthew would keep Ralph connected with social realities in English life that were wider than those known at Leith Hill. Richard became music director at the Passmore Edwards Settlement, an institution first founded by, and named for, a prominent Victorian philanthropist and which offered various social services, including musical ones, to the working class in central London. Later renamed the Mary Ward Settlement, it was housed close to Tavistock Square in one of the most impressive Art Nouveau buildings in London. The Settlement was the very first social charity to provide a school for children with disabilities. Into this milieu the idealistic Richard, who became the music director of its cultural programmes, introduced Ralph, who donated his services as a viola player. Richard, who subsequently made something of a name for himself as a composer, turned to an academic career at the Guildhall School and at the Queens College, Oxford, and was succeeded in his post at the Mary Wood Settlement by Ralph's friend of a later time, Gustav Holst.

During their years at the Royal College of Music both Ralph and Richard became pupils of Sir Hubert Parry in composition. But before he could be taught by Parry, Ralph had to achieve a certain proficiency in harmony. In this subject he was taught by F.E. Gladstone, a cousin of the Liberal Prime Minister who formed his final government (with a view to passing the Irish Home Rule Bill) some two years after Ralph first entered the Royal College. Ralph remembered that 'By a wise ruling of the College, which I fear no longer obtains, no one was allowed to study composition until he had passed grade 5 in harmony. So for two terms I did my theoretical work with Dr F.E. Gladstone. Under his guidance I worked through every exercise in MacFadden's *Harmony*, a discipline for which I have ever since been grateful.'[4]

In his third term Ralph finally became the pupil of Sir Hubert Parry, to whose work his cousin Stephen Massingberd had so excitedly introduced him at Charterhouse. Unquestionably Parry was one of the most important encounters and relationships in Ralph's whole life. When he wrote his teacher's obituary in 1918, well over a quarter of a century after they had first met, something of his intense, youthful feeling for the man remains palpable in his words. He began by recalling another powerful influence on him as a young man, the work of the American poet Walt Whitman. He remembers a line in 'Song of the Open Road' from *Leaves of Grass*. 'Walt Whitman says: "Why are there men and women that while they are nigh me the sunlight expands my blood?" Ralph states simply, "Parry was one of these".'[5]

He goes on to speak of Parry in messianic terms. 'You could not hear the sound of his voice or feel the touch of his hand without knowing that "virtue had gone out of him".' It would not have mattered what we wanted to learn from him – it might have been mathematics or chemistry – his magic touch would make it glow with life. Half-a-dozen of his enthusiastic, eloquent words were worth a hundred learned expositions.' Writing in his late forties Ralph confessed that 'I still often go out of my way to pass his house in Kensington Square in order to experience the thrill with which I used to approach his door on my lesson day.'

One of the founders of England's great musical revival towards the end of the nineteenth century, Hubert Parry was gentlemanly, generous and kind. The often acerbic George Bernard Shaw noted that 'Dr Parry sums up in his person every excellence that the best type of private gentleman can pretend to be'.[6] An Etonian who had not been permitted by his family to study music while at Exeter College, Oxford, Parry had gone on to try to become wealthy by working as an underwriter at Lloyds of London. This was in part to assist him in asking for the hand of a young woman whom he loved profoundly and who loved him but whose family considered him not good enough. He suffered humiliating rejections by her parents. But when they at long last relented, worse was to come. The marriage proved to be an unhappy failure. Parry then centred his life on two other passions: music and boats.

Parry's physical appearance was deceptive. Ralph commented on the way people 'entirely misunderstood Parry, they were deceived by his rubicund bonhomie and imagined that he had the mind, as he had the appearance, of a country squire.'[7] But Ralph came to see him differently. 'The fact is that Parry had a highly nervous temperament. He was in early days a thinker with very advanced views. I remember for example, how in the early nineties, he accepted Ibsen with delight. He was one of the early champions of Wagner when other thinkers in the country were still calling him impious.'[8]

Parry gained his position at the Royal College through his friendship with Sir George Grove whom he assisted in the compiling of the *Dictionary of Music*. He brought a fervent, evangelical enthusiasm to his teaching. He had been greatly affected by the moral fervour of John Ruskin, whom he had heard lecture at Oxford. Parry especially emphasized to his pupils the importance of local and national feeling in their music and also the right social and political attitude. Ralph long remembered, word for word, Parry's advice to him: 'Write choral music as befits an Englishman and a democrat.' Parry's Third Symphony composed some eleven years before Ralph became his pupil was called 'The English'.

When Ralph first had lessons with Parry, his teacher was very much involved with completing his cantata 'Job'. They must surely have discussed the text. And to such conversations must be dated some of the beginnings of one of Ralph's major future works. And Parry must have been interested to speak of Ralph's Darwin ancestry, because Parry was very much a Darwinian and inspired by Darwin's follower, Herbert Spencer. Sixty years later, Ralph recalled: 'Parry was a thinker on music which he connected not only with life, but with other aspects of life and science. When Parry was a young man the Darwinian controversy was in full swing. Inspired by Herbert Spencer he decided to find out how far music followed the laws of evolution. These thoughts he embodied in his great book, *The Evolution of the Art of Music*, in which he proves, conclusively to most people, that Beethoven's Ninth Symphony, for example, is not an isolated phenomenon, but a highly developed stage of a process of evolution which can be traced back to the primitive folk songs of our people.'[9]

Ralph was to retain throughout his long life a strong sense of a virtual apostolic tradition in English music to which Parry had connected him. In later years he wrote ringingly, 'We pupils of Parry have, if we have been wise, inherited from Parry the great English choral tradition which Tallis passed on to Byrd, Byrd to Gibbons, Gibbons to Purcell, Purcell to Battishill and Greene and they in their turn through the Wesleys to Parry.' Ralph concludes with an assertion of the moral responsibility of Parry's pupils to maintain this great legacy. 'He has passed on the torch to us and it is our duty to keep it alight.' Ralph and Winston Churchill, Britain's greatest orator of the twentieth century, were born within two years of one another. These words suggest how they share a similar rhetorical mode and the sense of history which it implies.

Besides inspiring in his students a missionary purpose Parry was also extremely generous to them. Ralph remembers how 'painfully illiterate' as a musician he had been at the age of eighteen when Parry first taught him. 'Parry could hardly believe that I knew so little music. One day he was talking to me about the wonderful climax in the development of the 'Appassionata' Sonata. Suddenly he realised that I did not know it, so he sat down at the pianoforte and played it through to me. There were showers of wrong notes, but in spite of that it was the finest performance that I have ever heard. So I was told to study more Beethoven, especially the posthumous quartets "as a religious exercise".'[10] Such linking of artistic activity with religion is characteristic of Parry and of Victorian high culture generally. It is prominent, for instance, in the literary criticism of Mathew Arnold, whose prose and poetry were well known to Ralph.

Parry also extended an endless patient generosity in helping his pupils to find their own voices, to express what was in them to express, to find their unique musical characters. 'Parry's great watchword was "characteristic". He was always trying to discover the character revealed in even the weakest of his students' compositions.' Ralph remembered with a pang of regret, 'I was very elementary at the time. I blush with shame now when I think of the horrible little songs and anthems which I presented for his criticism.' He relates an anecdote to illustrate Parry's relentless dedication to discovering originality in his pupils' work. 'Parry, not content with the official lesson, used to keep his pupils' compositions to look at during the week. One day, through pure carelessness, I had written out a scale passage with one note repeated and then a gap – (i.e. CDEFGGBC instead of CDEFGABC). Parry said, "I have been looking at this passage for a long time to discover whether it is just a mistake or whether you meant anything characteristic."'

In 1948, the centenary of Parry, Ralph composed a homage to him. Entitled 'Prayer to the Father of Heaven', it is a motet for mixed choirs, an *a capella* setting of a text by a Tudor poet John Skelton, whose work also supplied the words for Ralph's Five Tudor Portraits. The dedication to the centenary motet reads:

> To the memory of my master Hubert Parry, not as an attempt palely
> to reflect his incomparable art, but in the hope that he would have
> found in this motet (to use his own words) 'something characteristic.[11]

The profound commitment to helping his students discover their musical characters was accompanied by much practical generosity. 'Parry was very generous in lending scores to his pupils. This was long before the days of miniature scores and gramophone records. I borrowed "Siegfried" and "Tristan" and Brahms's "Requiem", and for some time after, my entire compositions consisted of variations of a passage near the beginning of that work.'

Parry's loans fed into his teaching. Ralph remembered that 'one day when I came in for my lesson I found ... Richard Walthew borrowing the score of the Prelude to *Parsifal*. Parry condemned it as the weakest of the Wagner preludes – "mere scene painting" was, I think, his description of it.' Ralph goes on to mention the moral element in Parry's judgement of music, the very same element that John Ruskin, who was a genera-tion older than Parry, brought to his sternly formulated judgements of architecture and paintings. Ralph goes on to recall that Parry 'was always very insistent of the importance of form as opposed to colour. He had an almost moral abhorrence of mere luscious sound.'[12]

Parry's strict, delicate moral sense extended to his personal dealings. Looking back in 1955 Ralph recalled how Richard Walthew as a student had shown Parry his setting of Robert Browning's poem *The Pied Piper of Hamelin*. Parry himself had also recently set this poem but quietly withdrew his version so that he might be in a better position to help Richard Walthew get his setting performed. It was not until over a decade later, in October 1905, that Parry's version was heard in public. It was well received. Appreciated as his first 'humorous' cantata, it was seen by one critic to occupy a similar position within Parry's oeuvre as *Die Meistersinger* in Wagner's.[13]

Other compositions by Parry have achieved a more lasting place in English musical culture. His settings of Blake's *Jerusalem* are familiar to a wider public that is not especially musical. Indeed, it is sometimes spoken of as England's unofficial national anthem. And Parry's setting of John Milton's 'Blest Pair of Sirens' has continued to appear on the programmes of choirs at various levels, including the one to which the present writer once belonged. Ralph singled out the work of his teacher for a very special, deliberated and formal salute: 'I hereby solemnly declare, keeping steadily in view the works of Byrd, Purcell, and Elgar, that "Blest Pair of Sirens" is my favourite piece of music written by an Englishman.'[14]

In the summer of 1890 Ralph's formal studies with Parry came to an end. It had been decided that he should leave the Royal College of

Music and begin his freshman year at Cambridge. It seems likely that the change was demanded by his family. They had long had doubts, of course, about the suitability of a musical career for someone of his, apparently, limited musical gifts and certainly for someone of his social standing. Nevertheless Ralph fought to keep a connection with the Royal College and on certain days during his Cambridge terms he would travel down to London for further musical tuition with Parry.

But it was Cambridge that became his base for the next three years until he completed his degree in history there. Here at Trinity College he would join a group of brilliant contemporaries who would accompany him in an exploration of what it meant to be an Englishman and a democrat. These young men in their generation carried further that urgently moral approach to life and to art that Ralph had first encountered with Hubert Parry in Albertopolis. In Cambridge he would be further educated in that philosophical, historical, political and very literary awareness that was to be an important, and distinguishing, condition of his development as a composer.

Chapter Three

CAMBRIDGE

When Ralph went up to Trinity College, he already had many connections in the university community. From his very first day he was part of an extensive network of relatives and family acquaintances. A distinguished fellow of Trinity College was George Darwin, later Sir George, who was a cousin of Ralph's mother. George Darwin was a brilliant polymath. A lawyer and a mathematician, in 1883 he became Plumian Professor of Astronomy and Experimental Philosophy at Cambridge. The year Ralph went up, George Darwin won the Gold Medal of the Royal Astronomical Society. His special field was the mathematical study of the tidal forces affecting the sun, moon and earth. He became famous for his fission theory of the origins of the moon which held that the moon had once formed part of the earth.

George Darwin was also an excellent example of that wide intellectual and cultural excitement that pervaded Cambridge in the 1890s and in which Ralph actively participated. George Darwin's elder daughter Gwendolen remembered how her father: 'loved travelling and always wanted to see absolutely everything in any country he visited; to learn the history and to speak the language and talk to everyone he met. Besides the ordinary European languages, he was always playing about with odd dialects – Provencal, Platt (sic), Deutsch, Romanche, Icelandic; and he liked to get all the technical terms of any craft right, and to find out the pedigrees of the words.' He read voraciously and greatly enjoyed reading to his children. 'The books he read to us were all in the romantic vein: Shakespeare's Histories, Chaucer, Percy's Reliques, Scott's novels. He adored a Roman road or a prehistoric fort, and no-one enjoyed a good dungeon, or a fine set of battlements, more than he did. To him the north was always more romantic than the south; so nearly every summer we went to Yorkshire for part of the holidays ... What fun it was, walking with him through the driving rain and mist, over hills and walls and bogs, while he told us stories about the Stone Age inhabitants of the moors.'[1]

Ralph encountered similar enthusiasms over at Downing College. Here in the West Lodge lived Frederic Maitland, Professor of the Laws of England. This eminent legal historian and jurist was a lively, witty man who had married Florence Fisher, daughter of Herbert William Fisher, the tutor and then secretary to the Prince of Wales, and a close friend of Ralph's father and uncles when they had all been undergraduates together at Christ Church in Oxford. Ralph was very much drawn to the Maitlands, an attractive couple now in their early forties. They had two young daughters, Ermengard and Fredegond (medievalizing Pre-Raphaelite names being fashionable in cultured circles in the 1880s). To the twenty-year-old Vaughan Williams, the little girls quickly became 'Gaga' and 'Vuff'. Fredegond grew up to be a poet and in 1922, thirty years after first meeting her, Ralph set four of her poems for baritone and piano.

Mrs Maitland was an accomplished amateur violinist and there were frequent evenings of house music at their home in Downing College in which the young freshman from Trinity with his viola was a regular and warmly welcomed participant. Sometimes, Florence Maitland's much younger sister, Adeline, who was a pianist but could also play the cello, would stay at the West Lodge and take part in these musical soirées. A Downing undergraduate who also took part in these lively gatherings was Nicholas Gatty, a violinist. He and his brother Ivor, who played the horn, were to stay important friends in Ralph's life.

Another Cambridge home into which Ralph was warmly welcomed was that of another of his mother's cousins, Francis Darwin, who was lecturer and then reader in the School of Botany at the university. His daughter Frances was six when Ralph went up but she retained a vivid memory of his first visit: 'I was told this was my new undergraduate cousin, Ralph. I remember it was a misty day in late autumn, of exciting, premature snow. He lifted me up to the window-seat to look out. I remember too how clumsily yet gently he did it, and also my sense that he really appreciated the snow in the field and liked the blue-grey afternoon just before tea time in the same way that I did.'[2]

Gentleness and a certain clumsiness seem to have been features that struck people in the young Ralph. Some five years later while allowing the possibility of genius in him, the novelist Virginia Woolf spoke of him as a 'calf'. Yet, for all his hesitancies, Ralph quickly made a number of friendships within Trinity College. Some of these were to be lifelong. With the future philosopher G.E. Moore and the future historian G.M. Trevelyan, he came to form a trio, which in sheer brilliance of achievement is unsurpassed in the history of undergraduate life in England. Each of the three became a (if not *the*) leading figure in his field in his time and generation. Each of the three was a recipient of the Order of Merit. They had many interests in common. George Moore, for instance, shared Ralph's love of music. On Ralph's very last birthday in 1957 George sent him a greeting and Ralph wrote to him saying, 'It carries me back to very old days when you used to sing Schubert and play Beethoven to us after Hall.'[3]

But during their student days George's chief developing interest was in the philosophical enquiry that would lead to his most famous work *Principia Ethica,* published in 1903, some eight years after the three friends had graduated. The book was to exert a powerful influence on the next generation of Cambridge undergraduates, among them Lytton Strachey and John Maynard Keynes, both of whom were at the centre of the Bloomsbury Group and its memorable achievements in thought, art and literature. For Bloomsbury, Moore's chapter entitled 'The Ideal' was particularly important. This urged the importance of love and friendship, maintaining that 'personal affections and aesthetic enjoyments include <u>all</u> the greatest, and <u>by far</u> the greatest, goods we can imagine.'[4] George Moore sent Ralph a copy of the book; Ralph found it 'difficult but wonderful'.

As an undergraduate George Moore organized 'reading tours' for his friends. The group would take the train to some remote, wild spot in the British Isles and there do long gruelling walks and sometimes climbs, and engage in intense intellectual discussion based on a large amount of preparatory reading. One of these excursions was to the Isle of Skye during Ralph's second year at Cambridge. Along with George and Ralph the group included: George Trevelyan; the future judge, Maurice Amos; George's brother, Bertie; and Ralph's friend and relative on his mother's side, Ralph Wedgwood, whom everyone called Randolph. The intellectual strenuousness that went into preparing for these tours is indicated in a letter to George Moore from Randolph. The last name on the book list is that of Wilhelm Windelband, an influential scholar of the day who had published several lengthy volumes on the history of ancient and modern philosophy. Randolph Wedgwood wrote, perhaps a little anxiously, 'I hope you are not starting too impatiently at your philosophy, as I shall not be beginning it till I get to Skye: At present I am busy at Psychology. The books I am going to bring are Locke's *Human Understanding*, Fraser on Locke (the serial edition), Berkeley (dialogues and other things), and Descartes. Pollock's *Spinoza* I will get and am willing to get two or three more if you will tell me what you have got. I have ordered Windelband's *History....*'[5]

More than forty years later Ralph had very happy memories of this excursion. But it was the place and its music rather than philosophical discussions that stayed in his mind. 'I was in Skye on a "reading party" in 1894!! It was a good place – we were in a farmhouse at Tothardrur (Struan) and we walked once to the Cuchillin Hills and climbed Skuranan Gillean and got lost in a fog. Have you seen Loch Coruisk – a wonderful place. Also if they have one of their big open air prayer meetings you should go to that – a wonderful sight and sound.'[6]

Ursula confirms the importance for Ralph of the Gaelic preacher whom he had heard during that holiday on Skye. Recalling what her husband had told her she writes 'not understanding the language, he listened to his voice and noted how emotional excitement, and having to speak so that the words would carry, changes speech rhythm into song.'[7] She adds that Ralph 'remembered the melodic formula into which the sermon grew ... and recognised it when he started work on folk songs....'

A very lively member of the party of young men on Skye was a student of history, George Macaulay Trevelyan. 'Trevy', as the others called him, was a forceful personality, intellectually aggressive with usually a serious, urgent expression behind his pince-nez. One of his biographers has written that 'during the first half of the twentieth century Trevelyan was the most famous, the most honoured, the most influential and the most widely read historian of his generation.'[8] And while conceding that George Trevelyan today belongs among 'the great unread', David Cannadine goes on to maintain, rightly, that Trevelyan was 'one of the towering figures in the political, cultural and intellectual life of twentieth century Britain.' When Ralph first met him, 'Trevy' was very much a young man in a hurry. He graduated from Cambridge at the age of twenty, in 1896, just a year after Ralph. 'Trevy' got a first in the Historical Tripos and very soon thereafter became a fellow of Trinity College. At the age of twenty-three, the first of his many books, *England in the Age of Wycliff*, was published. He went on to write a trilogy of books relating the career of the Italian freedom fighter and leader of the Risorgimento, Giuseppe Garibaldi. The *Garibaldi* was one of the great achievements of history writing in the Edwardian decade.

Like all of Ralph's friends at Cambridge, Trevelyan was a passionate Liberal. In the 1890s, before the Labour Party came into being, the political argument in Britain was one conducted between the Conservative and Liberal parties. To late Victorian and Edwardian Liberals, Garibaldi was a great hero and an icon. To them he was the embodiment of two of their most important political ideals: the right to self-determination of small nations (Ireland being the closest instance) and the repudiation of the principle of empire. Garibaldi was the leader of a successful revolt of a distinctive nation against its subordination to the vast imperial system of the Austro-Hungarian Empire run by the Habsburgs from Vienna. As Ralph would become aware, Garibaldi was seconded by Verdi and his music. Similarly the early music of Sibelius was a tacit protest against the Russian imperial system, and that of Leos Janáček against that of the German Empire.

When Ralph and 'Trevy' were undergraduates together and the British imperial system was at its zenith, history was a very attractive subject to publishers and to the reading public. There was widespread interest and pleasure in reading and considering the reasons for the astonishing success of this small island nation in creating a worldwide empire. George Trevelyan's uncle was Lord Macaulay who, in an earlier generation in the 1850s, had produced his *History of England*, one of the best received and best-selling works of non-fiction in the Victorian age. In grand, resounding prose which affected the prose style of many subsequent writers, most notably Winston Churchill, Lord Macaulay celebrated and explained England's conspicuously successful evolution in terms of a succession of creative constitutional settlements dating back to the Glorious Revolution of 1688. Lord Macaulay, like his nephew George, was a Trinity man and, such was his fame, the college was happy to commission a statue of him to stand across from that of one of another celebrated member of the college, Isaac Newton, in the antechamber of the chapel. Every time that Ralph, George Trevelyan and their friends entered the college chapel they would walk past this imposing image of the great historian. Lord Macaulay was a powerful inspiration to his nephew and, to a considerable extent, also to Ralph. Ralph studied history at Cambridge, and his concern with history shows itself in his subsequent career. One of Ralph's contributions to the musical culture of his time, albeit a minor one, was his steady sequence of writings: essays, lectures, criticism and journalism. In many of these there is a strong historical perspective. In words, as so often in his music, most famously, for instance, in his evocation of Thomas Tallis, he sought to indicate a new history of English music.

In the year that Ralph went up to Trinity, William Gladstone became Prime Minister for the fourth and last time. His prime purpose in taking office was to loosen Ireland's ties to the British Empire by granting the Irish Home Rule. He failed to do this and soon left office. The passionate, militant young Liberals who were Ralph's closest friends during his undergraduate years now had ten years to wait before another Liberal would become Prime Minister. The Tory, imperialist vision carried the country; it was also strong in Cambridge. One of its spokesmen was Sir John Seeley, who was the Regis Professor of History when Ralph went up. He was a very effective and popular lecturer and Ralph, preparing for the Historical Tripos, must surely have gone to hear him.

Seeley had made his name some thirty years before with his book *Ecce Homo*, an attack on Christianity that had involved him in a spirited, polemical exchange with Gladstone and Cardinal Newman. Two years before Ralph became a historian at Cambridge, Sir John Seeley produced what was to become another famous work, his *Expansion of England*. This was an imperialist work that proclaimed the importance and the value of the worldwide system that Britain had built up. It especially recorded and commended the process whereby Britain had taken control of that pre-eminent part of its Empire, India. Seeley's book was, in one important respect, a rebuttal of Lord Macaulay's. There is no mistaking the school of historical thought Seeley has in mind when he writes that certain historians 'make too much of the parliamentary wrangle and the agitations about liberty, in all which matters the eighteenth century was but a pale reflection of the seventeenth. They do not perceive that in that century, the history of England is not in England but in America and Asia.' Professor Seeley gained young George Trevelyan's lifelong enmity when he told the fervently Liberal undergraduate that his uncle, Lord Macaulay, was 'nothing but a charlatan'.

At this time, the two tutors involved in directing studies in history at Trinity College were more acceptable to 'Trevy'. One was Basil Edward Hammond whose best known work was *Political Institutions of the*

Ancient Greeks, which became a standard book in the field for many years. Hammond was working on it at the time Ralph matriculated and it was published in 1895, the year he graduated. Hammond's interest in the evolution of the Classical world would have been appealing to Ralph who had done well in Classics at Charterhouse. This element in his education would be helpful years later when he accepted an invitation to write the accompanying music for a production of *The Wasps* of Aristophanes put on at the Amateur Dramatic Company in November 1909. It must have been a pleasure to Ralph that in composing that music he was following in the footsteps of his admired teacher Sir Hubert Parry who, just over a quarter of a century before, in 1883, had written the music for the Cambridge production of Aristophanes' *The Birds*.

The other history tutor at Trinity during Ralph's undergraduate years was William Cunningham; he was one of the younger historians who were beginning to see history less in the traditional terms of kings and queens and more in terms of social – and more especially – economic forces. In a lecture of 1955, nearly sixty years after he graduated, Ralph's friend and fellow history student, George Trevelyan looked back on the course of his discipline and saluted William Cunningham as a pioneer in the writing of social history. To an audience at Christ's College he declared that in the emergence of 'social history, there is no doubt that it has now a much more solid base in economic history, which I consider was only begun as a serious academic subject by Dr Cunningham of Trinity at the time when I was an undergraduate.'[9] As will become evident, a shrewd awareness of social, economic and financial forces is an important feature in Ralph's writings on music and history. At university his political position moved more to the left than it had been at Charterhouse. He later recalled, 'When I got to Cambridge in '93, I and a few friends read the Fabian tracts and in opposition to the majority of undergraduates became Socialists.'[10]

The course of the close friendship between Ralph, George Trevelyan and George Moore proceeded within a web of other undergraduate friendships. Unquestionably the most important of these for Ralph was that with his distant cousin Ralph Wedgwood, who was always known to those close to him as Randolph. This very handsome young man and his brother Felix had an overwhelming effect on Gwen Raverat and her siblings. 'For, when I was about seven or eight, two Gods revealed them-selves to our worshipping eyes. They were our cousins, Ralph and Felix Wedgwood, and they came as undergraduates to Trinity, first Ralph and, soon after, Felix. Divine Beings, glorious in their condescension....'[11] Ralph Wedgwood's effect upon Ralph was not as overwhelming as this; nevertheless, it was extremely powerful.

After his freshman years when he lodged at 17 Magdalene Street, Ralph moved into 2 Whewell Court in the college, where he remained for the rest of his time at Cambridge. Here Ralph and Randolph lunched together (usually on biscuits and jam) just about every day. Ralph very much looked up to Randolph, who remained an important figure in his emotional life until years after Ralph was married.

Although almost two years younger than Ralph, Randolph was far more assured and self-possessed. An imposing, attractive young man, he had been head of school at Clifton College before going up to Trinity. He went on to be awarded a double first in the Moral Sciences Tripos. In that glamorous era of railways Randolph subsequently pursued a career which led him to a very senior position with the London North Eastern Railway and to a knighthood. At Cambridge one day Ralph and Randolph arranged to go to a photographer to have a double portrait made. Perhaps it was to be a gift to the several relatives the two cousins had in common. The photograph shows two very elegant, good-looking young men in wing collars. Randolph, his face brightly lit and in three-quarters profile, looks into the distance, a thoughtful, perhaps even spiritual expression on his face. Ralph in near half-profile stoops over his cousin's shoulder. He wears a striped waistcoat and sports a fluffy white handkerchief in his breast pocket. He grasps his pipe firmly in his mouth. Bending slightly over Randolph, Ralph looks to be sharing and respecting his companion's thoughtfulness. The moment the shutter of the camera is closed is a moment of great delicacy of feeling and of sympathy.

It offers a contrast to another moment when Ralph, that 'most determined atheist' as another Cambridge friend, Bertrand Russell, called him, swaggered into hall, demanding in a loud voice 'who believes in God nowadays I should like to know?'[12] Ralph's sense of himself while at Cambridge seems to have alternated a great deal. He could show a confidence approaching arrogance but he could also experience profound self-doubt, even self-loathing. In the latter moments, Randolph was a great help and inspiration to him. Shortly after leaving the university Ralph wrote his cousin a long, reminiscing and highly confessional letter.

He began with a tribute: 'I don't know why I shouldn't tell you how much being with you kept me up to the mark.' And then follows a spasm of self-disgust: 'I am naturally of a bestial, lazy, sensual, earthy, devilish nature but when I was with you a lot of that used to disappear, it was entirely your example that made me do what little work I did do.' There follows what Ralph himself refers to as a rhapsody of gratitude and indebtedness to Randolph. 'How splendidly you used to bear with my indecent or otherwise low remarks, or amazingly silly things I used to do and say, how you ever bore it I don't know. And so you see how necessary that I, who can never return your absolute goodness for its own sake, should occasionally see and converse with people for whose sake I think it worthwhile to make an effort, and I think you are the only man who has the desired effect.' The letter then becomes more sober: 'I hope you will excuse this rhapsody.... I have every intention of becoming more practical on the next page.'[13]

The practicalities all have to do with arrangements for Ralph and Randolph to get together. With hopeful enthusiasm Ralph writes, 'Why don't you come to London quite soon and stay several nights and then we'd go to theatres together and enjoy ourselves.' One possible date is unavailable to Ralph because of a promise to be with his mother. He has to keep it even though it means that two of his rivals for Randolph's company, Maurice Amos and George Moore, would have the charismatic Randolph to themselves. Compelled to reject, very reluctantly, a possibility of meeting, Ralph expresses his jealous annoyance in mock-biblical tones writing that 'filial piety wd drive me home even at the risk of making Amos skip like a ram and the little Moores leap like young sheep.'

Ralph's jealousy at seeing his other Trinity friends getting close to Randolph seems to have been intense. Perhaps one irritant for him was that George Moore, 'Trevy' and Randolph were members together of the Cambridge society known as the Apostles. Ralph was not a member. Several others of his good friends at Trinity belonged to the society. The strikingly handsome Llewelyn Davies brothers – Theodore, and Crompton who was the older and who would later on in life act as Ralph's solicitor – were both Apostles. And so too was the mathematician and philosopher Bertrand Russell, who would make a major contribution to Ralph's mental and emotional development by introducing him to the work of the American poet Walt Whitman. In the 1890s poetry was a far greater influence on general culture and on attitudes than it is now. Whitman's poetry would have a massive effect on Ralph's thinking and on his early musical compositions. Later in life Ralph would say of Whitman that, quite simply, he 'never got over him'.

The Apostles, sometimes referred to as 'The Society', had been founded in 1820 as the Cambridge Conversazione Society. A club for lectures and philosophical discussion, it gradually developed a tradition of keeping secret the names of its members and its procedures and rituals. Among its members in Victorian times were Lord Tennyson and his close friend Arthur Hallam. Those elected to membership in the early twentieth century included E.M Forster, Lytton Strachey, Leonard Woolf, Ludwig Wittgenstein, Rupert Brooke and John Maynard Keynes. Two later Apostles with Marxist sympathies, Anthony Blunt and Guy Burgess, were discovered to have spied for the Soviet Union during the Second World War and the Cold War.

The first step towards membership of the Apostles was to become an 'embryo'; Ralph advanced that far but did not progress further. It may have been that this large, slightly lumbering young man with his pleasing diffidence and occasional immaturities did not display the ostentatious verbal brilliance of his close friends who went on to become fully fledged Apostles. And although Ralph had a deep interest in philosophy and literature which were preoccupations of 'The Society', these were by no means his chief concern. This was music. As it always would be.

While an undergraduate at Cambridge he commuted regularly to London to continue his lessons with Hubert Parry. In fact, Ursula Vaughan Williams reported that he chose history as his subject because the history 'lectures at Cambridge did not conflict with Parry's teaching days at the RCM.' But Ralph was also extremely active in the musical life of Cambridge. Two important new friends were the Gatty brothers: Ivor, who played the horn, and Nicholas, who was a violinist and later became a composer and an assistant conductor at Covent Garden. Ralph would often go over to Downing College to join the brothers in their 'scratch' concerts of chamber music. Along with their brother Rene, who was also a musician and presently away pursuing his studies in Germany, Ivor and Nicholas were important participants in Ralph's musical education during his early manhood. The friendships were to be long lasting. Years after they all left the university Ralph would continue to visit the Gattys at their family home at Hooton Roberts, a village on the road between Rotherham and Doncaster in South Yorkshire where their father was rector at the imposing hilltop church of St John the Baptist. Here over the years Ralph would take great delight in the informal music-making which came so readily to the Gatty family.

At Cambridge Ralph received tuition that would enable him to obtain the Mus. Bac. as well as a history degree from the university. He took lessons in composition from Charles Wood of Gonville and Caius College. Wood had been one of the fifty inaugural class members of the Royal College of Music when it first opened its doors nine years before, in 1883. Ralph remembered him, a laid-back Ulsterman not many years older than himself, as the 'finest technical instructor I have ever known', adding 'I do not say necessarily the greatest teacher. I do not think he had the gift of inspiring enthusiasm or of leading to the higher planes of musical thought. Indeed he was rather prone to laugh at artistic ideals and would lead one to suppose that composing music was a trick anyone might learn if he took the trouble. But for the craft of composition he was unrivalled, and he managed to teach me enough to pull me through my Mus. Bac.'[14]

The phrase 'enough to pull me through' indicates the tendency to self-depreciation that was to last until late in Ralph's life. These doubts must have been fostered by another of those who instructed him in music as an undergraduate. At Cambridge Ralph continued to take organ lessons. These were given him by Alan Gray who, at the end of Ralph's first year, succeeded Charles Villiers Stanford as organist and master of the choristers at Trinity College. Gray was another of those who had serious doubts about Ralph's abilities. In a letter to Professor Parratt who was in charge of organ tuition at the Royal College, Alan Gray confided, helplessly: 'I cannot tell him that I think he is justified in going in for an organist's career which is his pet idea. He seems to me so hopelessly "unhandy". He has got to a certain point and sticks there. I can never trust him to play a simple service for me without some dread at what he may do.'[15] But Alan Gray's serious doubts about Ralph's musicianship do not appear to have harmed the relationship between teacher and pupil. Ralph even inherited Alan Gray's robes which he wore on grand occasions later in life, including the coronation of Queen Elizabeth II. A couple of years before that event Ralph wrote of Alan, 'Our friendship survived his despair at my playing and I became quite expert at managing the stops at his voluntaries and organ recitals.'[16] On one occasion the atheistic Ralph might well have referred to his long hours of service to Alan Gray in the college organ loft as a way of deflecting a disciplinary challenge from a senior member of the College.

'I did not see you in Chapel this morning, Mr Vaughan Williams.'
'No, Sir.'

'Perhaps, however, you were in the organ loft?'

'Yes, Sir, I was.'

'Well, you can pray as well in the organ loft as in any other part of the Chapel.'

'Yes, Sir – but I didn't.'[17]

The slightly portly and heavily moustached Hugh Percy Allen brought to Ralph the most important, long-term friendship in music dating from his Cambridge years. Less than three years older than Ralph, Hugh had begun a career as a church organist in Reading at the age of eleven. He had recently come up to Christ's College in Cambridge after having gained the B.Mus. degree at Oxford. Hugh Allen (later Sir Hugh) was to have a distinguished career at the Royal College of Music of which he would become director. All his life he would use his considerable energy and organizing ability to help to promote Ralph's music. Ralph long remembered the powerful effect Hugh Allen had upon the musical life of Cambridge upon his arrival. 'Allen at once took over the amateur University Musical Club, shook them out of their complacency and made them rehearse such things as the Schumann and Brahms piano-forte quintets and Schubert's string quintet.' Hugh Allen's programming became a part of Ralph's musical education. 'I got much musical instruction in listening to the rehearsal of these works.'[18]

Hugh Allen was also responsible for an important marker in Ralph's career in music. For the very first time he heard one of his compositions performed before an audience. He remembered, 'Allen also gave me an opportunity of hearing, for the first time, a semi-public performance of a composition of my own, a quartet of men's voices. The occasion was problematic but also an adventure. At the first performance the tenor got a bar out and remained so nearly to the end. Allen organized an encore and it was done all over again, this time correctly. The audience disliked it the second time even more than the first. This may seem a small episode but it was my first experience of an essential and salutary, though unpleasant form of composition lesson, a performance in public, something quite different from a private rehearsal.'[19]

A fellow graduate who long remembered this concert was George Frederick McCleary whose career was to be in medicine. In a memoir written some sixty years later in 1958, McCleary recalled, 'Soon after coming up to Cambridge, Vaughan Williams joined the University Musical Club, which then had its rooms in a high building near the south-western corner of the Market Place. The purpose of the club was chiefly to study chamber music.... Once a year the club selected a team to give a concert at the Oxford Musical Union ... and welcomed an Oxford team in return. Vaughan Williams took a keen interest in the proceedings of the club.... He was never himself a performer, but at one concert in my time a composition of his, a quartet for men's voices was performed....' George McCleary also recalled how Ralph was quick to give leadership in the practicalities of the club's music-making: '... after one club concert Vaughan Williams went round with a collecting box for a good cause.' The club committee had organized a performance of Beethoven's C minor symphony. But due to shortage of funds had decided 'not to incur the expense of bringing down a bassoon player from London to play the *contrafagotto* part. Vaughan Williams felt so strongly that such a mutilation of the symphony would be a public scandal that he resolved to raise enough money to prevent it.'

The club was not exclusively devoted to serious music. It also had time for popular and humorous music, especially the funny songs that Ralph enjoyed throughout his life. George McCleary remembered that: 'The club concerts were often followed by an informal extempore entertainment of comic songs. In this hilarious province of the great art of music the most brilliant executant was Sudley Taylor, an elderly Trinity don and distinguished physicist who, for some reason or other had incurred the enmity of Karl Marx, by whom he was violently attacked in *Das Kapital*. His most popular songs were 'The Polka and the Choirboy' and a parody of 'The Lost Chord' entitled 'The Lost Ball' and beginning with the line 'Batting one day at the Oval".'[20]

Another important recreation for Ralph in his Cambridge days was made available by the coming of the bicycle. Cycling was one of the great innovations of social life in the 1890s bringing a liberating sense of mobility, especially to the young. Ralph particularly enjoyed cycling over to the nearby cathedral city of Ely. He would set off early in the morning, speed along the quiet roads of the flat fenlands and be excited as the great octagonal lantern of Ely Cathedral came into sight. He would arrive just in time to hear the large choir singing the morning service. During one of his winters at Cambridge there was bitterly cold weather and undergraduates, including Ralph, had the exhilarating experience of skating over the flatlands to Ely.

The organist at Ely Cathedral was T. Tertius Noble who had previously been the assistant organist at Ralph's college, Trinity. He went on to produce some well-known compositions for the Anglican liturgy and had a distinguished career as organist and choirmaster in the Church of St Thomas in New York. In June 1894, at the end of Ralph's second year at Trinity, Tertius Noble supplied the music for a comedy review entitled *Jupiter, LL.D* and subtitled *An Original Mythological Musical Extravaganza*. A satire of college life, the piece begins on The Topmost Height of Olympus. The second act descends to the pastoral setting of a forest near Maida Hall and the third concludes in the Great Court of Trinity College, Cambridge. The principal character, Juno, duets with a variety of Cambridge types: The Bedmakers, Two Boating Men and Two Bloods. Ralph was cast in the role of one of the more contemplative characters; he appeared as one of Two Reading Men.

For all the uncertainty, awkwardness and occasional diffidence that witnesses perceived in Ralph during his undergraduate years, he was not at all withdrawn. He participated in many musical groups, founded his own choral club to sing Schubert masses and was obviously ready to participate in entertainments such as *Jupiter*. And there were girls!

Through the medium of the words of Ralph's second wife, Ursula, we have Ralph's memory of his first love in all its emotional uncertainty and evanescence:

All through his life Ralph was romantically susceptible to beauty, and, at Cambridge he was as liable to fall in love as anyone of his age. His first flame was a girl who, he said, was not conventionally pretty, but most deliciously attractive. He met her at dances, at Sunday tea-parties and at tennis parties. Once Ralph Wedgwood accused him of faking the toss so that he could be the one to partner her and Ralph brazenly agreed that he had. This springtime fancy never grew beyond the quivering expectation of meeting and the melancholy rapture of parting at the end of a dance. Nothing was said, and she remained a delightful memory. They never met again, though he knew when and whom she married, and even sixty years later the steps of her house recalled moments of tremulous expectation.[21]

Photographs of Ralph in his Cambridge years show this very romantic young man to have been handsome and also to have cultivated the style of the dandy which was so fashionable in the 1890s. Dr Frederick McCleary thought that despite the doubts people had about Ralph's abilities, especially in his life's vocation of music: 'he was not without distinction in his Cambridge days. His physique was imposing and, though he was not copious or fluent in talk, what he said was worth hearing. He gave an impression of latent power and a capable and original personality. Even in those early days he was evidently Somebody.'[22]

Yet one of the very last images we have of Ralph's undergraduate career is a reminder of the defensiveness, the uncertainty of this slow developer. At Easter 1895, Ralph, George Trevelyan, Maurice Amos and George Moore continued with their custom of going on a 'reading tour'. The practice had already taken them to Cornwall and to the Isle of Skye. On this third occasion they went to Seatoller, then a very tiny settlement in Borrowdale in the English Lake District just to the south of Derwent Water. They climbed the nearby hills, swam and went for long walks. They also kept a log-book of their activities including the formal discussions they undertook. These included the insufficiency of Natural Selection, the novelist Thackeray, and the Universe in Relation to God. There were also stories, rhymes and sketches containing a good deal of undergraduate facetiousness. Ralph contributed this limerick:

> There was a young man of Seatoller
> Who did nothing but guzzle and swallow
> For he found that the food
> Was so tasty and good
> That he frequently wished he was holler

The party remained at Seatoller for nearly three weeks but Ralph had to leave at the end of the first week. George Moore put into the log-book a mock epitaph which commended Ralph's gentle wit. But clearly not everyone in the party enjoyed Ralph's humour for he found it necessary to rebut, in the log-book, criticisms of his readiness to indulge in shallow, coarse jest. In a more controlled way than his soul-bearing outburst to Ralph Wedgwood, and showing something of his literary ability, Ralph wrote for the log-book a sonnet entitled 'To a philosopher who complains that I was not serious enough.' It is addressed to 'Sophistes', who was George Moore – or perhaps Randolph Wedgwood. (The members of the reading group all assumed Classical names.) The sonnet, signed 'R.V.W', with its conspicuously Latinate syntax reads:

> Sophistes, thou hast blamed me, as a drone
> Who have not stored sweet wisdom in my brain,

Nor wished to feed on wisdom's golden grain.
But clutched at shallow jest, and gained – a stone.

Think not that I place folly on the throne
Where great Philosophy alone should reign
Or that I would not, if I could, lie prone,
Where high thou standest, in her shining train.

Rather consider that thy balanced mind
Would weigh and wanting find my wisest word,
Which aping thy discourse, crow-like, would find
That peacock plumes but merriment afford.

If then my serious talk appear a jest
My jests alone will stand thy serious test.

The party returned to Cambridge for the third term of that academic year, the term in which they had to take their Tripos examinations. Ralph's conspicuously brilliant friends all fared brilliantly. Each of them gained a distinguished First. Ralph got a second in the Historical Tripos.

But he was now able to go back to what he knew without the slightest doubt to be the true business of his life – music. Having undergone the conventional tertiary education of a young man of his social class, he could now return to the Royal College of Music to resume his slow, but intensely focused and unending, progress as a musician and a composer.

Chapter Four

LONDON, LOVE and MARRIAGE 1895–7

When Ralph hastened back to Albertopolis for the midsummer term of 1895 he found that some important changes had taken place. The Royal College of Music itself had moved to a site immediately to the south of the Royal Albert Hall. Just over a year earlier, in May of 1894, its new (and present) home, the imposing, red-brick building, very much a late Victorian concoction in the Flemish mannerist baronial style, had been declared open by the Prince of Wales in a grand ceremony. Another change was that the administration of the College had been reorganized. Ralph's beloved mentor Hubert Parry had been promoted and had taken over as Director. This meant that Parry was no longer available to teach Ralph composition. This responsibility now fell to the ebullient Irishman Charles Villiers Stanford.

Twenty years older than Ralph, Stanford came from a very wealthy and musically minded family in Dublin. He had a long drooping face with a large moustache but no beard. He wore a tasselled pince-nez and sported a slightly raffish bow-tie. Like Ralph he had been an under-graduate at Cambridge and his conspicuous precocity had led to him being appointed to the position of organist at Trinity College even before he had received his degree. One occasion that had impressed the Fellows in the early 1870s was his flamboyant playing of the Overture to Wagner's latest opera *Die Meistersinger* from the full score on the college organ. Some, like the Master of Trinity, were uncertain about Stanford's avant-gardeism. The Master once introduced him as 'Mr Stanford, whose playing always charms us, and occasionally astonishes; and I may add that the less he astonishes the more he charms.'[1]

Stanford moved to London and energetically pursued a career as a composer of religious and secular works. But most of them failed to gain any lasting success. In the year Ralph became his pupil, Stanford was working on his comic opera, *Shamus O'Brien*. This was a setting of a libretto deriving from a play by George H. Jessop, an Irish writer who had emigrated to the United States of America and who had enjoyed several popular successes in the theatre there. Along with Stanford's *Much Ado*, it was an opera that Ralph long admired. Late in life he deplored its total neglect by opera houses that continued to 'shake the dead bones of *Norma* and *Samson and Delilah*.'[2] However Ralph's relationship with his new teacher was by no means an easy or comfortable one, certainly not as immediately inspiring or rewarding as his time studying with Hubert Parry had been. A few months before he died Ralph paid a handsome tribute to Stanford, declaring that he was 'a great composer, a great teacher, a skilled conductor, and as befits a true Irishman, a lovable, quarrelsome and generous man.' But a few years earlier Ralph had acknowledged the time-wasting, sterile tensions that had persisted between himself and Stanford. 'Stanford was a great teacher, but I believe I was unteachable. I made the great mistake of trying to fight my teacher.' Unlike Parry, Stanford neither sought nor found anything 'characteristic' in Ralph's compositions.

'The details of my work annoyed Stanford so much that we seldom arrived at the broader issues and the lessons usually started with a conversation on these lines: "Damnably ugly, my boy, why do you write such things?" "Because I like them." "But you can't like them; they're not music." "I shouldn't write them if I didn't like them." So the argument went on and there was no time left for any constructive criticism.'[3]

But for all his difficulties with Stanford, Ralph was to find that this teacher would do much to advance his career. Stanford helped him with the Mass he now set about writing for his Cambridge doctorate. And Stanford it was, along with Ralph's old university friend, the pushy Hugh Allen, who was to help get Ralph's first symphony performed at the Leeds Festival where Stanford held an influential position. In this same autobiographical essay Ralph goes on to make the point (that many would wholeheartedly endorse) that the teachers are not necessarily the most important part of a college education. He writes, 'The benefit that one obtains from an academy or college is not so much from one's official teachers as from one's fellow students', adding, 'I was lucky in my companions in those days.' He then lists among these 'Dunhill, Ireland, Howard Jones, Fritz Hart and Gustav Holst' – the second and pre-eminently the last of these contributing significantly to Ralph's life and to the history of music.

Extra-curricular activities in the college were also important to him. A few months after returning to London he was a member of the chorus, a be-robed priest, in a student production of Purcell's *Dido and Aeneas* conducted by Stanford and staged at the Lyceum Theatre in The Strand, with scenery lent by the great impresario and actor Henry Irving. Ralph would later make a more substantial and lasting contribution to the revival of Purcell's music that was gathering strength in the 1890s. He was also very active in the literary and debating society at the Royal College of Music. He gave papers on Purcell, Bayreuth, Didactic Art and the rise and fall of the Romantic school. And, in a year when the writings of Friedrich Nietzsche were increasingly a subject for student conversation, he was the proposer of the motion 'That the moderate man is contemptible'. After his three years at Cambridge Ralph appears to have come back to London with a new confidence, even flamboyance, dressing, as Ursula puts it, 'with a worldly dash remarkable among young musicians.' She repeats a story of one of his dandyish exploits that was often reported at the RCM 'that he appeared there after a wedding dressed in a morning coat and top hat; leaving later with some friends, they met a man playing a barrel organ, who told them that he had had a very bad day. Ralph pushed the organ into Kensington High Street and turned the handle and collected nearly a pound before he gave it back to its owner.'

The meetings of the college debating society were usually concluded with a motion to adjourn to Wilkins' tea shop close by in Kensington High Street. The motion was proposed musically. The students would sing in unison: 'Shall we go to Wilkins? Shall we go to Wilkins? Yes!' to the opening bars of the scherzo of the Fourth Symphony of Brahms. Then off they would go for refreshments. And in Wilkins' tea shop, Ralph recalled, they would 'discuss every subject under the sun from the lowest note of the double bassoon to the philosophy of *Jude the Obscure*.'

The first publication in book form of *Jude the Obscure*, which proved to be Thomas Hardy's final novel, was one of two very dramatic events in the literary world in 1895. To the Victorians, its explicit accounts of sex, class prejudice and the destructive powers of social conventions provoked a torrent of hostile reviews and a good deal of wider and angry controversy. The Bishop of Wakefield burned his copy of the novel. The hostility that greeted the book's appearance was widely believed to have brought about Hardy's decision to give up writing novels and to turn to other literary forms – the vast Napoleonic epic *The Dynasts*, for instance, a work that in later years was to impress Ralph greatly. But for him and his fellow students at Wilkins in the 1890s, *Jude the Obscure* provided much to stimulate interest and argument. Hardy would continue to be an important writer and reference point for Ralph all through his life. Ursula notes that 'Ralph read all Hardy's novels, and one summer followed Tess's footsteps in her walk from Flintcomb to Emminster. He thought *Tess* the greatest of the novels and his other favourite was *Far from the Madding Crowd....* When the cinema became 'capable of great themes' as he put it, Ralph 'longed for a film to be made of *The Dynasts*, so naturally suitable for the screen, and he would have liked to write the music for it.'[4] If Ralph lived to see film mature into an art form and 'become capable of many great themes' and to see himself contributing to it, he was also very much an adult at the moment the art form was born. His student year of 1895 saw many important occasions in the early history of film technology, most significantly the first screening of moving pictures to an audience by the Lumieres brothers in Paris.

The other historic event in London literary life in that same year was the arrest and trial of Oscar Wilde. In the February, Wilde's *The Importance of Being Earnest* opened in the West End. Four days later at the Albemarle Club the Marquis of Queensberry made allegations that led to Wilde's trial on the charge of 'sodomy and gross indecency'. Across the Channel at the same time another cause célèbre was unfolding in France. In January, Alfred Dreyfus, an artillery officer of Jewish origins who had been convicted of treason for supposedly betraying French military secrets to the Germans, was subjected to a ritual of public humiliation. He was made to undergo '*degradation militaire*' and be physically stripped of his insignia of officer rank in a grand ceremony on the Champs de Mars. He was then sent to brutal imprisonment on Devil's Island. But the case against him was seen more and more to have been inspired by anti-semitic groups in the French army and the larger society. His case would become one of the causes of the left in France. It would take over ten years for the innocence of Dreyfus to be established and his complete vindication to be confirmed. During that time the '*affaire Dreyfus*' created an increasingly bitter division between progressive and reactionary groups in French society.

Throughout Europe this was a time of stark conflict between

Liberalism and Conservatism. In 1895 the Tory party returned to office in Britain; it would retain power for the next ten years. For some of Ralph's Cambridge friends who were fervent Liberals (for instance, Theodore Llewellyn Davies, who had gone into the Treasury, and also his brother Crompton who had entered the civil service after leaving university), this made for difficult, even painful times. In some five years' time, events deriving from the political condition of the country would impinge dramatically and damagingly on Ralph's life. But in 1895 political events were still but a matter of teashop discussion. His vital concerns were elsewhere. He had his first job and he was becoming involved in a love affair.

Shortly after returning to London from Cambridge Ralph applied for, and was offered, the post of organist and choirmaster at the church of St Barnabas in south Lambeth. The salary was fifty pounds a year. Although he had private income deriving from the Wedgwood investments endowed on him, Ralph seems to have found that the small silver spoon with which, he said, he was born, was never entirely adequate to his needs. Occasionally, in the first forty or so years of his life he had financial worries, and earned income was always welcome. Also, the puritan work ethic of the Staffordshire Wedgwoods, which was so much a part of his character and directed his conduct throughout his life, drove him to seek employment. And there is no doubt that the work at St Barnabas on top of his obligations at the RCM must have been demanding. Here is how he described the job, in particular the weekly timetable for choir practice, in a letter at the time:

Monday: boys any time after 6.0
Wed: boys 7.0 service 8.0 – 9.0
Thurs: full practice 8.30 or 8.15 till 10 or past if you can get them to stop
Sunday: 11.0 with choral communion once a month 7.0 and children's service at 3.0 once a month.[5]

He also gave organ recitals at the church and founded a choral society and an orchestral society which became sufficiently skilled to perform a Bach cantata.

As an agnostic Ralph had a brief scruple about acquiescing in the vicar's requirement that he take holy communion. But already a determined careerist Ralph agreed, remarking that although he might by some be considered 'very wicked to have done all this', he nevertheless believed it 'more important to take every chance of improving one's talents (?!?) than to save one's soul.'[6] Also, he added, he enjoyed wearing the gown and hood to which he was entitled as a Cambridge graduate, 'in fact I always did it when there was choral communion because I thought it looked picturesque as I had a hood and went up first and was generally part of the show.'

The church of St Barnabas in south Lambeth had been completed and consecrated forty-five years before Ralph took up his post there. Architecturally it is similar to many of London's suburban churches erected in the early Victorian period, being built in the Gothic style, faced with square rubble with creamy-white stone dressing. But it is a good deal larger than most churches of its time and area. When Ralph looked out from the organ stool he could see a nave that could seat 1,500 people. With its jaunty tower and spire, on the righthand side of its west façade the church fronts on to a street flanked by nineteenth-century villas. By the early twenty-first century the church and vicarage had been converted into social housing. But in Ralph's day the immediate area would have suited prospering families aspiring to the middle class. But not many streets away there was another Lambeth of squalid, insanitary working-class tenements and noisy, showy and architecturally extravagant pubs and music halls, in one of which – the Canterbury Music Hall – the father of Charlie Chaplin sometimes performed. During Ralph's first year in Lambeth he may have crossed paths with the little cockney who was later to become one of the great figures of film. But not in his second and final year in his Lambeth job, for in 1896 the seven-year old Charlie Chaplin was removed from his impoverished, dysfunctional family and sent to a Cuckoo House, one of the dark, grim workhouses of late Victorian London where homeless children were brought up.

Ralph now had his own home for the first time in his life. Initially he had lodgings in Smith Square and crossed over Lambeth Bridge to his work. But then he found a place at St Barnabas Villas, South Lambeth Road, close to the church. Living south of the Thames Ralph found that his geographical and social awareness was widening. His Cambridge connections began to loosen. However, his friendship and esteem for Randolph Wedgwood were as intense as ever. Ralph was forever trying to get together with him and he still continued to be jealous of any time that he learned Randolph had spent with George Trevelyan or Maurice Amos. But other old Cambridge closenesses were starting to fall away. In April 1896 George Moore arranged another reading party, this time at

Penmenner in Cornwall. Along with Ralph, the group comprised George Trevelyan, Maurice Amos, Randolph Wedgwood and Moore himself. The party was together for three weeks and was joined at the Easter weekend by three Apostles, Arthur Verrall, C.P. Sanger and Crompton Llewellyn Davies. The gathering did not go well. George Moore found 'Trevy' 'intolerable'. In a letter he confided 'I did not like even to be in the same room with him … I disliked him very much and I hoped I should see as little as possible of him for the future….' Moore was also disenchanted with Ralph. 'For the rest, I did not like VW so much this time: he seemed more querulous and ill-humoured, and he couldn't walk fast.'[7]

The attempt to prolong undergraduate camaraderie had failed. But as friendships of only a year before weakened, Ralph was entering into new ones. And the one with a fellow student at the RCM, Gustav von Holst, became as important to him and, and over the longer course of his life, far more important even, than his early passionate friendship with Randolph Wedgwood. Two years younger than Ralph, Holst had been a student at the Royal College for two years before Ralph's return from Cambridge. He was the son of a music master in Cheltenham. The family surname was an indication of Swedish origins. Gustav's ancestors had moved about the Baltic lands and one of them had been court composer at the imperial court in St Petersburg. Gustav attended Cheltenham Grammar School where he early showed signs of the ill-health that was to afflict him throughout his life. A slight, frail but very intense young man, he had a weak chest and poor eyesight. More damaging to the musical career which he so passionately hoped and worked for, was the neuritis in his arm which finally led him to give up playing the piano and take up the trombone instead. But his passionate dedication to music showed early on in his schooldays. By the age of nineteen he was church organist at the small Cotswold village of Wick Rissington and then quickly took on the additional, more prestigious post of choirmaster, organist and director of the choral society in the larger community of Bourton-on-the-Water. Very early in his life Gustav also began to compose. By the age of twenty he had completed a two-act opera entitled 'Lansdowne Castle'. For its performance, Gustav enjoyed a still more prestigious location. The piece was performed at The Cheltenham Corn Exchange where it was a great success with both audience and reviewers. Gustav's father was sufficiently impressed that he took the difficult step of borrowing money to enable Gustav to go and live in London and study at the Royal College of Music. Here he studied composition with Stanford with whom, like Ralph, he was to have continuing disagreements. But Gustav also acknowledged the value of the teaching he received from the outspoken Irishman.

Until the end of his life Ralph remembered a detail from the occasion on which he first encountered this fellow student and took an instant liking to him. 'I first met him about 1895 when we were both at the Royal College of Music and he started the ball rolling by quoting Sheridan's *Critic*. This, for some reason, broke the ice and seemed to seal our friendship, and almost from that time onwards we used to meet at frequent intervals and give each other composition lessons.'[8] Richard Brinsley Sheridan's *The Critic*, a satire on theatre-folk and on the production of a heroic drama by the dramatist Mr Puff entitled 'The Spanish Armada', together with its mocking of a writer like Sir Fretful Plagiary and the critics Dangle and Sneer must have amused and interested the two young students. They were themselves keen theatre- and opera-goers and indeed, involved with Stanford's production of *Dido and Aeneas* at the Lyceum. And, of course, the two of them had aspirations to write stage music and opera. Gustav's interest in Sheridan's comedy may well have been inspired by Stanford, who was a great admirer of it and turned it into an opera which was performed in London in 1916.

When he first arrived in London from Gloucestershire Gustav quickly became involved with the group of artists and intellectuals who gathered around William Morris, poet, artist, craftsman and Socialist, at his home by the riverside at Hammersmith. Ralph later wrote of Gustav's first years in London after leaving his familiar Cotswold countryside. 'It was Holst's strong sense of human sympathy which brought him, when a young man into contact with William Morris and the Kelmscott Club. The tawdriness of London, its unfriendliness, the sordidness both of its riches and poverty were overwhelming to an enthusiastic and sensitive youth; and to him the ideals of Morris, the insistence of beauty in every detail of human life and work, were a revelation. No wonder then that the poetic socialism of the Kelmscott Club became the natural medium of his aspirations; to Morris and his followers "comradeship" was no pose but an absolute necessity of life.'[9]

Throughout Ralph's life people much less well off than he and without his social connections would attract his admiration. He was especially impressed by the way Gustav, very much in need of making a living, strode bravely into the hurly-burly of the music world in order to pay his way. 'Already in his student days he, like many others, had to be earning his living. He chose deliberately not to shut himself up in the organ loft or to give half-hearted pianoforte lessons to unwilling pupils, but to go out into the world armed with his trombone, playing, now in a symphony orchestra, now in a dance band, now in a Christmas pantomime in a suburban theatre.'[10] In those days when musicians were expected, even required, to be foreign, and if possible exotically so, Gustav worked for a season in a Magyar band which wore ornate blue uniforms. As he told Ralph: 'he spent his summer dressed up as a blue Hungarian, where he was admonished with a rude word by the manager to speak broken English.'[11]

That summer, seemingly that of 1896, supplied Ralph with an enduring memory of a student get-together. The first, and unnamed, student in the following sentences, who can afford to go perhaps a little superciliously on a Wagner pilgrimage but who is less inspired and inspiring about his summer than Gustav about his, is surely Ralph himself. Some forty years on he wrote: 'A reminiscence of those days still lives in my mind. At the end of our summer holidays some of us students met together to tell each other how we spent our vacation. One of us had been at Bayreuth and gave, I am sure, a highly critical appraisement of the proceedings. Others, perhaps had been to the Dolomites or to Brittany and were doubtless very poetical about it. In all this we listeners were mildly interested, but what remained in the memory of those who heard him was Holst's enthralling account of his experiences as a member of a seaside band, enthralling because of his great human sympathy, his unique humour, his strong sense of values.'[12]

Very soon after they met and so swiftly became friends Ralph and Gustav began their 'Field Days'. These were the occasions on which the two of them would meet, often for long walks in the countryside, and discuss very frankly their current compositions and the state of the music world in which each of them was starting a career. They were very open in their criticisms of each other's work. They each had an honesty of response that came from the affection and respect that each felt for the other. Ralph remembered that on their Field Days they would 'devote a whole day or at least an afternoon to examining each other's composi-tions ... these orgies must have started early and they continued to the end, that is to say, nearly forty years. I think he showed all he wrote to me and I nearly all I wrote to him. I say 'nearly all' advisedly, because sometimes I could not face the absolute integrity of his vision, and I hid some of my worst work from him. I regret now that I did not face even his disapproval.'[13] Ralph's career in music was blessed in several ways.

But there can be no doubt that highly prominent among these blessings was his close, mutually sustaining friendship with Gustav Holst. It stimulated, educated and confirmed him as a composer.

At the same time that his friendship with Holst was beginning Ralph was also starting to engage in what in those days would have been called a courtship. He began to call on Adeline Fisher who had been one of the participants at the music parties at Downing College, Cambridge. Adeline was the daughter of Herbert William Fisher, a historian noted for his book on the nature of slavery in the American Civil War. He had known Ralph's father at Oxford where they were undergraduates together at Christ Church. Fisher and his family, including Adeline, were regular guests of Ralph's uncle, Sir Roland Vaughan Williams, and his wife, Lady Laura, in their grand house in Queen Anne's Gate in Westminster. It seems likely that it was here, after his Cambridge days, that Ralph first called upon Adeline and later made clear his intentions towards her.

A very attractive young woman, Adeline had a long, narrow, sensitive face that had the Pre-Raphaelite style of feminine beauty that continued to be fashionable at the time Ralph began to woo her. A niece remembers that Adeline had 'fair hair coloured like spring sunshine in a winter world; soft and cool as snow, slender and very gentle, she breathed rather than walked into the house and then breathed away again.' The writer also recalled a less Rossettian side to Adeline. 'This gentleness fed a mind both humorous and acute. If other people's deficiencies played small part in her thought and none in her rare, deliberate speech, it was not for lack of a critical apparatus. She was in fact well equipped intellectually as well as by temperament to share in and foster the development of R.V.W.'s musical thought; and it was on this that her faculties were concentrated.'[14] Adeline's father was a man of some distinction. At Christ Church he was appointed tutor to the young Prince of Wales who, despite being reprimanded for loutish behaviour toward his tutor, made him his private secretary after he became king. Herbert Fisher also had a successful career as a lawyer and as a scholar. He was a Member of the Inner Temple and called to the Bar in 1855. Exactly ten years later there would appear the book that would establish his reputation as a writer on recent history – his *Considerations on the origin of the American War,* a description of attitudes to slavery in the Confederate and Union states and the importance of those attitudes in the coming of the American Civil War.

The Fishers had been established for centuries as a manorial family in the village of Brockenhurst, a few miles north of Lymington in

Hampshire. When the last of three maiden aunts died, Herbert Fisher inherited the ancestral home which, in its most recent form, was (and is) a very substantial early nineteenth-century mansion on the edge of Brockenhurst. In this remote, rural place, among the trees and wild ponies of the New Forest, Adeline grew up. Her mother, Mary Fisher, who was a great beauty and very artistic, made life in the nursery exciting. She painted the furniture with landscapes showing animals, birds and flowers. She made the children dresses so that they could act and imagine themselves into those dream worlds so much enjoyed by well-to-do children at the end of the Victorian period. The inherited house was full of ancient furniture and trunks full of old suits and dresses. Adeline's childhood was one surrounded by romance.

The family was an extremely large one; Adeline had seven brothers and three sisters. Several of them were to have an important impact on Ralph's life, none more so than Hervey Fisher who was some three years younger than Adeline. He wrote short stories, a volume of which, *A Romantic Man and other Tales* was published in 1920, a year before his early, long drawn-out death at the age of forty-eight. In one of them, 'An Afternoon', Hervey, portrayed as Kenneth, describes Adeline, who appears as Marjorie. There is some faint, delicate irony in the description of the young girl but it seems likely that this is very much how the family saw Adeline and how she saw herself.

> Marjorie was a flaxen-haired girl of sixteen ... with heavy-lidded grey eyes and the light of June in her cheeks ... to the brothers, the girls were on the whole Olympian and mysterious....
>
> Their beauty, virginal and dewy, gave a shape in his mind to those lovely Greek legends that already stirred in his heart a vague yet passionate desire. He saw in them the embodiment of myths, the rosy realisation of immortal shadows. Marjorie was a more human goddess. She played hide-and-seek sometimes, read aloud fairy tales, caught newts and butterflies, paddled in the river, sailing boats with the boys. Though sixteen, her hair still hung over her shoulders in a yellow cascade ... she was still a child's playmate with the warmth of the nursery yet upon her. Only her flashes of superior wisdom revealed to her brothers that she had descended from the heights.

The Pre-Raphaelite mode of perception intimated in the early sentences of Hervey's description was an important part of the growing up of the young Adeline and her siblings. One of Adeline's aunts, on her mother's side, was Julia Margaret Cameron, an important figure in the early history of art photography who had sought to present in photographs the same kinds of subjects as the Pre-Raphaelite painters. Many of her photographs showed staged occasions from Arthurian legend and other myths. She also photographed many of her eminent Victorian contemporaries. Her portraits include ones of family, friends and servants. She made a number of photographs of Adeline's eldest sister Florence, who married the law professor Frederic Maitland and resided with him in Downing College, Cambridge. Adeline was only five when Julia Margaret Cameron left England to live in what was then Ceylon, so she can have had very few memories of her energetic, bustling aunt. Nevertheless, until the end of her life she kept in her possession an album of photographs by Julia Margaret Cameron. When, very shortly before Adeline's death, a *Vogue* photographer came to take photographs of Ralph, Adeline reported excitedly that the visitor was 'a great admirer of Mrs Cameron and was thrilled with my album.'

Early in his relationship with Adeline Ralph composed settings of poems by Dante Gabriel Rossetti. These songs about love seem to confirm and to cater to Adeline's sense of herself as a Pre-Raphaelite figure and to the kind of love that both she and Ralph knew and understood. 'Willow Wood', a cantata for piano and baritone or mezzo-soprano, and Ralph's first major song sequence, is a setting of four sonnets taken from Rossetti's volume *The House of Life*. They are suffused by the melancholy that continued to be characteristic of the love poetry of Europe in the late nineteenth century, for instance in that of Paul Verlaine and the early W.B. Yeats. The sense of love devitalized by an awareness of loss and death and educated into spiritual understanding and sympathy runs through the Rossetti lines that Ralph chose to set.

And now Love sang; but his was such a song.
So meshed with half-remembrance hard to free,
As souls disused in death's sterility
May sing when the new birthday tarries long
And I was made aware of a dumb throng
That stood aloof, one from every tree,
All mournful forms, for each was I or she,
The shadow of those our days that had no tongue.

Was Ralph comfortable with this kind of sensibility? There is robustness and stolidity to his setting of the texts that are at variance with the very delicate, mournful flickerings of hope and hopelessness that run through Rossetti's words in these sonnets. But the discrepancy is reduced by the elegiac voiceless postlude that Ralph creates to conclude the song cycle.

As the courtship progressed, Ralph and Adeline would go and stay with Florence and Frederic Maitland. Adeline's sister and brother-in-law had a country home where they lived when they were not in Cambridge. This house was 'Horsepools' in the Cotswold countryside near Stroud in Gloucestershire. Here the two lovers were the objects of intense fascination to the Maitlands' two little daughters, Fredegond who was now eight and Ermengard who was a year older (and who were known in the family as 'Gaga' and 'Vuff'). Many years later, Ermengard remembered how 'we crept through bushes in the Horsepool gardens to see them sitting in an arbour and the shrub called by us Bridal wreath held the sum of our experience.' She also remembered Ralph supplying a piano accompaniment to her mother as she played her violin. But for the little girls the visits of the young couple were their 'first step into Romance – a very short step for he and Adeline were much like our prince and princess in grace and beauty and [we] were wide-eyed in excitement over their engagement.'

In mid-July 1897 Ralph wrote to Randolph Wedgwood announcing the engagement. In an awkward, stumbling, syntactically incoherent, opening sentence he writes, 'so that you think it is possible for people to care for each other and when they do find it out they ought to tell each other – That is what Adeline Fisher and I have done and we have agreed to marry.' He clearly thinks that this news will surprise his old friend for he continues, 'take a long breath and then read on.' Ralph then proceeds to explain, in a notably passionless way, how the friendship between he and Adeline (of which Randolph was surely aware) had suddenly resulted in an engagement. 'She is two years older than I am; you know, I think, that for many years we have been great friends and for about the last three I have known my mind on the matter.' The last words indicate that Ralph had wished to marry Adeline since he was twenty-two and in his last year at Cambridge. A very youthful commitment.

In the same letter Ralph is anxious to assure his close friend that the coming marriage will not affect their friendship. In another nervous, scurrying, slightly fudging sentence that is a whole paragraph long he writes:

It is sometimes said that when a person is going to be married his rela-
tions with his friends alter – do not let this be so in this case because
she cannot hold <u>more</u> the first place than she has done before with
me because that is impossible and you and I have never been greater
friends than we are now – may I think so at all events – and now you
and she will be cousins and great friends too.

Ralph also had to inform the head of the Vaughan Williams family, his
uncle, Lord Justice of Appeal, Sir Roland Vaughan Williams. He was slow
to write this letter; he sent it approximately one month later than that
to Randolph. He addresses it to Uncle Roland's wife Aunt Laura in their
early eighteenth-century house in fashionable Queen Anne's Gate that
had a view over St James's Park. It was a very stiff, formal letter mitigated
only by the gentle, reproachful sarcasm of the first sentence. 'I think
that important steps taken by even the most insignificant members of a
family should be communicated to the other branches of that family.' The
announcement, which is a mere four sentences long, ends curtly: 'I will
only ask you and Uncle Roland to wish me well as I hope you will.' He
then signs his full name.

Ralph made his successful proposal in London, at 22 Hyde Park
Gate which was very close to the Royal College of Music and the home
of Adeline's Aunt Julia. She was the second wife of Leslie Stephen, an
eminent literary critic and editor of the *Cornhill Magazine* in which he
published leading late Victorian writers such as Henry James, Robert
Louis Stevenson and Thomas Hardy. Both in his residence and his influence, Leslie Stephen was at the centre of Albertopolitan culture. The two
Stephen daughters were soon to achieve success in the arts: Vanessa,
who married Clive Bell, as a painter, and Virginia, who married Leonard
Woolf, as a novelist and essayist. Virginia and Vanessa were not kindly
disposed towards their cousin Adeline or to her mother, their Aunt Mary.
But Stella Duckworth, the Stephen girls' half-sister, the daughter of Julia
Stephen by her first marriage (and thus Leslie Stephen's stepdaughter)
was Adeline's very close friend. Stella had been pursued by Jack Hills, a
young former Etonian who was preparing to become a solicitor. To the
relief of her father she rejected his many proposals of marriage. But then
she suddenly accepted him. Stella was married on 10 April 1897 and then
immediately travelled to Paris with her new husband for the honeymoon.
On her return, Stella was taken seriously ill with what, after some delay,
was diagnosed as pregnancy complications. Adeline rushed to London to

be with her friend. Stella appeared to recover. In early June, Ralph went to the Stephen house and made his proposal of marriage to Adeline. She accepted. The next day, after receiving the news, Mrs Fisher, but not her husband, travelled to London from the new Fisher residence, a large early Victorian villa close to the sea at 19 Second Avenue, Hove, East Sussex, to congratulate her daughter and her new fiancé Ralph.

Adeline and her mother returned to Hove; Ralph remained in London to do his job at St Barnabas and to continue with his efforts as a composer. On Adeline's birthday (14 July), he cycled all the way from London to the Sussex coast to bring her a birthday gift. But on that very same day the news reached Hove that Stella Duckworth had suffered a serious relapse. Adeline immediately set off for London. Three days later, with Adeline beside her, Stella died.

Adeline was utterly distraught. For a time it looked like her marriage to Ralph would have to be cancelled. But now Aunt Laura, wife of Sir Roland Vaughan Williams, who had only recently been informed, in Ralph's brusque note, of the engagement, took a hand in stabilizing it. She invited Adeline to come and stay with her in the house in Queen Anne's Gate. In those opulent surroundings Lady Vaughan Williams calmed the distressed young woman whom she had known since she was a child. It appears likely that she also encouraged Adeline to proceed with the marriage, a commitment about which some close onlookers, especially in the Fisher family were extremely doubtful. Adeline finally began to come to terms with her intense grief and returned to her parents' house near Brighton. The marriage was once again confirmed.

The wedding took place on 9 October 1897, in Adeline's parish church, All Saints in Hove, a grand building which in that year was still in the process of construction. All Saints, designed by an eminent London architect, was being built to service the needs of the well-to-do people like Adeline's family, who were settling in this expensive, fashionable suburb of Brighton. The marriage ceremony was performed not by the incumbent vicar Thomas Peacey, though he was in attendance, but by an old friend of Adeline's father. They had known each other since under-graduate days at Oxford. This was the Reverend W.A. Spooner, now Fellow of New College, Oxford, who was to give his name to the kind of joke based on a comic speech error, the Spoonerism. The marriage certif-icate records that the witnesses were Adeline's father, Herbert W. Fisher who styled himself 'J.P. Sussex' and Ralph's uncle, Sir Roland Vaughan Williams. In that same year Sir Roland, who some seventeen years before had published, what was for decades a standard work of jurisprudence, *The Law and Practice of Bankruptcy,* had become a Lord Justice of Appeal. He presumably was the leader of the Vaughan Williams family 'authorities' who had prevented Ralph from becoming an orchestral player when he had left school some seven years before. A third witness at the wedding was listed simply as R.L. Wedgwood, Ralph's old and dear friend Randolph who acted as his best man. Ralph himself is styled not choirmaster or church organist but rather 'Gentleman'. This term for his 'Rank or Profession' was chosen seemingly to indicate his social standing and perhaps his independence as one financially self-sufficient. Certainly *not* a musician.

Gaga and Vuff were the bridesmaids. In a letter, now in the British Library, Ermengard recalled, years later, how awkwardly she and her sister had conducted themselves at the grand family ceremony. 'We were their very badly behaved bridesmaids – just told to do as they did. So when they knelt, we sat on the floor. I can see and feel our stiff benzaline silk frocks now.' Ermengard later burnt her copy of the wedding photograph. And later still greatly regretted doing so. The reason she gives for her action clearly indicates the snobberies of the day, deriving from the great division between anyone in small business and those socially eminent such as the Fishers and the Vaughan Williamses. The photograph was an embarrassment; it did not portray the wedding party sufficiently as members of their station in life. Ermengard writes: 'I so wish I still had the wedding group but it was supposed to make them 'look like shopkeepers!' and in middle-aged respectability I burnt it.'

The acceptability of Ralph as a husband for Adeline appears to have been questioned in the Fisher family. Her niece, Mary Bennett, recalled that: 'Adeline was not thought to be making a good match. The more romantic members of the family might think it very splendid that she and Ralph should be married and turn their backs on the world of visiting cards and dinner parties, and live so austerely and for music alone; the elders found it odd that she should prefer this awkward and silent fellow, younger than herself and without a proper profession....' Adeline's sister Cordelia remembered the response of their father to the letter Adeline sent from the Stephen house in London announcing her engagement to Ralph. Herbert Fisher opened it at the breakfast table and was much cast-down, remarking gloomily, 'So it's a fait accompli.' From Ursula's biography and therefore very likely from Ralph himself, we hear that, 'The Fishers were not anxious for their daughter to marry, home life seemed to fulfil every demand. "Adeline could have married anyone" was often said, but quite obviously she didn't want to, and no-one succeeded in touching what many must have believed to be a heart of ice. Besides her beauty she had a quick wit, a lively intelligence, and an ability to be cruelly critical.'[15]

'Adeline could have married anyone.' But, in the event, by the age of twenty-seven she hadn't. She was of an age that in those days began to promise a future as a spinster. Virginia Woolf, when she met her cousin Adeline's fiancé, found him immature. Perhaps he did not understand Adeline's situation very clearly. Certainly he cannot have imagined the impact that his large family of in-laws would have upon his life. Not long before he died, Ralph seems to have confided to Ursula the hurt that he experienced from the Fisher family. Since Ursula was not even born when these relationships were established, we must assume that this assessment of the Fisher family came from Ralph himself. She reports that the Fishers practised 'a cult of family so passionate and intense that even the husbands and wives they married remained outsiders although officially accepted and loved'.

Arguably Adeline's most successful and most eminent sibling was her brother Herbert Fisher. Some two years older than she, he distinguished himself both at his public school, Winchester, and as an undergraduate at New College, Oxford. He went on to pursue careers as a historian and a politician. A Liberal, he became an MP and then Minister of Education and a member of Lloyd George's cabinet during the First World War. (In this capacity he would appear to have played an important part at a very painful juncture in Ralph's life.) In his memoirs Herbert Fisher suggests that at the time of Adeline's marriage their family had come down in the world since the days in which they had hobnobbed with the Royal Family. The chief cause was the long-lasting illness of their brother Hervey which had 'culminated in a serious but temporary mental breakdown. "Hervey's years of suffering" cast a shadow over family life. My mother, and after her death my sister Adeline Vaughan Williams, spent their lives in his sick room.' It also brought about a pointed lowering of the family's social position. It was 'the cause of our giving up our house in the New Forest, for Brighton, a town in which we had no friends and where my father was forced at an advanced age to seek for new and less congenial occupations.'[16] Herbert Fisher's only child, Adeline's niece, was Mary Fisher, who also became a historian. After a career in the Civil Service and marriage to a colleague there, she became Principal of St Hilda's College, Oxford.

In the late 1950s she corresponded with Ursula, assisting her in her research for her biography of Ralph. In one of her letters she says of the Fisher family's attitude to Adeline's choice of husband: 'I'm sure no overt line against VW marriage was ever taken – family would have been officially enchanted. But some at least thought it (a) odd (b) disappointing.'

She goes on to remark of Ralph's numerous brothers- and sisters-in-law, 'As you will have realised, Fishers can be sharply divided into the wild and the sane! With Hervey as the leading wild and I think of my father and Aunt A[deline] (who were very like each other to look at) vying as the leading sane. The sane ones adored the wild ones and probably wished they were more like them.' Mary Bennett continues: 'My mother ... always thought that A[deline] and R[alph] took on all family crises and responsibilities – she was always deeply impressed by RVW's saintliness over miscellaneous in-laws of varying degrees of tiresomeness – from the straight boring to the raving mad....'[17]

The wild Fishers as well as the sane Fishers would alike greatly affect Ralph's life. In the latter category along with a cabinet minister was an admiral who received a knighthood, two military heroes and a chairman of Barclay's Bank. In the former group were two who had had severe mental health problems leading in one case to attempted suicide and sectioning. One of Adeline's siblings was to be the victim of what can be considered the greatest hoax of the Edwardian period. 'In the twentieth century the family story was to continue to be marked by a great deal of suffering. During the first thirty years of the marriage of Adeline and Ralph the Fishers were devastated by tragedy after tragedy, terrible blows that must surely resonate in Ralph's life and music. In the midst of this suffering it was the partnership of Ralph and Adeline that, despite initial reservations about their marriage, became the rock of family life. Outliving all but one of the original eleven, it was they who kept in touch and came to the rescue; who were the first to receive news of tragedy and success; who provided the point of stability to which each brother and sister or nephew or niece might return.'[18]

These developments lay in the future as did Ralph's great achievements in music, of which the Fishers at that time had not the faintest suspicion. But at that time of the marriage, Adeline's father, despite his reservations about the young church organist with his uncertainties and gaucheries and his second-class degree (the Fishers invariably got Firsts), may well have been somewhat reassured to receive a solicitor's letter dated exactly a week after the wedding confirming that Ralph, like each of his two siblings, was a beneficiary of the residuary estate of their Bagot grandmother, Dame Jane Margaret Vaughan Williams. They each inherited a third of her estate. Most of the inheritance came from investments in the British imperial system. There were shares in the East India Railway and, far more substantially, in the Madras Railway Company. Dame Margaret also bequeathed a large number of domestic shares in the Great Western Railway. Ralph's small silver spoon was paid for not just by the Wedgwoods but by his father's family too.

But while the Fishers pondered their doubts and the two families engaged in correspondence about financial matters pertaining to the marriage, the bride and her younger groom seem to have been very content together. Ralph's letters and other testimony suggest it was a happy couple who, towards the end of that year, 1897, prepared to set out on their wedding journey.

Chapter Five

BERLIN AND AFTER

In the late autumn of 1897 the newly married couple set off for Berlin. Their stay in the imperial German capital was both their honeymoon and Ralph's last period of formal tuition as an apprentice musician. They remained in the city for close on six months

The year 1897 was an eventful one in the history of music. Gustav Mahler took up the directorship of the Vienna Court Opera, Richard Strauss completed *Till Eulenspiegel* and Rachmaninov produced his First Symphony. But most affecting for Ralph and for his teacher Hubert Parry, was the death of Brahms in the April of that year. In response, Parry composed his Requiem for Brahms, and Ralph, in one of his first attempts at music journalism contributed to *The Musician* an article entitled 'The Romantic Movement and its Results', which, confidently and robustly, assesses Brahms's place in the history of music. Quickly resolving the long-standing disagreements between the admirers of Brahms and Wagner, the young writer establishes that: 'if we trace the course of the romantic movement we shall find that though its day is over, yet it has not perished in the wilderness, but that it has reached its goal and done its work, and that this work was the creation of the New Art of Richard Wagner.'

He concludes: 'The next musical pioneer after Wagner must be a man who will start again on the lines from which the romanticists broke away, and who will write pure music out of a pure musical heart – and who has done this if not Brahms, the first whole-hearted classical composer since Beethoven? True, there has been an interregnum, but that does not make Brahms a reactionary, it only means that he has waited his time.'

Ralph's passionate interest in German music was a worry to his former teacher Charles Villiers Stanford. He urged Italy as an antidote and suggested that Ralph go and hear opera at La Scala in Milan. But Ralph was determined to go to Berlin to complete his studies. Here alone, except for Bayreuth, was Wagner's *Ring* cycle performed without cuts. And Ralph, like so many young people at this time was avid for the music theatre of Wagner. With Adeline he had carefully worked through the scores of several Wagner operas 'so that she might set out properly prepared for a forthcoming excursion to Bayreuth.'[1]

He got in touch with Heinrich von Herzogenberg, the head of the Department of Theory and Composition at the Hochschule für Musik in Berlin. This contact linked Ralph directly with the great and near apostolic tradition in German music running from Mozart and Haydn to Beethoven, Schubert and Brahms. Von Herzogenberg was, in fact, a friend and correspondent of Brahms and married to one of Brahms's favourite students, Elizabet von Stochhausen, the marriage reportedly causing some irritation, even jealousy on the part of the composer. We do not hear what compositions of his Ralph submitted to von Herzogenberg but Ralph remembered that the Professor commented that they reminded him of the composer of the opera *Cavalleria Rusticana*, Pietro Mascagni. Upon consideration he recommended that Ralph should study composition with his colleague, Professor Bruch. The advice proved to be good.

Max Bruch was a portly, genial, heavily bewhiskered 60-year-old with a high domed forehead. Nearly twenty years before he had taken up the directorship of the Liverpool Philharmonic Society, a position he retained for nearly three years. His perennially performed Violin Concerto No. 1 in G minor was completed around the time he went to England.

The specifics of what Bruch taught the 25-year-old Ralph remain unknown. Only his remarking on his student's fondness for the flattened seventh has been recorded. But unquestionably Bruch's overall influence on the young man was benign and creative. Remembering his studies in Berlin Ralph remarked many years later: 'it is difficult to say what one learns from a teacher. I only know that I worked hard and enthusiastically, and that Max Bruch encouraged me and I never had much encouragement before.'[2]

Berlin itself was an education for the two young honeymooners. In the year 1897 the second German Reich was at its zenith, created just over twenty-five years before by the 'Iron Chancellor' Count Otto von Bismarck. That year the empire of the Hohenzöllern Kaisers was just about half-way between its inception so proudly proclaimed by Bismarck at Versailles after Prussia's humiliating defeat of France in 1871, and its demise after the armistice that ended the First World War and brought about the Weimar Republic. In 1897 the young German Empire was experiencing rapid economic expansion. It was also becoming a powerful political and military force that was causing anxiety in the governments in Paris, St Petersburg and London. Germany's capital city as Ralph and Adeline knew it during the months they lived there was a busy, thriving place that exuded confidence and a sense of purpose.

The arts too were vibrant. Just two years before their arrival the novelist Theodor Fontane had published *Effi Briest*, a classic work in German fiction dealing with the morality and culture of the Junker aristocracy from which the Prussian officer corps, which had fought for Bismarck in his expansionist wars, was recruited. The leading German dramatist of the day was the future Nobel Prize winner Gerhart Hauptmann. Ralph and Adeline went to see what is now regarded as one of his major works *Die Versunkene Glocke* (The Sunken Bell). Still improving his German, Ralph understood the play as 'the dramatis personae of Hans Anderson talking Ibsen as hard as they could.' Conversations with German acquaintances, usually jokily reported by Ralph in his letters, helped him see the Nietzschean themes of the play. He and Adeline also got to know something of the German classical theatre. The two parts of Goethe's *Faust* were being performed in Berlin at the time. They attended a performance of Part One but apparently did not make it to Part Two. Ralph also had a go at the great classic of the German eighteenth-century Enlightenment, Lessing's *Nathan the Wise*. However, he found it 'very dull'.

But of course the couple went eagerly to the opera and to concerts. And there were lots to go to. In the middle of October 1897 they saw a complete performance of Wagner's *Ring* cycle at the grand State Opera on Unter den Linden. Ralph reviewed it admiringly in an enthusiastic 'Letter from Berlin' which he contributed to *The Musician*. He particularly enjoyed the singing of the famous soprano Lilli Lehmann as Brunnhilde. He and Adeline also went to *Robert le Diable*, one of the grand operas of Giacomo Meyerbeer. It was a very popular and much performed piece in the nineteenth century but less so in the following one. Ralph was an admirer of Meyerbeer's work, particularly his grandest of grand operas *Les Huguenots*. Later in life he made an arrangement of 'The Blessing of the Swords' from that epic piece. The young couple went to numerous concert venues. At the Singakademie, the concert hall in which Schumann and Brahms had performed, they heard Bach cantatas. And Ralph long remembered a performance of Brahms's Double Concerto which they heard performed at the Hochschule für Musik at which he was enrolled.

During their near half year in Berlin, the honeymooners' social life was also very active. René Gatty, a brother of Ralph's Cambridge friends, Nicholas and Ivor Gatty, was living in Berlin and was extremely helpful to them. René was a fluent speaker of German and Czech, and later became Reader in English at the University of Prague. Ralph remembered him as 'a delightful person and a genius in his way', 'a very good and keen musician, a first-rate composer in the light style'. In one of his recollections of Berlin Ralph offered an image of René as a young man about town, assessing the ladies and 'pacing the Potsdamer Platz and exclaiming "Donnerwetter ein reizendes gesicht" as some schones Madchen passes you or going on to Schultheiss and saying "Ha-Champagner".'

René Gatty it was, the young bon viveur, who helped Ralph and Adeline find somewhere to live. This was at 6 Eichhorn Strasse, an imposing apartment building close to a major social and commercial hub of Berlin, then as now, the Potsdamer Platz. Well over a hundred years later, despite the heavy bombing of Berlin during the Second World War, the devastation accompanying the Russian capture of the city in 1945 and the creation of the wide, barren, no-man's land either side of the Berlin Wall in 1961, Eichhorn Strasse still exists. Bordered on both sides by post-modern office buildings, it runs north from Felix Mendelsshohn Park to the Marlene Dietrich Platz. But in the late 1890s when Ralph lived there, it was a residential, fashionable street inhabited by members of the upper middle class.

Ralph and Adeline lived well in their Berlin flat. They were able to employ someone to tutor them in German, a rather fat, fussy, tendentious man whose teaching was the subject of many jokey references in their letters home. They ate out and enjoyed drinking. At a meal at Friedrich's, a modish restaurant on the Potsdamer Strasse, they drank champagne cocktails and then devoted themselves to hock. When Ralph returned home and set about writing a letter, he knocked the ink all over the table-cloth, an accident he blamed on the drinks. Inexpertly, he and Adeline attempted to boil the tablecloth to bring out the stain.

They did not always eat at expensive restaurants. On some occasions they ate much more modestly. In a letter of late November 1897 Ralph reproduced the menu for a homemade meal which though written in the style of Potsdamer Platz haute cuisine amounts, amusingly, when translated into English, to little more than eggs boiled or scrambled.

In the gay nineties the conventional English view of Berlin was that it was dour, even grim, certainly when compared to the Paris of the day. But Ralph and Adeline came to like and to enjoy the city. Ralph wrote home to Randolph Wedgwood protesting that 'All that has been said against Berlin is absolutely untrue – it's of course not a picturesque place but very bright and cheerful and delightful canals with trees planted all along them.' They also enjoyed visiting the country residence of Frederich the Great at Sans Souci. It had, Ralph enthused to his friend:

> the most wonderful artificial garden with its statues and fountains and terraces all on an autumn afternoon with the leaves falling which fitted in beautifully with the general feeling of sentimental decay. Then across the valley on the other side rise beautiful sheer ruins making a classical landscape in the style of Claude.

The Prussians were not invariably bureaucratic and unbending. Ralph went on to tell Randolph of a small incident that had charmed him. One evening, he and Adeline were walking home from a concert just as a policeman was starting to extinguish the gas-lit street lamps. But the officer was not quite tall enough to reach up to one of the lamps. The tall, young English gentleman was most pleased to go over and offer his services. Ralph told Randolph that the officer 'was trying to do it with his sword but was not tall enough so I offered to help him whereupon the servant of the Kaiser handed me his sword and I turned it out.'

Adeline's parents were spending Christmas of that year in San Remo, the then prestigious resort town on the Italian Riviera that was the home, at various times, of Tsar Nicholas II of Russia, the Empress Elisabeth of Austria, the Swedish philanthropist Alfred Nobel and the English humourist Edward Lear. Adeline's mother and father invited the young couple to join them there for the holiday. So they set off from Berlin on the long journey south, changing trains at Bolzano. In this Tyrolean city they had a long stopover so they were able to go for a walk among the hills with the snow-topped Alps behind. When they rested for a while, Adeline took a photograph of Ralph. Rather posed, it shows him reclining on the hillside, a cigarette held negligently in his right hand, his left supporting his head as, sunk in meditation, he is indifferent to the scenery round him. They proceeded to Genoa and joined the family the following day. In San Remo they rented bicycles and went riding together in the hills over the Mediterranean coast. But more frequently Ralph took off on his own, while Adeline enjoyed the company of her mother and her sister.

Then it was back to Berlin. And for Ralph the hard grind of preparing compositions for submission to Max Bruch. There were also social calls to be made, or at least, according to middle-class practice at that time, cards to be left at the residences of personages known to family and friends in England. One such introduction was arranged for them by Albert Venn Dicey, Vinerian Professor of Law at Oxford and a colleague of Adeline's brother-in-law Frederic Maitland, Professor of the Laws of England at Cambridge. The introduction was to the widow of Hermann von Helmholtz, the former Professor of Physics at the University of Berlin and a highly distinguished scholar famed for his research into optics, human eyesight and also the mechanical bases of thermodynamics. Frau von Helmholtz lived in a grand building on the Rauch Strasse, just south of the wide, green expanses of the Tiergarten. Ralph and Adeline broached contact by leaving their card. But (was it after another vinous meal at Friedrich's?) they left their card at the wrong address. To their great embarrassment they received a curt note the following day denying any knowledge of the Diceys, signed 'Clara Goldberger'. A more successful social venture was their attendance at one of Max Bruch's 'At Homes'. Ralph reported that the kindly Bruch said to him that 'he hoped I should be as successful as I was courageous.'[3] And in February 1898 as Adeline and Ralph began their preparations for returning to England, Max Bruch supplied a succinct and strong letter of reference.

> Mr Vaughan Williams, who in the winter of 1897–98 attended the master class in composition led by me, is a very fine musician and a talented composer. He deserves to be warmly recommended to all music societies, church choirs, etc.
>
> *Director Max Bruch, Member of the Royal Academy of Arts, Berlin*

Before they left Germany, Ralph and Adeline had one last treat: a quick excursion to the historic and highly cultured city of Dresden. They had a room at Weber's Hotel, which Ralph told Rene Gatty, was where Paderewski, the superstar pianist of the time, would stay. At the opera house they heard a performance of Beethoven's Ninth Symphony and on the following day Verdi's *Otello* was performed. They also had an opportunity to indulge the taste for painting which they shared; at the Zwinger Gallery in the city Raphael's *San Sisto Madonna* was on show.

This outing marked the end of the honeymoon and by mid-April they were back in England. After a brief visit to Leith Hill Place and then to Adeline's family in Brighton the couple set off for London. It was time to set up home together in the city in which Ralph could pursue his musical ambitions. They found very modest lodgings in a Georgian terrace house at 16 North Street in Westminster. In comparison to Leith Hill Place this was very squeezed accommodation. In a letter to the family Adeline described it as 'Three very small rooms in a curious old panelled house ... close to Westminster Abbey, and closer still to Queen Anne's Footstool Church in Smith Square....'[4]

Ralph was expected to resume his duties as organist at St Barnabas in South Lambeth. On one of their first Sundays back in England he and Adeline went over to the morning service there. The reunion was not a happy one. Adeline reported that the young composer, John Ireland, who had taken Ralph's place during his honeymoon and who was probably hoping for a permanent position was 'very much upset' to see Ralph reappear. The vicar preached a poor sermon. And when Ralph went to the vestry after the service there was another difficult moment. Well meaningly, but misunderstanding the reason for Ralph's six months absence, the members of the choir expressed the hope that he had enjoyed his holiday in ... Switzerland.

Ralph was very keen to see Randolph Wedgwood again and soon after their return he and Adeline made the long train journey up to Durham to visit him in West Hartlepool where he was pursuing his career as an engineer and manager for the North Eastern Railway. As usual, time with this special friend was for Ralph a great pleasure and a great stimulus. On his return to North Street he exclaimed in a letter 'how awfully jolly (and amusing and instructive) it was being with you at W Hartlepool.'[5] He also enthused about the two candlesticks which were Randolph's wedding present to them:

> how beautiful the candlesticks are and how good it was of you to have
> them packed up and how unkind it was of us to refuse to take them
> with us, one in each hand. They make such a blaze in our room that
> we decided on the spot to spend the sum of £1-0-0 (one pound) on
> dark blue linen hangings....

Ralph was now working on several fronts to establish himself in the world of music. He was composing and was also submitting articles to music magazines. He also decided to work for a doctorate in music at Cambridge. When in this same letter he told Randolph of this new plan, he again felt a sense of youth and immaturity in comparison to Randolph who still seemed very much to him the 'big boy'. Using the metaphor of the grown man's safety bicycle he wrote: 'it makes me feel very young still going in for examinations when you have probably forgotten what an examination is; it makes me feel as if I was still on a toy bicycle while you were on in safety.'

The tenancy of the flat in North Street was not a happy one. It lasted just a few weeks. Adeline developed influenza and the landlady, probably fearing that it might be infectious tuberculosis, promptly asked them to leave. They searched urgently for new accommodation thinking they might find something in Battersea Park, which would be convenient for Ralph's work in south Lambeth. But they eventually settled for another place close by in Westminster. On 30 May 1898 they moved into rooms at 5 Cowley Street; they would live here for some eight months. They were still close to the centre of the political life of Britain and its vast empire, which was then at its peak. Living in the street that now houses the national headquarters of the Liberal Democrats, they were less than five minutes' walk from the Houses of Parliament. Every day of their lives there, amidst the loud noise of the horse-drawn traffic on Millbank, the carriages, the wagons and the hansom cabs, Ralph and Adeline heard the hourly chiming of Big Ben.

Though unsure of himself in some ways, especially in relation to Randolph Wedgwood, Ralph was determined and extremely hard-working in his pursuit of his calling. He continued to try his hand as a musical journalist but for the most part received rejection slips. Early that summer he wrote from Cowley Street, proudly telling Randolph that he had become an Associate of the Royal College of Music in theory and composition and 'am allowed to affix to my name the letters A.R.C.M.' He also reported proudly that his name and that of one of his lighter compositions had been printed in a programme. Announcing that 'The orchestra will perform the following selection', the theatre programme contained the words, according to Ralph, 'in an obscure corner', 'Scenes de ballet ... Williams'. He was also doing more serious work. He was making progress with his Cambridge degree exercise which, he had decided, would be a Mass. This work, the manuscript of which is still kept in Cambridge, was a pleasure to him to write. The text inspired him: 'they're such fine words and you get such good climaxes out of them.'[6]

But despite his happy marriage and his intense hard work with his music, he fretted about his separation from Randolph Wedgwood. In one letter to him Ralph burst out: 'I never see you and we are becoming strangers – and you mustn't think that because I am married I don't hate not seeing you just as much – it makes it worse because there are now two of us that want you and never have you.'[7] His frustration was aggravated by knowing that George Trevelyan was at that moment on his way to see Randolph. He admitted that he was filled with a jealousy that threatened to explode. 'I'm jealous of Trevy – he came here today – ate a large tea and then announced with the utmost satisfaction that he was going to see you at West H'Pool – I almost pulled his nose off.' He fumed on: 'why don't we ever go to you or why don't you ever come to us – of course, opulent freelances like Trevy can go off at any minute like a pop-gun.'[8] Adeline must have seen how upset Ralph was becoming as he wrote because she took the pen and put into the letter, 'I am scolding Ralph for writing like a spoiled child....' She was witnessing an instance of that emotional turbulence that often seethed within Ralph and that was usually concealed behind his quiet, withdrawn, somewhat awkward demeanour but could, on certain sensitive occasions, erupt.

In a letter written a week or two later, Ralph apologized to Randolph for what he said about George Trevelyan even though he was aware that George was visiting him again, this time at Hallsteads, one of the Wedgwood properties near Stoke-on-Trent. '... I spoke very harshly of Trevy (in my) last letter, but you must understand I was speaking of Trevy not as a person but as a cause – because I like him very much.' In the early months of his marriage a good deal of his emotional life was a continuation of those intense friendships and jealousies that had come into being in his set at Cambridge. He was touched to meet Crompton Llewellyn Davies, one of his more peripheral Trinity friends at a concert in London.

The young couple had a break from London, in the August of 1898, with a trip to Holland. They heard the organ at Haarlem and saw the great paintings at the Rijksmuseum in Amsterdam. Ralph also took time from his work to accompany his mother on a short country holiday at Birdlip in Gloucestershire. His mother later treated him and Adeline to a trip to Prague. The fifty pounds she gave them also allowed them to make return visits to Dresden and to Berlin. Ralph's steady and robust determination to advance his career shows in his remark to Randolph Wedgwood that he went to Berlin 'to keep up with the influential people there.'[9]

In Prague, the couple found that Dvořák's operas were very much the staple fare of the national Bohemian theatre. Ralph and Adeline went to see *The Devil and Kate*. The future composer of *Hugh the Drover* thought that the first part dealing with Bohemian village life was 'tremendously good'.[10] He was less impressed by the underworld section which he found 'very dull' and thought 'Bagged from the "Niebelheim" in Wagner's *Rheingold*.' When they returned to London, Adeline reported in a letter to Rene Gatty, that Ralph was writing 'a new serenade for orchestra, which is turning out rather Dvořák-y....'[11]

Rene was still in Berlin and Adeline was acting as his unpaid literary agent, copying and recopying his poems and sending them off to London editors. She also told him of an afternoon string quartet made up of his brother Nicholas playing first violin, Ralph the viola and Mr von Holst and herself taking the other parts. These musical afternoons seem to have been their last social occasions in the Cowley Street flat. For some time they had been looking for something larger and more suitable and towards the end of the year they found it. This was a whole house to themselves, though by the standards of their social class at the time a small one, at 10 Barton Street, again in Westminster. It had a late Georgian exterior and limited facilities. 'There was no bathroom so hot water had to be carried from the kitchen to fill a brown tin bath, and the lavatory was in the back yard, but it was quiet and there was a spare room for visitors.'[12] There was a drawing room on the ground floor which Ralph used as a study. He signed the six-year lease for the house in December 1898. Randolph Wedgwood seems to have been annoyed that he, now a practical man of business, had not been consulted in the taking of this decision. Apparently he wrote a 'withering' letter questioning the wisdom of what they had done. On 15 December 1898 Adeline wrote back defending their leasing a house that was not in very good condition. 'I have survived your "withering fire" – of course we did not ask your permission before we invested all our savings in No 10 Barton St. for of course you'd never have given it – it is such a shaky investment – we shall be lucky if the roof and walls outlast our 6 years ...'[13] But despite these worries Ralph and Adeline happily set about furnishing their new home. They did not share the mid-Victorian taste of their parents for the imposing and the fussy. Rather they were influenced by the example of William Morris and the contemporary Arts and Crafts movement; thus, they 'furnished very simply with rush mats and white curtains, oak furniture they had picked up at sales, and two ancient chests from Hooton Roberts.'[14] They moved into the Barton Street house in February 1899. This was their first settled home as a married couple. Ralph was twenty-six. Adeline reported that her husband took his role as man of the house very seriously. 'Ralph gives himself very important airs as a house-holder, turning off the gas and locking every window and door every night.[15] He and Adeline would live in this house for nearly seven years. Here his career in music would be firmly established.

Chapter Six

BARTON STREET, WESTMINSTER

In the early weeks and months at Barton Street Ralph worked at the most easily performable and saleable kind of composition, the song setting. He set texts by Shakespeare and by the poet laureate who had died just five years before, Alfred, Lord Tennyson. At this early, uncertain stage of his career Ralph, who always possessed a strong writerly side and gift, also had ambitions as a music critic and journalist. The titles of three of the essays he wrote indicate the subjects in his thoughts at this time: 'How to play Brahms', 'A School of English Music', and 'Bach and Schumann'. In a letter to Randolph Wedgwood Ralph announced his very ambitious intention of making a collection of these and other essays and submitting them as a book to the then very prestigious publishing house of Smith, Elder and Company; their list included works by George Eliot, Robert Browning, John Ruskin, Thomas Hardy and Lord Tennyson. As he feared, Smith Elder quickly returned the manuscript to him. But some three years later some of these pieces were published in a short-lived music periodical *The Vocalist*.

Ralph and Adeline continued a lively correspondence with the friend they had made together in Berlin, Rene Gatty, of whom they were both very fond. Adeline wrote to Rene about their music-making, together and with others, in their new home. They also attended, and reported on, a first performance of 'Serenade' by Rene's brother, Nicholas, which, Ralph enthused, 'came off most tremendously.... Awfully jolly tunes in it too – and those not isolated but welded into a whole – altogether a complete success....'[1]

Adeline also wrote to Rene about the books they were reading. There was a strong literary bent to their lives as they settled down in Westminster. Ralph read the nineteenth-century Russian novelists who were just then becoming known and admired in England. Imogen Holst in her memoir of her father wrote that 'he read all the novels of Turgenev, which he borrowed, one after another, from Vaughan Williams'.[2] Ibsen's plays and the novels of Anatole France were among the books Ralph mentioned to Rene. He, in return, strongly recommended the poetry of Paul Verlaine. Ralph took a keen interest in French literature. After he ended his association with St Barnabas church (a new vicar insisted he take communion and that for Ralph was the last straw in his dissatisfaction with the job), a collection of French books was found in the organ loft of the church, books which Ralph had read during his quiet times during services and then forgotten about. Accompanied by a curt letter from the vicar, the books were forwarded to Barton Street. In an Anglican setting in late-Victorian England the books must have been considered risqué; they included works by Balzac, Maupassant and Zola.

Adeline continued to devote her time to acting as Rene Gatty's literary agent in London. Generously, she wrote out numerous copies of his poems and tirelessly sent them out, with little success, to editors and publishers. Around this time Ralph and Adeline also paid a visit to the Gatty family at their vicarage home at Hooton Roberts, a village near Doncaster. The Reverend Gatty was bluff, very down to earth and extremely fond of the country people of the West Riding who were his parishioners. He greatly amused Ralph by telling him that whenever anyone came to communion looking a bit poorly, he made sure he got an especially 'good swig' of the communion wine. The vicar and his wife and the younger siblings of Ralph's old Cambridge friend, Nicholas, quickly took a liking to Adeline. Their younger sister Margot, then in her early teens, could still convey nearly sixty years later, in a letter of August 1957, her excitement when Ralph and Adeline came to Yorkshire. The hyphenated phrases recreate the intensity of her feelings as a young girl:

when you are very young, as I was, two grown-up people arrive –
15–16 years in age older – you are utterly out of your depth – afraid
and adoring – never can two more wonderful young people have
arrived in a country – Rectory than they – R more than good looking
– strong – gentle – kind to the young and old – Adeline too exquisitely

lovely for any words – and it was Adeline who took a youngster's hand
– to walk hand-in-hand downstairs (no one else as a guest ever had!).
I was lost.[3]

It was a very joyous visit for all who were there and Ralph and Adeline
were to be invited back on several occasions. On this first visit they all
went for walks in the country, had picnics and played a good deal of
music together including recent compositions by Ralph and Nicholas
Gatty. There exists an old faded photograph of their music-making. The
group is gathered in the sunshine before the door of the stone-walled
rectory; Adeline is playing the cello.

Just over a month after the move into the Barton Street house Ralph
travelled back to Cambridge to take the examination for his doctorate in
music. In partial fulfilment of the requirements for this degree he had
submitted a composition, in his case a Mass. The doctoral examination
went off successfully and now Ralph became Dr Vaughan Williams. He
was happy to use the title throughout his life. It must have helped him
in those early days in his career to obtain the occasional teaching job
which he needed in order to supplement his private income. At about this
time he gave lectures on music in the extension programme of London
University; he also did some teaching in a small girls' school in Ladbroke
Grove in west London. One of the girls, Maud Brackenbury, remembered
how they all liked him. His brown suit, his shyness and his choice of
music were reasons they came to refer to him as 'the nut-brown maid'. At
the same time that he was teaching, Ralph was also continuing to study.
He paid for singing lessons from Madame Careno, a huge imposing lady
whose tuition greatly helped his writing for choirs and for individual
voices.

Just a few hundred yards from the new Vaughan Williams home stood
the Houses of Parliament. On at least one occasion Ralph and Adeline
went to watch the procession of lords and commons in the state opening.
They lived at the centre of a great worldwide empire. In the October of
that first year in Barton Street parliamentary debates became dominated
by a controversy that would increasingly, and ever more bitterly, divide
Westminster and then Britain as a whole. For some time the Afrikaans-
speaking Boer farmers of South Africa had grown increasingly restive
at their subordination to Britain's world-wide imperial system. In this
they had counterparts and sympathizers among the Irish who at this
same time continued to fight for Home Rule. Incidents of tension and

confrontation between the British and the Afrikaaners increased and in October 1899 the Boer War began. It would prove to have a profound effect on Ralph's marriage and his life.

The two wars that lay far in the future – the world wars of 1914–18 and of 1939–45 – would bring radical change to Ralph's life, career and art. But it is also the case that this earlier, much more limited war at the turn of the century brought him his first experiences of suffering and horror. This was because of the devastating effect that the Boer War was to have on Adeline. It brought her the first of the many ugly, agonizing tragedies that were to beset her life.

Her brother, Arthur Alexander Fisher, known in the family as 'Jack', was four years older than she and a career soldier. As a child he had been photographed by his aunt, Julia Margaret Cameron, in his sailor suit. It was such a charming image of a Victorian childhood that when the photograph came into the possession of the National Portrait Gallery it was chosen to be used as an image for a jigsaw and to embellish a mug. Jack served in the West Yorkshire Regiment and the Prince of Wales Own; he rose to the rank of captain. Prior to the Boer War he was in Egypt and India. Then he was sent to the rebellious colony of Uganda to operate in what would later be called counter-insurgency. His niece, Mary Fisher, later revealed family talk about the atrocities which Jack had witnessed when seconded to the Uganda Rifles, 'shooting tribesmen ... poisoning wells'. When the Boer War began, he was sent to South Africa. Here he began to suffer seriously from mental illness. By the end of the war worse still happened to him. He was sent back to Britain in a straitjacket and subsequently sectioned. His family was devastated.

When the war began in 1899, Ralph was not against it. His friend Randolph Wedgwood seems to have been one of the 'jingos' as the aggressive supporters of the war were called, and Ralph in a letter to him expressed admiration for his 'outbreak of military spirit.' Blaming Joseph Chamberlain, the Colonial Secretary in the Tory government for getting 'us into this damned mess', Ralph went on to take the view that 'we've all got to do our best to get ourselves out of it – besides we've got to win, whatever the disgusting beginnings of this horrible business may be we've got to <u>win</u> it now – thems my sentiments.'

In their strong pro-war attitude, Ralph and Randolph differed from their Liberal friends from Cambridge days. 'Trevy', for instance, was ferociously opposed to the militant imperialism of Joseph Chamberlain. 'Trevy' would later write an influential letter to *The Times* protesting the inhumane conditions in the military institution, invented by the British command in the course of this war, the concentration camp.

To Ralph's great pleasure, Randolph Wedgwood and Adeline always got on well. Around this time the three of them holidayed together in Yorkshire. Ralph long remembered how they had walked, and sometimes rowed, in glorious summer weather. He liked to recall how, a little dishevelled and perspiring, they had turned up at a country pub one evening. Facing a slightly sceptical landlord, Ralph who had spotted a piano in the bar, sat down and played dance tunes. Randolph and Adeline encouraged the other customers to get up and dance and suddenly a party was on the go. It continued for the rest of the evening. The landlord supplied the newcomers with free beer and food and finally offered Ralph a job. He gave Ralph and Adeline his son's bed for the night and made up a bed for Randolph in the bar. The following day he was sad to see them leave; and they to go. It was one of Ralph's happy memories of country outings, country pubs and country people. It was a taste shared by Ralph's Trinity contemporary Edward Marsh and was at the centre of the poetry he anthologized and published some years later in the succession of volumes entitled *Georgian Poetry*.

About four months before the Boer War began there occurred an event of major importance in the history of English music. At St James's Hall in London, the distinguished conductor, Hans Richter, an associate of Richard Wagner, successfully conducted the first performance of the 'Enigma' Variations by Edward Elgar. This work brought a reputation to its 41-year-old Worcestershire composer and to English music, the renaissance of which then progressed dramatically. The work quickly gained admirers across Europe, especially in Russia where it impressed both Alexander Glazunov and Rimsky-Korsakov. It would receive its premier in New York in a concert conducted by Gustav Mahler. As Ralph began and continued his career as a composer he would be impressed and a little awed by the work and achievement of Edward Elgar who was fifteen years older than he. He later wrote to Elgar asking for lessons, in orchestration especially. But Elgar had too much other work and recommended that Ralph approach Granville Bantock who was closer to him in age and who would succeed Elgar as Peyton Professor of Music at the University of Birmingham. Ralph was in Birmingham in October 1900 and heard the first performance of Elgar's *Dream of Gerontius* in the Town Hall there. The premiere was generally considered to be a failure. But Lady Stanford, who was in the same party as Ralph, murmured to

him as they left, 'Is that not a fine work?' Ralph was later to acknowl-
edge the influence of Elgar's oratorio on his own First Symphony, 'A Sea
Symphony', which would have its first performance in Leeds Town Hall
almost a decade later.

In the same year that Ralph went to Birmingham to hear the new
Elgar work, he completed his own first orchestral work of any substance.
This was his Bucolic Suite. It was given its first performance by the
Bournemouth Municipal Orchestra in March 1902 almost a year after
they had premiered Ralph's much slighter piece, his Serenade in A minor
for small orchestra, a very pleasing work with an especially charming
fourth movement, entitled 'Romance'. The conductor of this prominent
orchestra was Dan Godfrey who would also be an important figure in
Ralph's early career. He was the son of the bandmaster of the Grenadier
Guards and extremely enterprising. Seven years before he launched
Ralph's career in orchestral music, Dan Godfrey had agreed a contract
with Bournemouth Council to create an ensemble of thirty musicians to
augment the attractions of the fast-developing seaside resort. It was to be
something far better than the familiar, slightly clownish band on a pier
in which Gustav Holst had sometimes had to play. Dan Godfrey worked
hard and imaginatively to develop the band which we know today as the
Bournemouth Symphony Orchestra. He quickly established himself as
a figure in the national music; a photograph of 1910 shows him posing
confidently with leaders of the profession, Edward German, Stanford and
Parry. His brilliantly successful initiative was another part of that great
renewal of English music in the concluding decades of the nineteenth
century which made obsolete any justification to the statement, sometimes voiced in Germany, that England was 'the land without music'.
The renewal took place in provincial towns as well as in the recently
funded colleges and concert halls in London. The first great artefact and
marker of the revival, the 'Enigma' Variations, was the work of a provin-
cially trained, mainly self-taught musician, the son of a shopkeeper in
Worcester. In late Victorian Bournemouth Dan Godfrey created an
enduring orchestra from nothing. This was the ensemble which gave
Ralph's Bucolic Suite its first performance.

It is a more substantial piece than Ralph's Serenade in A minor. Julian
Rushton has remarked that 'the form of the Bucolic Suite is comparable to
symphony.'[4] Ralph appears to be becoming more ambitious with orchestral forces. And in this he was not alone. As Lewis Foreman has noted,
as Ralph was working on the Bucolic Suite, his very close friend Gustav

Holst was composing his 'Cotswold Symphony'. Ralph seems quickly to have come to regard the Suite with its several reminiscences of Max Bruch and Dvořák, as a piece of juvenilia. By the end of the Edwardian period he seems to have made no further efforts to get it performed.

The same is true of another more important, two-part orchestral composition worked on in 1900 and continued during the next couple of years. This is the ambitiously titled Heroic Elegy and Triumphal Epilogue. On the manuscript of the first of these two related works, the Elegy, Ralph wrote 'Finished 1.40 a.m. Jan 22, 1901'. Which is to say in the very early hours of the day on which Queen Victoria died. Perhaps we can regard the Elegy, which is very much the music of public occasion, as a response to the sense of loss marked by the ending of her long reign of well over sixty years. Some writers have suggested that the mounting dirge-like music is also a lament for the losses which at that very moment were being sustained in the war in South Africa. One of these, involving the hospitalization of her brother Jack Fisher, was already affecting Adeline and would cause her increasing suffering during the composition of the companion piece to the Heroic Elegy.

She had other very painful troubles and distractions. She was now living away from Ralph, helping her mother to nurse her brother Hervey who continued to suffer from both mental and physical illness. On 25 March 1901 she wrote to Randolph saying that Ralph was 'very encouraged by the way in which it (Heroic Elegy) has impressed his musical friends'; she went on to add elliptically: 'My mother and I are still alone here nursing Hervey – calamity … He is his own wonderful self. Through it all we have always got happiness from being with him – I have been separated from Ralph for Hervey is only allowed to see my mother and me – but I hope he is coming into lodgings at Easter and then I shall see him. He has been having a rather miserable time with sciatica.'[5]

The ailing Ralph provided an epigraph for his Elegy; it reads 'terrible as an army with banners' and comes from the fourth chapter of the Song of Solomon. Initially this may seem to refer to the jingo militarism of the military parades and embarkations then proceeding apace as Britain continued to send troops to the Cape. A resident of central Westminster must have surely seen a good deal of military ceremony in those war years. But the context, in the 'Song', of the six words chosen by Ralph evokes something else; the state of a *love* relationship. It is one from which one of the lovers has begun to withdraw. The first verse of the chapter begins with urgent, anxious questions: 'Whither is thy beloved gone, O thou fairest among women? Whither is thy beloved turned aside?' There follows a passionate outburst in which the beloved is compared to a famous Jewish heroine and then characterized by three adjectives, the third of which introduces some emotional complication into the attitude of the lover: 'Thou art beautiful, O my love, as Tirzah, comely as Jerusalem, terrible as an army with banners.'

A distancing between Ralph and Adeline may be one of the sources of this music of gathering regret. Certainly they were turning to different objectives at this time. Ralph was working strenuously at his music and Adeline was devoting more and more time to her parents, to assist them in their urgent needs. Adeline's younger brother Hervey was suffering increasingly from mental illness. A young man now in his late twenties, Hervey, who characterized Adeline so admiringly in his short story and for whom she in turn felt a deep affection, was now confined to care in his parents' home. Mrs Fisher, his mother, felt greatly burdened by the responsibility. Adeline spent more and more time in Brighton helping her parents with their difficult, demanding task. Bad news about 'Jack' continued to come from South Africa.

Ralph's Elegy was first performed some two months after its completion by the orchestra of the Royal College of Music. Stanford agreed to conduct. In the same concert, pieces by Ralph's contemporaries John Ireland and Nicholas Gatty were also played. The Elegy was well received. Stanford himself admired the work written by the young man whose work had once so provoked his impatience. John Ireland who had taken over Ralph's job at St Barnabas was in the audience that day. After the performance he had a conversation with Stanford. In his characteristically bluff, unhelpful, provoking way Stanford said of Ralph's Elegy 'That's better than anything you could write, me bhoy.'

Ralph proceeded to work on the Triumphal Epilogue. He added another, second section in what he had originally envisioned as a 'Symphonic Rhapsody in Three Parts'. On the finished score of this next part he wrote 'Finished Nov 6 1901 / Revised Aug–Sept 1902.' This means that the Elegy and Epilogue taken together are music from a very pronounced juncture in British history. The first is explicitly associated with the death of Victoria and the revision and completion of the second are ascribed to the month in which the coronation of her successor, Edward VII, took place. The Epilogue is a longer, richer, more instrumentally textured work than that which precedes it. Made up of several, discontinuous sections and repeating more than once the trombone

98

theme that pervades the Elegy it finally works its way to an expression of winning through that is promised in the title. Perhaps in the second section of this two-part piece can be heard feelings of hope, liberation and new confidence inspired in part by the new reign. Certainly the lingering *fin de siècle* melancholy of the first part has been energetically, if not entirely, set aside.

This work was the first of Ralph's to attract the serious attention of music journalists and this meant an important step forward in his career. Most important amongst those who now started to write about his work was Edwin Evans who continued to be so impressed by Ralph's work that he took it upon himself to help promote and push for performances of his compositions. In 1902, Evans, like Ralph, was just beginning to establish his career. At this time he was writing criticism for the *Musical Standard* and would go on to write for the *Pall Mall Gazette*. At the end of his career he was the music critic of *The Daily Mail*. As a young man he was a great champion of Maurice Ravel and Diaghilev and the Ballets Russes. Through the good offices of Edwin Evans, all three would figure in Ralph's later career. But at the beginning of the Edwardian period Evans's prime concern was to promote the work of the young, emerging English composers including Ralph and his friends, Arnold Bax and Gustav Holst. Bax remembered that 'for years I received very little sympathy or encouragement from any of the Press, with the exception of Edwin Evans, always my sponsor through pre-war German thick and the Franco-Prussian thin of "the silly twenties".'[6]

The year 1902 which brought both the end of the bitterly divisive Boer war and the coronation of the new king, Edward VII, led to new hope and expectations in the country. It also confirmed Ralph's progress as a composer. He worked especially hard at song settings and this year saw the first performance of what was to prove an ongoing 'hit' for him: his beautiful setting of 'Linden Lea' to words by the Dorset poet, William Barnes. But amidst all this promise, Adeline and her family were dealt a devastating blow. Her brother Jack was sent home from South Africa in an acute state of mental illness. On the troopship bringing him home he had been kept under physical constraint throughout the voyage. Family friends awaiting him at the dockside were horrified to see him carried down the gangplank strapped tightly from head to foot on a stretcher. The youngest of the brothers, Edwin Fisher, a future chairman of Barclays Bank, who at that time was a teenager, fainted at the pitiable condition of his elder brother.

Jack's parents found it painfully difficult to receive him and look after both him and his mentally ill brother, Hervey. His niece Mary Fisher recalled, in a letter now in the British Library, that Aunt Adeline and Uncle Ralph bravely attempted to receive Jack into their home, 'The VWs took on Arthur ('Jack') when he came back from the Boer War off his head until Aunt A found him fingering a razor and he had to be incarcerated.' Certified insane and sent to what in those days was known as an asylum, Jack was allowed no visitors. His mother and sister Adeline rented a room in a nearby house which had a view into the grounds of the institution; their hope was to catch sight of him during his exercise periods. Then came the news that he was trying to starve himself to death. He developed appendicitis and underwent surgery. He died not long after the operation on 12 March 1902.

Almost two months later Ralph's part song 'Rest', an *andante sostenuto* setting of a sonnet by the Pre-Raphaelite poet Christina Rossetti, had its first performance; this was in St. James's Hall in London. The funereal words of the poem, though referring to a woman are clearly apposite to the grief and feeling of a blessed relief that Jack's death must have brought to all associated with the Fisher family.

> O Earth, lie heavily upon her eyes;
> Seal her sweet eyes weary of watching, Earth
> Lie close around her; leave no room for mirth
> With its harsh laughter, nor for sound of sighs.

The piece, which *The Times* reviewer, probably Fuller Maitland, found 'refined and musicianly' was sung at a concert given by the Magpie Madrigal Society to which the piece was dedicated. This choral group was composed of well-to-do amateurs including Diana Massingberd (who was related to Ralph's contemporary at Charterhouse), the Countess of Cavan, Herbert Gladstone and Lady Lygon who was the figure alluded to in the thirteenth of Elgar's 'Enigma' Variations.

For all his many connections with high society Ralph still needed to eke out his income with occasional teaching. Presumably it was through Dan Godfrey and the enthusiastic young musicians of the Bournemouth Orchestra that he obtained an invitation to give a series of lectures at the Technical School at Pokesdown near Bournemouth in the winter of 1902. The content of these lectures was very probably, in great part, a restatement of the ideas expressed in Ralph's flurry of essays of a year or two earlier and which now finally appeared in print in the pages of *The Vocalist*. Above all he stressed the importance of locality and community as the basis of a healthy, truly creative music culture. After a talk with the title 'Are we a musical nation?', Ralph proceeded to give one describing 'The Characteristics of National Song in the British Isles.' He always liked to illustrate his lectures with live performances, that is to say he would sing or play relevant passages himself. In this particular lecture he was assisted by Lucy Broadwood, a member of the Purcell Society, who with *The Times* music critic Fuller Maitland had co-authored *English County Songs*. This was a historic work in the folk music revival that took place in England, as in many other European countries, at the end of the nineteenth century. Born and brought up in Scotland Lucy Broadwood was the great-granddaughter of John Broadwood who had been the founder of the highly successful and, for musicians, influential piano-manufacturing company. She was very active in music circles and a skilled piano accompanist and was a prominent adjudicator at the many provincial music festivals that were coming into being at this time. A little later in life in association with Ralph's sister Meggie she would help to found the Leith Hill Music Festival in Dorking.

Never married, Lucy Broadwood was middle-aged when she helped Ralph by singing and playing at his lectures. She had a fine voice and a very pleasing presence. She charmed the students. A vivid detail stayed with Ralph until his very last years when he remembered how at the end of his last lecture the students quite unexpectedly presented her with a bouquet of chrysanthemums and maidenhair fern with orange streamers.

The concluding lecture in the course was called 'The Importance of Folk Song' and was a strong reiteration of his growing enthusiasm for this tradition in music. His penultimate lecture also dealt with a music that existed outside the concert hall and the recital room, the music of the church. Ralph was especially concerned with hymns. These, like folk songs, would come to be a major influence and a subject in his compositions. In this early treatment of the subject, in what amounts to an early position statement, he roundly criticized the sentimentality and falsity of many contemporary Victorian hymns and asserted the dignity and value of forgotten ones from earlier times. Such views would, in the near future, attract an important patron.

Ralph, a teacher for many years of his life, was pleased with his first major venture into lecturing. A few weeks later, in January 1903, he repeated the lectures, this time in Gloucester. But that month was clouded by another death in the Fisher family. On 17 January Adeline's father died in the family home at Hove. Six days later he was buried in the hillside graveyard of the parish church at Brockenhurst. It was a very large funeral. The King sent a representative to the solemn occasion that marked the passing of his former tutor and secretary. It was the second bereavement that the Fishers had suffered within a year. After the funeral Adeline did not return to Barton Street. She stayed to help her distraught mother to dispose of the Hove property and to acquire a home in London. She also assisted in the tending of Hervey whose mental instability continued.

The strong presence of death in the lives of Adeline and Ralph as they entered their thirties, appears to show itself in some of the compositions of this year. 'Sound Sleep' is another setting by Ralph of a poem by Christina Rossetti; it is a graveside meditation for women's voices. The death-tinged sequence of love poems 'Willowwood', settings of words by Christina's brother, Dante Gabriel Rossetti, was performed in March at St James's Hall in London at one of the concerts organized by Lucy Broadwood. The music of one of these poems, 'Silent Noon', is heard again in the Quintet in C minor for piano, violin, cello and double-bass on which Ralph was working in the spring months of 1903. There is a tension in this piece. A Brahmsian largeness in the first movement is followed by an *andante* which recalls the melodic, long lingering melancholy of the Rossetti song. The third and final movement completes the quintet in quiet meditation.

In February Ralph travelled to Oxford to play the piano part in a performance of an earlier quintet, the one in B major which he had written for clarinet, horn, violin and piano some five years before, shortly after his marriage. There is a lightness, playfulness and humour to the piece that contrasts markedly with the sombreness of the C minor quintet written in those early months of loss. A comparison of the two quintets shows Ralph's music moving into darker, more painful feelings about experience in the years consequent on the war in South Africa.

In April he went to stay with the Massingberds at Gunby Hall, their Queen Anne mansion on the edge of the Lincolnshire Wolds. Here he heard his part-song setting (for three female voices and piano) of Christina Rossetti's deeply elegiac 'Sound Sleep' performed at the Lincolnshire Music Festival. His name would from now on become increasingly well-known in the growing number of provincial music festivals. At the same time Ralph was completing 'Solent', a work with a title that alludes to that area of Hampshire to which Adeline and her family belonged. It was performed in June with Adeline and her mother in the audience; Hervey Fisher, recently allowed home from a mental hospital was also able to be there. Ralph was dissatisfied with the piece and immediately withdrew it. But material from 'Solent' appears again, in Ralph's First Symphony ('A Sea Symphony') and also, nearly half a century later, in his very last symphony, the Ninth.

In the summer of 1903, Ralph and Adeline took her bereaved mother for a holiday in Salisbury. Randolph Wedgwood took the train south to be with them and the three young people set off on a boating trip down the River Avon from Salisbury to Christchurch. They also made an afternoon excursion to Stonehenge. As they ate their picnic in the summer sunshine, Ralph found the ancient site less menacing than he had a few years before when he had bicycled to Gustav Holst's family home in Cheltenham. He was always sensitive to the English landscape and its sacred places.

A little later in that year, after they had settled Mrs Fisher in her new home in London, Ralph and Adeline set off on another holiday, this time with Ralph's mother and his sister Meggie. They went to stay by the sea, in Thomas Hardy's country, at Swanage on the Isle of Purbeck in Dorset. It was an area that was special to Ralph because of his deep interest in Hardy's writings. On their return to London there was suddenly more activity in the Barton Street house. While Adeline had been away helping to tend her dying father, her ailing brother and her often distraught mother, Ralph often had a silent house to himself. But now, with Mrs Fisher established in nearby Chelsea, Barton Street became more of a family centre. Mrs Fisher's diary records a long series of lunches, teas, visitors and family occasions.

But Ralph seems to have held himself apart from much of this activity, keeping to his music room upstairs. He was preoccupied with his composing and his career. In particular his interest in folk song, at that time, like other country arts and skills being obliterated by industrial culture, was intensifying. He set about visiting country villages to hear and to make a record of the old songs. During the later months of 1903 he gave a series of lectures on folk song at Brentwood in Essex. And here occurred what Ralph was to look back on, and to write about, as one of the most important experiences of his life.

At the end of one lecture two middle-aged ladies approached him and announced that they had a new source for him. Their father, the vicar of the nearby village of Ingrave, was soon to give a tea party for his older parishioners. The sisters thought that several of these villagers knew ancient country songs; they invited Ralph to come and meet the old people. Shy, as always, Ralph hesitated, but finally was unable to resist the opportunity. On the day, the sisters introduced him to an elderly labourer, Mr Pottipher. For Ralph the meeting was momentous. Mr Pottipher refused to sing publicly but he agreed to meet Ralph the following day and to sing for him then, in private. This was 4 December and the day Ralph first heard the song 'Bushes and Briars'. The old man's singing was for Ralph an epiphany, the final, overwhelming confirmation of his developing love of folk song and the start of what became his now relentless activity as a collector.

The hunt for disappearing songs became a consuming passion with him. It was an enthusiasm that was shared by many others in those Edwardian times. In the summer of that same year, 1903, an identical experience was had by Cecil Sharp, some twelve years older than Ralph, and a former Principal of the Hampstead Conservatoire of Music, and now a peripatetic lecturer and writer on music. Visiting his friend, the Reverend Charles Marson, a prominent Christian Socialist, in his parish of Hambridge in Somerset, Sharp happened to overhear his host's gardener singing 'The Seeds of Love'. As with 'Bushes and Briars', for Ralph this was a turning point in life. Now Sharp, who had already developed a keen interest in folk dance, became a zealous collector of folk songs. He and Ralph soon became close collaborators.

At Christmas time 1903, Adeline and Ralph spent some time with his mother and sister at Leith Hill Place. Ralph was anxious to get out of the house and cycle into the countryside to see if he could discover more songs. He was surprised and delighted to find that the country neigh-bours of his childhood had numerous songs for him to transcribe into his notebook. A neighbour recalled that initially Ralph '... had the singers come to him at Leith Hill Place, but subsequently he worked in the field, or more accurately in the pub.... Among the places listed in his folk song notebooks are The Plough, Rusper, The Wheatsheaf at Kingsfold, and the inn at Lambs Green. Mostly the words and music were noted down on paper, but on a couple of occasions Vaughan Williams used a phonograph....'

One of the local singers remembered, 'This was the first time I had seen or heard one of these marvellous machines and I was amazed beyond expression to hear my own songs thus repeated in my own voice'. Ralph's special helper around Leith Hill was the local butcher. 'He delivered meat in the Rusper area by horse and cart and R.V.W. occasionally went with him. On the way they would call at various hostelries where ... "the locals" were only too pleased to sing the well-known folk songs. As they sang, R.V.W would quickly set the tunes down'.[7]

Early in the New Year he was back in Essex, anxious to hear more songs from Mr Pottipher. He was there again in February. Adeline did not accompany him. She, her mother and her sister Emmeline were now devoting their time to nursing Leslie Stephen, Mrs Fisher's brother-in-law who lay mortally ill in his house in Kensington. After the famous literary critic and editor died in the last week of February, Adeline and Emmeline went off for a holiday in Rome together. They returned just in time to go to a concert in Bournemouth in which Dan Godfrey conducted Ralph's Symphonic Rhapsody, an orchestral piece based again on a poem by Christina Rossetti (her 'Come To Me In The Silence Of The Night'), a call of longing to a dead beloved which again would have had a poignant resonance for the women of the Fisher family in their ongoing experiences of death.

But at the end of that month there was a flurry of excitement at Barton Street. From his upper window Ralph suddenly heard street singers down below him performing ballad songs such as had been heard on the streets of London for generation upon generation. For once, the music of the people had come to him and not the other way around. He hurried down and greeted the singers on the street. He bought copies of each and every broadsheet they had to sell. They also sang the song 'William and Philis' for him to copy down.

He continued with song-seeking expeditions into Sussex, Surrey, and, yet again, Essex. But he was unable to devote as much time to his passionate quest as he would have wished. He found it necessary to take on another teaching job. This time it was at James Allen's Girls' School at Dulwich. Part-time he taught classes here for about a year, at the end of which he managed to arrange for Gustav Holst to take over the work. Ralph also took on the task of editing the 'Welcome Songs', one item in the Purcell Society's voluminous enterprise *The Works of Henry Purcell*. This commission, which probably came to him through his acquaintance with two prominent members of the Purcell Society, Lucy Broadwood and Fuller Maitland, entailed long days working in the Reading Room of the British Museum. He also had to work in the library at Buckingham

Palace. Barclay Squire who was in charge of printed music at the British Museum and a contributor of numerous entries to the *Dictionary of National Biography* sponsored and escorted him on his visit to the King's Library. Adhering to dress code was far more stringently enforced at that time than today. Squire was embarrassed to find that Ralph turned up for the appointment wearing an everyday suit and not a morning suit and top hat as was the custom for Palace visitors in those times. Squire judged it best to conduct the young, would-be scholar in and out of the Palace through the kitchens.

Ralph's work as a scholar continued when he was invited by Fuller Maitland, editor of the second edition of *Grove's Dictionary of Music and Musicians*, to write the entries on fugue and on conducting. In preparing the latter piece Ralph sought the help of Henry Wood, a near contemporary and son of an Oxford Street pawnbroker, who had made a name for himself as conductor of the orchestra of the Carl Rosa Opera Company. Over a decade earlier he had established a name for himself when he conducted the British premiere of Tchaikovsky's *Eugene Onegin*. Another important young figure in Britain's musical renaissance, Henry Wood was presently engaged with the impresario Robert Newman in conducting his newly devised Promenade Concerts at the Queen's Hall in Langham Place, London's leading concert venue since its opening some ten years earlier. The aim of the two men was evangelical; gradually to develop and improve the public taste for classical music in this country. Henry Wood took great interest in Ralph's compositions and did much to assist him in getting them performed and promoted. A very cordial relationship developed between the two.

Ralph's musical ambition, like his reputation in the musical world, was increasing. He was now working seriously on a large orchestral piece which he called 'The Ocean' and which in its final version would become his first symphony. In the summer of 1904, perhaps to escape the hubbub of family, he left Barton Street and travelled on his own to the North Yorkshire coast. He rented rooms, hired a piano and worked every morning and evening on this new project. In the afternoons he went for long walks and, of course, was always on the look-out for folk songs. He found a few in Westerdale, close to Scarborough, and in the little town of Robin Hood's Bay. For Adeline's thirty-fourth birthday in July, almost seven years after their wedding day, he sent a short piano piece as a gift. He swam a good deal, on one occasion over-extending himself and almost failing to make it back to the shore. Each evening, just before his Yorkshire landlady brought in his solitary meal, he would play over what he had written during the day. On one occasion she remarked that Ralph's music reminded her of 'what our postman plays but he plays it much faster'.

At the end of the summer Ralph joined the Fisher ladies at Salisbury where they were holidaying. Quickly after his arrival he cycled off to such villages as Coombe Bissett and Stratford Tony, in the Hardy country to the south of the city, in search of yet more folk songs. He also followed up a suggestion that he visit the Salisbury workhouse and find out what the residents, many of them older people, had to offer. They were happy to sing long remembered songs to him and there was much for him that was new to note down.

In early December 1904 two new song sequences by Ralph had their first performances at the same concert in the Bechstein Hall in London. Present in the well-to-do audience was Ralph's uncle, Lord Justice Vaughan Williams, who may have helped his nephew sponsor the concert. The contrasting song cycles marked a distinct change and development in his song-making and, it seems, in his view of the world. It was appropriate that piano accompaniment at the concert was provided by the upcoming young Irishman, Hamilton Harty, another member of Ralph's generation to assist in the revival of music in Britain. Hamilton Harty was soon to receive recognition, and a knighthood, for his reinvigoration of the Hallé Orchestra in Manchester.

The first song sequence was a setting of six poems from Dante Gabriel Rossetti's *The House of Life*. They are among Ralph's very last versions of Pre-Raphaelite texts articulating the experience of love, characteristically tinged with the shadow of death and loss. Ralph's other sequence at the concert was strikingly different. This was Songs of Travel, settings for baritone voice and piano of nine poems selected by Ralph from Robert Louis Stevenson's collection of the same title. His preferences in poetry were shifting. He was moving away from the psychologically claustrophobic poems of the Pre-Raphaelites to the more open-air, breezy verses of Stevenson. And then from them on to the expansive poetry and democratic vistas of the poet, who more than any other, would affect Ralph's sensibility and his compositions, the great American poet Walt Whitman.

The dominant motif in Songs of Travel is the open road and the freedom and solitariness to which it beckons:

And the road before me.
Wealth I ask not, hope nor love
Nor a friend to know me;
All I ask, the heaven above, And the road before me.

So insists the heavily tramping piano in the first song. The words are a celebration of the idea of the vagabond which was an important male fantasy in the Edwardian period and which would long remain with Ralph. The third song, 'The Roadside Fire', imagines the company of a lady vagabond who close to the roadside would wash her linen and keep her body white. But the sequence as a whole presents the vagabond as a roving man alone who has, for good reason, left his love behind him. He says to her:

He came and went. Perchance you wept a while
And then forgot.
Ah me! But he that left you with a smile
Forgets you not.

The penultimate song, 'Bright Is The Ring Of Words', a piece that is both rousing and touching and which Michael Kennedy rightly identifies as the best in the sequence, also ends with remembrance of a love lost.

And when the west is red
    With the sunset embers
The lover lingers and sings

In the ninth and concluding piece the protagonist, in words and in the music he is given, is emphatic and unambiguous in his awareness that he is moving on from love.

I have trod the upward path and the downward slope
I have endured and done in days before;
I have longed for all, and bid farewell to hope;
And I have lived and loved, and closed the door.

During his lifetime Ralph suppressed the concluding part of the cycle; it appeared with the permission of Ursula only in 1960. Was this because he was reluctant to make so very plain to the public, and especially to

Adeline, his recognition of a now finished period in life? Ralph would be utterly committed and loyal to Adeline until her death nearly fifty years later. But the music and the words of Songs of Travel indicate an ending, a love not renounced but left behind. They also, stirringly, announce a beginning. One which means for Ralph a travelling along the country roads of England, in quest of its past and the musical artefacts of that past.

Yet folk song was not the only vital music concern for Ralph in this year. However, this time he did not go in search of it; literally it appeared on his doorstep. Years later he remembered:

> It must have been in 1904 that I was sitting in my study in Barton Street, Westminster, when a cab drove up to the door and 'Mr Dearmer' was announced. I just knew his name vaguely as a parson who invited tramps to sleep in his drawing room; but he had not come to me about tramps. He went straight to the point and asked me to edit the music for a hymn book. I protested I knew very little about hymns but he explained to me that Cecil Sharp had suggested my name, and I found out later that Canon Scott Holland had also suggested me as a possible editor, and the final clinch was given when I understood that if I did not do the job it would be offered to a well-known Church musician with whose musical ideas I was much out of sympathy.

A flamboyant, energetic figure, the Reverend Percy Dearmer was a lifelong Socialist and a prominent figure in the Alcuin Club which had been founded a few years earlier to promote the detailed liturgical propriety considered so important by the Anglo-Catholic wing of the Church of England. He was the vicar of St Mary's, Primrose Hill, in north London. Here the organist was Martin Shaw, who would be a part of Dearmer's plan to put together a collection of hymns more acceptable than those in the recently updated and controversial edition of *Hymns Ancient and Modern*, the hymnal first compiled half a century before. Hymnody was very much an issue in Edwardian church life. In this same year, Martin Shaw began the first of what were to be a number of collaborations with Ralph. Shaw was also developing a career outside church music. In 1899 he had helped found the Purcell Operatic Society and had been the musical director of a production of *Dido and Aeneas*. The year before he began to work for Ralph, Shaw had joined Ellen Terry's company at the Imperial Theatre in Parliament Square, Westminster, where he supervised the music in a production of *Much Ado About Nothing*. He would continue throughout his life to have a career both in show business and in the church, as organist at St Martin in the Fields. He later became the conductor for Isadora Duncan's dance group and he composed the music for T.S. Eliot's pageant play *The Rock*. Through his association with Martin Shaw, Ralph would have access to areas of music which he had not known before.

Ralph accepted the position as musical editor of the new hymn book, the overall project being controlled by a number of churchmen headed by Percy Dearmer. The musical task was large and daunting; it involved finding a great number of new settings for hymns. Ralph turned to his friends in music, Nicholas Gatty and Gustav Holst in particular, to assist him. The participants in the making of the hymnal turned into something of a committee with long, lively, argumentative meetings in Ralph's workroom upstairs in Barton Street while the ladies of the Fisher family conversed more quietly in the sitting room. One of the theologians was the hymnwriter Athelstan Riley, a passionate Anglo-Catholic who would sometimes halt the discussion and call upon Ralph to entertain at the piano and thus provide 'something to act as a musical olive to clear our artistic palates.'[8] Athelstan Riley would make dramatic appearances in Barton Street riding a beautiful white horse. It was the task of Adeline's youngest brother Edwin, (the future banker) to hold the horse by its bridle until the very rhetorical owner was ready to leave.

Now in his early thirties Ralph was showing an impressive amount of energy. Accepting Percy Dearmer's invitation was to entail some two and a half years of hard work. Shortly after agreeing to become the musical editor of *The English Hymnal* he also accepted an invitation to work on another major project. The Shakespeare Club of Stratford-upon-Avon had decided to mount a revival of Ben Jonson's masque *Pan's Anniversary or The Shepherd's Holyday*. The Club secretary wrote to Barclay Squire at The British Museum enquiring about the original music. Barclay Squire reported that none of the original music could be found but suggested that Nicholas Gatty or Vaughan Williams had the ability to compose music appropriate for the revival. He described Ralph as a 'very rising and able young man who is especially interested in folk music'. After making sure that he was to receive a fee and forcefully negotiating a long list of practicalities that he drew up, Ralph accepted the commission. Again, he got Gustav Holst to help him. He went to Stratford for the rehearsals and conducted the first performance on 24 April 1905. It was another illustration of the new concern with the forgotten music of England's past; it was the first performance of *Pan's Anniversary* since it was first staged on New Year's Day 1625. It took place in the open air in the Bancroft Garden, the area just behind the old Shakespeare Memorial Theatre. It was Ralph's first experience of writing music for dramatic performance; there were to be many more. His interest in the masque long remained with him. He was to compose music for several examples of the form, most notably his great masterpiece of a quarter of a century later, *Job, a Masque for Dancing*.

Almost three weeks after this event in Stratford came another occasion which involved considerable effort on Ralph's part. On 10 May 1905 the first Leith Hill Music Festival took place in Dorking, the town closest to Ralph's childhood home in rural Surrey. The music was performed in Dorking Public Hall, which later became the town fire station and then, when I last saw it, housed a large pet shop. The festival continues to flourish well over a century later in the Dorking Halls, further down the same street. The idea of creating such a festival came from conversations between Ralph's sister Meggie and her neighbour, Lady Farrer of Abinger Hall, who had been Ralph's contemporary at the Royal College of Music. A crop of music festivals had appeared recently in the northern counties of England (another manifestation of the nationwide musical resurgence) and one had also been founded in nearby Petersfield in Hampshire. The two young women had gone there together and been impressed and inspired by what they heard. They set about planning a festival of their own. They enlisted the help of three collaborators: Sir Walter Parratt, the organist at St George's Chapel Windsor and the Master of the Queen's (and then the King's) music, Colonel Lewin at whose house Ralph had joined in chamber music in his student days, and Lucy Broadwood. They met regularly at Abinger Hall to design their festival. They decided to establish a public competition between local choral societies and to follow this with a combined performance by all the choirs. It was a format that has endured to this day. For the first festival in 1905 the work chosen for the performance by the joint choirs was Handel's *Judas Maccabaeus*. A minute from the Festival records states that 'The Committee decided to ask Mr. R. Vaughan Williams if he would conduct the evening concert and would coach the various choirs in the combined music beforehand.' And so began an association which despite the disruption of two world wars would be an important part of Ralph's life until close to his death.

For him, it was a great pleasure and pride to help contribute fine music to the life of the area in which he grew up and which he loved.

When they returned to London after the festival, Ralph and Adeline began to look for a new home. Their six-year lease of the Barton Street house was now approaching its end and they decided not to renew it. Despite the lack of an inside lavatory and a proper bathroom the landlord was demanding a higher price. And Adeline was keen to move closer to her mother who was now living in Chelsea. So, when in early summer they discovered that 13 Cheyne Walk was available they decided to take it. A much grander dwelling than that on Barton Street, the large Chelsea terrace house (which has been re-fronted since Ralph's time there), stands on a corner and has a front garden behind a stylishly wrought-iron entrance way and garden railings. It stands five storeys high with a white stucco front and yet more ironwork across the first floor. The gateway pillars once supported urns and the fourth storey had a balustrade. The home of numerous celebrities, both before and since he lived there, Cheyne Walk was a very visible sign of Ralph's progress in life.

He and Adeline moved in on the first day of November 1905. They would remain for some twenty years, until they were both into late middle age. Here Ralph would work on his first major compositions: the Fantasia on a Theme by Thomas Tallis, The Lark Ascending, his first opera, *Hugh the Drover,* and his first three symphonies. During the more than two decades that he lived in Cheyne Walk Ralph became a national figure.

Chapter Seven

CHEYNE WALK, CHELSEA

R alph was excited about moving into his new, much larger, house. He urged Randolph Wedgwood, now living in Newcastle-upon-Tyne, to come and see it. In a letter written less than two weeks after he and Adeline had moved in, he enthused, 'You must come and see the new house soon, I've got a grand study in the attic with a grand view of the river and a bridge and 3 great electric light chimneys and a sunset.' Then he drew a sketch of the four stacks of the Lots Road Power Station and Chelsea Bridge at sunset. There were also new furnishings: 'I've got a roll-top desk, a writing table and a new piano.' Another old Cambridge friend Crompton Llewellyn Davies was one of the first dinner guests at Cheyne Walk. And at a party for members of the Fisher family, Ralph's Quintet for piano, violin, cello and double bass was performed.

Hervey Fisher's mental illness continued and Adeline spent a good deal of her time away from the new home helping to tend and entertain him. Ralph went on with his journeying into the different parts of the country in quest of more folk songs. One product of those travels was the May issue of the *Journal of the Folk Song Society*, which contained a collection of songs that Ralph had put together after visits to seven different counties. He contributed a preface that contains a paragraph picturing the very special pleasure that he took in spending time with older country people and listening to their ancient songs.

I could imagine a much less profitable way of spending a long winter evening than in the parlour of a country inn taking one's turn at

113

the mug of 'four ale' .... in the rare company of minds imbued with that fine sense which comes from advancing years and a lifelong communion with nature – and with the ever-present chance of picking up some rare old ballad or an exquisitely beautiful melody, worthy, within its smaller compass, of a place beside the finest compositions of the greatest composers.

Ralph and Adeline did manage to have some time together in the summer of 1906. They rented The Warren, a house at Meldreth, not far from Cambridge. Here Ralph worked at the second movement of his 'Sea Symphony'. And here one day he received in the post a packet from Gustav Holst which contained Holst's Two Songs Without Words, a work for chamber orchestra showing the interest in folk idiom that Holst shared with Ralph. The piece was dedicated to 'RVW'. Ralph was touched by this gesture from his old friend; he replied stating, 'if I ever do anything worth doing it will be greatly owing to having such a friend as you ... always ready to help and advise....'

That summer of 1906 Ralph was much involved with developments in the life of another important friend. Randolph Wedgwood, now thirty-two years old, after putting Ralph 'off the scent – talking about thin ice when ... fully intending to tumble all the time' – suddenly announced his engagement to the 19-year-old Iris Pawson. They were married in St Margaret's, Westminster, on 24 October 1906. Ralph was delighted for his old, close friend who, he sensed, lived a lonely life on Tyneside. He quickly reassured Randolph about the new unknown bride. 'Of course we shall like your heroine first off – anyone who is in love with you and with whom you are in love – what more?' He went on to say, 'you call Adeline and me your best friends – and I can't say what it means to me to have you say that.' He was eager to help his friend with the musical arrangements for the wedding. He warned him about Reginald Goss-Custard, the organist at St Margaret's and one of several members of the musical world towards whom Ralph felt utter scorn. 'I should love to go and beard the brute at St. Margaret's with you. I advise you to make out a <u>complete</u> programme of all the music you'd like played and tell him to play that and <u>nothing else</u> – otherwise he'll play muck and make everyone sick.'

The English Hymnal, which was Ralph's great effort to improve the standard of music in church, appeared in this year. The commission from Percy Dearmer had taken some two and a half years to complete and had cost Ralph far more time, effort and expense than he had bargained for at the outset. As music editor Ralph took final responsibility for all the settings whilst Dearmer had editorial control over the words. Ralph enlisted other musicians such as John Ireland and Gustav Holst to supply and arrange settings. These came from various countries and, provocatively at the time, from folk songs. He also contributed four original melodies, two of them given titles with private, autobiographical significance. One of these, to the words 'Come Down O Love Divine', is named for his birthplace, 'Down Ampney', the other for the most important friendship of his early years, 'Randolph'. The opening line of this hymn is, significantly, a blessing: 'God Be With You Till We Meet Again'. The dedicatee of 'In the Fen Country', Randolph Wedgwood, was also given the dedication of 'A Sea Symphony' on which Ralph was working in the same year as the publication of the hymnal. The two old friends of Cambridge days were, after some years of going their separate ways, again growing close.

Ralph's compilation of hymn settings had the ambitious aim, as he later remembered, of being 'a thesaurus of all the finest hymns in the world'.[1] It also constituted a campaign to renew music in the church. In the preface to the book he deplored 'the miasma of the languishing, sentimental hymn tunes which so often disfigure our services'. Such settings might pass for 'correct music'. But, declared Ralph simply, briefly and emphatically, 'the only correct music is that which is beautiful and noble'. He added, 'it ought no longer to be true anywhere that the most exalted moments of a churchgoer's week are associated with music that would not be tolerated in any place of secular entertainment.'

Many of the hymns in Ralph's compilation have become established favourites throughout the English-speaking world, for instance, 'For All The Saints Who From Their Labours Rest', 'He Who Would Valiant Be', and 'Come Down Oh Love Divine'. And the *English Hymnal*, as it slowly gained a reputation, contributed greatly to the fame that was now coming to him. The years of work on the collection also affected markedly Ralph's development as a composer. Michael Kennedy has rightly identified 'five tunes which he included in the hymnal and which, in varying ways, were to haunt him all his life.' The Scottish Psalter tune 'York' was to appear in the opera *Hugh the Drover* and *The Pilgrim's Progress*. 'Dives and Lazarus' is treated again in Five Variants. The 'Old Hundredth' and also 'Our Captain Calls', a tune which Ralph had collected in Sussex and which he used for 'He Who Would Valiant Be' are audible in several subsequent works. But unquestionably the most important find in the research for the *English Hymnal* was Thomas Tallis's Third Mode Melody, which Ralph adapted for the setting of the eighteenth-century text 'When rising from the bed of death' by John Addison. This fine melody became the basis of one of Ralph's most loved and admired works, the Fantasia on a Theme by Thomas Tallis, first performed in September 1910 – just a month before Ralph conducted the first performance of 'A Sea Symphony' in Leeds Town Hall.

Wilfrid Mellers has observed that:

> There is a Tallis-like element in the very concept of a new English Hymnal in so far as it was a minor Counter-Reformation. For just as the Protestant Reformation had clipped the wings of Tudor polyphony in the interests of verbal communicability, so in the early years of this century Vaughan Williams sought to reanimate communal hymnody with the spirituality it had surrendered. Often he succeeded, himself creating at least half a dozen tunes that are among the finest in the Anglican tradition, simple enough to be relished and sung by plain men and women, yet an inspiration to spirit as well as lungs. He offers release from the military harmonic and metrical concordance of Victorian hymnody ... and achieves, if not the ecstasy of monadic plainsong or Tudor polyphony, a spiritual humanism relatable, modally, harmonically and rhythmically, to the metrical psalms set by Thomas Tallis.'[2]

If the *English Hymnal* was in part a way of helping to redefine and revitalize the great tradition of English music, so important to Ralph, that same tradition, as he came to know it better, invigorated his own compositions.

In the autumn of 1906 around the time that the *English Hymnal* was being published, Ralph's Norfolk Rhapsody Number 1 had its first performance conducted by Henry Wood in London. Numbers 2 and 3 were performed just over a year later in Cardiff with Ralph invited to conduct the London Symphony Orchestra. The score of the third Rhapsody has long since disappeared; the second exists as an incomplete manuscript. The Rhapsodies clearly show the entrance of folk song into Ralph's symphonic music. The first, for instance, uses 'The Captain's Apprentice' which Ralph had collected in Kings Lynn in January 1905 from the Norfolk fisherman James Carter. In his Rhapsodies Ralph is following in the pioneering steps of Liszt and then Dvořák, relating rural song and dance music to the sounds and textures traditional in the concert hall. The Norfolk Rhapsodies evoke the mistiness and evanescence of the landscape in Impressionist music, suggesting melancholy and moodiness; then comes brightening, cheerful folk melody to alleviate and contextualize them. In America that year, Ralph's close contemporary Charles Ives was writing his *Central Park in the Dark,* a work which has affinities with Ralph's Rhapsodies. Ives evokes musingly the mysteriousness of the woodlands of Central Park, while occasionally admitting the martial music from the nearby bandstand and the popular songs from the vaudeville theatres of Upper Manhattan.

That autumn Ralph was invited to take on a subject to which he would return throughout his life. Joanna Hadley and Evelyn Ouless had dramatized a series of scenes from John Bunyan's *Pilgrim's Progress.* Their play was to be performed at Reigate Priory in Surrey on the first day of December. They wrote to Ralph asking whether he would supply some incidental music for the production. He had been recommended to them by their mutual friend Lucy Broadwood. *Pilgrim's Progress* had long been, and would forever remain, one of Ralph's favourite books and he wrote back saying that he would be delighted 'to arrange and invent some music' for their play. Here was another instance of his readiness to join in, and contribute to musical initiatives at grassroots level. He pushed forcefully for 'real' folk song and the inclusion of 'Who Would True Valour See'. As he proceeded to correspond with the two ladies, his lists of 'wants' grew more emphatic and finally sounded more like demands. The first performance was a success. And in the following spring it was repeated at the Imperial Theatre in Parliament Square and in the hall of Lincoln's Inn. The project began Ralph's near career-long series of attempts to create a musical work based on Bunyan's book. In 1922 he would return to the subject and create the pastoral episode *The Shepherds of the Delectable Mountains.* Twenty years later in the middle of the Second World War he would supply the incidental music for Edward Sackville-West's BBC radio version of the book. And in 1951 his full-scale opera or 'morality' setting of the book would be performed at Covent Garden. Unfortunately, in 1906 Ralph's interest and involvement in the project were interrupted by bad news concerning another member of Adeline's family. Frederic Maitland, the husband of her elder sister Florence, had been ill for some time. He suddenly grew worse. It was decided that to improve his health it would be wise to take a house on Grand Canary for the duration of the winter. Florence and her two daughters Gaga and Vuff travelled over to Las Palmas and rented and made ready a villa. Shortly after Frederic sailed over to join them, he suddenly died. Adeline and Ralph prepared to go out to console her sister and nieces and to help them with the sad task of unpacking the house and preparing for the return to England. But Adeline grew uneasy about leaving her mother alone to take care of the ever unstable Hervey. So Ralph agreed to go on his own.

He sailed in the first week of January 1907 and was away until the end of the month. On board ship he wrote a long letter describing condescendingly his fellow passengers and the 'very dull and shoddy crew'. Disappointingly there were no opportunities for flirtation, an activity which from now on, and with Adeline's acquiescence, he enjoyed until the end of his life. 'I can't even flirt with the ladies – There's only one who is possible from this point of view – and she is fearfully dull – also she much prefers the chief engineer....' So Ralph devoted himself instead to some of the classics of English literature. '*Tom Jones* (for the second time) and ... Shakespeare's historical plays and a lot of Browning.' His literary tastes were vastly different from those of his fellow passengers. They were all keen readers of the highly successful writer of romances, Marie Corelli. 'The whole company discussed Marie Corelli last night-and I realised for the 1st time what it was to be really out of it'.

Arrival in Las Palmas must have begun a sad time for Ralph. He helped his sister-in-law and his nieces, the 16-year-old Fredegond and her younger sister Ermengard, close down the house and prepare for their unexpected return to England. Ralph had affectionate and admiring memories of Frederic and would have recalled how kind, warm and hospitable he had been when Ralph as a rather awkward freshman had been welcomed to Downing College. A Cambridge Apostle, a distinguished professor of jurisprudence and the author of a biography of Leslie Stephen (another Fisher in-law), Frederic Maitland was one of the most sociable of Adeline's family members. When Ralph died, there were just two photographs in his bedroom: one of Gustav Holst, the other of Frederic Maitland.

Ralph dedicated the first composition that he completed after returning to England, to Maitland's widow Florence. This was Toward the Unknown Region. It is a setting for choir and orchestra of fifteen lines by Walt Whitman. Charles Edward McGuire has pointed out the literary tact and skill underlying the work: 'the care Vaughan Williams took with the text is particularly evident. The first four of Whitman's five verses are separate syntactical units, with Vaughan Williams providing a sense of closure for each before moving to the next'. And another commentator has observed, 'Vaughan Williams possesses in common with the visionary poets a prophetic sense which enables him to penetrate the meaning of spiritual values'.[3] A mystical and visionary work, its opening words and music enquire of the soul, tenderly and tentatively, whether it has the daring to proceed to an entirely unknown region of new consciousness, an ontological state in which there is:

> No map, there, no guide,
> Nor voice sounding, no touch of human hand,
> Nor face with blooming flesh, nor lips, nor eyes are in that land.

On one level the poem and the singing allude to the solitariness and the deprivation brought about by grief such as Ralph knew his sister-in-law to be experiencing (and in which he surely shared). But they also have a far broader reference. Ralph here musicalizes Whitman's ambitious and very American projection of a new mode of being for humanity. The music moves on from its opening uncertainty and then sounds out new confidence, hope and, in a rousing ending, elation, exultation and – an emotion cardinal to Romantic aesthetics – joy.

The new, liberated consciousness, having the courage to travel into the unknown, is promised freedom from all constraints other than Time and Space and a new experience of these two themselves.

> Then we burst forth – we float,
> In Time and Space, O Soul – prepared for them;
> Equal, equipt at last – (O joy! O fruit of all!) them to fulfil, O Soul.

The music powerfully conveys the grandeur of this vision. It is, as McGuire has rightly said, 'an exercise in triumphant rhetoric, including several climaxes, a grand pause before a homorhythmic choral declaration and a copious use of exclamatory brass and percussion'.[4] The evocation of the progress to the great concluding assertion in less than a dozen minutes is a remarkable achievement. The prospecting of a new awareness of time is very much a feature of this first decade of the twentieth century. In the same year that Ralph completed this composition, Einstein was beginning to initiate new thinking about time in his developing theory of relativity. And now, too, a radically new relationship with space was envisioned when the New York financier J.P. Morgan met with the directors of the White Star Line. Their discussions led to the planning of an unprecedented liner for the crossing of the Atlantic. This was the *Titanic*. The Edwardian decade was, in one respect, a period of daring, expectation and hope; these are very audible in Toward the Unknown Region.

As a result of Stanford's influence Ralph was invited to conduct the first performance of the work at the Leeds Festival in October 1907. Stanford himself conducted the first London performance two months later in a concert at the Royal College of Music. The piece was well received. Ralph was starting to build a reputation in provincial England. *The Yorkshire Post* of 11 October 1907 reported:

> Dr Vaughan Williams, who has given evidence of being one of our younger moderns of distinctive individuality ... took the conductor's place and directed a most exhilarating performance of his new work.... The merit of the work lies in the way in which the composer used choral effects in the way usually referred to when speaking of modern orchestral music as the quality of colours. Not only does he clothe the imaginative words with musical meaning, but the music moves along with a certain spiritual form that ends with a splendid effect, the soul's flight to fulfil its destiny. Sung not only with power, but with understanding, the very striking work ... met with immediate and hearty approval, the chorus, who evidently found the work much to their taste, joining lustily in the cheers that were accorded to the composer.

This was some compensation for a summer in which Hervey Fisher's condition had seriously deteriorated. When, slowly, he started to recover, Ralph and Adeline were able to have a few weeks' break at Temple Elfande, a half-timbered Tudor house close to Capel, south of Dorking and near to the area in which Ralph had spent his boyhood. Here he completed the first draft of his 'A Sea Symphony'. Writing to Randolph Wedgwood Ralph credited his old friend with ordering him to move away from the melancholy poetry of Robert Louis Stevenson and to write 'something healthy'. Randolph seems always to have urged Ralph to show his hearty side. A good friend of Randolph and his wife Iris was the 23-year-old Richard Curle, a Scots publisher and future devotee and promoter of the Polish novelist Joseph Conrad. Curle called on Ralph and Adeline at Temple Elfande. Through them Curle would meet Adeline's sister Cordelia whom, a few years later, he would marry. This meant a further reinvigorating of the relationship between the two couples: the Wedgwoods and the Vaughan Williamses.

Ralph was now approaching his thirty-fifth birthday. With his first 'magnum opus' now completed and, as he said, despondently to Randolph, about to 'go into its drawer and remain there forever', he seems to have entered a period of great uncertainty about the direction of his career and the quality of his work. After hearing Frederick Delius's Piano Concerto in October, Ralph sent off a brief, rather desperate, self-deprecating letter asking whether he might show Delius some of his work or come and visit him so that 'you might be able to suggest ways in which I cd improve myself – either by going to Paris or not'. He concludes nervously, 'I don't know if I ought to ask this on so slight an acquaintance'. Such periods of self-depreciation and self-doubt were to recur during his long career.

Paris seems very much to have been on Ralphs's mind at this time. He later recalled that 'I came to the conclusion that I was lumpy and stodgy; had come to a dead-end and that a little French polish would be of use to me.'[5] He probably discussed the idea of study in Paris with his long-time supporter, the critic Edwin Evans, who suggested that Ralph might benefit by studying with Vincent d'Indy who taught at the Paris Conservatoire. (His pupils included Joseph Canteloube, Erik Satie, Isaac Albeniz, Arthur Honegger and Cole Porter.) But Evans also seems to have discussed Ralph's musical needs with a fellow music critic, Michael Calvocoressi. From him came the suggestion that Ralph should approach a highly controversial figure in French music, Maurice Ravel. For Ralph's career and confidence this proved to be a very helpful piece of advice.

Calvocoressi was a Frenchman of Greek parentage; he was fluent in several languages. He wrote articles on musical events in Paris for various British and American periodicals and in 1907 he was also lecturing on contemporary music at the Ecole des Hautes Etudes Sociales. At the age of twenty-eight, two years before he helped Ralph, he had published his first book, which was on Liszt. Currently he was working on one on Mussorgsky. As a critic he was an early enthusiast for the Russian tradition which would become so influential on the classical music of the twentieth century. Around the time that Ralph was in Paris Calvocoressi was drawing close to Diaghilev and members of the Ballets Russes. He was also a member of Les Apaches, one of the several groups of artists, musicians and writers to be found in Paris in the first decade of the century, the Bande à Picasso being the most famous. The Apaches were all very progressive in their thinking about music and, perhaps at Calvocoressi's suggestion, adopted the theme in Borodin's Second Symphony as their call to order. They were strong supporters of Claude Debussy on the occasion of the first performance of his extremely controversial opera *Pelleas et Melisande* at the Opera Comique in 1902, five years before Ralph set off for Paris. Two of Calvocoressi's slightly younger contemporaries, Manuel de Falla and Igor Stravinsky, were occasional visitors to the meetings of Les Apaches. Otherwise, only one member of the group is remembered today and that is Maurice Ravel.

More than two years younger than Ralph, Maurice Ravel was a short, slight, dapper man of indeterminate sexuality. When Ralph chose to go and study with him, most of Ravel's major works had still to be written. The *Bolero, Daphnis and Chloe, La Valse*, his two piano concertos and his orchestration of Mussorgsky's *Pictures at an Exhibition* all lay in the future. In 1907 what fame he enjoyed had much to do with the scandalous number of times the Paris Conservatoire had denied him the prestigious Prix de Rome. But Ravel also had a few discerning admirers such as Calvocoressi who recognized the quality of works such as *Pavane for a Dead Infanta* and *Miroirs*, a sequence of five piano pieces, each one dedicated to a member of the Apaches. (The fifth and technically very difficult piece in the set, the *Alborada del gracioso*, is dedicated to Calvocoressi.) The sequence was completed two years before Ravel accepted Ralph as a pupil. At the time of their first meeting Ravel was working on his *Rapsodie espagnole* and his charming one-act opera *L'Heure Espagnole*. Ravel was very conscious of his family's Spanish origins and his roots in the Basque country. A keen awareness of nationality was something he shared with Ralph.

With his elegantly trimmed moustache and beard and his impeccable high collar, Ravel was a familiar figure in fashionable, artistic circles in Paris. In the course of his long-lasting and increasingly publicized struggles over the Prix de Rome he had received the support of Alfred Edwards, the editor of the American-owned newspaper, *Le Matin*. Edward's wife at this time was Misia Godebska, a pianist of East European origins who had studied with Fauré. She was a great beauty and her portrait was painted by most of the leading painters of the time, including Toulouse-Lautrec, Renoir and Picasso. Two years before he took on Ralph, Ravel had been one of the guests of the Edwards on their yacht the *Aimée* on a cruise lasting several weeks through Holland and

Belgium. The important contacts Ravel made on such occasions he would try to pass on to Ralph.

As they got to know each other the pupil and his younger teacher developed a friendship, one that was to be long lasting. But at their very first meeting Ralph was made uneasy; he felt he had to assert himself:

> When I had shown him some of my work he said that for my first lesson I had better 'ecrire un petit menuet dans le style de Mozart'. I saw at once that it was time to act promptly, so I said in my best French, 'Look here, I have given up my time, my work, my friends and my career to come here and learn from you, and I am not going to write a petit menuet dans le style de Mozart. After that we became great friends and I learned much from him'.[6]

At the lessons, Ralph recalled, 'I practised chiefly orchestration with him. I used to score some of his own pianoforte music and bits of Rimsky and Borodin to which he introduced me for the first time.' Ralph identified Ravel's chief gift to him in this course of tuition as a new perspective on orchestration. 'He showed me how to orchestrate in points of colour rather than in lines. It was an invigorating experience to find all artistic problems looked at from what was to me an entirely new angle.'

Ralph was in Paris until March 1908. Adeline came over from London for a few brief visits. He lived in a room at the inexpensive Hotel de l'Univers et du Portugal, a building which still stands on the Rue Croix des Petits Champs, today a non-descript street running north from the Louvre towards the banking district of Paris. He enjoyed eating at the nearby cafes and creameries. But he felt uncouth beside the suave and sophisticated Ravel when it came to ordering from up-market Parisian menus. On one occasion, Ravel, kindly trying to assist Ralph's career, brought him together with a publisher in a restaurant. The discussion between the two Frenchmen about what to order lasted well over twenty minutes. Ralph felt embarrassed that he could make no informed comments on the choices and was grateful that his host and the publisher were forbearing with their large, baggily suited and very English guest. When the elaborate meal came to an end, the publisher turned formally to Ralph, nudged him in the ribs and suggested 'Now we go see some jolly tarts, ha?' Ralph went along with the idea but, as he later told Ursula, he found the girls 'disappointing', and 'guaranteed' he assured her 'not to tempt any young man to lose his virtue.'

Musically Ralph's months in Paris were a great success. Writing to thank Michael Calvocoressi for his excellent advice, Ralph was in no doubt whatsoever about the suitability of Ravel as a teacher and adviser for him at the present stage of his career. Ravel was 'the man who is <u>exactly</u> what I was looking for. As far as I know my own faults he hit upon them all exactly and is telling me to do exactly what I half feel in my mind I ought to do – but it just wanted <u>saying</u>.' Ralph's first two compositions after he returned to the comparative comfort of 13, Cheyne Walk in the spring of 1908, very much under the influence of Ravel, were his first string quartet, in G minor, first performed by the Schwiller Quartet in the November of that year, and 'On Wenlock Edge', a sequence of six songs for tenor, piano and string quartet, setting poems by A.E. Housman whose collection *A Shropshire Lad* was immensely popular at the time. Years later, Ralph recollected that he returned '... home with a bad attack of French fever and wrote a string quartet which caused a friend to say that I must have been having tea with Debussy, and a song cycle with several atmospheric effects, but I did <u>not</u> succumb to the temptation of writing a piece about a cemetery, and Ravel paid me the compliment of telling me that I was the only pupil who 'n'ecrit pas de ma musique.'[7]

The unwritten cemetery piece appears to be a reference to *Gaspard de la Nuit*, the very difficult piano piece that Ravel was working on in 1908 and which the two composers must have surely looked at together. All three of the settings of poems by the *poete maudit* Aloysius Bertrand have nocturnal, deathly subjects, especially the second, 'Le Gibet' which ponders the image of a dangling corpse. Not a subject for English Edwardian taste.

The musicalizing of such radical, morbid features of the human condition were beyond Ralph at this time and despite the very audible influences of Debussy and Ravel, his first string quartet shows pervasively a continuing relationship with the music that he had written over the last ten years and more. The delicate dancing in the second movement, Minuet and Trio, has modest traces of folk song and the following movement, occasionally seeming directionless, shows an evolution from gentleness into soaring intensity that is typical of Ralph's music earlier and later. His hearty, definitely non-morbid side appears in the racing, emphatic conclusion to the Finale.

The song sequence 'On Wenlock Edge' is a much more considerable work. After its first performances in November 1909, reviewers detected

French influences, one suggesting that there were reminiscences of 'the manner of Ravel's *La Vallée des Cloches*. Certainly there is some delicate articulation and interaction among the strings of the quartet, piano and voice, but the overall impression conveyed by this fine song suite remains essentially English in its sound as well as in the words that evoke and explicitly refer to a very Midland setting. At least one of these songs, 'Bredon Hill' belongs in any competent anthology of English art song. Ralph's persistent denigrator, the influential critic Ernest Newman, saw in the sequence an attempt at Wagnerian word-painting, 'another of Dr Vaughan Williams's disastrous attempts to imitate folk song'. But in the same issue of *The Musical Times* Ralph's continuing champion Edwin Evans insisted that:

> The musical sentiment of 'On Wenlock Edge' is as sincere and unso-phisticated as that of the poems themselves. Nowhere is it marred by the self-indulgence of excess and nowhere does it show signs of being studied or self-conscious. It is fresh and spontaneous and therefore convincing.... It expresses, as it were, in the colouring of his own climate, the clean faith of the healthy young English man.[8]

This is surely correct. The period in France clarified rather than coloured the sound of his compositions. Perhaps Ralph himself best summarized the abiding effect of his study with Ravel. In a trenchant, single sentence paragraph he wrote 'My French fever soon subsided but left my musical metabolism, on the whole, healthier.'

On his return from Paris Ralph returned to his bread-and-butter activities in the English music world. In May 1908 he spent several days as an adjudicator at the Bucks, Beds and Oxon Festival. One of his fellow judges was Walford Davies who, Percy Dearmer had threatened, would have been made musical editor of *The English Hymnal*, if Ralph had declined the job. The following month Ralph conducted *Towards the Unknown Region* at Cambridge and it was probably then that he was asked to write incidental music for *The Wasps* of Aristophanes, a perfor-mance of which was being planned at the university for the following year. He also continued his various collaborations with Gustav Holst who was now teaching at the Morley Memorial College for Working Men and Women, founded some eighteen years before and named for a wealthy philanthropic textile manufacturer. Ralph donated his services helping his dear friend mount performances of Rossini's *Stabat Mater* and in

1909, Purcell's *King Arthur*. During the winter of 1908–9 Ralph also gave a series of extension lectures 'From Haydn to Wagner' at the college. And of course, whenever he had the time, Ralph would set off into the country in search of yet more folk songs. Em Marshall in her book *Music in the Landscape* reports that around this time Ralph:

> also joined a walking group called the Sunday Tramps. Founded in 1879 by Virginia Woolf's father [the author, critic and mountaineer Sir Leslie Stephen], and the jurist Sir Frederick Pollock, the group caught trains to villages twenty-odd miles out of London and then walked back into town from there. They no doubt discussed highbrow subjects en route, for fellow members included Lord Haldane [later to become Lord Chancellor], The Bloomsbury Group artist Roger Fry, the author John Buchan, the historian Goldsworthy Lowes Dickinson, the critic Desmond McCarthy, the three Trevelyan brothers and Geoffrey and John Maynard Keynes.[9]

Ralph's life in these years continued as a very divided one; he was increasingly busy in the music world of London but he also had a passion to leave Cheyne Walk behind him and set off on his own into the English countryside. He would stay in country inns, drink in public bars, walk the roads and encounter fellow vagabonds and also members of the other community of the wayside who fascinated him deeply – the gypsies. Occasionally he would stay with some of the many middle-class folklorists and collectors of folk songs and folk dances active at this time. During one particular summer, after a visit to the Three Choirs Festival at Hereford, he went to stay with Ella Mary Leather, the wife of a solicitor, who lived in nearby Weobley. Mrs Leather, who was slightly younger than Ralph, was a passionate folklorist. She had immersed herself in local country life, joining in hop-picking with the casual labourers and learning their songs and stories. Her findings were the basis of her book *Folklore of Herefordshire* which Ralph greatly admired. Especially exciting for Ralph was that she had managed to become accepted among the local gypsies. These were people to whom Ralph would feel drawn throughout his life. His favourite novel, Ursula notes, was George Borrow's *Lavengro*, the classic novel of Romany life along the roads of Britain during the early decades of the nineteenth century before the coming of the railways and the full onset of industrialization. Of Mrs Leather, Ralph wrote:

... one only had to accompany her, as was more than once my privilege, on a folk song collecting expedition among the gypsies of Herefordshire, to be astonished at her friendly reception by these proud and suspicious people. She understood them and they understood her; they knew that both she and Colonel Leather were willing and anxious to help and advise them in all their difficulties, and in return they gave her of their best.[10]

Ralph long retained a very vivid image of one of the visits to a gypsy camp which Ella Mary Leather made possible for him.

One of these expeditions remains clearly in my memory. It was a cold, clear September night and we stood by the light of a blazing fire in the open ground of the gypsy encampment; the fire had been specially lighted to enable us to note down tunes and words in the growing darkness. Then out of the half-light there came the sound of a beautiful tenor voice singing 'The Unquiet Grave'. It was a memorable experience.[11]

Sometimes Ralph's excursions from the metropolitan world into that of Romanies and simple country people turned into escapades rather than poetic images. One evening at closing time outside a pub in Ledbury he was suddenly aware of a girl singing a ballad to two men. To Ralph, as Ursula recorded the incident, the three figures 'standing in the road outside in the light of the still open door, looked like a group in a story.'[12] Ralph approached them and asked if they knew any other songs. One of the men said that his father did and offered to take Ralph to see him. They set off into the countryside and the rain came on. It grew heavier. They went on down narrow lanes and then on to a muddy track where they came upon two tramps sheltering in a barn. Ralph was intrigued to hear one tramp ask the other 'Did you ever hear the harmonium?' Receiving the answer 'No', he told him 'It's sweet music'. Ralph's companion decided to give up and go home. The tramps proceeded to ignore him. And so there, in a desolate muddy farmyard in Herefordshire in the dark and in the rain, Ralph's quest came to an uncomfortable end. Not all his excursions produced results.

Ralph's increasing preoccupation with his search for folk song increased his geographical and mental separation from Adeline. And she for her part was more than ever concerned with her troubled family.

Early in 1909 her mother had a fall. Adeline, despite being ill herself, and running a very high temperature, insisted on going to tend her. To onlookers and especially Ralph this seemed strange, even perverse, since Adeline's sisters Emmeline and Cordelia were already in their mother's house. It seemed to at least one witness that Adeline was determined to maintain her position as the controlling figure among the family members surrounding her mother and the still ailing Hervey. Around this time Adeline also began to suffer from arthritis. It swiftly grew worse and soon prevented her from walking. Ralph took her to Weymouth for a few days at the end of March. By early April she had recovered enough for them to be able to stay with the Holsts at their home near the Thames at Barnes, from which they watched Cambridge lose to Oxford in the university boat race.

Ralph continued to correspond with Maurice Ravel who, generously, was making an effort to get his English friend's music performed in Paris. Ravel's own career was progressing very well and he had recently moved from his modest home in the Rue Chevalier in an industrial suburb of north-western Paris, where Ralph had known him, to a grand apartment on the fashionable Avenue Carnot close to the Arc de Triomphe. He was presently composing his *Mother Goose* suite and *Daphnis and Chloe*, the ballet intended for Serge Diaghilev. But he interrupted his work to accept Ralph and Adeline's invitation to stay at Cheyne Walk in late May. The visit confirmed and strengthened the friendship. To Ralph's great relief Ravel was relaxed about English food especially enjoying the steak and kidney pudding and the stout at Waterloo Station. Ravel shared Ralph's keen interest in painting and he made a point of asking to be taken to the Wallace Collection to see its fine collection of seventeenth- and eighteenth-century French pictures.

Shortly after Ravel's departure Ralph was caught up in the hectic activity that for him always went along with the Leith Hill Music Festival. Then in late June he went to Cambridge to attend the centennial celebrations of Charles Darwin and was taken aback by the high esteem, even reverence, that was expressed towards the figure whom he remembered as the kindly great-uncle of his childhood. Adeline was having an ongoing course of massage for her arthritis but it was not getting better, so they spent time getting different treatments for her at the grand Victorian spa at Woodhall in Lincolnshire. Her condition was not greatly improved.

In the autumn they had another exciting opportunity to indulge their interest in paintings. On 9 October along with Mrs Fisher and Richard

Curle, the future husband of Adeline's sister Cordelia, they went to the National Gallery to see the National Loan Exhibition in Aid of National Gallery Funds. This was a major event in that year's art and social calendar and the larger 'season'. It was a show made up of paintings lent by wealthy owners and rarely seen in public. It contained major works by Reynolds, Holbein, Gainsborough, Watteau, Rubens, Goya, Velázquez and El Greco. A year later in 1910 there would be a contrasting exhibition at the Grafton Gallery. This one was organized and curated by Roger Fry, the lover of Adeline's cousin Vanessa Bell. This famous event in art history was the exhibition 'Manet and the Post-Impressionists' which introduced into Britain the work of the radically innovative artists of turn of the century France including, besides Manet, Cezanne, Gauguin, Van Gogh, Matisse and Picasso.

Just over a month after the visit to the exhibition of old masters came an important occasion in Ralph's career as a composer. His Housman song sequence 'On Wenlock Edge' had its first public performance in the Aeolian Hall in New Bond Street. The strings were the Schwiller Quartet headed by Isidore Schwiller, a former colleague of Gustav Holst in the Carl Rosa Opera Orchestra. Ralph was delighted by the sensitivity of their playing and by the performances of the pianist and the tenor, Gervase Elwes whose wife Lady Winefride recorded that after the concert 'Ralph Williams came up to me, his eyes shining with delight. By nature he is far from effusive and I have never seen him look so excited'.[13] Reviewers were enthusiastic too. They were very aware of the French influences in the sequence; more so than most listeners would be today. One jokingly suggested that with all the Debussyan, impressionist atmospherics in the instrumental parts the work might be renamed *L'Apres Midi D'Un Vaughan*. It was one of Ralph's earliest works to find an ongoing place in recital rooms. ('Linden Lea' was, of course, another.) Ravel also liked *On Wenlock Edge* and succeeded, a couple of years later, in getting the work performed in Paris with Fauré playing the piano part.

The day after the heady evening at the Aeolian Hall, Ralph travelled to Cambridge to help with the rehearsals for *The Wasps*, the comedy by Aristophanes. He had been commissioned by the Cambridge Greek Play committee (which continues to the present day) to provide an overture and incidental music for the production. (Hubert Parry had been given the same commission exactly a quarter of a century earlier.) The performance took place on 26 November in the New Theatre. Charles Wood of Gonville and Caius College, who had taught Ralph when he was an undergraduate, was the conductor. Again Ralph had a great success. The brisk, breezy overture quickly established itself as a concert hall favourite. Unfortunately the subsequent incidental music, witty and entertaining though it is, fell into neglect. Three years later, in 1912, Ralph revived it in a five-minute suite. But it was not until the full text and score of *The Wasps* became available in 2005 in the excellent CD version scripted by David Pountney and conducted by Sir Mark Elder, that the totality of this charming, allusive music became generally available. On the whole it is light-hearted stuff with jokey allusions to Offenbach's *Le Roi Carotte* and the famous 'Merry Widow' waltz which was introduced to London the year before *The Wasps* was heard in Cambridge. Far more abstruse is the passage that quotes from Parry's Greek play music of 1883 to which Ralph added the note, 'with apologies to a great English composer'. There is also an implicit reference to Ralph's origins. In 'The March Past of the Witnesses' section which in the suite is re-titled 'March past of the Kitchen Utensils', a timpanist is asked to shake a bag full of broken china. One of the players who knew of Ralph's ancestry asked if it should be Wedgwood. 'Of course', came the reply, 'it's the only china that would make the right sound'. The influence of Debussy and of Borodin (who greatly interested Ralph) is audible in this music. But it also has a very English breeziness. The work overall is one of Ralph's several achievements in light music, its popular appeal tinged, verbally and musically, with donnish humour from the time of Edward VII.

As the year 1909 drew to an end, the year that had seen the completion of the *Elektra* of Richard Strauss and Mahler's *Das Lied von der Erde*, the 37-year-old Ralph found himself ever busier with an increasing number of music projects. He and Adeline spent Christmas with his mother at Leith Hill Place. This enabled him to tackle the mass of work involved in the coming Leith Hill Music Festival. The preparations meant dealing with such mundane tasks as the writing of programme notes, checking and correcting hired parts and scores, planning rehearsals, hiring soloists and teaching inexperienced conductors and singers how to come together as a choir. To all these jobs he brought unceasing energy and enthusiasm.

And then it was 1910. One of the great landmark years in Ralph's career as a composer. In the midst of the now familiar, ongoing whirl of musical activity there came three outstanding achievements. This year he suddenly made his venture into opera and by the autumn of 1910 had completed sketches for his first one, *Hugh the Drover*. In September at the Three Choirs Festival at Gloucester there was heard for the first time his Fantasia on a Theme by Thomas Tallis, one of his works most loved by the public and most often played. A week after this, amidst the Victorian grandeur of Leeds Town Hall, his 'Sea Symphony', which had been several years in the composing, was at last performed. With these three major ventures, all within the one remarkable year, Ralph started to become identified as one of the promising composers of his generation.

THE EDWARDIAN ACHIEVER

Chapter Eight

THE FIRST TWO SYMPHONIES 1910–14

Adeline's somewhat estranged cousin, Virginia Woolf, famously remarked that, 'On or about December 1910, human character changed'. What initially prompted her statement was Roger Fry's historic, highly controversial exhibition 'Manet and the Post-Impressionists' at the Grafton Gallery. But in this year that was also such a turning point in Ralph's career, radical, often shocking innovations were occurring in many walks of life. They were to have a profound effect on his life and his music.

The year marked one of the most momentous changes in British political history. In May with the death of Edward VII, the Edwardian age came to an end. More consequentially the intensifying class tensions in the country finally brought about, formally and actually, the ending of the political power of the aristocracy. There had to be two general elections, one in January and one in December. These were necessitated by the policies of the Liberal Chancellor of the Exchequer, the Welshman David Lloyd George. Highly energetic and voluble, and brought up in North Wales, he had begun life working for a lawyer and was the first solicitor ever to become Chancellor *and* Prime Minister. A passionate advocate of the cause of 'the common man' against 'the Dukes', Lloyd George had, in 1909, introduced the People's Budget, which proposed heavy taxation of the wealthy and large landowners. Passed by the House of Commons, the legislation was rejected by the predominantly Tory House of Lords. This brought about the first general election of 1910, one which kept the Liberals in power. The budget eventually became law. But

135

during 1910 Lloyd George and the Prime Minister H.H. Asquith were working on what was a radical, even revolutionary, constitutional change. This was the Parliament Act, which would deny the House of Lords its ancient right to veto laws approved by the Commons. Passed in the lower house the Parliament Act was, as expected, rejected by the Lords. The country was in political deadlock. Dramatically, the Liberals asked the new king, George V, to create sufficient Liberal peers to outvote the Tories. But before this took place the issue was taken to the people in the general election of December 1910. Again, the Liberals regained power. It was a dramatic moment in British political history. The King's hand was not forced because the Tories eventually backed down. The Parliament Act finally became law in August of the following year. It marked the first of several great shifts in the political and social ordering of Britain during Ralph's lifetime.

The political passions of 1910, the heated controversy, especially that surrounding the suffragette campaign for the vote for women, are very palpable in the fiction of the time. The 'condition of England novel' had been a category in English fiction since the mid-nineteenth century; contributors to it included Dickens, Disraeli and H.G. Wells, whose novels greatly impressed Ralph. The year 1910 produced another important example, *Howard's End* by E.M. Forster, Virginia Woolf's good friend and associate in the Bloomsbury Group and a future friend and collaborator of Ralph's. A theme of the novel is the political and cultural emergence of the working class. Significantly this year also saw the publication of *The White Peacock* by D.H. Lawrence, the first, and by far the greatest novelist of this previously inarticulate section of society. Lawrence would take up the rainbow theme from *Howard's End,* using it for the title and concluding image in his masterpiece *The Rainbow,* which is also, to some extent, a 'condition of England' novel.

Members of the Bloomsbury Group, such as Roger Fry, Duncan Grant and Adeline's cousin Vanessa Bell, were especially interested in the striking, radical changes in painting and sculpture that were continuing in Paris. This was the year that Picasso completed the Cubist portrait of his dealer Daniel-Henri Kahnweiler and that Matisse produced the two great canvases *La Musique* and *La Danse.* Also in Paris that year came the first performances of Stravinsky's ballet *The Firebird* written for Diaghilev's Ballets Russes. It was Stravinsky's breakthrough into fame. Ralph's friend Michel-Dimitri Calvocoressi was one of many to write enthusiastically about the work. Excitedly, he asserted that Stravinsky was the heir and developer of the achievements of the Russian school known as 'The Mighty Handful', which included Borodin, Balakirev, Rimsky-Korsakov and Mussorgsky. Calvocoressi admired them, as he admired Stravinsky, for their efforts to renew the music native to Russia. Like Ralph they were inspired by a musical nationalism. *The Firebird* and Ralph's *Fantasia on a Theme by Thomas Tallis*, both first performed in 1910, have, of course, conspicuous differences. But they have in common a keen, passionate desire to revivify the ancient music of their composer's homeland.

In May of that year there was at Cambridge a retrospective concert of Ralph's works over the last decade and more. It was the first such tribute and flattering to a 37-year-old. It was a clear confirmation of the standing he had now achieved in the music world. The concert was organized by Edward Joseph Dent, an old Etonian who had been an undergraduate at King's College, Cambridge, while Ralph was at Trinity. Like so many friends of Ralph of that time, Dent had strong links with the Liberal Party. His father was a wealthy landowner who was a Liberal member of Parliament for some seventeen years. E.J. Dent, as he was generally known, went on to have a distinguished career as a musicologist, writing books on Mozart's operas, Alessandro Scarlatti, Busoni and Handel and becoming Professor of Music at Cambridge. An influential member of the music establishment, he became another important booster of Ralph's music. When, out of the blue, he wrote proposing the idea of an all Vaughan Williams concert at Cambridge, Ralph replied expressing his 'intense pleasure', saying 'I can't say anything to tell you how touched I feel by all this.'[1] During the early months of 1910 the two men conducted a very active correspondence as Ralph helped with the organization of the concert, settling on the works to be performed, booking performers and determining the fees to be paid.

In a letter of late March 1910, after he had confirmed three of the songs to be sung at his concert, Ralph reported to Dent a recent happening that was to have a major effect on his career as a composer. It was an epiphany for him; one that introduced an entirely new strand into his musical activities. That month he had been to the Savoy Theatre in The Strand to see a production of Glück's opera *Orfeo*. The title role was taken by Marie Brema, the first English singer ever to perform at the Wagner Festival in Bayreuth, who had also sung the part of the angel in the first performance of Elgar's *The Dream of Gerontius* in Birmingham. Now in her fifty-fifth year Marie Brema was approaching the end of her singing career. But for Ralph the experience was overwhelming. Never before had he realized the potential of opera as a form. Excitedly he wrote:

> I admit the singing was bad.... but I saw what cd be done with opera
> (for the 1st time) with real rehearsal and an attempt to illustrate every
> moment in the music – and I thought it was awfully successful – and
> the dance and staging was wonderful – quite modern of course – but
> if the music can bear it why not? and that girl that danced – had no
> idea it was possible to express so much emotion by means of the arms
> and legs....'[2]

Ralph quickly set about composing an opera. He had in mind a subject
that he was extremely keen on but he needed a librettist. He discussed
the matter with his brother Hervey Vaughan Williams, who was now in
the colonial Civil Service and recently returned from Nigeria. Hervey
put his brother on to a friend of his, Bruce Richmond, a lawyer who
had been educated at Winchester and New College, Oxford, and who
was in the process of becoming one of the most influential figures in
English literary culture during the first third of the twentieth century.
After writing for *The Times* for a period, he took over the editorship of
the recently created *Times Literary Supplement* in 1902. Holding this
position for well over thirty years Bruce Richmond became very much an
establishment figure and arbiter of literary tastes. Ralph told Ursula that
one day when Richmond was staying at Leith Hill Place, Ralph turned
to him, demanding 'I want to set a prize fight to music – can you find
someone to make a libretto for me?' Bruce Richmond suggested someone
he knew who wrote leaders for *The Times*; this was Harold Child, who
was also a theatre critic.[3]

In the summer of 1910 Ralph wrote a long letter to the journalist
thanking him for agreeing to collaborate and describing the subject he
had in mind. The letter was sent from a hotel by an Alpine lake near Bozen
in the Austrian Tirol where Ralph and Adeline were having a few weeks'
holiday. After thanking Harold Child for his enthusiasm for the project,
Ralph immediately cautioned him about the prospects for the proposed
work, 'I see hardly any chance of an opera by an English composer ever
being produced, at all events in <u>our</u> lifetime....'[4] Given the low state of
English opera at this moment Ralph's utter pessimism seems justified and
his spirited effort to improve the situation a very creative and admirable
initiative. Enthusiastically he tried to set down the 'nebulous ideas' he
had for an opera. His plan was 'to write a musical, what the Germans

call 'Bauer Comedie' – only applied to English country life (real as far as possible – not sham) – something on the lines of Smetana's *Verkaufte Braut* – for I have an idea for an opera written to real English words, with a certain amount of real English music and also a real English subject....'[5] In the following paragraphs Ralph proceeds to sketch some of the scenes in the opera he envisages. The first is set in a village fairground 'with all the paraphernalia – merry-go-round, cake-stalls, shooting gallery, fat-woman ... a ballad-monger, small boys with whistles, etc. etc.' All the activity begins to come to a climax when a prize fight is announced. There is to be suspense while a challenger to the village champion is waited for. Then 'at last a stranger rides (or walks up) (possibly a gypsy – see one of the opening chapters of Borrow's *Zincali*).... Defeat of the village champion.... heroine feels relieved to transfer her affections to the stranger – disgust of the village hero'. Ralph is in some doubt whether 'it is in the nature of things for a gypsy to run off with a non-gypsy'. He and Harold Child can settle this later. But Ralph's keen desire to relate his opera to the world of the Romanies is clear enough.

I Zincali was one of the most successful books of the Victorian period. First published in 1841, it was continually republished throughout the reign. Subtitled 'an Account of the Gypsies in Spain', it is a memoir of George Borrow's close involvement with the Romany people – the Zincali – during the 1830s when he worked in Spain for the Bible Society, founded a quarter of a century earlier by William Wilberforce and other evangelical Christians. The book has many anecdotes about the Iberian Romanies including some that deal with what was seen as the dark side of their culture: sorcery, cursing, cattle poisoning and thievery. Containing a dictionary of the Romany language, the book also places the Romanies and their history in a European and world context. The section of *I Zincali* entitled 'The English Gypsies' especially interested Ralph. It contains the story of 'the terrible Thurtell', a prominent figure in the prize-fighting business, whom Borrow remembered promoting a fight in a village near Norwich. The fight attracted a trio of gypsies. Two of them left a lasting and unprecedented impression on Borrow. In his description they appear as figures of operatic charisma. Ralph was powerfully affected by Borrow's presentation of them. Of the first gypsy Borrow writes:

It is impossible for the imagination to conceive anything so perfectly beautiful than were the features of this man, and the most skilful sculptor of Greece might have taken them as his model for a hero and a god. The forehead was exceedingly lofty, – a rare thing in a gypsy; the nose less Roman than Grecian, – fine yet delicate; … his complexion was a beautiful olive; and his teeth were of a brilliancy uncommon even among these people, who have all fine teeth. He was dressed in a coarse waggoner's slop, which however was unable to conceal altogether the proportions of his noble and Herculean figure.

To Borrow the other gypsy was similarly prepossessing but in a different way:

> … Gypsy Will, was, I think, fifty when he was hanged, ten years subsequently (for I never afterwards lost sight of him), in the front of the jail of Bury St Edmunds. I still have present before me his bushy black hair, his black face, and his big black eyes fixed and staring. His dress consisted of a loose blue jockey coat, jockey boots and breeches; in his hand was a huge jockey whip, and on his head …, a broad-brimmed, high-peaked Andalusian hat…. In stature he was shorter than his more youthful companion, yet he must have measured six feet at least, and was stronger built, if possible. What brawn! – what bone! – what legs! – what thighs!

At Thurtell's ordering, these two figures of outstanding male beauty clear away the fairgoers in order to make space for a ring. They easily, quickly, defeat all challengers. When no more seem forthcoming, Gypsy Will, backed by Thurtell, tries another tack. With a very tempting purse of twenty pounds he offers to fight any comer for the title 'The best man in England'. No one steps forward. But then yes! A strong country boy wished to win the stakes, and was about to fling up his hat in defiance, but he was prevented by his friends, with – 'Fool! He'll kill you!' With some contempt the spectacularly handsome gypsies mount their horses. 'They pressed their horses' flanks, again leapt over the ditches, and speedily vanished, amidst the whirlwind of dust which they raised upon the road.'

This was the episode that was the inspiration and the kernel of Ralph's first opera. So keen was he to use the scene that in a letter later that summer he sent Harold Child a copy of I Zincali with the relevant passages marked. He also suggested that their next opera might be based on Borrow's classic novel of gypsy life, Lavengro. 'I've always had this in my mind,' he wrote.

Vagabond impulses often showed themselves in Ralph's life. In the summer of 1910 he went to Oxford to show the early drafts of his opera to Hugh Allen, his good friend from their undergraduate days in Cambridge. Allen, now organist at New College, brought along some of his young colleagues, Henry Ley, organist at Keble College, and George Butterworth, the handsome young music master from nearby Radley College whom Ralph may well have met already through Cecil Sharp and others in the burgeoning folk dance movement. The future composer of 'The Banks of Green Willow' was a very keen and gifted dancer. He and the other two listeners were delighted by Ralph's opera score. At nightfall Ralph suddenly wanted to walk out into the summer night. The others were not enthusiastic, but Henry Ley agreed to accompany him; 'to shouts of "Madmen" we set off',[6] he recalled. They roamed the lanes on the edge of the city and tramped down country tracks. As the night grew blacker, Ralph decided that he wanted to see the dawn break over the spires of Oxford. The two of them sat on the top of a poultry shed to watch the sunrise. Some time after half past six they arrived back in Hugh Allen's house in Keble Road.

Another of Ralph's companions in Oxfordshire ramblings was the early music scholar Dom Anselm Hughes, who was also a member of an Anglican monastic order. Hughes remembered how his clerical clothes put off one of the country people who, after a pint or two, were ready to sing old songs for Ralph.

'Oh Sir, I can't go on', looking at my monkish habit. ''Tis rude words'. Ralph would drag me to my feet and push me out of the door 'Come on, Hughes, get out.' ... as he closed the door on me I would see him take a 10/– note from his pocket and offering it to the singer say, 'NOW!'[7]

Back in London, as he continued to compose his opera (which, in the event, would take another fourteen years before it was completed and performed), he was also working on an important and prestigious commission. It had come from the Three Choirs Festival, which was to be held in Gloucester that year. At one of the concerts the main work was to be *The Dream of Gerontius* conducted by Sir Edward Elgar himself. The festival committee invited Ralph to contribute a short opening piece. What he presented was his Fantasia on a Theme by Thomas Tallis. It was to prove to be one of the works that made the year 1910 outstanding in the history of the arts.

It is a work which has long since established itself as a classic of English twentieth-century music. Composed for a string quartet and double string orchestra it has a grave beauty. As Michael Kennedy has observed, 'The great spread string chords give the work power, massive spaciousness and a four-square solidity'. Though only some twenty minutes in length, it is a great monument of spiritual profundity and enduring nobility. As the title indicates, the work refers back to the spirit of Tudor music and was a product of Ralph's years of work on the *English Hymnal*. After the two ancient introductory themes have been established there follows an intricate interweaving of string sound. Amidst the developing grandeur in the music there are gentle lyrical moments but the abiding effect is one of enduring power. There is a spiritual authority to the piece that makes it an important milestone in Ralph's career as a composer and in English music as a whole. The first major work of his long career was now achieved.

Ursula reports that onlookers remembered how on that historic occasion of the first performance Ralph stood before the large audience 'looking taller than ever on the high platform, dark haired, serious, inwardly extremely nervous'. Just over a month later he was the conductor of another new work of his and was even more nervous, being unable to sleep for the preceding few days. This composition was 'A Sea Symphony', another historic career achievement of 1910. The performance took place in Leeds Town Hall. Ralph's tension was very obvious as he stepped up on to the podium. Henderson the timpanist did his best to steady him, calling out 'Give us a square four in the bar and we will do the rest.' But the similarly nervous Campbell MacInnes, the baritone soloist, did not help matters when he whispered to Ralph, 'If I stop, you'll go on, won't you?' For those present that day the performance went well. Lady Stanford, for instance, touched Adeline's shoulder and murmured 'You must be very proud of him'. Ralph himself was less sure of how it had gone. But he was grateful to his friend Hugh Allen for ensuring that the symphony was performed very soon afterwards in Oxford. The organizing committee at Leeds had proposed a fee of thirty guineas for 'A Sea Symphony'; this was twenty more than had been offered for Toward the Unknown Region in 1907. But Ralph was still some distance from those who commanded the highest remuneration. At that same festival in Leeds in 1910 Rachmaninov was given 100 guineas to perform as a piano soloist. And for the same sum, Elgar conducted his first symphony which had been premiered some two years before.

'A Sea Symphony' was Ralph's most ambitious work to date. Setting four passages from the poetry of Walt Whitman and taking well over an hour to perform, the work is a musical response to the profound issues that are encountered in Whitman's lines as in the work of the other American transcendentalist writers, Thoreau and Emerson. The late nineteenth century had produced a number of large expressions of cultural and philosophical synthesis. Alongside Whitman's very long sequence of poems *The Leaves of Grass* stand Karl Marx's *Das Kapital* and Richard Wagner's *Ring* cycle. And exactly one month before 'A Sea Symphony' was performed in Leeds, Gustav Mahler conducted the first performance of his Eighth Symphony, his choral symphony of a 1,000 in Munich. All these works offer in different ways an interpretation and understanding of the totality of human experience. There is to them an ambitiousness that came to seem grandiose as the twentieth century progressed.

The vast choral and orchestral range of Mahler's Eighth Symphony shows up the modesty, the delicacy even, of Ralph's symphony of synthesis. The soundings of experience heard here relate to just three images, and thence metaphors, from Whitman: the sea, the sailor and the ship.

'Behold the sea itself' is the exciting, commanding, exulting opening. Alain Frogley is surely correct when he maintains that the 'dramatic shift from B flat minor to D major harmony at the word "sea" conjures a visceral sense of space opening up before us, and surely constitutes one of the great opening gestures of musical history'.[8] The listener's attention is immediately seized. There follows an apostrophizing of the ocean which quickly becomes a metaphor for all life processes. The second movement of the symphony, 'On the Beach at Night, Alone' turns from such large forces to the individual consciousness; it is a nocturne in which the baritone soloist moves from subdued meditation to a vast cosmic vision supported by horns over pizzicato strings. Five lines in, we come upon Whitman's, and (we must assume) Ralph's, concept of what is the underlying synthesis of all the variegated life processes.

A vast similitude interlocks all.
All distances of space however wide,
All distances of time,
All souls, all living bodies though they be ever so different,
All nations, all identities that have existed or may exist.

In the third movement, 'The Waves', a beautiful, rippling *scherzo*, we turn from such difficult abstractions to the very sensuous-sounding reality of the movement of the waves and to their eddying displacement as a 'stately and rapid ship' passes through them. The fourth and final movement 'The Explorers' turns back to vast, cosmic contemplations. This time, in the lengthy conclusion, the apostrophizing is to something larger than the sea, which was the subject of the first movement. Now it is the planet itself and its cosmic context which are addressed.

> O vast Rondure, swimming in space,
> Covered all over with visible power and beauty,
> Alternate light and day and the teeming spiritual darkness
> Unspeakable high processions of sun and moon and countless stars
> above.

There follows a summary of the evolution of human consciousness from Adam and Eve down to that of 'the noble inventors'. Then the singer/poet interrogates his soul, in a passionate duet, about their readiness to move on into a yet newer level of consciousness. (The same prospect had been faced in Toward the Unknown Region.) There is a celebration of a new form of self-hood; it is expressed and dramatically musicalized in five crucial and affirming syllables: 'O thou transcendent'.

After these five slow, emphatic syllables, sung in moving celebratory fashion, the choir is quickly swept up into excited sea-shanty rhythms as the great unprecedented voyage is prepared for.

The final lines of the symphony assert a new, perhaps dangerous destination of awareness.

> Reckless, O Soul, exploring, I with thee,
>   and thou with me,
> For we are bound, where mariner has not
>   yet dared to go,
> And we will risk the ship, ourselves and all.
>   O my brave Soul!

The penultimate line is given a powerfully dramatic percussive setting. The conclusion is a quiet ecstasy trailing away at the last into a calm, confident, contemplative silence.

'A Sea Symphony' has a vastness of explicit philosophical dimensions

144

that is not excelled in any of Ralph's subsequent works. The choral writing keeps up with the soaring verbal range, the orchestral accompaniment less so. (The orchestral riches of Mahler's Eighth Symphony are a revealing comparison.) But 'A Sea Symphony' is unquestionably a fine and, in the concert hall, an enduring work. Emotionally evocative, it succeeds at the critical moments in its development in conveying musically a profound and inspiriting sense of secular sanctity.

For some years now Ralph's concern with the musical utterance of spiritual experience had drawn him to the work of the seventeenth-century poet George Herbert. In 1911 Ralph completed his song cycle 'Five Mystical Songs' setting Herbert's texts for baritone, chorus and orchestra. The sacramental and mystical are expressed in these poems in carefully managed stanzas with delicate rhyming and assonances. The highly crafted lines are very different from the roaming expansive lines of Walt Whitman in 'A Sea Symphony'. They convey a more simple, down-to-earth mysticism of the kind that T.S. Eliot refers to when he quotes Dame Julian of Norwich in *Little Gidding*. Ralph's achievement in these settings was recognized by *The Times* reviewer who attended one of the early performances and wrote that 'the spirit of the words is reproduced with extraordinary sympathy; and the words themselves are declaimed in a way which indicates a true musical descendant of Lawes and Purcell'.[9]

'Five Mystical Songs' was first performed at the Three Choirs Festival at Worcester in September 1911. Again Ralph's pieces served as a preface to a much larger piece by Sir Edward Elgar, his violin concerto. The soloist in the Elgar was the most famous violinist of the day, Fritz Kreisler. As Ralph, very nervous as usual, began conducting his Herbert settings he was taken aback to see a figure playing the violin at one of the back desks. He later recalled: 'When I looked at the fiddles I thought I was going mad, for I saw what appeared to be Kreisler at the back desk. I got through somehow, and at the end I whispered to Reed [a violinist], "Am I mad or did I see Kreisler in the band?" "Oh Yes", he said, "he broke a string and wanted to play it in before the Elgar Concerto and couldn't without being heard in the Cathedral."'[1]

One of the violinists remembered that Kreisler whispered as he slipped into the orchestra, 'Nudge me if there's anything difficult and I'll leave it out.'

Ralph may have been shaken up by the intrusion but many onlookers at that festival saw him and also Adeline as glamorous, charismatic figures. The young Clare MacKail, a granddaughter of Burne Jones, was one such. She was studying with Gustav Holst at Morley College where that year, with his choir of working men and women, Holst was organizing a performance of Purcell's *Faery Queen*. Clare remembered that 'Ralph was a kind of god-father or patron saint of Morley and was, of course, adored there.... To see him and Gustav together at any time was a delight, but to see them at Morley was pure joy.' Clare also long retained a very vivid image of Ralph and Adeline at that festival at Worcester: 'with the sun shining through the window on her hair which looked like pure gold. It was an unforgettable sight, the two of them. He had a thick thatch of dark hair, a tall, rather heavy figure, even then slightly bowed; and his face was profoundly moving; deep humanity and yet with the quality of medieval sculpture – timeless, ageless, noble, balanced, calm, simple, TRUE.'[10]

George Butterworth was another young admirer, albeit a gruff, abrupt one. Ralph's friendship with the 25-year-old composer and now professional folk dancer was quick to develop after that early meeting at Oxford. With Butterworth Ralph shared another vagabonding adventure. At the end of 1911 they went together to the Norfolk Broads on a hunt for folk songs. One night in a pub where the drink was flowing abundantly, one of the volunteer singers offered to row them across the Broad to save them a long cycle ride. Once out in the boat they found that the singer was quite drunk. Waving his oars about he would indicate 'Southwold' or 'Lowestoft', invariably contradicting himself. George Butterworth insisted on taking the oars whereupon the singer immediately fell asleep. Reaching the shore they left him in his boat and made their way down the muddy tracks back to the pub. But the following day the singer was there again, and ready to sing for them. For Ralph and George, collecting folk songs was as much adventuring together as scholarship.

Ralph was still very much in touch with an older friend Percy Dearmer, the energetic, enterprising vicar of St Mary-the-Virgin on Primrose Hill. In the spring of 1912 when there was widespread starvation in Russia, Ralph agreed to become Secretary of the Russian Famine Relief Fund which Percy Dearmer had set up. It was probably through Martin Shaw, the organist at St Mary's that Ralph also met Gordon Craig the pioneering theatre director and dramatist who in 1911 published his highly influential *On the Art of the Theatre*. Ralph also met Isadora Duncan, one of Craig's lovers and the mother of his daughter Deirdre. Isadora was a very important figure in the development of modern dance. Born and brought up in California she worked in dance companies in Chicago and New York City but then moved to Europe hoping to be able to develop a more liberated, less constrained mode of dance. In London, in fashionable drawing rooms Isadora performed dance with movements suggested to her by the bas-reliefs in the British Museum. Ralph greatly admired her dancing and she, in turn, was an admirer of his music. She asked him to write a piece for her to dance to. She invited him to her studio to demonstrate to him some recently developed dance movements. Isadora was very much a free spirit. Had they been in Paris, she apologized, she would have danced for him 'without costume' but unfortunately this would have caused great embarrassment to the London pianist who was her accompanist. Ralph who so admired the long roving lines in Walt Whitman (at that time a great innovation in English poetry), was greatly taken by this other example of American style, Isadora's loose, fluid and, to a great extent improvisatory, dancing. He had never cared for classical dancing 'on point'. He readily agreed, however, to compose a dance sequence for Isadora. Perhaps encouraged by the success of the Greek play at Cambridge, he proposed a Greek subject *The Bacchae* of Euripides. Isadora agreed and Ralph set to work. She would arrive at his Chelsea house in her chauffeur-driven limousine after a performance and take him for late-night rides around London. Sometimes she would order the driver to stop so that she and Ralph might walk along the Embankment and see the River Thames by moonlight. She was a great admirer of her compatriot, Whistler, and of his paintings of the river. Isadora was impulsive and very generous. Ralph recalled to Ursula how beggars and the homeless sleeping rough on public benches were taken aback when Isadora made her way up to them and gave them each half a crown, a considerable sum in those days. To them as to Ralph she appeared 'like some eccentric fairy in her pale evening dress, waking them from their newspaper-wrapped sleep to press a coin into their hands.'[11]

Isadora also introduced Ralph to her brother Raymond Duncan who was similarly exotic. Himself a dancer and also an artist, poet, craftsman and educationist, Raymond had a villa just outside Athens and dressed as an ancient Greek. He would arrive at Cheyne Walk in time for tea, wearing a white cloak, chiton and sandals, even in the rain. After tea he would declaim long passages from Whitman with grand, theatrical gestures. He must have presented a great contrast to his hostess, Adeline who was now wearing sombre, even dowdy clothes. As Ursula reports, 'she made no concession to the fashion'. This must have been a sadness to Ralph who always had a keen interest in the way women dressed and was a lifelong reader of *Vogue*. Adeline was also becoming socially withdrawn, genuinely happy only in the company of members of her own family. At a party at Cheyne Walk attended by Gordon Craig and Martin Brown, Adeline was heard to mutter wearily 'I shall give a party some day and not be there.'

Through Gordon Craig Ralph had his first encounter with Serge Diaghilev of the highly successful and fashionable Ballets Russes. His star dancer and lover, the twenty-one-year- old Vaslav Nijinsky, was also present at the grand lunch Diaghilev gave at the Savoy Hotel but said very little. Diaghilev wanted a ballet score for the subject of Cupid and Psyche and so did Gordon Craig. But Ralph was uneasy with the subject. Eventually the project fell through. So too did Ralph's music for Isadora Duncan's proposed ballet. Only one of the choral numbers he composed for her, 'Where is the home for me?' was ever published.

As a man and as a composer Ralph was more comfortable with native English dance traditions. He was a regular and enthusiastic participant in the meetings of the English Folk Dance Society, which his friend Cecil Sharp founded in 1911. Prominent among the first members was Sharp's sometime lover Maud Karpeles who was twenty-five that year. Maud had, like Ralph, studied music for a time at the Hochschule für Musik in Berlin. She was a keen Fabian Socialist and pioneered the teaching of folk dancing in the women's settlement in Canning Town where she was a social worker. Her sister Helen was also an active member of the society, as was Helen's husband Douglas Kennedy. A co-founder of the Society was Ralph's friend George Butterworth. He was now beginning to write music but at this time, the future composer of 'The Banks of Green Willow' regarded himself primarily as a student, performer and proponent of folk dance.

There is extant footage, taken on a Kinora machine in 1912, of the four founding members dancing. The two sisters, Maud and Helen, wear white shirts, black gymslips and dark woollen stockings with garters. The much older, and balding Cecil Sharp swings about in a slightly baggy three-piece suit and a tie. At one moment he collides with the trim, bushily moustachioed George who wears a bright white suit with Morris attachments. The folk movement caught on with the public and a six-member team from the Folk Dance Society performed with their swirling white handkerchiefs at the fashionable Savoy Theatre in December 1912.

Ralph long remembered an important indebtedness to George Butterworth who was some seventeen years his junior. It had to do with the origins of his Second Symphony, 'A London Symphony'.

One of my most grateful memories of George is connected with my London Symphony: indeed I owe the whole idea to him. I remember very well how the idea originated. He had been sitting with us one evening, smoking and playing (I like to think it was one of those rare occasions when we persuaded him to play his beautiful little pianoforte piece, Firle Beacon) and at the end of the evening, as he was getting up to go, he said in his characteristically abrupt way: 'You know, you ought to write a symphony.' From that moment, the idea of a symphony – a thing which I had always declared I would never attempt – dominated my mind. I showed the sketches to George bit by bit as they were finished, and it was then that I realised that he possessed, in common with very few composers, a wonderful power of criticism of other men's work, and insight into their ideas and motives.[12]

During 1912 as he proceeded with the work on what would become his Second Symphony Ralph was again in touch with Ravel. His former teacher had succeeded in arranging for Ralph's song sequence 'On Wenlock Edge' to be played at a concert in Paris. Himself overworked and especially wearied by his work on his ballet *Daphnis and Chloe,* Ravel was greatly cheered by the enthusiastic reception which 'On Wenlock Edge' received in France. He forwarded to Ralph a highly complimentary letter from Xavier Godebski, the brother of Misia Sert, the Parisian socialite who was the patroness who long helped to sustain Ravel. Ravel himself wrote that 'In everyone's opinion your lyrical settings were a revelation'.[13] Ralph went over to Paris for the concert. He was surely pleased with the enthusiastic reception though years later he is said to have remarked, with the ungraciousness of which he was sometimes capable, that 'it was the worst performance he had ever heard, which was probably why the French liked it.'[14]

Another promoter of Ralph's career at this time was Bruce Richmond of *The Times Literary Supplement,* who had earlier found him a librettist for his first opera *Hugh the Drover.* In 1912 Richmond recommended Ralph to Sir Frank Benson, a famous actor-manager, who was looking for a musical director for a season of Shakespeare plays he was organizing at Stratford-upon-Avon. Always interested in the theatre, Ralph was happy to accept Benson's invitation. He and Adeline took rooms in Stratford for the spring and summer seasons and greatly enjoyed being among theatre people. *The Merry Wives of Windsor* was one of the plays being produced and Ralph developed a keen interest in it. Here was the germ of what was to be one of his later operas. That spring Ralph and Adeline were also invited to a party at one of the great sights of Stratford – and indeed of Edwardian England – the opulently palatial home of Marie Corelli, the famous, best-selling novelist. The extensive gardens of her house were filled with replicas of Venetian palaces with canals running between them. She also had her own personal gondola propelled by an authentic Venetian gondolier. Ralph must have remembered his voyage to the Canary Islands five years before when his fellow passengers had argued at length about the propriety, the 'profanity' even, of Marie Corelli's wildly romantic and highly successful novels. Her sales are reported to have exceeded those of her famous contemporaries, H.G. Wells, Rudyard Kipling, and Conan Doyle combined.

Ralph and Adeline found the imitation Venetian palazzo 'Perfectly awful'. And though they thought their hostess 'Perfectly awful too', they also found Marie Corelli 'impressive in her belief in herself'. This was a quality which, together with a dedication to hard work, was some-thing that Ralph, the descendant of Josiah Wedgwood and Erasmus Darwin, shared with the wealthy authoress. It was a quality that impressed Adeline also. It was shared by several of her siblings; not all of them were afflicted by illness and tragedy. Her eldest brother Herbert Fisher was establishing a name as a historian at Oxford and was being seen as a promising member of the Liberal Party. Edmund, just two years younger than Adeline, was already a successful young architect, completing among other commissions, a building at Somerville College, Oxford. And a future admiral, William Wordsworth Fisher was already a high-ranking officer in the Royal Navy. In 1910 he was in charge of the gunnery on board HMS *Dreadnought*, at the time Britain's most advanced battleship. As such, he was one of the prime victims of the Dreadnought Hoax involving his cousin Virginia Woolf. Along with her brother Adrian and friends, Virginia had sent a telegram to the Captain of HMS *Dreadnought* purporting to come from the Foreign Office. It announced that the Emperor of Abyssinia would pay a formal visit to the new, vast and technologically sophisticated battleship. Virginia blacked her face, wore a turban, an elaborately embroidered kaftan and a long gold chain. She stuck on a handsome moustache and a substantial beard. She and her similarly disguised courtiers were received at Weymouth station with military honours and then conveyed by steam launch to the battleship. They were piped aboard and ceremonially welcomed to the bridge by the senior ship's officers, including William Fisher who did not recognize his cousin. Emperor and retinue were then given an extended and detailed tour of the 'hush hush' battleship. After tea the imperial party was escorted back to the station. Virginia, who never much cared for the Fishers, was delighted with her success. But when the news reached the press, there was widespread public consternation that, in the context of the accelerating arms race with the German Empire, such a breach of security could occur. The right-wing press demanded explanations; there were questions in the House of Commons.

In Stratford in 1912 Ralph had his own comedy to ponder, *The Merry Wives of Windsor*. He decided to write music linking the episodes; he based these entr'actes on some of the folk songs he had collected, 'Lovely Joan', which he had collected in Lincolnshire being especially striking. The fashionable enthusiasm for folk culture was very palpable in Stratford that summer. Cecil Sharp, Douglas Kennedy, George Butterworth and Maud and Helen Karpeles, together with other members of the English Folk Dance Society, were giving demonstrations and classes in the town. Ralph happily and readily danced with them. Now forty years old, Ralph never had good physical co-ordination. His dancing, Michael Kennedy tells us, was 'something which those who did not see it can only dimly imagine'.[15]

For the Stratford theatre season Ralph also arranged music for some of Shakespeare's history plays. He created accompaniments for *Richard II* and for *Henry IV Parts I* and *II*. For these latter two he took music from Gustav Holst's 'Songs Without Words' which his good friend had dedicated to him. The stage manager of the festival later recalled Ralph's sheer hard work and also his interest in composing a hit. 'I well remember the opening of Act II Scene 2 of *Richard II*. Off stage effect of a harmonium and a woman's voice singing something like "Greensleeves". By the matinee on Saturday VW had rehearsed and produced what became, as he told me, his "best seller". He must have worked all that night.'[16] Ralph's prophecy turned out to be correct. This version of 'Greensleeves', albeit one of his lesser works, has, like 'Linden Lea', enjoyed an enduring fame and popularity.

As Ralph pondered Shakespeare's Histories, contemporary history was producing its own dramas. In April of 1912 there was the sinking of the ss *Titanic*, an event which stunned the western world and called into question its long-standing confidence in progress through science and technology. Three months earlier there had been another shock, particularly for the British. Captain Robert Falcon Scott and his party of explorers had arrived at the South Pole to find that their great competitor, the Norwegian Roald Amundsen, and his team had arrived there first. Public disappointment turned into a sense of tragedy when, some time later, Scott and his men lost their lives in the Antarctic cold. The sharp poignancy attaching to these deaths was intensified by the publication of Captain Scott's diaries, which revealed the courage, stoicism and nobility which he and his companions had shown as they faced the end. Certain of his sentences quickly achieved the status of quotations. The story of Scott's expedition long remained in Ralph's thoughts. It became the inspiration of his seventh symphony, completed nearly forty years later, after he had composed the music for a film about Scott, the making of which itself showed the enduring fascination of the story.

The increasing tensions within British society in the years 1912–13 began to explode dramatically. The campaign for women's suffrage grew ever more violent. Early in 1912 suffragettes smashed many shop windows in London's Oxford Street; they also chained themselves to public buildings. For her protest activities Emmeline Pankhurst was sentenced to three years of penal servitude, the harshest and most degrading form of punishment practised in the prison system. Two months later, in early June 1913, her comrade Emily Davison, another well-to-do lady, ran out in front of the King's horse at the Epsom Derby and was trampled to death. In the following month 50,000 women joined a protest march in Hyde Park. In the national consciousness the Pre-Raphaelite woman whom Adeline had mimed and Ralph had musicalized was a figure of the past. Time and the passing of time were very much themes in the symphony that Ralph was now writing.

The long-standing problem of a political settlement in Ireland was also threatening to turn violent. Home Rule now appeared to be a possibility in Parliament. But with the likelihood of a parliament in Dublin, Unionists of Ulster founded the Ulster Volunteer Force under the leadership of Edward Carson in order to resist the creation of such a government. In Belfast was heard the chant 'Ulster will fight, and Ulster will be right'. Yet the looming unrest in Ireland did not deter Ralph from going on a bicycle tour there in the company of his old friend Randolph Wedgwood. They arranged to meet at Waterford on 3 September and to bike and hike westwards into Munster, although Ralph would have preferred to go north and 'to have seen the Wicklow mountains where the Neo-Kelts come from'.[17] Staying in the pretty village of Killaloe on

152

the banks of the River Shannon in County Clare, they fell into conversation with an Irishman who was much concerned with the threatened disturbances in his country. He later sent Ralph a copy of W.E.H. Lecky's standard work *A History of Ireland in the Eighteenth Century*. As he had finally come down on the imperial side in the war against the Boers, so too now Ralph expressed his support for the imperial order. He expressed a willingness 'to volunteer (if they'll have me) on the side of law and order when the fight comes'.

The Irish holiday with Randolph was something of a compensation for Ralph for an annoying experience in London earlier that year. He had received a commission from Philip Sassoon, a prominent member of London high society, to write some incidental music; this time to accompany a play *Death of Tantagiles* by Maurice Maeterlinck, whose *Pelleas and Melisande* had provided the text for the opera by Debussy. Sassoon, a multi-millionaire and a member of the Rothschild family, wished to stage the play at a grand supper party in his large house in Park Lane. The meal and entertainment were to follow a State Ball attended by the King and Queen. But the refined literary taste of the aesthetically fastidious Philip Sassoon was not shared by his wealthy guests. The expensive occasion was a disaster. The socialite Edward Marsh, Ralph's contemporary at Trinity and now prominent in the literary world as editor of *The Georgian Anthology*, recalled 'the flash of stars and tiaras, revealing the fact that all the Ambassadors and Duchesses in London were present'. But, he continued, the delicate poetry of Maeterlinck and Ralph's mostly sombre, mournful music were 'not the sort of thing to hold the attention of a fashionable London audience after a superb dinner'. The audience was restive, fidgety and noisy. Sassoon's sister Sybil, the Marchioness of Cholmondeley, was in despair, and kept whispering 'You can't imagine the anguish I'm suffering' and 'never again will I ask a soul inside the house'.[18] Not even the second entertainment, a comic one-act piece by John Masefield about the Irish rebellion of 1798 could save the evening. Compounding Ralph's disappointment and annoyance was the attempt to send his band of musicians downstairs for cheaper refreshments rather than those prepared for the important guests. Feeling very much himself a fellow musician, always ready to supply leadership, Ralph boldly and huffily led them into the grand reception room to have their share of the champagne and strawberries.

There was a far happier occasion in Leeds in early October. The Shropshire Lad rhapsody by his friend George Butterworth had its first and very successful performance. The orchestra was under the baton of the distinguished Hungarian maestro Arthur Nikisch, who was presently instructing a young Englishman, Adrian Boult, in the art of conducting. Ralph was greatly pleased to see his young friend beginning to establish his name as a composer. A few months later he wrote, 'I believe he is going to be a great man – if he is not so already'.[19]

Adeline's brother Hervey continued to be unwell. She, her mother and sisters decided that Ospedaletti, then a very quiet, unspoiled resort on the Italian coast near the French border might be a good change for him. Ralph went with them for the Christmas holidays of 1913 but returned to London on his own early in the New Year. Adeline remained in Italy with family members for the next three months. Alone in Cheyne Walk, Ralph worked hard preparing for the first performance of what would become his second symphony, the 'London'. Before, on 23 March, came the first performance of another work, the Phantasy Quintet. This had been commissioned by Walter Cobbett, a successful and extremely wealthy industrialist who was also an amateur violinist and a keen musicologist. He devoted four years of his life to creating *Cobbett's Cyclopaedic Survey of Chamber Music* to which Ralph, ever the capable writer, was a contributor. The Phantasy Quintet is a very pleasing piece, but far less considerable than other works of these very productive years. At the same concert was performed Ravel's *Gaspard de la Nuit* and a quartet version of *Molly on the Shore* by Ralph's fellow folk-song devotee, Percy Grainger. An advertisement in the programme announced a concert at the Queen's Hall four days later. It listed Three Songs by the rising young composer Arnold Bax and also the *Valses Nobles et Sentimentales* of Ravel. But the longest offering by far was 'A London Symphony' by R. Vaughan Williams. The evening would confirm Ralph as, beyond doubt, a leading figure in contemporary English music.

This important concert of innovative music was subsidized by Bevis Ellis whom Ralph's friend Arnold Bax described as 'one of the de Walden family, a charming young man about town and an amateur of the arts'. Bevis Ellis took over his 'Maecenas' role from the wealthy Balfour Gardiner of whom Bax wrote that, years before, 'the princely generosity and selfless enthusiasm of Balfour Gardiner set on foot the most ambitious plan for the encouragement and dissemination of native work that had ever been devised'. Bax continued, 'He had saved Holst from neglect and a weighty sense of personal failure, and had fairly launched me on my orchestral career'. As the war approached Balfour Gardiner was ready to give way to Bevis Ellis. Bax reports that Ellis too soon found the act of patronage too difficult to sustain; 'at the close of 1913 he discontinued his venture. He may have been chagrined and disillusioned himself, but Vaughan Williams, Percy Grainger and I owed him a debt of gratitude impossible to pay'.[20] As a staff officer in the coming war Bevis Ellis would be killed, and his body utterly destroyed by an explosion in the trenches. Ralph's first symphony owed its initial performance to the world of the provincial music festival. His second owed its premiere to the tradition of patronage for new English music that was continuing to develop in London.

'A London Symphony' constitutes a strong clear contrast with the preceding 'Sea Symphony'. Hope, confidence, exaltation are no longer the controlling feelings in the piece. Now the supervening, controlling mood is one of melancholy and sadness as the composer ponders his city, which despite very audible moments of pleasure, excitement, pomp, drama and humour, is heard as but a figment of time, gently alluded to by the chimes of Big Ben in the opening and concluding movements. Ralph's most revealing comments on this symphony are in a letter he wrote to his friend and biographer Michael Kennedy in September 1957. Ralph refers him to the conclusion of *Tono-Bungay*, a substantial novel by the then highly renowned novelist H.G. Wells. The narrator sails down the Thames and through London towards the sea as night comes on and the bright lights of the metropolis are gradually extinguished. 'Light after light goes down. England and the Kingdom, Britain and the Empire, the old prides and the old devotions glide abeam, astern, sink down upon the horizon, pass – pass. The river passes – London passes, England passes....' Similar musings occur in other fiction of the time, for instance at the end of *Heart of Darkness* by Joseph Conrad, the close friend of Ralph's future brother-in-law, Richard Curle.

The acute sense of the transitoriness of things, things even as vast and substantial as London, is at the heart of the symphony. The first movement may well quicken, gradually from a dull early morning rumbling into the sound of urban bustle and purposefulness and end with a rousing finale that conveys the excitement that urban life can have; however, the second movement, a *lento*, develops, with considered emphasis, a moving sense of all things passing. A solo instrument recalls the blues; there is the melancholy of the Salvation Army band playing in the street. From the middle of the nineteenth century, from the *Tableaux Parisiens* in Baudelaire's *Les Fleurs du Mal*, artists, writers and composers have contemplated, often ambivalently, the exploding metropolis, the 'immonde cite'. 'A London Symphony' belongs in this tradition. But the mutations and ultimate transience of the city are but metaphors for the human condition itself. Towards the end of the second movement any programmatic references disappear into a grand, swelling funeral march. There is in the movement an extreme, almost unbearable tenderness and compassion for London and its noisy people, as they are contained within the larger process of transience.

The third movement, the *scherzo*, brings some diversion from the tenderness. We return for a comparatively brief period to the blaring of horns, to the scurry and hectic busy-ness of the streets of London. For this central London nocturne the listener should imagine himself, Ralph recommends in his programme note, 'on Westminster Embankment at night, surrounded by the distant sounds of The Strand, with its great hotels on one side, and the "New Cut" on the other, with its crowded streets and flaring lights ...' But the glamorous excitements of the London night inevitably fade away. The *scherzo* ends with the last, slow flickers of late night activity and, like the second and final movements, concludes in silence. Ralph was to tinker with the score of the symphony over the years. The redaction confirmed in 1936 is the one usually played today and here the *scherzo* and final movement are both much shorter than in the first version of 1913. In that, first recorded by the London Symphony Orchestra conducted by Richard Hickox in 2001, the last two movements bring a much greater weight of Edwardian melancholy to the work. Arnold Bax especially regretted 'the loss of a mysterious passage of strange and fascinating cacophony with which the first version of the *scherzo* closed'.[21]

The final movement remembers passingly the pulsing, drumming activity of the first. It also recalls, and resounds with, the music of London's pomp and ceremonial. But then comes the second *tempus fugit* reminder from Big Ben. An eerily gloomy meditation follows, then, at the last, a concluding sweep of melancholy resignation with the final chord confirming the fade into nothingness. A radical shift in outlook and feeling had occurred since the appearance of 'A Sea Symphony' of just three years before.

In 1913 as he completed his 'London Symphony', Ralph published 'Five English Folk Songs', a work for unaccompanied mixed chorus. Musically, he was living a double life. His unceasing quest for folk songs took him into rural England and its past and into the lives of country people. In his current symphony he looked inwards, into the deepest, most painful depths of his own highly troubled consciousness as these were reflected to him by the London which was his home and base, his other ambience.

'A London Symphony' was warmly and excitedly received. Gustav Holst exclaimed: 'You really have done it this time. Not only have you reached the heights, but you have taken your audience with you. I wish I could tell you how I and everyone else was carried away on Friday'.[22] On 28 March 1914, the day after the great occasion, George Butterworth wrote more soberly to Ralph to express his admiration, 'among all the debauch of last night's congratulations and mutual pattings on the back I really had nothing much to add, but should now like to tell you how frightfully glad I am that you have at last achieved something worthy of your gifts'.[23]

Ralph was characteristically modest about his achievement. He was always ready to speak of the way others had contributed to his work. He once recalled, for instance, how his new found friend, the composer Arnold Bax, had helped him with his Second Symphony: 'We were discussing my then new London Symphony. One passage disappointed me and I asked his advice. He suggested the addition of a counter melody on the oboe. Indeed he sat down at the pianoforte and improvised one. This actual passage was obviously too Baxian to make its inclusion possible. But following his advice, I made up another which, though not nearly so good as his, was more in keeping with the rest of the movement.[24]

Adeline was still in Italy at the time of the first performance of the Phantasy Quintet and of 'A London Symphony'. Her elder sister Florence, the widow of Frederic Maitland, was present and was powerfully affected by the work. She was also upset that Adeline had not come to hear it. A niece later remembered that: 'Florence wrote in misery that Adeline hadn't been there because the Symphony was the most wonderful experience and that London would always be that to her after hearing it'.[25] It may well be that some of the sadness that infuses the symphony derives from the distance that was widening between Ralph and his wife.

In the weeks that followed, Ralph was disappointed that he could not find a publisher for the new symphony. Ravel was also having difficulties and annoyances in promoting his own work. That summer he wrote to Ralph bemoaning what was happening to his major work, the ballet music *Daphnis and Chloe*. He had been promised a performance of it at Covent Garden, but then discovered that it was to be done in a truncated, 'makeshift arrangement' that he found entirely unacceptable. There was only one redeeming feature in the proposed programme; the companion piece was Stravinsky's *The Nightingale*, which Ravel declared 'a real masterpiece musically'.[26] Ralph, when he heard it, strongly agreed.

The international situation was growing worse. War between Britain and Germany looked ever more likely. But as the possibilities for publication of 'A London Symphony' in England dwindled, Ralph decided to try his luck in Germany. He sent the manuscript, possibly care of the eminent conductor Fritz Busch, to the music publishers Breitkopf and Härtel in Leipzig. It was never to be seen again. After two world wars attempts were made to find it, but unavailingly. It was only a very thoughtful act of friendship on the part of George Butterworth that saved the work. Knowing that Ralph himself had not had the time or inclination to make a second copy, Butterworth got together with another of Ralph's friends, E.J. Dent, to copy the orchestral parts. And thus the work was saved.

On 4 August 1914 war was declared between Britain and Germany. The entire western world was never to be the same again. The war changed Ralph's life profoundly. For the four years of its duration he composed virtually nothing. He also lost many of his closest colleagues in music. As with many of his contemporaries in the arts, his outlook was radically changed.

Just three weeks after the declaration of war George Butterworth came to see Ralph at Cheyne Walk. Ralph told him the story of his recent arrest on the cliffs at Margate whilst having a brief holiday there. He had sat down on a spot overlooking the Channel and was making some jottings in his notebook. A boy scout approached him. He proved to be zealously patriotic and very war-minded. He announced that he was formally arresting Ralph on suspicion of being a spy. Ralph eventually agreed to be escorted to the nearest police station. Here officers searched his notebook and finally let him go with a caution.

When George Butterworth, who had recently enlisted as a private in the Duke of Cornwall's Light Infantry, left Cheyne Walk that day, it was for the last time. He and Ralph would never meet again. In August 1916 at the climax of the Battle of the Somme, Lieutenant Butterworth (as he had become) was leading his men in the defence of what, in his honour, they had named 'Butterworth Trench'. During an assault sortie George Butterworth was shot through the head by a sniper. This was just three weeks after his thirty-first birthday. His men hastily buried his body in the trench. The area was heavily bombarded in later weeks and months. His remains were never recovered.

THE SOLDIER AND EX-SERVICEMAN

Chapter Nine

WORLD WAR ONE

In August 1914 the atrocious horrors that were to come in the war were unimaginable. Many of Ralph's younger friends and colleagues, inspired by intense patriotic zeal, hurried to enlist. War fever spread throughout Britain. The young Harold Macmillan, a future Prime Minister, was anxious 'to get in quick before it was all over'. Approaching the age of forty-two, Ralph was not young enough to be considered for combat but he was keen to serve. His highly developed public spirit was such that within weeks he had joined the Special Constabulary. But for him this was definitely not enough. A few weeks later he presented himself at the headquarters of the Royal Army Medical Corps in what is now Duke of York Square in the King's Road, Chelsea, not far from his house in Cheyne Walk. Despite his flat feet he was accepted as an ambulance orderly with the rank of private. Training began immediately. He and his fellow volunteers were taught drill on the parade ground at the Duke of York barracks and given medical instruction at Guy's Hospital on the other side of London. At night Ralph was able to return to Cheyne Walk to sleep. Some days he was free to teach at Morley College. In his spare time he continued to work urgently to create another score of 'A London Symphony' to replace the one which had been sent to Germany for consideration for publication by Breitkopf and Härtel, and which was now assumed to be lost. He was grateful and touched by the help given him, not only by George Butterworth but also by Edward Dent and by Denis Browne, a colleague at Morley College who was a close friend of the poet Rupert Brooke. In less than a year Browne would be killed in the war in the Dardanelles, in the campaign against the Ottoman Empire that was allied with the German Empire and Habsburg Austro-Hungary.

On New Year's Day 1915 Ralph's rather disorganized unit was ordered to leave London for billets near Dorking, where they did route marches and practised stretcher drill up and down nearby Box Hill. They were now consolidated as the 2/4th London Field Ambulance. Ralph proved to be an untidy soldier. He did not fare well at kit inspection, had difficulties keeping his puttees straight and wearing his cap at the correct angle. Most of his fellow ambulance orderlies were much younger than he but Ralph's cheery, unassuming, egalitarian manner allowed him to get on well with them. One of the group, Harry Steggles, a generation younger than he, quickly became a friend and remained so long after the war had ended. A bond between them was music. Harry had a mouth organ which he played expertly. He could also sing. Their performances together of music hall songs such as 'When father papered the parlour', with Ralph playing the piano, were greatly enjoyed by their fellow soldiers.

In the spring their unit was moved around south-eastern England, first to Watford, then to Saffron Walden and thence to Bishop's Stortford. Here they had the good fortune to be billeted with the Machrays, a large family most of whom were musicians. They rigged up many happy concert evenings in the Machray house with Harry Steggles arranging 'an early jazz drummer's outfit of flower pots, fire irons and a borrowed drum'.[1] Ralph taught the family Morris and country dance tunes. Their training as ambulance men continued. In November Ralph was granted brief leave to go and play the organ at the wedding of his Leith Hill neighbour and lifelong friend, the publisher Robert Longman. Ralph retained very happy memories of his time at Bishop's Stortford. He was so content and comfortable there that he volunteered to stay at the Machrays over Christmas to cover for Harry Steggles who went home for the holiday. Clearly, there were no festivities in Cheyne Walk to compel Ralph's presence.

Early in 1916 Ralph was posted to Salisbury Plain where the unit lived a more austere life in a camp of wooden huts, at Sutton Veny, very near Warminster. The training intensified as spring came on and then came the long-expected order to sail to France. On 22 June they set off south and crossed to Le Havre in the night. On disembarking they were put into cattle trucks and transported north to Maizières. From here they marched on to the hamlet of Ecoivres where they could hear the gunfire from the battle being fought on the nearby River Somme. Today

Ecoivres is the site of an extensive cemetery run by the Commonwealth War Graves Commission; it was Ralph's base for some three months. His unit replaced the ambulance auxiliaries of the 51st Highland Division. The company lived in the outhouses of a large villa which served as the first receiving hospital for those casualties brought back from the trenches. The place was protected from the gunfire by the rising ground crowned by the badly shelled towers of the abbey church of Mont-Saint-Eloi. Ralph, as Harry Steggles recalled nearly forty years later 'was on the motor ambulances between the trenches and our dressing station'.[2] Harry added, 'The trenches held no terrors for him – on the contrary, he was thrilled one day when he was allowed a peep at the German front line trenches'. In one of his letters home, to Gustav Holst, Ralph wrote: 'I am "Wagon orderly" and go up the line every night to bring back wounded and sick on a motor ambulance – this all takes place at night – except an occasional day journey for urgent cases'.[3] Ralph must surely have seen some horrendous sights. Certainly his experience during his first three months at the Front remained scored in his memory and affected his later work, particularly his Third Symphony.

As autumn approached there were rumours and counter-rumours about what lay ahead for the company. They were marched to Eaucourt sur Somme close to Abbeville and taught to use gas masks and prepare for the newly developed gas warfare. It looked like they might be returning to the trenches for the coming winter. But at short notice they were again packed into cattle trucks and sent on a long, slow, train journey south to the port of Marseilles where they embarked for what proved to be Salonika in central Macedonia in Greece. Ralph's next experience of the First World War would be in a completely different theatre.

The Salonika Campaign was an endeavour by Britain and its allies to support Serbia on the eastern front of the war against the combined forces of Germany, Austria-Hungary and Bulgaria. This war in south-eastern Europe has been overshadowed in western historical memory by the dramatic and horrific events in northern France. In part this is because the Salonika Front was comparatively quiet until the final British offensive of 1918, which brought about the defeat of Germany and its Balkan allies. Also, the war in northern France was far more of a subject for the arts. The war in the trenches produced the paintings of John Nash, David Bomberg and Wyndham Lewis. It also produced memorable works of literature. There was the great documentary poem

In Parenthesis by David Jones, an epic quickly recognized by T.S. Eliot as a masterpiece; there was also memorable lyric poetry by Wilfred Owen, Siegfried Sassoon, Isaac Rosenberg and Ivor Gurney. (This last, after his gassing and mental wounding or shell-shock in the war and his subsequent committal to an asylum, would become one of Ralph's personal concerns in the post-war years.) There were also memorable prose works such as Frederic Manning's *Her Privates We* and Robert Graves's *Goodbye To All That*. The Salonika campaign was less important in the arts. The most important products were paintings such as *Travoys Arriving With Wounded* by Stanley Spencer who, pre-war, had been like Ralph, a home counties commuter to the arts world of London. Stanley Spencer arrived in Greece after Ralph had been sent to another posting.

Ralph sailed from Marseilles to Salonika in late 1916 just as winter was setting in. The troopship was crowded and the food poor but Ralph nevertheless enjoyed the long leisurely voyage through the warm Mediterranean. They arrived in Dudular, a small Greek town near Thessalonika, and were then ordered to Vromeri, a coastal village where they camped on a hillside with Mount Olympus dominating the skyline. There was little ambulance work for them to do. The fighting in this theatre of war was sporadic and remote. Ralph and Harry Steggles explored the wine shops in Katerini where they would occasionally watch Greek soldiers dancing. Ralph duly noted down the dance melodies.

By Christmas-time the days were still bright but nights became extremely cold. Harry Steggles described their living conditions in the Greek December:

> in the confined space of a 'bivvy' a little less than the area of a double bed we had a ground sheet, a blanket apiece and all our worldly goods including razor, comb, lather brush, also Isaiah and Jeremiah. I must explain these for it was the name given by R.V.W. to two empty pineapple tins in which we lit charcoal and after whirling them round and round like the old fashioned winter warmer we rushed them into the bivvy and sealed up any air intakes we could find. I think we slept more from our rum ration plus carbon monoxide from Isaiah and Jeremiah than fatigue.[4]

Harry went on to remember 'a filthy night in the Balkans when he and Ralph were indulging in consoling visions of what might happen, "when this lousy war is over" [as the popular song put it]. Harry recalled that

Ralph suddenly said: 'Harry when this war ends we will (a) dine at Simpsons on saddle of mutton, (b) see *Carmen*'. Years after the war, Harry was surprised suddenly to receive a postcard proposing precisely such an evening. Both at the Royal Opera House and at the expensive restaurant on The Strand, Ralph immediately put Harry at his ease. Now a struggling sales representative, Harry was again impressed by 'the terrific personality of R.V.W.' Like so many others before and afterwards he was keenly aware that Ralph was *somebody*.

After New Year 1917 Ralph started to become bored and frustrated by the military routine at Katerini. He was irritated by the absurd exercises created by the officers to keep the men busy. Harry Steggles described Ralph's state of mind:

> Salonika was too dilatory for him. He went on mosquito squad work, which consisted of filling in puddles to prevent mosquitoes breeding; he thought this was useful in an abstract way. But what caused him the most anguish was to sit down and wash red bricks, which were laid on the ground to form a red cross as protection from German planes. He swore one day, saying 'I will do anything to contribute to the war, but this I will not do'.[5]

Stanley Spencer created a painting of this activity which was one of the characteristics of the Salonika Campaign.

There were still more trivial and demeaning tasks for Ralph's unit. One of the Leith Hill retainers recalled that 'Mr Ralph ... told me in front of his mother, the last three weeks he was in Salonika he was doing latrine fatigues all the time'.[6] Above all he had a biting sense of the futility of being in the campaign in Greece. Eventually he managed to get around the censorship rules and let Adeline, and perhaps others know, of the frustration he was experiencing. Adeline was recovering, but very slowly, from a hammer-blow of loss. At the beginning of the previous summer her brilliant younger brother Charles Fisher had lost his life in the naval battle at Jutland at the age of thirty-eight. A tall, attractive, extremely gifted man, Charles was a Classical scholar of considerable achievement. He was also a fine cricketer, who had gained a blue at Oxford and also played for Sussex. A brilliant academic career at Oxford looked to lie ahead of him. He was serving as a lieutenant on the battlecruiser HMS *Invincible* when she was sunk off the coast of Denmark with a loss of more than a thousand lives.

In the misery of her loss Adeline would seem to have appealed to her elder brother Herbert Fisher to help extricate Ralph from the futility in which he felt himself trapped in the Salonika theatre. An active Liberal, Herbert had become MP for Sheffield Hallam in December 1916. He would soon become a member of the government of the new Prime Minister David Lloyd George. It seems very likely that Adeline and Ralph used this highly placed connection to pull strings and get him moved to a more useful area of the war effort. In any event, he received an order singling him out from his unit and commanding him to return to England and to report at the War Office rather than at the Royal Army Medical Corps. He arrived back in London, dirty and unshaven, to find Adeline, with whom he had been unable to communicate, gone from home and the house in Cheyne Walk locked up. He went round to nearby Phene Street to the house of Bruce Richmond, who was continuing as editor of the *Times Literary Supplement*. Bruce and his wife Elena gave him a home while he awaited his appointment at the War Office. Here he was informed that he was to undergo training that would give him the possibility of passing out with a commission in the Royal Garrison Artillery.

In August 1917 Ralph duly presented himself at the Officer Cadet School at Maresfield in East Sussex, on the southern side of Ashdown Forest. Far older than his fellow cadets, Ralph found that the noise and lack of privacy in the camp seriously impaired his studying for the examinations in gunnery theory which he had to take. Fortunately, he had the money to rent a room in a cottage just outside the camp. He made a hole in the perimeter hedge and camouflaged it with moveable branches and so could come and go without having to pass the camp sentries. His companion in this arrangement was John Tindall Robertson, a fellow cadet who also wanted to take his exam preparations seriously. He later recalled that he did his best to help Ralph 'both with his work and seeing that he got his equipment and so on right for parades. He was not one to whom the proper arrangement of straps and buckles and all those things on which the sergeant major is so keen, came easily. Nor was it easy for him, then in middle age, to learn and retain all the miscellaneous information which was pumped into us. But he achieved it by dogged perseverance and toil.'[7]

The two of them were successful in their examinations and received their commissions. In late November, Second Lieutenant Vaughan Williams was ordered to Lydd on Romney Marsh in Kent for a practical course in firing. With other newly commissioned officers he was also made to do physical jerks in shirtsleeves in the midst of a blizzard. After Christmas they were sent to the Royal Artillery's St Lucia Barracks in Bordon in Hampshire to await an overseas posting.

On his occasional leaves during this period of waiting Ralph was able to visit London. On one such occasion he went to the Queen's Hall where, he had been excited to learn, his 'London Symphony' was to be performed. The enterprising young conductor was the 28-year-old Adrian Boult. Virtually a generation younger than Ralph, he was just then beginning the career that would make him a central figure in British concert life well into the 1950s. A strong advocate of British composers, Adrian Boult had studied first history and then music at Christ Church, Oxford, before going on to Leipzig to work with the distinguished Hungarian conductor Arthur Nikisch. Declared medically unfit for military service in 1914 he had worked as a translator in the War Office and organized concerts with financial help from his wealthy father, who had shipping interests in Liverpool. The conducting of 'A London Symphony' on 18 February 1918 was one of Adrian Boult's reputation-building successes even though he later wrote of the performance as being 'rather spoilt by a Zeppelin raid'. In the audience Ralph admired intensely what he had heard, writing enthusiastically to the young man, 'may I say how much I admired your conducting – it is real <u>conducting</u> – you get just what you want and <u>know</u> what you want – and your players trust you because they know it also.... I look for great things in the future when such musical ability and such public spirit go hand in hand'.[8] The concert at the Queen's Hall was the beginning of a lifelong friendship which would be of central importance in the careers of both conductor and composer.

A fortnight after the concert Ralph and his unit were sent to France, sailing from Southampton to Le Havre on 1 March 1918. After a few days Ralph was sent to join 141 Heavy Battery, an artillery unit that still used horses to pull their massive guns. They set off, as Ralph told Gustav Holst, 'slowly trekking towards Germany, not a job I relish, either the journey or its object'.[9] He went on to give his friend a description of the life he was now leading:

We usually march about 10 Kilos or more a day and rest every 4th day – it's a tiresome job watering and feeding horses in the dark before we start (though I must confess that there being 8 subalterns in this [Battery] my turn of turning out early for this only comes once a week). Then usually 2 or 3 wagons stick fast in the mud at the 1ˢᵗ start off and worry and delay ensues, and finally when one gets to one's destination one has to set up one's horse lines and find water and fill up nose bags etc. and if <u>this</u> has to be done in the dark it beggars description. So you see there's not much music writing going on at present. But I've started a singing class....[10]

In April 1918 the British were forced to fall back. One of Ralph's fellow subalterns, W.A. Marshall, recalled:

the retreat which began on March 21ˢᵗ, when the gun position was near Fontaine-les-Croiselles, some miles south of Arras and north of Bullecourt. We had retired twice and, when I first met Vaughan Williams, the guns were in position behind a wood, Athers Wood. I remember the Guards passing us in open order with fixed bayonets. Vaughan Williams had not been with us for long and was in charge of the horse lines – not a 'cushy' job by any means, especially at that time.[11]

This was Ralph's closest involvement in combat since he had looked across at the German trenches at Ecoivres two years before. Within some weeks the British were able to resume their advance.

Through the autumn of 1918 Ralph's cumbersome unit lumbered its way across northern France in pursuit of the campaign against the Germans. They passed through Charleroi and Namur and on through villages which, after the armistice in the second week of November, were decked with welcoming flags and triumphal arches celebrating victory. Ralph spent his spare time organizing concerts even though the musical talent available to him was limited. Another of Lieutenant Marshall's memories was that Ralph 'spent a lot of such spare time that he had in getting up concerts, vocal, by and for the troops, mostly drivers. I can't think he enjoyed them much, in view of the talent available. I saw him once or twice, drooping despondently over the keyboard of a ghastly wreck of a piano while drivers sang sentimental songs – execrably as a rule, to his accompaniment'.[12]

But it was not long before Ralph's abilities and dedication as a musician were recognized. Soon after the armistice in November 1918 Ralph was transferred from the artillery and given the title of Director of Music in the First Army of the British Expeditionary Force in France. The military authorities recognized that it would take some months for the army in France to be demobilized in an orderly way. They therefore set about creating a programme of recreational, sporting and cultural activities to fill the time before hundreds of thousands of soldiers returned to Britain and to civilian life. Ralph was assigned an important role in this post-war initiative. He settled into quarters in the ancient, badly damaged city of Valenciennes, the headquarters of the First Army, close to the Belgian border. He worked at his new job with great energy and enthusiasm. One of his colleagues in the Officers' Mess remembered how he devoted his time 'to visiting the Divisions over a wide area, finding officers and other ranks from various units who were interested in music and getting them to act as conductors to a choral society, orchestra or to take a class in music'.[13] Ralph's characteristically energetic public-spiritedness brought results. 'At the time of his demobilization, in February 1919, there were already nine choral societies, three classes, an orchestra and a band. Included in these was the Head Quarters Choral Society of which he was the conductor.' Ralph took every opportunity to promote, and evangelize for, music. His colleague remembered how 'once after a church service in the town, [he] came forward [rather an incongruous figure in uniform] and spoke of its activities'.

Later in life he would look back with affection on 'those happy old days at Valenciennes'. To found and participate in a grass roots musical culture, as he had helped to do with the Leith Hill Music Festival, gave him great pleasure. But these three happy months were but an intermission in his life and career. In the second month of 1919 he received his demobilization papers. His time as a soldier was over. The next step was for him to return to England and, after four years' absence, to take on the challenge of re-entering the musical life of London.

Chapter Ten

IN LODGINGS

After his demobilization in February 1919 Ralph returned to his house in Cheyne Walk. There was no one at home. His neighbour and sister-in-law, Emmeline, the wife of R.O. Morris a fellow soldier and musicologist, told him that Adeline was still in Sheringham on the Norfolk coast, taking care of her brother Hervey. Ralph duly travelled north and joined his wife in the furnished rooms she had taken in 'Northern Light', a house in the old fishing village which, since the coming of the railway some thirty years before, had developed into a small resort. Ralph seems to have been very conscious of his distance from London, 'In this out of the way place'. Some '5 hours by rail', he regretfully told Philip Webb, the secretary of the Handel Society, who had written to him to say that the society wanted to invite him to become their conductor. Ralph accepted the post expressing the hope that he would have 'only a temporary absence from London'. In the event he would be based in Sheringham for well over two years.

Towards the end of Ralph's first year in Norfolk he and Adeline found new accommodation, moving into rooms at 'Sundial', another house in the town. From here, with some difficulty, Ralph negotiated a timetable for a sitting with the fashionable London artist William Rothenstein for a portrait to be used in the second issue of *Music and Letters*. The drawing was to accompany a study of Ralph's work and career by the editor A.H. Fox Strangways. The feature in this new and progressive periodical was a help in restoring him to public awareness after his four years of absence. This kind of attention also constituted a conspicuous tribute to Ralph's achievement. The previous issue had focused on Sir Edward Elgar, unquestionably Britain's leading composer of the day, with an essay on him by George Bernard Shaw and, again, a portrait by William Rothenstein. Ralph himself contributed an article, 'The Letter and the Spirit'. In this he gently distanced himself, though in his characteristically robust polemical fashion, from two of the leading figures in the musical establishment: Henry Hadow, the chief inspector of music in schools and Vice Chancellor of Sheffield University, and Dr Arthur Somervell, a noted musicologist. Ralph deplored their insistence, fashionable at the time, on the importance of experiencing music through the reading of it, the view 'that the really musical man prefers not to hear music, but gets at his music silently by reading it to himself as he would a book'. Ralph insisted that music was first and foremost something to be heard, a sensuous experience. He began with the principle that 'the object of the art is to obtain a partial revelation of that which is beyond human senses and human faculties – of that, in fact, which is spiritual'. But, he immediately added, 'the means we employ to induce this revelation are those very senses and faculties themselves'. Music is for the ear. And for the hearing. Ralph defended his position eloquently and at some length, seeing definite dangers in the attitude of the believers in 'reading'. 'Why is it that it is always the dull unimaginative music which gains the prize in competitions? Is it because the adjudicators are content to look at the music and not to hear it – with the result that anything that looks right on paper is judged to be good, and everything that looks unfamiliar and awkward is rejected?'[1]

The following year – 1920 – Ralph again disagreed with Henry Hadow, this time on a less theoretical issue. The two were on a Carnegie Trust Committee which was asked to assess a Chamber Rhapsody by the young composer Arthur Bliss with a view to its publication by the trust. Henry Hadow gave the piece a 'C', which would have prevented its acceptance. But Ralph awarded it an 'A', praising its 'great beauty of theme, harmony and colour'. The work was eventually published.[2]

The newly founded *Music and Letters* was not the only institution to honour Ralph on his return from the war. In the summer of 1919 he travelled to Oxford where on 19 June the university conferred on him the honorary degree of Doctor of Music. Following the ceremony there was a performance of 'A Sea Symphony' in the Sheldonian Theatre as part of the celebrations to commemorate the 250th anniversary of Sir Christopher Wren's building. The Oxford Bach Choir was conducted by Hugh Allen, Ralph's old Cambridge contemporary who had worked so hard to promote the work when it had first appeared nearly a decade earlier.

The year before Ralph's return to civilian life, when Hubert Parry died, Hugh Allen had taken over as Director of the Royal College of Music. It must have been around the time of the Oxford ceremony that he offered Ralph a job at the college. It is reported that Hugh Allen, wishing to alleviate his old friend's exile in Norfolk, simply said to him, 'Come up to the RCM and be yourself one day a week'.[3] To Ralph's delight, Gustav Holst (whose *The Planets* had received its first performance in February) was also given a teaching job at the college. For the next twenty years or so teaching was to be an important part of Ralph's life. His relationships with his pupils were to prove a great pleasure and invigoration for him over the years. At the start of his teaching career, some of his students – Patrick Hadley and the badly shell-shocked Ivor Gurney – were, like himself, ex-servicemen. But he was soon working with the younger generation of musicians that included Imogen Holst, Grace Williams, Elizabeth Maconchy and Ina Boyle. It was soon a commonplace of college life that Ralph especially appreciated his young women students.

In 1919 Ralph also picked up the threads of his career in composition which he had been compelled to abandon in 1914. In the year of his demobilization he published his 'Eight Traditional English Carols' settings which he had for the most part composed before the war. In 1920 he published more carols. Also originating before the war was a piece that was to become one of his most successful and beloved works, The Lark Ascending. It was first performed at Shirehampton in rural Gloucestershire by a choral society organized by Philip Napier Miles, a Bristol businessman, who from his fine Vanbrugh house at King's Weston, financed a good deal of musical activity in the West Country. He was one of the several very wealthy music lovers in provincial England who were enablers of Ralph's career.

The Lark Ascending has long been recognized as a small scale masterpiece. This romance for violin and orchestra perfectly exemplifies Ralph's view so strongly emphasized in his essay 'The Letter and the Spirit' that the purpose of music is to intimate the spiritual. The piece was inspired by a poem by a writer much read by Ralph in his youth, George Meredith. The poem exploits the sound semantics of language. The evocation of the skylark begins:

He rises and begins to round,
He drops the silver chain of sound
Of many links without a break,
In chirrup, whistle, slur and shake,
All intervolv'd and spreading wide
Like water-dimples down a tide
Where ripple ripple overcurls
And eddy into eddy whirls;
A press of hurried notes that run
So fleet they scarce are more than one,
Yet changingly the trills repeat
And linger ringing while they fleet,
Sweet to the quick o' the ear, and dear
To her beyond the handmaid ear, who sits beside our inner springs,
Too often dry for this he brings.

A musical transcription of these lines, The Lark Ascending, is an inter-play between the lark song sung by the violin and the earthly sounds of the world, conveyed by the orchestra. These are, at times, dull rumblings; at others they lilt into folk music and dancing. The interchange concludes with the violin leaving the orchestra behind and soaring off, on its own, into that ultimate inaudibility and silence which for most listeners will be heard as that spiritual realm which Ralph's art and thinking so often pondered. This is how Meredith described the moment of going beyond sound:

As he to silence nearer soars,
Extends the world at wings and dome,
More spacious making more our home,
Till lost on his aerial wings
In light, and then the fancy sings.

Ralph's concerns with the spiritual were very much assisted at this time by a new and formal involvement with the work of Johann Sebastian Bach. Hugh Allen decided that his many responsibilities as Director of the Royal College of Music would not allow him to continue as conductor of the Bach Choir. The position was offered to Adrian Boult but he was unable to accept. So Hugh Allen turned to Ralph who, ethically scru-pulous as always, agreed to take part on condition that he would not be expected to leave the Handel Society in the lurch. He took over the directorship on the last day of the year. His dedication and responsibilities to the choir would be a very important part of his musical life for many years to come. Two weeks before he took over, he very successfully conducted his first concert with the choir, a programme centring on three Bach cantatas.

A few weeks later, at the end of January 1922, there occurred an event which was the definite confirmation of Ralph's return to the centre of British musical life. It was the first of a number of achievements that made the year 1922 so auspicious in his life. The event was the first performance of his Third Symphony (the 'Pastoral') with Adrian Boult conducting the Orchestra of the Royal Philharmonic Society in the Queen's Hall. The work was the most important achievement of Ralph's two years of seclusion in Norfolk.

Today we can see this symphony as one of the major works of art deriving from the experience of combatants in the First World War. As a precipitate of that horrific period in British history it belongs with the lyrics of Wilfred Owen, the war paintings of Stanley Spencer (particularly those painted for the memorial chapel at Burghclere), and *In Parenthesis* by David Jones, which T.S. Eliot was swift to recognize and to publish. The year 1922 also saw the publication of Eliot's *The Waste Land* which, along with *Hugh Selwyn Mauberley* by Eliot's close friend and mentor Ezra Pound, is one of the major works in English deriving from the war and written by non-combatants. Ralph's symphony is also, in one respect, about a waste land. It has rightly been called 'A dream of sad happiness – a requiem for Pan'. With its bugles, marches and laments it is also a symphony about war.

The initial reactions to the work were not positive. Philip Heseltine (aka Peter Warlock) mockingly commented that it was 'like a cow looking over a gate'. Even Ralph's close, long-standing friend and promoter Hugh Allen said that 'it suggested VW rolling over and over in a ploughed field on a wet day'. And Sir Thomas Beecham, as he finished conducting 'A Pastoral Symphony', is said to have laid down his baton and confided to the orchestral players, 'A city life for me, then'. Certainly the Third Symphony in its evocation of a pastoral world is less arresting, less immediately compelling, than the evocation of the sea in the First Symphony and of the city in the Second. For long stretches it is more laid-back, more unassuming than either of its predecessors. But as we continue to listen to it we become aware, as we do in that highly, auditory prose-poem *In*

Parenthesis, of its subtlety and restraint. The influence of Ravel is very audible in the symphony.

The first movement, *Molto Moderato,* like the second and the fourth, is one of long lingering melancholy and mournfulness. But here these emotions are carried along by, and assimilated into, a rather English, quick flowing cheeriness. This is eventually swept aside by a swiftly strengthening and more complex lyrical impulse that contains within it a special complex of deep felt emotions: loss, pride and sadness which at the deepest level underlie the symphony as a whole.

The second movement, the dark-toned, nocturnal *Lento Moderato,* establishes with unmistakeable audibility that Ralph's pastoral world is not that of Beethoven, nor of his contemporary Wordsworth, nor of the latterday nature Romantics in Edward Marsh's *Georgian Anthology.* The cadenza for natural trumpet brings to our ears a characteristic sound of the First World War in the fields of northern France, the army bugles sounding out at nightfall over no-man's land and the trenches. As Ralph said to Ursula, speaking of the origins of the composition: 'It's really war-time music – a great deal of it incubated when I used to go up night after night with the ambulance wagon at Ecoivres and we went up a steep hill and there was a wonderful Corot-like landscape in the sunset.'[4]

It makes the haunting bugle sound all the more poignant for the listener (and most probably for the composer) to recall that it was at Ecoivres that George Butterworth lost his life.

The third movement, *Molto Pesante,* interrupts the mournfulness with the uproar of a *scherzo.* Heartiness enters into the music. We hear the brassy cheeriness of a folk song or perhaps a regimental march. The final movement brings another contrast and surprise, a woman's voice wordlessly keening. After this elemental human sound there comes from the orchestra a solemn hymn for the dead. And then a panicky, stricken dialogue and questioning duet between the strings and the woodwind. The keening soprano returns, a very ancient primitive response to the terrible deaths in this modern war. We usually think of Ralph as a composer deriving from the Romantic tradition in music. But the great power of this concluding movement of 'A Pastoral Symphony' derives from a quiet restraint that is eminently Classical.

By no means all of those who heard the first performance of the symphony in January 1922, (the year of T.S. Eliot's *The Waste Land*) were lukewarm in their responses. Three days after the premiere, Ralph's long-standing colleague in the folk-song movement Lucy Broadwood wrote to him exuberantly, 'Thank you a million times for the gorgeously beautiful symphony you gave us on Thursday ... The trumpet stirred me desperately – and how finely it was played. And surely the voice was perfection?' She hoped that Ralph was pleased by the excited response of the audience and of the orchestra players themselves. 'I hope that some of our joy returned, reflected, to you, and that to have the "Old Philharmonic" shouting and waving to you across the dour bust of Beethoven was a happy thing, and a funny thing too, for you'.[5]

At this time there also arrived a letter from an old friend from Cambridge days, Crompton Llewellyn Davies. Crompton was now a successful barrister and a close friend of the Prime Minister Lloyd George. Through his Irish wife he had become involved with the revolutionary politics of Ireland which, in this year, finally achieved the status of a Free State. Crompton was greatly impressed by Ralph's achievement and by how far he had progressed in his career since they had been undergraduates together; 'remembering walks and talks with you I can understand in some sort of way how promises have come true and high intentions carried out'. With both pride and modesty Crompton declared 'I have felt a sort of triumph in the work you have planned and carried out'.[6]

For all his newly achieved eminence, Ralph persisted in his hard-working commitment to music at grassroots level. In the spring, as usual, he was very active at the Leith Hill Music Festival which, with lively local interest, was continuing to expand. At a previous festival he had met one of the visitors, the youthful Diana Awdrey, an enthusiast for music who was very keen to establish a similar festival in her home area around Stinchcombe in Gloucestershire. Ralph, who increasingly enjoyed the company of lively young women, agreed to help her. So that year, when the Stinchcombe Festival was launched, Ralph went there to assist with the choral preparations and to judge the entries.

Shortly afterwards Ralph made a brief visit to the Netherlands to attend 'a big performance' of Bach's St Matthew Passion, which, in the event, did not fit in with his view of the work. Percy Grainger was in Holland at this time and reported to be deeply depressed by the recent suicide of his mother whom he had loved intensely. Ralph made a point of going to see him. The two happily reminisced about the times, some two decades earlier, when they and other young musicians had met at Mrs Grainger's London home, listened to each other's compositions, shared their enthusiasms, (for instance, their shared passion for the poetry of

Walt Whitman), and had discussed their ambitions and hopes for the future.

By this time Ralph and Adeline had been able to return from their lodgings in remote Norfolk to their house in Cheyne Walk, Chelsea. In May 1921, Adeline's brother Hervey whom she had helped to tend for many years, died at Mainsail Haul in Sheringham. His death certificate lists the durations of the several illnesses that brought about his passing at the age of forty-six: 'Tuberculosis of spine 20 years. Abscess Albuminuria 2 years. Uraemia 3 days'.[7] But for all his protracted suffering Hervey had managed, a year earlier, to place his collection of short stories, *A Romantic Man and Other Tales*, with the progressive young publisher Martin Secker. The stories show some of the gentle humour that so endeared him to all those around him. Several of them are set in the Chelsea in which Adeline and Ralph lived and in which 'ladies talked with a drawl about Cubists and the Russian Ballet'. The story 'The Battle of the Blondes' tells of two ladies living in a state of great hostility in Oakley Street. 'Neighbours were soon aware of the friction between the two ladies. Some even found the contest of more interest than the Great European War'.[8] The climax comes when one of the protagonists is denounced as a 'beastly vixen'.

Hervey Fisher's death certificate contains the phrases: 'Ralph Vaughan Williams Brother-in-Law. Present at the death'. As an ambulance orderly in the First World War Ralph must have seen many horrific deaths. But witnessing Hervey's end must surely have been especially painful to him. For Adeline it was yet one more devastating bereavement. Perhaps Hervey, the enduring sufferer from the war years and earlier, was also remembered in the keening at the end of the Third Symphony.

Not long after the first performance of his 'Pastoral Symphony' Ralph received a surprising and exciting letter from America. It came from Carl Stoeckel who ran a music festival in Norfolk, Connecticut. The son of the first professor of music at nearby Yale University, Stoeckel had, like Koussevitzky, married a very wealthy heiress. This was Ellen Battell whose forebears had been cheese merchants and then highly successful land speculators in the developing western states. The Stoeckels decided to use some of their vast financial resources to commemorate Ellen's father by founding a music festival which would, as Ralph was informed, 'honour the memory of Robbins Battell ... with the object of presenting to the people of Litchfield County, choral and orchestral music in the highest forms'. To this end the Stoeckels had built a special auditorium,

The Music Shed. Sibelius had been the invited composer in 1914 and had there given the first performance of his Oceanides. Now Ralph was invited, with all expenses paid, to come and conduct 'A Pastoral Symphony' in the small New England town.

He and Adeline sailed on the liner *Berengaria* at the end of May. They arrived in an America that had prospered greatly since the end of the war. It was now strongly Republican, conservative and, ominously for current geopolitics, isolationist. In the year of Ralph's visit three major public sites were opened. Each in its own way confirmed a new sense of American self-concern, identity and confidence. They were: the Lincoln Memorial in Washington DC, the Hollywood Bowl in Los Angeles and Yankee Stadium in New York City. Ralph was utterly overwhelmed by New York. Seeing it for the first time was one of the greatest experiences of his life. The Stoeckels had arranged for him and Adeline to be installed in a luxurious suite of rooms with two bathrooms on the sixteenth floor of the expensive Plaza Hotel on Fifth Avenue. The city impressed him even more than Niagara Falls to which the Stoeckels had also arranged for them to be taken. From New York he wrote to Gustav Holst: 'I've come to the conclusion that The Works of Man terrify me more than The Works of God – I told myself at the time that Niagara was the most wonderful thing in the world – and so it is – especially when you get right under it – but I did not want to fall on my knees and confess my sins – whereas I can sit all day and look out of my windows (16 floors up) at the sky scrapers'.[9]

The hotel meals arranged for them by the Stoeckels were lavish and delicious: 'oh the American food – it's beyond powers of expression'. The Stoeckels themselves were 'nice and simple' people but after a while Ralph began to find their relentless hospitality overwhelming. He decided that, 'I never want a patron, it's too wearing'. Adeline noted that Ralph now 'knows how Mozart and his contemporaries felt living under a patron'. From New York he and Adeline were whisked off to Norfolk, Connecticut, where they stayed in the Stoeckels' thirty-five room mansion, The Whitehouse, in the centre of the little town. The Stoeckels, Adeline told her sister Cordelia, 'live in the "ancien regime", beautiful horses instead of motors, Swiss maids, an English gardener and an English parlour-maid! a very happy feeling in the house. Meals are too rich and wine flows all the time!'[10]

Ralph's 'Pastoral Symphony' was performed with great success before a very appreciative audience, with some fifteen hundred extra listeners camped on the grass outside The Music Shed. Presented with a large laurel wreath at the conclusion, Ralph was greatly pleased with the stay in America, which had lasted just less than two weeks. He and Adeline sailed home from New York on 26 June. It was the first of three very happy visits to the United States.

A fortnight after their return there was the first performance of Ralph's one-act opera *The Shepherds of the Delectable Mountains*. It took place in the recently named Parry Theatre at the Royal College of Music. The piece is a chapter in the story of Ralph's near lifelong concern to make an opera from John Bunyan's *The Pilgrim's Progress*. This 1922 setting of part of the book looks back to the incidental music he had written to accompany the Bunyan episodes staged at Reigate Priory in 1906. And most of it would be assimilated into the full-scale opera first produced at Covent Garden in 1951. The single act work begins by showing the Pilgrim being greeted by somewhat ethereal psalm-singing from the four shepherds. They then give accounts of the Delectable Mountains, the Celestial City and the Pilgrim's journey to that longed-for destination. Opinion has long been divided over the question of whether this music is oratorio rather than opera. But whatever the view there is unquestionably music to move the listener, particularly in the passage in which the First Shepherd celebrates the natural world, the birdsong, the flowers and the mountains. Three rondels with the title *Merciless Beauty*, some words attributed to Chaucer, which were published this same year have a similar delicate power.

The Shepherds of the Delectable Mountains shared the programme at the Royal College on 11 July with another one-acter, a cameo piece 'Scenes from Pickwick' composed by Charles Ives. The conductor was Arthur Bliss. The occasion and the college were honoured by the presence of Queen Mary, the consort of King George V. Ralph was duly presented to her by his old friend Hugh Allen, the Director of the college. Adeline reported to her sister Cordelia the comically inconsequential conversation initiated by the Queen. Adeline, repeating Ralph's account, related 'the interview after shaking hands':

QUEEN Are you the composer? I mean the composer of the first opera?
R. Yes, Mam
QUEEN I thought the dresses were very nice – and the scenery quite charming.
R. The students did it all themselves.

Then he received a gracious bow of dismissal and the next man was presented. Then everyone settled down again to listen to the Dickens opera but had hardly done so when the Queen got up from her chair and of course everyone got up too but R says as far as he could see she only wanted to shake or scratch herself and soon settled into her chair again.[11]

Ralph went on to say that as a result of the royal visit he had had a 'snob' dream in which he had gone to tea with the King and Queen at Buckingham Palace and, when it came time to leave, Queen Mary had walked with him to the door, winked broadly, and whispered 'Thursday'.

In July Ralph and Adeline had a holiday at Cordelia's house at Tetsworth a few miles east of Oxford. Cordelia, whose marriage to Richard Curle had broken up, was holidaying in France with her son Adam, who that same month, celebrated his sixth birthday. Ralph greatly enjoyed his time in the Chilterns countryside. He walked and cycled a good deal, became a great friend of Cordelia's dog, Julius Caesar, and enjoyed seeing the badgers who had taken up residence close by. He also looked again at his opera *Hugh the Drover* which he had finished scoring in May 1914, a few months before he had gone off to war, and which he had worked on again in 1920 during his many free hours in Norfolk. He was now able to send off a lengthy summary of the work to the music journalist Percy Scholes. Presumably Ralph hoped that this energetic writer and publicist might help to bring about a staging of the piece. If so, Ralph was to be disappointed. He had to wait two more years for a production of the opera. He was also very aware of how 'pre-war' the piece was. The life of vagabonding which the hero, Hugh, offers the heroine, Mary (and which found its passionate celebration in 'Songs of Travel') was not so appealing after the tent-life in Flanders fields; 'we used to imagine that we liked that kind of thing before the war when we had not experienced it'.[12]

Ralph was keenly aware of the radical changes that were taking place in post-war England. The political, social and cultural set-up was now in rapid flux. In 1922, following the conceding of independence to the new Irish Free State, Tory backbenchers brought about the end of the coalition government under the Liberal, David Lloyd George, that had been in power since the most difficult days of the war. Lloyd George was the last Liberal to be Prime Minister. British politics now began to evolve into a contest between the Conservative Party and the young Labour Party founded just over twenty years before. This was a new ordering with which Ralph, with his many Liberal connections was, within a few years, to become acutely uncomfortable.

Another change that was to greatly affect him also began in 1922 when a consortium of electrical companies took rooms in Marconi House opposite Somerset House on the eastern edge of the Aldwych and began experiments with radio broadcasting. Their initiative was a runaway success. Within a year they had to take larger premises in Savoy Hill just off The Strand. And within ten years the organization had to move again to the large landmark building erected in Portland Place, for what was by then the British Broadcasting Corporation (BBC). The first half of Ralph's career had run its course in a pre-radio society. From 1922 onwards the BBC became an increasingly important part of his life in music. He was invited to give his first broadcast talk on Christmas Eve 1924. He gave a short lecture entitled 'Carols and Waits' that introduced a programme of Christmas music. He would continue to broadcast, intermittently, until the last years of his life.

In the autumn of 1922 Ralph had his fiftieth birthday. Among the many greetings he received there was a very special one from Gustav Holst and the students with whom he and Ralph worked at Morley College. On the evening of 12 October the diminutive, bespectacled Gustav Holst, leading a group of students, stole silently into the front garden of Ralph's house at 13 Cheyne Walk. They stood beneath his window and greeted him with a choral serenade. One of the singers was the 28-year-old Jane Joseph, a composer and arranger who was a close associate and sometimes pupil of Gustav Holst. An enthusiastic admirer of Ralph and his work, she had composed a special choral part song which the singers in the garden now proceeded to perform. Jane, who had studied Classics at Girton College, Cambridge, headed the scroll on which she had carefully copied the score with a salutation in Latin.

Radolpho Guilielmo
natalicam hanc cantiunculam
d.d.
Joanna Josepha
Iv Id. Oct. A.D. MDCCCCXXII

Jane Joseph was a strong, very active advocate of women's rights. She was also on the left in politics. In the words of her birthday song to Ralph

Jane addressed him as 'Comrade'. At this time when political tensions in Britain were starting to develop to the point at which the stability of the state eventually came into question, the word 'Comrade' had a very strong, even dangerous, resonance. Revolutionary politics were very much in the air. Just five years before, the Bolshevik Revolution in Russia had brought to power Comrade Vladimir Ilyich Lenin. Less than six months after Ralph's birthday Lenin would be dead and replaced subsequently by Comrade Joseph Stalin. Jane is surely joshing Ralph in addressing him as 'Comrade', or perhaps, a progressive herself, she has hopes of him. How much of a 'Comrade' Ralph was, is very doubtful. But the affection of the young woman who composed for him and of the students who sang for him that evening in the Chelsea garden is beyond question.

(Maestoso)
    My comrades! Rejoice and sing
    Upon this day of thanksgiving
    Give honour
    And greet the mighty one
    Who added grace to song
    For he is the friend of all joy-loving folk

    Comrade of all knowing him:
    So, comrades, give homage
    Rejoice and sing
    Upon this day of thanksgiving.

Ralph and Adeline stood at the first-floor window to listen to the birthday greetings. The singers were then invited inside for refreshments and Jane Joseph handed over the scroll on which the score of his birthday song had been meticulously copied out.

There remained one more event to complete this year, 1922, which for Ralph was so outstandingly rich in experiences and achievement. This was the first performance of the Mass in G minor for soloists and double chorus. It was sung in Birmingham in the first week of December by the City of Birmingham Choir and conducted by Joseph Lewis, soon to be famous as a conductor on radio and, at that time, the Director of the Wolverhampton Music Society. This was the choir with which at the Queen's Hall in a few months' time Joseph Lewis would give the first London performance of the Mass in G minor. Ralph's music was now being taken up in an industrial town in the Midlands as well as in music festivals in country towns and villages. Ralph would continue to maintain a relationship with Wolverhampton and its musical life until his very last years.

The Mass was dedicated to Gustav Holst and to the choir he had created at Morley College, the Whitsuntide Singers. Lasting a little under twenty-five minutes, it is a beautifully poised, elegant work. It blends music from very audible sixteenth-century sources with music with modern sounds and textures. The Tudor sounds are part of a structure which is a version of Ralph's other Tudor inspired work, the Fantasia on a Theme by Thomas Tallis. The four solo singers conversing with the two separate four-part choirs constitute a dialogue similar to that created by the dispositions of the strings in the Thomas Tallis. But along with the gravitas recalling the Tallis there is also here a beautiful airiness and spaciousness. It has an effect similar to that which Bauhaus furniture and interiors must have made when they first became known during the same decade. From the bright hopefulness of the Kyrie and the bursting joyousness of the Gloria right through to the severity of the Benedicite there is a supervening coolness that makes this a memorable work. Its first performance in December was an appropriate way to conclude this year which was one of the most outstanding in Ralph's long career.

Chapter Eleven

A CAREER RE-ESTABLISHED

In the first week of 1923 the BBC – still less than a year old – experimented with its first-ever broadcast from an outside studio. To the swiftly and exponentially growing number of crystal sets and valved radios the organization successfully transmitted from Covent Garden a performance of Mozart's *The Magic Flute*. At the same time Ralph was beginning rehearsals for an ambitious, early project with the Bach Choir, a performance of Bach's great St Matthew Passion. It took place at the Queen's Hall on 7 March with two further performances that same month. Benjamin Britten and some others might disparage Ralph's conducting but this, his first venture with this demanding piece, proved to be a great success. Audiences responded enthusiastically. Ralph was particularly gratified by a complimentary letter from his crusty old teacher Sir Charles Villiers Stanford. Other letters were far less qualified than Stanford's; nevertheless, they conveyed the vibrant power of these concerts. Vally Lasker who played the violin in Gustav Holst's orchestra at St Paul's School and later participated in the Leith Hill Music Festival wrote that the performance of the St Matthew Passion was 'the greatest spiritual and musical experience I have ever had in my life.... I congratulate myself and us all for being privileged to be born in the same generation as you'.[1] And Dorothy Longman, a neighbour of the Vaughan Williamses at Leith Hill Place, whose husband Robert was a prominent London publisher, wrote 'to thank you for our hearing of the lovely performance last night. Again the magic land was entered and lived in for a space'.[2]

Dorothy, like Vally, was an accomplished violinist. To Dorothy, whom he had known since before the First World War, Ralph dedicated his Two Pieces for Violin and Piano, which he published this year. The little work is a Pastorale preceded by a Romance that has a passionate pulse to it. Dorothy and Ralph played the piece together, though there is no suggestion that their duetting had elements of Tolstoy's *Kreutzer Sonata*. The Longmans and the Vaughan Williamses had a long-lasting couples' friendship. Ralph had played the organ at their wedding during the war. But Dorothy liked to play and ponder the pieces on her own and in early April wrote tenderly to the composer, who, at the age of fifty still had recurrent doubts about his music: 'I've been playing them today, alone. You have sometimes doubted, if I should care for your music apart from our friendship – but you and your music are not apart they are one and that is why both mean what they do to me; will you not understand this?'[3]

Ralph conducted more Bach this year. He went on to perform the St John Passion and, at the Leith Hill Music Festival, three more cantatas. Workaholic that he was, he also had time to produce less weighty works. He responded to an invitation from Colonel John Somerville, the Commandant of the Royal Military School of Music, to write a piece for a military band. Ralph produced his *English Folk Song Suite* which quickly entered the repertoire of the parade grounds, the bandstands and, an important venue for musical entertainment in those days, the seaside piers. The piece had its first performance on 4 July at the home of the Royal Military School of Music in the grand Kneller Hall in Twickenham. A month earlier another of Ralph's lighter works had been performed in Cambridge. This was his ballet *Old King Cole*.

On a visit to Cambridge in 1920 when he had seen an undergraduate production of *The Fairy Queen*, Ralph, perhaps still affected by the pervasive enthusiasm for Diaghilev's Ballet Russes, is reported to have made an offer: 'if any of you like to write the story of a ballet, I will write the music'. A competition for an outline was then organized by the Cambridge branch of the English Folk Dance Society. The winning proposal was submitted by one of the members Mrs Edward Vulliamy. She proposed a dance sequence based on a particular passage in Edmund Spenser's *The Faerie Queene* that relates the story of Old King Cole, a monarch of one of the ancient British tribal kingdoms whose capital was at Colchester. King Cole's daughter Helen had married the Roman Emperor. And Ralph's ballet picks up the story when she returns to Britain to pay her father a visit. She brings him a present which one member of the

Cambridge audience remembered as 'a huge Hookah, sent from the East'. King Cole samples it but decides he prefers a drink and calls for his bowl. He then also calls for his fiddle-players and organizes a song and dance competition for the entertainment of his daughter. First comes a gypsy fiddler dancing to a Morris jig; the second offers a romantic tale of love, based on the folk song 'A bold young farmer'. The third contestant offers a version of the folk melody 'The Jolly Thresherman'; its lively humour is a contrast with the piece that went before. King Cole, in true British style, awards the prize to this last, very hearty dancer. But it is clear that Helen would have chosen the second. In compensation she throws him a rose which, as he dances his farewell, he does not notice. Understandably, the music was well received by the audience on that pleasant spring evening. The hookah dance with its reedy woodwinds is pleasingly druggy and the three competition dances contrast entertainingly. The ballet, which is often funny, ends touchingly as the second contestant plays his haunting theme and fails to see the flower that is thrown to him.

The ballet was performed during May Week of 1923 in the open air in Neville's Court in Trinity College, where Ralph had completed his under-graduate career exactly thirty years before. There was an elaborate set on which 'two fantastic thrones were set up for King Cole and his daughter the Empress Helen. They were designed by Mrs Sydney Cockerell'. (Kate Cockerell, then well known as an illustrator and illuminator, was the wife of Sydney Cockerell, a sometime associate of John Ruskin and William Morris, and by then the energetic and innovative director of the Fitzwilliam Museum in Cambridge.) The hookah made a very dramatic entrance. 'A gorgeous page [Justin Vulliamy] and six little black slaves carried it, on a long tube', the same member of the audience continued to recall. And as the ballet drew to its conclusion and 'as the light faded, the windows of the Dining Room were lit up and servants came out carrying magnificent dishes for the Banquet which was to follow. R.V.W. himself told Mrs Vulliamy that nowhere but in Cambridge could such a spec-tacle have been carried through'.[4] *Old King Cole* marked a very happy theatrical return to Cambridge for Ralph nearly fourteen years after his success there with *The Wasps*.

That same spring he and Adeline went on holiday to Venice. In beau-tiful evening light they were rowed down the Grand Canal in a gondola to their hotel. But almost immediately Adeline fell ill and was confined to their room. With some difficulty she prevailed upon Ralph to do some sightseeing without her. They soon travelled to the Dolomites where

186

Adeline felt well again. A few weeks later they followed their usual yearly pattern of taking a place somewhere in the English countryside for a short summer stay. This year they took a furnished house in the remote woodland village of Danbury, in the Chelmsford area of Essex. It had been found for them by the young composer Armstrong Gibbs who had been Ralph's pupil and was now his colleague at the Royal College. Here in the country quiet Ralph began work on *Sancta Civitas*, his first major work since the Mass in G minor and a grand visionary piece which, as Michael Kennedy has suggested, gives the impression of being 'in the form of a homage to Bach from the twentieth century'.[5] As Ralph assimilated the various shocks of the recent war and had to face the instabilities of the post-war world, Bach's music of transcendence was very much a part of his thinking and his musical activities. He must have been both gratified and touched when in the November of this year his Mass in G minor was performed in Bach's church, the Thomaskirche in Leipzig.

In the spring of 1924 Charles Villiers Stanford died and the Chair of Music at Cambridge became vacant. Ralph was now confronted with a decisive career choice. He was a keen advocate of his old friend and promoter Edward J. Dent, who was at the time President of the recently founded International Society for Contemporary Music, as the best candidate to take over the professorship. But there were also those who believed strongly that Ralph himself should take the position. Choosing between teaching and creating is often a difficult decision, a temptation even, for those with artistic ambitions. Ralph in mid-life was in no doubt whatsoever about what he wished, and intended to do. To a Fellow at Trinity who was one of those urging him to go for the vacant professorship he wrote, with both candour and self-criticism, 'my whole life has been taken up (in the intervals of earning my living) with trying to become a composer – and I look forward now that I can drop some of my outside work to trying to learn the job of a composer – which I have yet failed to do – before I am too old to do anything'. He concluded with the clear simple emphasis which often characterizes his writing style, 'To put it shortly – at my time of life I've got to settle whether with the rest of what remains to me I am to write or to teach – I want (rightly or wrongly) to write – I can't do both'.[6] In the event the professorship was assumed by Ralph's old teacher, the Ulsterman Charles Wood, who was well known for his compositions for the Anglican Liturgy. On his death, some three years later, the Chair went to Edward Dent.

In early July of 1924 Ralph, seeking to move beyond academe, ventured again into the world of entertainment. Some ten years after its first drafting, *Hugh the Drover* was finally performed and published. It was staged at the Royal College of Music on 4, 7, 9 and 11 July. Each of these 'private dress rehearsals' was enthusiastically received. A few days later it was performed again, this time in the West End, at His Majesty's Theatre, by the British National Opera Company, an organization that derived from the opera sessions which Sir Thomas Beecham had organized during the war. This performance was under the baton of the exciting new conductor Malcolm Sargent, a young man of working-class origins who had made his debut at the Proms just three years before at the age of twenty-six. Ralph was grateful to him for saving a performance which was greatly under-rehearsed.

There have been other performances since, at Sadlers Wells and at lesser venues, but it seems unlikely that this 'Romantic Ballad Opera' as Ralph termed it, will find a secure position in the repertoire of major opera houses. It is too slight. As a product of the opera-less England of pre-1914 it was unquestionably a brave, constructive venture. But it has obvious limitations. It is based on a very hackneyed, reach-me-down operatic situation. The attractive heroine, Mary, is being forced into a loveless marriage by her father, the constable of the small Cotswold village in which they live. Her father's choice for her is John the Butcher who is very well-off. He is also loutish, arrogant, brutal and dishonest. But the tenor hero, Hugh the Drover, arrives, sweeps Mary off her feet and wins her in (what is a very stageworthy section of the opera) a prize-fight with John. But this very stagey, double-dyed villain denounces Hugh as a spy for Napoleon and gets him put in the stocks. Mary devises a plan to help her new lover. She joins him in the stocks, and in consequence, is disowned by her father and John for thus lowering and humiliating herself. There is even the titillating suggestion that John will henceforth regard, and even treat, Mary as a 'trull', the words 'whore' and 'prostitute' not suiting the distinctive 'olde worlde' rhetoric of this libretto. But through Mary's dramatic action, the lovers are united. Then Hugh is quickly recognized to be a heroic patriot and the opera ends happily.

Yet the pantomime character of the narrative is mitigated at the end when Mary experiences a troubling tension between the claims of love, freedom and vagabonding adventure with Hugh, on the one hand, and the claims of her lonely, loving aunt Jane, her family and her community on the other. At the end, *Hugh the Drover* has a poetic and musical delicacy to match this new thematic complexity. And this to some extent redeems the crudities that have gone before: the melodically coarse self-congratulation of the villagers, the vulgar francophobia, the clunking rhymes and the lumbering archaisms in the libretto. The gentle, thoughtful finale reminds us that there was also a pleasing music in some of the earlier scenes, particularly in the series of interchanges between Mary and Hugh. The piece certainly impressed those choral students at the Royal College in 1924 who hastened over to His Majesty's Theatre to offer their services when the first professional production fell into difficulties.

After all the hard work and excitement of staging *Hugh the Drover* Ralph and Adeline again set off on their customary summer holiday in the country. Dorothy Longman's sister, Mary Fletcher, lent them 'Martinscote', her small house in the village of Oare, near Marlborough in Wiltshire. They were extremely happy there, Adeline telling Mary: 'I can't say the hundredth part of how pleased we are to be here ... we do so love the garden following the lines of the lane – and the hedgerow trees and the house from every aspect....'[7] Mary Fletcher later remembered that in the course of this happy summer stay Ralph was much taken with one of the books on her shelves, *The Romance of Words* by Ernest Weekley. The author was a Professor of English Language at Nottingham University whose German wife, Frieda, had notoriously abandoned him and three young children in order to elope with D.H. Lawrence. Fascinated by the book, Ralph took it away with him, asking Mary if he might keep it. His action is further testimony to the intensely lexical, verbal and literary element in his powerful intelligence. His mind was very active and excited at Oare. As Adeline reported, 'Ralph went about saying "I shall write here...."' And write he did, his principal work during these June weeks being *Flos Campi*. Years later Mary Fletcher told Ursula, 'Ralph composed *Flos Campi* in my little house at Oare ... and sent me by Adeline an autograph copy of the principal theme in it – I stuck it into my Visitors' Book and should like to show it to you.'[8]

A suite in six movements for solo viola, wordless mixed chorus and small orchestra, *Flos Campi* is in the context of Ralph's overall output, a distinctive, highly unusual, and very puzzling work. Each of the movements is headed by a quotation from the Song of Songs. Biblical scholars have disagreed as to whether this book in the Old Testament is about loving God or loving a woman. But most listeners who have written about Ralph's settings of the selected passages hear it very much as a work of sensuous, sexual feeling. After the very masculine marching

189

sounds of the fourth movement, at the centre of the piece, comes the great following section led by Ralph's instrument, the viola; a movement of which Simone Packenham has observed that 'the viola, its voice husky with passion, sings its ecstatic rhapsody. This is surely the musical apotheosis of longing!'[9] Yes, *Flos Campi* centres on a hymning and a celebration of physical love, but a love that comes to pass and then is ended. The final thoughtful movement gives an impression that the relationship was very much a brief encounter. As this twenty-minute piece comes to its impressively delicate conclusion a biographer is prompted to ask whether this was a love remembered or a love imagined. In the former case there is a temptation to *chercher la femme*. And certain possibilities present themselves. But as yet there is insufficient evidence to assist in pursuing them. But what is unquestionably clear from the work, which is so atypical within Ralph's oeuvre, is that in the summer tranquillity of Oare he was recollecting some very powerful, earthy emotions. The viola sings of the evolution of a relationship through its varying phases until it reaches its end. And the wordless chorus sounds out the connections and reverberations of this love to a larger soundscape. It recalls a similar, non-verbal chorus in Ravel's *Daphnis and Chloe* in which individual sensuous impulses are heard to have a wider, larger imminence.

In the arts generally in the early 1920s there was what has been called a *rappel à l'ordre*, a movement away from the *non a priori* experimentalism from before the war and a recall to firm established forms. The about-turn is very visible in the paintings of Picasso at this time and also in the poetry of T.S. Eliot and his close collaborator, Ezra Pound. Another composition that Ralph worked on in the summer of 1924 at Oare was a work of this kind of retrenchment. It contrasts markedly with what was, for Ralph, the strikingly innovative, sometimes exotic soundscape of *Flos Campi*. This other piece was the violin concerto which Ralph wrote for the beautiful Hungarian violinist Jelly d'Aranyi, an assistant of Béla Bartók, who, with her similarly striking sister Adila Fachiri was a conspicuous figure in the music world of 1920s London. Originally called the *Concerto Accademico*, a title which was perhaps meant to recall the Italianate titling of the eighteenth century, the piece which is now known as the Violin Concerto in D minor is far more traditional and formal in its structures than *Flos Campi* of the same year. It is a pleasing, melodic piece with reminiscences of Bach that shares the fashionable concerns with neoclassicism. There is a bounding, opening movement, its high spirits somewhat disturbed by a passage of counter melody from the soloist, and then comes a thoughtful, ritualistic adagio and, to finish, a romp of a reel and a jig. All very engaging. But it has not the depth of the *Flos Campi* and seemingly Jelly D'Aranyi was not much impressed. Some ten years later Ralph recalled that 'I gave Jelly a 6 months run of my violin concerto (not that she made much use of it)'.

At the end of a very creative summer of composing in Wiltshire, Ralph had to return to conducting. He had accepted an invitation to perform his 'Sea Symphony' at the recently revived Norwich Festival. Queen Mary was again a member of his audience. Uncomfortably he remembered that when she had attended one of the performances of *Hugh the Drover* she had had him summoned and had demanded sternly why Hugh and Mary had not been married before setting off on their life of vagabonding. After all, the village church was a conspicuous part of the set and thus eminently convenient for them. Alas, Ralph had no answer. Fortunately, at Norwich the conversation proved to be less awkward. The Queen simply congratulated him on his symphony and the performance of it.

On another occasion that year came a display of the unassuming, seigneurial confidence and leadership of which Ralph, a former head of house at Charterhouse, was so readily capable. It was at a concert given by the Royal Philharmonic Society and conducted by the young, handsome debonair Malcolm Sargent in his debut year. The programme included Ralph's 'Pastoral Symphony' and the *Fantaisie Espagnole* by Lord Berners, the most eccentric and colourful figure in English musical life during the inter-war years. Also performed was the piano concerto of Herbert Howells. When the pianist and Malcolm Sargent:

> were acknowledging the applause, a man stood up in the circle. 'What I say is, 'Thank God it's over!' he shouted. Two others in the audience got to their feet – a lady in the stalls yelled 'Take that man out, he's drunk!' and Vaughan Williams from a seat in the circle immediately over the orchestra, clapped demonstratively, leading what grew to be an ovation when Howells appeared on the platform.[10]

It turned out that the demonstrator was a passionate and militant advocate of E.J. Moeran whose work he thought the London music establishment ignored. This seems to have been the first time that Ralph was seen to be associated with such an establishment. It was a perception that was voiced increasingly in future years.

Ralph now teamed up again with Percy Dearmer and Martin Shaw and spent a good deal of time and effort with them, producing a new hymn book to succeed the *English Hymnal* which they had worked on together nearly twenty years before. The publishers, Oxford University Press, had decided that a collection less high church in its associations and one that would make a special appeal to young people was now desirable. Ralph and his colleagues accepted the new commission and duly set to work and produced *Songs of Praise*. The new collection was a great success, being taken up by many churches and, most importantly from a commercial point of view, by numerous education authorities. During the coming decades, *Songs of Praise* was revised in a succession of new editions. It was an important supplement to the income brought by the small silver spoon.

Ralph's connections with Oxford University Press (OUP) were further strengthened by the relationship he struck up with the young man whom OUP had appointed to be the first director of its newly established music division. This was Hubert Foss, a keen admirer of Ralph's work. In 1925 Foss published *The Shepherds of the Delectable Mountains*. From now on, OUP was Ralph's regular publisher. During the Second World War Hubert Foss would complete a book about Ralph's music for which the composer would supply the important essay 'A Musical Autobiography'.

In May 1925, the month in which OUP accepted *The Shepherds of the Delectable Mountains*, Ralph and Adeline set off to Prague to attend some of the sessions of the International Society for Contemporary Music (or what Ralph, always rather guarded and sceptical about Modernist music, alluded to as 'the Freak Festival'). It was announced that there was to be a formal occasion at the gathering. So Adeline hastened to Frederick Gorringe's, a highly fashionable department store in Buckingham Palace Road much patronized by courtiers. Here she bought herself a silk tussore dress, the kind of purchase that always gave Ralph great pleasure. The weather in Prague was excellent and Adeline wrote to Cordelia that Ralph's *Pastoral Symphony* 'got a good reception', though Ralph himself didn't think so. They were received at the British legation and a Czech film company shot some footage of him. But his greatest pleasure in Prague was a performance of Janáček's *Cunning Little Vixen*. For all his uncertainty about innovative music, Ralph was entertained and impressed by the Czech composer's celebratory evocation of the processes of nature and of the lives of country people.

But he was dismayed and a little embarrassed to find he could not feel a similar enthusiasm for the *Choral Symphony* by his old, dear friend,

Leith Hill Place near Dorking, Surrey – the childhood home of Ralph Vaughan Williams.

The Leith Hill servants were an important part of Ralph's boyhood. His nurse, Sarah Wager (*second from the left, front row*), had a great influence on him, particularly in political matters.

Ralph at the age of 14. In January 1887, in his fifteenth year, he joined his elder brother Hervey at Charterhouse School.

Hubert Parry, composer, Ralph's beloved teacher at the Royal College of Music.

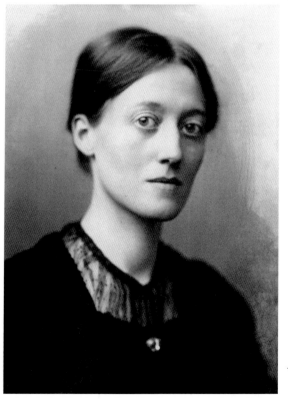

▲ Charles Villiers Stanford, an Irish composer and teacher with whom Ralph had a more troubled relationship at the Royal College of Music.

◄ Adeline (née Fisher), some ten years after she married Ralph.

Ralph in 1910, at the time of the premiere performance of his first symphony, *A Sea Symphony*.

Ralph and Adrian Boult in 1935, the year Ralph received the Order of Merit.

Haymaking near Dorking in the 1930s. The spire of St Martin's parish church is visible in the background.

Ursula Wood, 1935, the wife of Captain Michael Wood, RA, three years before meeting Ralph.

Ralph with E.M. Forster (*to Ralph's right*), collaborators on the pageant 'England's Pleasant Land', which they wrote for the Dorking and Leith Hill Preservation Society in 1938.

Ralph and Ursula attending a concert in the Civic Hall, Wolverhampton, in 1950.

Ralph tending an ailing Adeline in 1950, some months before her death.

The wedding of Ralph and Ursula in the crypt of St Pancras Church, London, in February 1953.

Ralph and Ursula in the USA for a lecture tour, autumn 1954. Ralph held a visiting professorship at Cornell University in New York state.

Ralph and Ursula leaving for a holiday in Austria, 1957.

Gustav Holst which had its first performance at the Leeds Festival that year. In part due to the success of *The Planets*, Holst now had a standing in the music world comparable to Ralph. With the straightforward honesty that always characterized their friendship, Ralph set about trying to explain 'why I felt vaguely disappointed'. He continued, 'I felt cold admiration – but did not want to get up and embrace everyone and then get drunk like I did after the H[ymn] of J[esus]'. He was quick to admit that his failure in appreciation might well be his own fault. 'I think it is only because it is a new work and I am more slowly moving than I used to be and it's got to soak in'. He concludes the letter by speaking of his pain at the lack of responsiveness to his old comrade's latest work. 'I couldn't bear to think that I was going to "drift apart" from you musically speaking. (If I do, who shall I have to crib from?) – and I don't believe it is so – so I shall live in faith till I have heard it again several times and then I shall find out what a bloody fool I was not to see it all first time'.[11]

The musical divergences between the two men were confirmed when Holst wrote back. He, in his turn, had not taken to *Flos Campi*. But he saw no problem for them in taking separate paths. 'I couldn't get hold of Flos a bit and was therefore disappointed with it and me. But I'm not disappointed in Flos's composer, because he has not repeated himself. Therefore it is probably either an improvement or something that will lead to one'.[12]

Towards the end of 1925 Ralph was working on two other works which would show further and pronounced movement away from the idiom he had shared with Gustav Holst. They were both masterworks. The first was his great, visionary oratorio for chorus, soloists and orchestra, *Sancta Civitas*, which was virtually completed by the end of the year. The other, still a work in progress, was the setting of *Riders to the Sea* by the Irish writer John Millington Synge who had created a name for himself (and also a scandal) with the production of his *Playboy of the Western World* at W.B. Yeats's Abbey Theatre in Dublin. It was an important moment in the Irish cultural renaissance that accompanied the movement to independence. Very probably Ralph had been introduced to Synge's work by Elizabeth Maconchy, a lively teenager of Irish descent and upbringing, who had become a student of his at the Royal College just a couple of years before. He may also have discussed the play with Ina Boyle, an older Irish woman of extensive literary interests, whom he also taught and whose compositions he admired and championed.

Riders to the Sea ranks among Ralph's finest achievements. As Wilfrid

Mellers has succinctly observed, 'it is a masterpiece – its composer's most perfectly realised theatrical work'.[13] It is unfortunate that, being a one-acter, the piece is infrequently performed. Its grim, even harrowing subject matter is also a deterrent to producers. The opera treats of keen painfulness in the human condition like Alban Berg's *Wozzek* which was also first performed in 1925, under Frank Kleiber in Berlin. Ralph's opera also shares with Berg's work a use of song-speech or *Sprechgesang* as he establishes on stage the archaic lifestyle of the fisher-people of the Aran Islands, off Ireland's west coast, around the turn of the century. From the outset their elemental world is immediately evoked by the prelude in which the small orchestra, assisted innovatively by a sea machine, sounds out the raging storm. Nora and Cathleen, daughters of the principal character Maurya, the old woman who has lost so many of her menfolk to the violence of the Atlantic, wonder anxiously whether the last of her sons, Michael, may also have been a victim to it. Clothes that look to be his have been washed up on the coast, away up in Donegal. With the entrance of Maurya there is heard a new music, that of human fortitude, which resists the surrounding violence. And the fortitude endures as, excruciatingly, another son is claimed by the sea. The music now alludes to depths of feeling far removed from the easy, picturesque manageability of *Hugh the Drover*.

From now on, Maurya dominates the opera as its tragic heroine. She becomes an archetype of human grieving. She sings a threnody of lamentation not only for those of her own flesh whom she has lost but for those of all mankind. Choral keening accompanies her as she finally comes to a statement of one of the crucial inevitabilities of the human condition: 'No man at all can be living for ever and we must be satisfied'. Those concluding five words in Ralph's setting of them, have a power that is subtle, understated and yet piercing. And so ends this profound, compact piece which is one of those that show Ralph moving beyond the soundscape that he had shared with Gustav Holst and much closer to that of the continental Modernists who were so active in the 1920s. As one commentator on this impressive work has observed, 'innovation and expression find a harmonious union in this otherwise disquieting composition, compelling us to challenge the received notion of Vaughan Williams as a conservative "pastoral" composer out of step with his time'.

At the same time as he started to explore new possibilities in composition, Ralph was also very much involved with the tried and the true and the long familiar. The Gatty family, his old friends from Cambridge days, were suddenly very much back in his life again. Ralph was there to see Nicholas Gatty's opera *The Tempest* when it was given a performance at the Royal College of Music in November. A few weeks later he was at the Forest School in Sussex which was run by Hugh Parrington and his wife Margot Gatty, Nicholas's sister who as a child had so deeply appreciated Adeline's kindness years before. The school was putting on a Christmas performance of *The Taming of the Shrew*. The school orchestra played incidental music and Ralph readily and happily became a member of it. He and Margot were together in the orchestra's viola section and Nicholas Gatty was one of the second violins. Margot remembered that Ralph's passion for playing: 'was quite tremendous so that always bow hairs would become broken and wave up and down as he bowed. Then in a very vigorous section (his bow must have been a little short for him) he would bring it down so far to the point that it would slip under the bridge. This always sent darling Adeline in the front row into silent tears of amusement.'[14]

Such get-togethers will have reminded Ralph of the happy times when they had all made music together in the welcoming Gatty home in the old Yorkshire parsonage in the years well before the scarifying sufferings and shake-ups of the First World War. But as the New Year 1926 began, there developed yet one more rending crisis in British life. It was another grim confirmation that those peaceful, happy times at the old Rectory at Hooton Roberts were a thing of a remote past. The General Strike of that year upset Ralph profoundly as it did countless others. As a man and a composer he would be racked painfully by the profound and suddenly violent divisions within the country. He was shocked to find himself in an England that had come to a virtual standstill, that was panic stricken at the prospect of a revolution similar to that in Russia less than a decade before and, that unbelievably, was placed under military rule. One of Ralph's greatest visionary works had its first performance in the midst of this crisis.

Chapter Twelve

PONDERING APOCALYPSE

In the worsening economic and financial crisis of the mid-1920s the colliery owners of Great Britain bluntly informed the miners that they would have to accept a substantial reduction in their wages. Coal, the chief energy source of the nation, was – and not for the last time in the twentieth century – in a state of crisis. The miners refused to accept the proprietors' diktat. Under the leadership of their eloquent and very Left-wing union leader A.J. Cook, they were soon on a nationwide strike. When the owners responded by locking them out, the Trade Union Congress took the momentous step of calling on other unions to join a General Strike in support of the miners. It began at a minute before midnight on 3 May 1926.

Ralph's close contemporary, Winston Churchill, now Chancellor of the Exchequer, feared and vigorously warned that this radical disruption in everyday life could be the prelude to a Communist Revolution such as had occurred so very recently in Russia. He proposed putting tanks and machine guns on to the streets to protect strike-breaking food convoys. The Prime Minister, the more moderate Stanley Baldwin, argued for greater caution. To deflect Churchill's reactionary energies Baldwin made him responsible for *The British Gazette*, the government newspaper which, together with the TUC's *The British Worker*, was the only press to appear during the strike. As the headline over the central column in *The British Gazette* of 5 May, Churchill published, and encapsulated in a phrase, what he saw as the stark choice: 'The Constitution or a Soviet'. Two days later the army was used to escort the lorries which were forcing their way through the dockers' picket lines in the East End of London to bring food into the capital. At the same time, artillery pieces and barbed wire appeared in Hyde Park. In the North East an express train drawn by the record-breaking locomotive The Flying Scotsman was derailed by strikers.

As Ursula has reported, Ralph was 'deeply troubled' by the crisis dividing the nation. To settle his conflicting thoughts and to try to decide what he would do if the country were to fall into revolution and class war, he made the effort to write out, in a page and a half, his complicated, ambivalent attitude to the strike. 'On the whole I am with the miners in this dispute', he began. He mistrusted Churchill and his 'gang in the cabinet'; and 'the beastly rag the National Gazette which is trying to inflame evil passions is theirs also'. He proceeds to ask himself directly, 'isn't it our duty to support the govt as such even if in the end it has to resort to armed force?' Then he puts the same question another way: 'is it wrong to be on the side of revolution if it came to that?' At this stage in his meditation he decides that, 'I should not be against revolution by violence in the last resort (I don't think the status quo anything to be proud of).'

But immediately an important proviso came into his mind. Before envisaging 'the temporary anarchy which would follow I must be fairly certain that a <u>better</u> state of things is going to emerge'. And this he doubted. 'Much as I dislike the govt I mistrust the labour leaders ... Cook is an empty wind-bag.' Another simple fact gave him pause too. 'Also I cannot deny the duty of the govt to see that people do not starve if the food is to be had.' The problem was frustratingly insoluble. 'The simplest thing for a man of my age is to do nothing.' But such an abdication was unsatisfactory too. Ralph continued to meditate about the issue but without coming to any resolution.

He was struggling with these questions while he and Adeline were staying in Oxford with her brother, the historian H.A.L. Fisher, formerly a Lloyd George cabinet minister who was now Warden of New College. Doubtless the crisis was the subject of intense discussion during the visit. Ralph was in Oxford to attend the concluding rehearsals and the first performance of his oratorio *Sancta Civitas*. The premiere took place on 7 May, the day before the government used troops to effect entry into the London docks. What an irony that Ralph's musical evocation of the coming of a *sancta civitas*, a holy city, a divine polity, should be first heard at such a dangerous, historic moment!

197

The oratorio is about the Apocalypse. It is a setting of a selection of passages from the final book of the Bible. In the aftermath of the horrors of the First World War and among the dizzying series of dislocations, financial, economic and social, that subsequently ravaged Europe, a sense of approaching apocalypse informed a number of the major artistic enterprises of the time. It is conspicuously there, for instance, in T.S. Eliot's *The Waste Land* of 1922. It is also present in D.H. Lawrence's *Women in Love* which in one redaction took its title from the *Dies Irae*, the thirteenth-century Latin hymn about the Apocalypse, the Day of Judgment, as envisaged in the last book of the New Testament. It is characteristic of Ralph's literary and linguistic sophistication that when he too turned to this imposing subject he chose his texts, not only from the King James version of the Bible but also from the much earlier Taverner version which is marked by a lexical preference for the Anglo-Saxon, the concrete and the earthy rather than the Latinate.

The passages which Ralph collaged present a vision of devastation followed by one of human, planetary and cosmic salvation. The epigraph on the first page of the score, a passage from Plato's *Phaedo*, deflects the listener's thoughts from the Bible to this other text which enlarges the work's frame of reference, yet also confirms the existence and the ultimate durability and triumph of something that can be termed the spiritual. In Ralph's copy of F.J. Church's translation from the Greek the passage is heavily marked.

> A man of sense will not insist that things are exactly as I have described them. But I think he will believe that something of the kind is true of the soul and her habitations....The venture is a fair one and he must charm his doubts with spells like these.

Ralph's attempt to banish his agnostic doubt falls neatly into four sections. The auditory vision emerges from silence, cellos and basses having a slow, rising progression. Into the stillness and mystery emerges the voice of the protagonist, John of Patmos, declaiming the imminent marriage of the Lamb of God to his people. Distant, then ever nearer, the choral voice of humanity joins him. In the second section, as there develops a complexity of metaphor, the divine figure mutates from the Lamb to that of the warrior, Faithful and True, astride a white horse. Introduced by urgent drumming he makes war against the kings of the earth and destroys them. His 'fierceness' is expressed in a powerful triple forte chord of G minor and there follows a passage of disturbing ferocity and brutality. In the third section these martial and then victorious sounds are replaced by ones of loss and regret. Babylon has been vanquished but as human beings we are in two minds about its destruction and the loss of all its 'things which were dainty and goodly'. The recent, just war of 1914–18 may have been won but the destruction which the victory has cost is also an occasion for sadness. We have here, as Michael Kennedy has so well expressed it, 'masterly pages of choral writing like a vast symphonic sigh'.[1] The sounds of *Sancta Civitas* do not constitute a simple vision; there is here ambiguity and doubt too.

Finally, in the fourth section, there comes the slowly dawning prospect of a new earth and a new heaven, a *sancta civitas*. A solo violin furthers the hushed vision. Then a trumpet sound announces the Holy, Holy, Holy and the music takes on a growing urgency and compelling emphasis. It culminates in a memorable understatement, the simple, one-line declaration from the Redeemer: 'Behold, I come quickly. I am the bright and the morning star. Surely I come quickly'. And then the conclusion of the vision, after these simple, succinct, affecting words, is a trailing away into the quietness and then the silence in which this powerful complex vision of salvation first developed.

Sancta Civitas, which was completed and rehearsed in the politically fraught months leading up to the General Strike, and for many, to the seeming apocalyptic prospect of revolution, was the work which Ralph considered his greatest choral achievement. A rich, subtle work, it claimed a great deal of creative energy. In the following months he turned to less demanding projects. Some three weeks after the first performance of *Sancta Civitas*, with the General Strike having collapsed due to a lack of support from the public, his Six Studies in English Folk Song, a pleasing sequence for piano and cello was performed in London. He also turned back to an old favourite, the poems of A.E. Housman, and set eight of his texts to a fugal violin accompaniment in the sequence Along the Field. He also began sketching the first movement of the piano concerto that would only be completed and performed some seven years later. But in general the months after the first hearing of *Sancta Civitas* were comparatively quiet ones in Ralph's characteristically busy, driven career as a composer. It was a time when he would continue, even more regularly, to set off on walking holidays in the English countryside he loved so much.

Since Adeline was often not well enough to accompany him, he would arrange to join a party, usually a foursome that included Dorothy

Longman and her husband Robert, the publisher. The fourth walker was usually Frances Farrer, who had taken over as secretary of the Leith Hill Music Festival in 1923. Her father was the second Baron Farrer and her grandfather had been made a peer in 1893 as a result of his energetic activities as a Liberal polemicist and thinker. Now in her early thirties, some twenty years younger than Ralph, Fanny Farrer had grown up at Abinger Hall and so was a close neighbour of Ralph's mother and sister who had continued to live at Leith Hill Place. She was a gifted, enthusiastic organizer and contributed a great deal to the success and steady expansion of the Leith Hill Music Festival during the inter-war years. She continued as secretary until 1940 when she felt compelled to resign in order to devote her considerable energies to her other great commitment, The Women's Institute.

In his film *The Passions of Vaughan Williams*, John Bridcut described Fanny Farrer as having been 'burnt by the Vaughan Williams flame'. In an interview given to the *Vaughan Williams Journal*, the film-maker goes on to speak of evidence supplied by members of the Farrer family.

It became clear that certainly within the family there was a belief that it was a very intense friendship and that she never married and that the family put it down to the strength of feeling she had for Ralph which she never got over ... She was obviously a very attractive woman with enormous spirit and ultimately unfulfilled.[2]

Her great-niece Emma Corke reported that 'Fanny wanted all Vaughan Williams's letters to her burned after her death', describing the request as 'one of the tell-tale signs of her having a broken heart'.

The country walks of Ralph, Fanny Farrer and their companions were often related to his literary passions and inspired by them. His enthusiasm for discovering the England of George Borrow never flagged and he took a special pleasure in walking in areas that figured in the works of Thomas Hardy. For Ralph another favourite novelist and nature writer, famous at the time, was W.H. Hudson. A book Ralph particularly admired was Hudson's *A Shepherd's Life – Impressions of the South Wiltshire Downs*, and for one of their walking excursions he and his three friends set off for this part of the country. Another added incentive for Ralph was that the area was also rich in Hardy associations. The four walked along the Wylye valley, and, as often happened on these rural wanderings, Ralph had something of an adventure. Arriving late in the village of Chitterne, the foursome could not find lodging together. They sought help at the police station and were sent to separate cottages. As Ralph ate his supper his landlady pondered his face with interest. She took a photograph from the mantelpiece and asked if he were one of the army ambulance men in it. Ralph recognized himself and an old comrade, just as that same man, hearing and recognizing Ralph's voice, came hurrying downstairs to greet him. They sat up late into the night, drinking tea and remembering their wartime experiences together. All his life Ralph enjoyed remembering such Borrow-like incidents as he walked the highways and byways of England.

An important country destination for Ralph from this time on was Poynders End near Hitchin in Hertfordshire. Here in 1927, the young Cambridge X-ray crystallographer and enthusiastic musician Bernard Robinson organized the first Music Camp. This was an enterprise inspired by a passionate belief, very much shared by Ralph, in the importance of amateur music. Participants came from all over the country, bringing their tents, living in the most Spartan conditions and sharing the household chores as well as the hectic music-making. Ralph wholeheartedly endorsed the enterprise and often went there, and readily did his bit in the cooking and washing up as well as in the performances.

During 1927 Ralph's interest in composing large musical works revived. At this time he was especially attracted to opera again. Back in 1913 when he had worked as music director for Sir Frank Benson's Shakespeare Company at Stratford-upon-Avon, *The Merry Wives of Windsor* was one of the plays for which he supplied a musical accompaniment. In 1927 he worked to complete an opera based on this play. It would have its first performance some two years later at the Royal College of Music. He trusted to his own, very considerable literary skills for the creation of the libretto, adding to Shakespeare's words other Elizabethan lyrics. He originally intended to entitle the work 'The Fat Knight' but after he had considered the Shakespearean passages he had chosen and the extraneous love songs he had introduced, he decided instead to call his opera *Sir John in Love*. The work inevitably invites comparison with several other operas about the Falstaff character: by Salieri, Nikolai, Holst and Verdi. The version by Verdi has, for well over a century, continued to retain a presence in the opera houses of the world. The same cannot be said of *Sir John in Love*. The comedy here is rarely more than gentle or picturesque. Like his other operas, with the striking exception of *Riders to the Sea*, it does not rank among Ralph's great works of music. Yet undoubtedly the piece has a pleasing charm. It contains excellent tunes and settings both for choir and individual voices.

The other opera that Ralph undertook to compose in 1927 proved far less successful. This was *The Poisoned Kiss*, the text of which had been prepared for him by Evelyn Sharp, the sister of Ralph's old friend and colleague in the English Folk Song and Dance Society, Cecil Sharp. Her libretto was based on a short story from a collection by Richard Garnett, the founder of an early-twentieth-century literary dynasty. This included his son, Edward Garnett, the influential publisher's reader, who encouraged writers such as T.E. Lawrence, Joseph Conrad and D.H. Lawrence. Edward Garnett's grandson David Garnett was a well-known figure around the Bloomsbury Group and the author of *Lady into Fox*, like *A Poisoned Kiss*, a work of fantasy fiction. Evelyn Sharp herself was a well-known figure in the progressive circles with which Ralph, like Gustav Holst, had long been in contact. A very active Socialist and Communist she had been sent to prison for her activities as a suffragette. She was an energetic campaigner on behalf of children and working-class women. She was also a writer of standing and had contributed to *The Yellow Book* back in the 1890s. She had a keen taste for fairy tale fantasy and was well known as a writer of stories for children. *The Poisoned Kiss*, which Richard Garnett based on a Nathaniel Hawthorne story 'Rapaccino's Daughter', strongly appealed to her. It tells the story of a magician who, jilted by a woman of nobler rank than he, has brought up his daughter on a diet laced with poison so that, when one day she meets the son of the arrogant noblewoman, she may with her lips kill him with a kiss. But true love foils this vile plot and all ends happily. The opera shows yet another side of Ralph's multifaceted personality as a composer: his readiness to turn to the lightest, flimsiest of subjects. Here he shows his aptitude for very light opera and operetta. There are also passages that recall the music of pantomime, review and Gilbert and Sullivan. During his collaboration with Evelyn Sharp he was continually trying to lighten the piece, asking her not to be 'high falutin' and 'grand operaish'. But the real problem with the libretto is that many of the lines are clunkingly bad. But Ralph remained committed to it. In the last months of 1927 and indeed for years afterwards as the prospects for the piece grew ever dimmer, he continued to correspond with her about it. After her death in 1955 he even bought the rights to the text from her estate so that, with Ursula's assistance, he might attempt yet again, to make it stageworthy. But Ralph was not destined to revive the English musical. This would be accomplished some eight years after Ralph began *The Poisoned Kiss* by Ivor Novello (the composer of the great World War One hit 'Keep the Home Fires Burning') with the first of his runaway successes *Glamorous Night*. But although it has failed as theatre, *The Poisoned Kiss* is entertaining to listen to. It is melodic throughout and has tunes in a light, lyrical vein such as 'Love breaks all rules', 'Long have I waited', and 'Blue larkspur in a garden' that have great charm.

In early October 1927 when Ralph was very much involved in his collaboration on the opera, Adeline, now fifty-seven, had a very bad fall and broke her thigh. The fracture was so bad that her body was put into a large heavy plaster that extended from her chest to her toes. Her bed had to be brought downstairs and a nurse employed to tend her. At this time, however, Honorine Williamson came to help in the house. She was the charming, bubbly niece of R.O. Morris, husband of Adeline's sister Emmeline. Honorine would become very much a part of the Vaughan Williams household, taking on the role of adopted niece, chauffeur and trouble-shooter for the next twelve years until the time of her death in an air-raid in London in 1940. Adeline's recovery was slow; it was not complete until well into the following year. In the early months of 1928 she and Ralph decided that they should leave the large, several-storeyed house on Cheyne Walk with its many staircases and move into either a flat or a bungalow. They decided to look for somewhere in the Dorking area adjoining Leith Hill where Ralph had grown up. That year they took their summer holiday in a house called The Old Barn in the village of Holmbury St Mary not far from Leith Hill Place and the village of Abinger Hammer where the writer E.M. Forster who had recently completed his most ambitious novel, *A Passage to India,* was then living. From here they set about house-hunting. They eventually decided on White Gates, a large, unusual residence on the western edge of Dorking, a little to the north of the Guildford Road. It was a very modern bungalow-style house having been built some six years before for a family that had returned to Britain from India. Long since demolished, White Gates was one big central and galleried room surrounded by a corridor with smaller rooms leading off, each of them with a large window and window seat. Ralph's study, facing west and south, had a French window opening on to the garden. In here he had a large kitchen table on which to pile scores, manuscripts and music paper. There was also his little upright piano, a desk and a huge armchair. On the walls he hung reproductions of Italian paintings and two landscapes by Ivor Gatty, his friend from his undergraduate days. The big central room of White Gates, known as the hall, contained the grand piano and the dining table. The many books were in shelves in a gallery that ran around the room about ten feet above the floor. Since this was the 1920s the house was one of the first to have been built with a garage. Above was a loft where Ralph stored cat baskets, gardening tools, travel trunks and boxes and boxes of band parts made for the Leith Hill Music Festival.

In the first week of October 1929 Ralph and Adeline sent their friends a printed postcard announcing their change of address. It was a great milestone in Ralph's life. The near thirty years in Chelsea were at an end and the two decades and more in small-town Surrey were beginning. The removal took place at almost the precise moment at which the North Atlantic world underwent one of its most damaging crises. A fortnight after the change of address cards were posted, there came the Wall Street Crash. Ten times the annual budget of the United States was wiped away in days. Economic depression and resulting unemployment spread rapidly across North America and Western Europe. The catastrophe was to sweep away the second Labour Government headed by Ramsay MacDonald which took office that year. The social and political tumult which had so affected Ralph back in the General Strike of 1926 now markedly increased apace. For the next two decades of his life economic depression and then world war provided the context in which his art proceeded.

Ralph had now become a commuter. On his teaching days at the RCM he would take a morning train up to Waterloo and return to his Surrey home in the early evening. Those he taught typically remembered him with affection and gratitude. Elizabeth Maconchy recalled:

> I was a pupil for 6 years. He was not a conventional teacher – and I find it difficult to describe his methods of teaching – his other pupils would probably find the same difficulty. But we should all agree that he was an inspiring teacher – by which I mean that he stimulated us to write better music than we should have done otherwise. And he set an example of absolute musical integrity and complete and uncalculating devotion to music. He had little respect for the rules and conventional methods of teaching composition and never followed a formal scheme.[3]

Elizabeth Maconchy was first taught by Ralph when he 'was in his early

50s and I was 18. It was the beginning of a friendship that lasted to the end of his life'. She went on to remark that:

> perhaps the thing that strikes me most in looking back is how little he changed over all those years. Even his appearance remained almost unchanged. The large looming figure so familiar at the R.C.M. only became a little more stooped and the always rather shuffling walk a little slower. Otherwise he never grew old and was just as he had always been with his lively sympathy and interest in other people and his quick enjoyment of a joke'.

Another student around this time was Michael Mullinar who in later years would greatly assist Ralph in major compositions. When still a young man Michael Mullinar reported: 'Dr Vaughan Williams never forces his own ideas on you when giving instruction in composition.... If he considers that a work which falls short of being satisfactory could possibly be improved, he will offer his ideas, but only as suggestions, and he will not allow you to adopt them unless you really feel that way and can make the ideas your own.' One hears Ralph passing on a central tenet of Hubert Parry's teaching philosophy when the young man continues: 'His leading advice is "That one must always write what one <u>feels</u>, and never what one thinks one ought to feel". He directs you to be yourself, and it does not matter how old you are before you really find yourself.'[4]

Ina Boyle, who between 1928 and 1936 made a point of travelling over from Ireland for intermittent lessons with Ralph, remembered how, in February 1928, he did his utmost to help her when she first submitted her 'Psalm for Cello and Orchestra' for his assessment:

> I was so dreadfully nervous that I could hardly play a note – everything was out of tune and time – it was a perfect nightmare. I think Dr VW was aghast, but he was gentle and patient beyond words and did everything to make it easy for me. He never said a word about it being out of time, though it must have been agonising ... he then went over it again bit by bit, altering anything that seemed necessary.... I felt so dreadfully sorry to have gone so entirely to pieces ... yet in a way it was one of the most helpful lessons I ever had, and I never felt more grateful to anyone than I did for the consideration and sympathy he showed about it.[5]

In the early days in the new house in Surrey correspondence with Evelyn Sharp about *The Poisoned Kiss* went on unabated. It is an indication of Ralph's great versatility as a composer that at the same time he continued to work on this lightweight piece, he was also involved in negotiations about what would become of one of his major works, his *Job, A Masque for Dancing*. The subject was very much in keeping with these times of trial and suffering. The project originated back in 1927, which was the hundredth anniversary of the death of William Blake. Geoffrey Keynes, a Blake scholar, surgeon and balletomane, set out to commemorate the centennial by creating a ballet based on Blake's *Illustrations of the Book of Job*. Keynes wrote a scenario relating the story of Job's life and trials. He then turned to his wife's sister, the artist Gwen Raverat, the author of *Period Piece*, to design the stage sets. Geoffrey Keynes's brother, the economist Maynard Keynes, was one of those who agreed to help with the financing of the ballet. The project was also supported by the Camargo Society, an important new organization in the history of the art of dance in Britain. During the 1920s the Camargo Society, comprising numerous wealthy and prominent people, sought to establish and promote ballet in London by mounting productions that employed dancers from the Marie Rambert and Ninette de Valois groups. A very active member of this group was the music critic Edwin Evans, Ralph's advocate of years before. For the music for the ballet, perhaps at Evans's suggestion, Geoffrey Keynes turned to Ralph who was quickly stimulated and inspired by the subject. He had intense, lengthy discussions about the music for *Job* with his friend Gustav Holst, writing, years later: 'I should be alarmed to say how many "Field Days" we spent over it … he came to all the orchestral rehearsals…. I owe the life of *Job* to Holst.'[6]

Geoffrey Keynes submitted the ballet to Serge Diaghilev whose Ballets Russes was now, after the upheavals of the war, based in Monte Carlo. But the famous dance impresario rejected it for being 'too English' and 'too old-fashioned'. However, Ralph was not greatly dismayed by this rejection. Writing to his collaborator and distant relative, Gwen Raverat, he commented:

I never expected Djag [*sic*] wd look at it – and I'm glad on the whole – the reclame wd have been rather amusing – but it really wdnt have suited the sham serious really decadent and frivolous attitude of the R.B. [Russian Ballet] toward everything – can you imagine Job

206

sandwiched between *Les Biches* and *Cimarosiana* – and that dreadful pseudo cultured audience saying to each other 'My dear, have you seen God at the Russian ballet?' No – I think we are well out of it'.[7]

Nevertheless, it is clearly the case, as Percy M. Young has maintained, that *Job* arose from the vogue for ballet which, after Diaghilev, greatly affected English musical development both in respect of creation and appreciation. And as the same critic allows, the masque was an art form that had developed a very distinctive tradition in England.

> Masquing was a part of the development of civilisation which in England culminated in the courtly entertainments of the Tudors and, more especially, the Stuarts. The masque of the seventeenth century was a blend of poetry – most gracefully represented in the works in the genre of Campion, William Browne and Milton; drama, allegory and topical comment – as in Ben Johnson; mise en scene in which the achievements of Inigo Jones reached a peak of imaginative design; and dance. Vaughan Williams interprets an aspect of (this) English tradition, albeit the tradition went underground three centuries ago.

Becoming more specific, Young comments that 'The Satanic music of the masque recalls the implications of the symbolised Evils of Ben Johnson's *The Golden Age Restored*'.

Despite the Diaghilev rejection of this 'too English' work, Ralph pressed on with the completion of what was becoming a very substantial composition. Rehearsals were held at the RCM in October 1930 and that same month *Job* had its first performance at Norwich. In the following February Ralph again conducted a performance broadcast from the original studios of the BBC on Savoy Hill. In July 1931 the Camargo Society gave the first stage performance at the Cambridge Theatre in London. The sometime Ballet Russes dancer Anton Dolin danced the role of Satan and the young Constant Lambert conducted the orchestra. The choreography was by Ninette de Valois. The first public stage performance of *Job* took place later in the year at the Old Vic where there would be further performances into 1932.

The work requires more than fifty minutes to perform and is made up of nine scenes. It contains memorable orchestral effects and colouring with some striking passages for individual instruments, some of them (the xylophone and the tenor saxophone, for instance) still unusual in concert orchestras at the end of the 1920s. Yet the soundscape also contains within it a subtle structuring that brings before the listener challenging, philosophical, religious and ultimately metaphysical issues.

Following the Old Testament narrative, the ballet begins with an introduction in which slow, steady orchestral rhythms and then rustic passages for flute and viola evoke the pastoral well-being of the patriarch Job and his family. But there comes a dramatic disturbance. Descending octaves on strings and bassoon introduce the Satan figure that will seek to disturb and destroy such human contentment. There follows the 'Saraband of the Sons of God', a movement which announces a countervailing power; it is set in music that has a beautiful stateliness. Yet the Satanic returns still more forcefully and aggressively in the second scene. Satan's Dance of Triumph is made up of mocking yet menacing sounds, prominent among which is the raucous, irreverent clatter of the xylophone. The scene builds to a magnificent climax in an *alla marcia* driven by blaring trombones. The third scene is the Minuet of the Sons of Job and Their Wives. The courtly dance reveals the assured, elegant complacency of the young things who are the sharers and inheritors of the Job patrimony. But their graceful life is slowly undermined, then violently racked, by the shrill destructive discords that are the sounds of Satan. The fourth scene – the middle one, entitled 'Job's Dream' – brings us to the very centre of the drama; it evokes the very nadir of Job's downfall, his loss of his possessions, his family and, as a result of his loss of his trust and belief in God, his own selfhood. The thudding pizzicato and the frenetic 1920s jazz sounds give us Job's dizzying panic and mental disorder. The fifth scene begins the second half of the ballet, the journey back, the journey to redemption. Here, a delicate cantabile melody for the first violin emerges from the heavy, throbbing percussion to offer some tenuous reassurance. The sixth scene shows a failure to develop this; here comes the music of self-pity, with blues-style whining on the saxophone. But this in turn is swept away by the thundering of the Almighty which resonates in the powerful, dominating organ sound. A more human voice of redemption introduces itself in the seventh scene, Elihu's Dance of Youth and Beauty; Job is here reassured by his neighbour Elihu, in a lyrical, then increasingly excited and finally ecstatic violin solo. The Satan theme attempts one more entrance only to be swept away by God in music of calm command. Scene Eight, The Galliard of the Sons of the Morning is an assured, stately music of triumph that is in no way triumphalist. The penultimate scene, Altar Dance, an *allegretto* of controlled joyousness, culminates in one last concluding surge of happiness. The ninth scene, the final one, takes us back to the quiet, steady contentment evoked by the very first movement of the ballet. The effect of this return is no less than a subtle intimation of the eternal. It is a fine example of Ralph's profound, laid-back ambitiousness as an artist. The first and last movements of *Job* constitute a frame that contains and ultimately supervenes man's struggle with the Satanic and the destructive. Before, after and (the musical structure implies) above human doubt, despair and conflict there can be heard the sounds of another reality. It is surely significant that Ralph as an act of his particular kind of faith chose this passage to be played at his funeral. At the end of *Job* we are very much aware of Ralph not only as a composer of music but as, however soft-spokenly, a philosopher and visionary.

Chapter Thirteen

WHITE GATES

Amonth before *Job* had its first performance in Norwich came the
shocking news of a dramatic election result in Germany. The
National Socialists led by Adolf Hitler had established themselves as
the second largest party in the Reichstag. In the aftermath of the Wall
Street catastrophe world economic conditions continued to worsen.
In Germany inflation was rampant and became terrifying. In Britain
the Labour government lost the confidence of the markets and had
to consider drastic reductions in public spending. The Labour leader
Ramsay MacDonald went into coalition with the Conservatives and
some Liberals to create what was called the National Government. In the
general election of 1931 the coalition heavily defeated the remnant of the
Labour Party which had refused to join the National Government. But
economic conditions in Britain, as elsewhere in the North Atlantic countries, continued in a state of depression. Unemployment was widespread.
The high hopes that had accompanied the ending of the First World
War and that, for Ralph, had been dimmed in the perplexing confu-
sions of 1926, were now obliterated by far worse and more frightening
prospects at home and abroad. During the early 1930s Ralph would also
encounter a series of personal difficulties. In such hard times he began
and completed his major work of the decade, the Fourth Symphony.

For their first few years at White Gates, Ralph and Adeline lived there
as renters. Perhaps they were unsure (Ralph especially) about the right-
ness of leaving London and settling in the country. In November 1930
they were back in the capital enjoying a stay at the Eversleigh Hotel at 105

Cromwell Road, where, for some years, they would stay when in London. Because of her arthritis Adeline found it difficult to leave the hotel, so various female friends accompanied Ralph to entertainments in central London. Fanny Farrer went with him to a performance of Gustav Holst's *The Planets*. And the lively Peg Richie who years before had taken him off to fancy-dress balls at the Slade School of Art and who was now a qualified doctor, was his occasional companion for a theatre evening. They went to the Old Vic to see *The Jealous Wife* by George Coleman the Elder, an eighteenth-century comedy based on Henry Fielding's *Tom Jones*. It has a rollicking, earthy humour which Ralph would have enjoyed. The high point of the London stay was the concert Ralph helped to organize to showcase the compositions of his brother-in-law, Emmeline's husband R.O. Morris, a fellow musician who also now taught at the Royal College of Music and was a specialist in counterpoint. Ralph had long felt that 'Morris', as the Fisher sisters called him, had been handicapped in his advancement by his extreme shyness. There had also been the disappointing episode of a few years before when Morris and Emmy had returned to England after a dispute that made them feel unable to continue on at the Faculty of the Curtis Institute that had been founded in Philadelphia in 1924.

With characteristic energy, enthusiasm and generosity Ralph threw himself into the concert of music by his old housemate at Cheyne Walk. It was a great success. The two beautiful sisters, Jelly d'Aranyi and Adila Fachiri, were the star soloists. Jelly played Morris's Concerto in G minor and the two of them together played his Concerto for Two Violins. Writing of the London visit to her young friend Rosamond Carr, Adeline reported: 'The climax was the Morris concerto – lovely. We feel so satisfied – we were so happy about the music itself – the hall was almost brimming over.... Morris was angelic, a surprise to us all! It was most warming to my heart to see him on the platform bowing to the outburst of shouts and clapping – a real ovation'....[1]

After the concert, family members were among those invited to the new home of Edmund Fisher, Adeline's youngest brother, who years before had minded visitors' horses outside the house in Barton Street but was now rapidly progressing in what proved to be a highly successful career in banking. At the party, according to Adeline, Ralph eagerly ate and drank everything in sight. And when smoked salmon appeared later on, he ate a good deal of that too. His eating would become excessive and one of his difficulties during these years was his struggle to control his weight. Another of the happy occasions during this London visit was a tea-party ('just the perfect party' according to Adeline) which Dorothy Longman put on for them. But, Adeline insisted after their return to Dorking, 'he is glad to be in the country again and I see it is best to live among the cabbages and have an orgy now and again....'[2]

Whether Ralph saw it that way may be doubted. As Ursula has commented of the departure from Chelsea, it was not long before Ralph realized:

> just how much more bother it was going to be, however excellent the train service, for him to enjoy from Dorking the musical life he had had for the past thirty years. He loved the country for walks, expeditions and bicycling – but to go back and live in it, which he had not done since he left Cambridge, was a very different matter. He had long felt himself essentially a Londoner and he never ceased to miss the town life, 'the pleasure of wandering into the Tate gallery for an hour, the river in front of his window, and most of all the Bach Choir rehearsals.'[3]

The necessary giving up of the conductorship of the Bach Choir in London was a particularly painful loss for Ralph. Bach, of course, was the composer whom he revered before all others. He also greatly enjoyed the fellowship and the fun involved in the rehearsals. As he regretfully handed over the conductorship to his friend, Adrian Boult, he gave him advice that clearly suggests his own brisk, purposive, down-to-earth approach to preparing the choir. He wrote, 'Don't wait to start practice till everybody is ready or you will never start at all. I always used to kick off at 5.30 sharp whoever was or wasn't there and however much row was going on in the bargain centre behind the curtain. Always insist on 2 band rehearsals. The extra rehearsal only costs about £25 which is a drop in the ocean compared with our own total loss on each concert.'[4]

Ralph's troubled ambivalence about his leaving London is very likely another of the emotional triggers of the Fourth Symphony now well into its composition, a work which takes on the subjects of impatience, frustration and rage. Nevertheless, if he was now prevented from continuing with his beloved Bach Choir in London, his profound commitment to the music of Bach could still be lived out in Dorking. He was now settled in the town that was the home of the Leith Hill Music Festival. Early in 1931 the building of the Dorking Halls was completed and the festival began to be held there. In January, Ralph's sister Meggie died. She had been one of its founders and long-time sustainers. In her memory there was a very special performance of the St Matthew Passion. The choir was drawn from all the competing groups in the festival and amounted to nearly eight hundred singers. They greatly outnumbered the audience; the large new hall could only accommodate five hundred.

During 1931 no new music by Ralph was performed, though he continued to work on the new symphony and on the piano concerto which he had first sketched out some five years before. But this year he did see the publication of a new and enlarged edition of *Songs of Praise*; among the new, original hymn tunes was one entitled 'White Gates' and another 'Abinger', the home of the Farrer family. During the hot, oppressive summer of that year Ralph, encouraged by the young and lively Honorine, played a good deal of tennis and went for long walks and bicycle rides, often with Fanny Farrer. He also sought solitude. On the last day of August Adeline reported: 'Here it is steamy heat. R off on his bicycle [*sic*] ... a few cheeses in his pocket and means to be out til tea'.[5] At this time, Ralph's mother, bereaved and lonely at Leith Hill Place after the death of Meggie, came over to stay at the Dorking house. Adeline told Rosamond Carr that: 'she has brought a little dog with her which gives her an interest and help [*sic*] her to feel more at home in this house. I have moved my bed into Honorine's room, R. into his work room,' Adeline added, 'quite amusing'.[6]

In the autumn Ralph was approached by the Dean of the Anglican Cathedral in Liverpool, on behalf of the Archbishop of Canterbury with a view to conferring upon him a Lambeth Doctorate in Music. The proposed honour was very likely a recognition of Ralph's long-standing work in hymnology. Ralph declined the doctorate, commenting that he '... drifted into hymns more or less by accident'. He also stated unequivocally that 'I have no real connection with anything ecclesiastical and no longer count myself a member of the Church of England.'[7] Nevertheless, he was prepared to accept a secular honour from the city of Liverpool. Just before Christmas 1931 he travelled there to accept an honorary degree of Doctor of Laws from the university. In presenting Ralph to the Chancellor, Lord Derby, the University's public orator, described his achievement as one that appealed to conservative, musical taste:

In music, as in other arts, we have our innovators: who believe that to be original it is necessary to be difficult. Austere and self-denying, they pursue a strenuous and unlovely Muse along uncharted ways, and panting amateurs tail after them in vain. Ralph Vaughan Williams worships at the shrine of a less athletic beauty. His melodies and harmonies are not less original for being comprehensible. He is no mere imitator. He is the author of many works, songs and symphonies, choral works and operas, and they are all unmistakably his own. But his novelty is based on antiquity; growing freely, though rooted in the past. He is a scholar as well as an artist, a learned, though never a pedantic, musician, he has refreshed our memory by his study of the early music of our country, folk song and the formal composition of the masters created when delight in ordered sound was common among us.

Exactly a week after the ceremony there was, as Adeline noted, 'a quiet Christmas day' at White Gates. There was a bottle of Australian port given by Robert Trevelyan, a Surrey neighbour and a poet and scholar who was the brother of Ralph's old Cambridge friend, the historian George Trevelyan. Honorine 'cooked a fine Turkey [sic] and we browsed over our presents. As was customary Ralph read aloud to the company, on this occasion Dickens's A Christmas Carol, a story for which he had plans to compose a ballet. After that we listened to the wireless ending at the King's speech (that might have been better?).'[8]

On Boxing Day Ralph took the train to Cardiff in order to conduct Toward the Unknown Region and 'Four Hymns' before an audience in a nearby coal-mining village. Were these inspirational works offered as a gesture of sympathy and support for working people threatened with increasing privation and poverty at this moment of intensifying economic and political instability? Adeline insisted that Ralph, usually somewhat careless in his dress, made a special effort for this holiday concert in front of Welsh coal-miners in what was termed at the time a 'distressed area'. 'He has taken his white waistcoat and will be wearing his very best.' Ralph remembered the beauty of the singing by the Welsh choir and also the extremely strong tea which he shared with his hosts, staying late to talk to them. It was an occasion on which he would see the realities of the Depression at first hand.

The following day his strenuous generosity led him to London where he took the singing class at the Christmas School organized by the English Folk Dance and Song Society. On New Year's Day Gustav Holst, who was shortly to set off on a visit to the United States, came to White

Gates to help Ralph with the fully emerging Fourth Symphony. Vally Lasker and Helen Bidder, another colleague from St Paul's Girl's School, played the score on two pianos. A few days later when Ralph had returned to his duties at the RCM the two women again played the piece for him, this time at the school. Ralph invited his young friend Gerald Finzi to come and hear it. A week or so later Ralph extended his characteristic kindness to another young composer, the 18-year-old Benjamin Britten, then studying at the Royal College. Ralph sent two psalm settings by the young man to Ivor Atkins, the organist at Worcester Cathedral; they were performed there that autumn.

During the spring and summer of 1932 Ralph worked on a series of lectures which he had been invited to give in the United States. These were the Mary Flexner Lectures, recognized as a prestigious, annual academic and intellectual occasion and delivered at Bryn Mawr, a liberal arts college for women, ten miles west of Philadelphia. The previous year the lectures had been given by the philosopher Alfred North Whitehead. Ralph's successor the following year would be Erwin Panofsky, the eminent art historian. On the occasion of this second visit to America, ten years after the first, there could be no question of Adeline accompanying her husband. Her arthritis and her difficulty in moving about made it impossible for her to travel. So in the late autumn he sailed on his own, on the *Empress of Britain*, from Southampton to New York. He found the city 'more classically and tragically beautiful than ever' and again 'had a wonderful experience at the top of the "Empire State", first sunset over the river and all the skyscrapers suddenly lighting up. Then all the street lights came out and the moon!'

In the small college town of Bryn Mawr his hosts installed him at the College Inn where, he told Gustav Holst, 'I am fairly happy and everyone is v. hospitable'.[9] He seems to have found his audience of female undergraduates somewhat daunting. 'I have to stand up before a class the day after each lecture and be heckled by a crowd of young women – who ask me 'what I mean by' then they refer to their notebooks'. A little apprehensively he added, 'I've come off fairly unscathed to the present'.[10]

Ralph entitled his series of lectures 'National Music'. He later published them as a book. The argument was a familiar one in his early writings. Music has its roots in a particular place and a particular people and folk song is the origin of much that comes later, both in ecclesiastical and secular music. Important references in Ralph's developing thesis are to Cecil Sharp, his old friend and fellow folklorist and to his old teacher

Hubert Parry whose Darwinian perspective, *The Evolution of the Art of Music,* supplies several important quotations. Very much in Ralph's mind too was the distinguished Classicist and close friend of H.A.L. Fisher, Gilbert Murray, who had helped him back in 1911 when he was working on his *Bacchae* ballet for Isadora Duncan. More than once he cites Gilbert Murray's aphorism that 'the genius may be a rebel against tradition, but at the same time he is a child of it'.[11] Murray helps Ralph broaden his argument about music as an evolutionary phenomenon into a broader contention: 'Thus you see it is possible to ascribe communal authorship even to a book. To quote Professor Murray once again, "The *Iliad* and the *Odyssey* represent not the independent invention of one man, but the ever-moving tradition of many generations of men." If this can be true of the book, how much more so of purely oral music and poetry.'[12]

As the lectures progress and Ralph comes on to the present and to the future in music, he begins to sound less confident. There is an ambivalence in his argument. On the one hand he finds Emerson and Whitman helpful allusions in front of his American audience as he seeks to envision a new music of the people: 'We are too apt to divide our music into popular and classical, the highbrow and the lowbrow. One day perhaps we shall find an ideal music which will be neither popular or classical, highbrow or lowbrow, but an art in which all can take part.... When will our art achieve such a triumph? Is this popularisation of music merely a Whitmanesque fantasy? At present it is only a dream, but it is a realisable dream.'[13] But, on the other hand such a fusion is hard to reconcile with Ralph's repeated insistence on the spiritual component in music: 'music cannot be treated like cigars or wine, as a mere commodity. It has its spiritual value as well. It shares in preserving the identity of soul of the individual and of the nation.' And what about American soul, the particular contribution of the United States to the evolution of music? On this subject Ralph is uncertain. At one point he refers to jazz as 'Negroid emetics'. This phrase is an instance of the kind of casual contempt, sometimes found in Ralph's writings, which could alienate his readers, his lifelong critic Ernest Newman being a conspicuous example. Later on in his lectures Ralph is more moderate in his comments on the subject, but still sceptical. He maintains that people are 'wrong in despising jazz, but I do not go so far as to say as some thinkers do that it has in it the seeds of great further development'. He adds that 'musical vitality in America ... may manifest itself in some other form which has in it the elements of greatness.'[14]

Like W.B. Yeats, another near contemporary visiting an institution for female education, Ralph, lecturing at Bryn Mawr, presents the persona of the 'smiling public man'; he also refers to his views as those of 'an old fogey'. Nevertheless, at the same time he proposes some innovative ideas for the future of music. Improbably, he even contemplates a Soviet-style 'five year plan'. In such a planned period 'only indigenous music would be allowed for five years'. He recognizes that 'the objections are obvious', but does not stay to tackle them. He concludes instead with two rhetorical quotations: one in prose, one in verse, and both of them of German origin. The latter is three lines sung by Hans Sachs at the end of Wagner's *Meistersinger* which raises 'to its highest power all that is best in the national consciousness of his own country':

Honour your own masters;
Then even when Empires fall
Our sacred nation's art will remain.

The prose quotation which Ralph chose for his conclusion is from Gustav Stresemann, a German of more liberal views than Wagner, who was a prominent statesman in the Weimar Republic, the polity which had governed Germany after its defeat in the First World War. His attempts to promote reconciliation with France in the post-war years had brought him a Nobel Peace Prize. In his 'Some Conclusions' lecture at Bryn Mawr Ralph ends by quoting, with obvious approval, the liberal humane nationalism expressed succinctly in a single sentence of Stresemann: 'The man who serves humanity best is he who rooted in his own nation develops his spiritual and moral endowments to their highest capacity, so that growing beyond the limits of his own nation he is able to give something to the whole of humanity.'

Just a few weeks after Ralph quoted these words in a small college town in rural Pennsylvania, President Hindenburg appointed Adolf Hitler Chancellor of Germany. The Weimar Republic together with its liberal aspirations was a thing of the past. The Nazi vision of nationhood was now at the centre of European politics.

In the weeks following his return to Surrey from America, Ralph put the final touches to a concerto which he had written for the glamorous and famous pianist Harriet Cohen. Some two weeks before his departure for the United States he had conducted at the Three Choirs Festival at Worcester the first performance of his *Magnificat* written for another well-known female performer, the contralto Astra Desmond. The sparking of this composition had occurred a year earlier at the Gloucester Festival, when Ralph's old friend, the tenor Steuart Wilson, had commented on the Virgin Mary's hymn of acceptance of the divine will. With the fastidious *pudeur* characteristic of the English middle class as late as the 1930s Wilson had remarked that 'It is not quite nice that young, unmarried women should always be singing *Magnificats*'. The distinguished recitalist and sometimes opera singer, Astra Desmond, who was with them retorted 'I'm a married woman with three children so why don't you write one for me?' Ralph said he would and he kept his promise. He dedicated the work to Astra who was the first to sing the solo part. To express musically the presence of the Holy Spirit is an immense challenge for a composer. Ralph here manages to meet it in his characteristically laid-back way. The divine command, encouragement and will are intimated in the flute cadenzas that contrast tellingly with the nervous ambivalence in the vocal part expressing the responses of the submissive girl. The *Magnificat* is a delicate, touching composition which subtly conveys the happiness and uncertainty of the Virgin Mary at the time of the Annunciation.

The Piano Concerto in C major, which Harriet Cohen premiered in January 1933, is a much longer work and had a far longer gestation. The work derived from one of Ralph's more rhetorical, avuncular flirtations. When the 'Dearest Harriet' of the correspondence prompted him in November 1931 to complete the work for her, the remuneration she offered was apparently 10,000 kisses. Ralph replied, 'How can I say "no" – when such a reward will be mine if I say "yes"? I shall claim it to the full....'[15] Harriet was the long-time lover of Ralph's friend, the composer Arnold Bax, and an early version of the work contains a quotation from Bax's Third Symphony. Ralph wanted the two bars cited played in a special way: 'the two bars of Arnold – I like them slower ... quite slow and very far off like a dream.'[16] After the first performance Ralph decided that the quotation did not fit in and he removed it. But clearly the work was born of a trio of human relationships, two lovers and their good friend. Harriet Cohen, who was thirty-seven years old when she gave the first performance of the concerto, was a very attractive woman. She was something of a socialite and was prominent not only in the music world of the time but also in literary and political circles. At different times she had friendships with D.H. Lawrence, George Bernard Shaw and H.G. Wells. Her closeness to the newspaper proprietor Max Aitken,

Lord Beaverbrook, was a reason she was one of the most publicized and photographed performers of classical music. Arnold Bax created works specifically for her and so did other composers, including Ralph's close contemporary John Ireland and slightly younger ones such as Ernest Bloch, E.J. Moeran and Béla Bartók. Perhaps Harriet's keen interest in the music of Bartók may have encouraged the emergence of the striking new, jagged and percussive soundscape of Ralph's concerto. When Bartók himself heard the concerto a few years later, he admired it.

Ralph completed the first draft of the work by the end of May 1931 when he heard it played through on three pianos at St Paul's Girls School by three of Holst's associates: Helen Bidder, Nora Day and (Ralph's correspondent over a number of years) Vally Lasker. On 14 July he sent a corrected score to Harriet, writing: 'If you don't like it send it back. If you do like it I will come and claim my reward.' Ralph later had misgivings about this version telling Adrian Boult 'what I am frightened about in this concerto is the balance; it may be overscored.... I give you carte blanche to thin out the score all you wish if you do not think the pfte [pianoforte] will come through enough....' The work which was dedicated to Harriet was finally performed at a BBC Symphony Concert on 1 February 1933, the day after Hitler came to power. The programme included other modern works: Delius's *Sea Drift* and Bax's *The Garden of Fand*.

The concerto is an exciting work which reveals a conspicuous expansion of Ralph's musical range. It is the music of upset, very much a work of the 1930s. The toccata which opens the work sounds out a violence previously unheard in his compositions. Beginning with the first notes there bursts out a relentless, at times strident, pounding that expresses anger, frustration, destructiveness. Does this refer to personal, social or political experiences? In any event it shows Ralph widely distancing himself from the traditionalism for which he was so highly praised at the degree ceremony at the University of Liverpool. Now we hear Modernist idiom that shows Ralph's awareness of the music of Bartók and Hindemith and, perhaps too, a new understanding of the experiential disruptions which lay behind their compositions.

The thunderous agitated opening bars are curtailed by the entry of some British cheerfulness; in comes a pacy, jaunty theme that is not far from the sounds of British light music. (In a few years' time Ralph will be musically explicit about his respect for the work of the highly popular radio conductor Henry Hall.) But this too is but a phase in the concerto;

there next comes a development of the piano's repeated note figure and a building up to an intense and difficult tension. This is finally released into a rippling piano cadenza that slows into quietness. The ending is a great contrast with the beginning. We are aware of an emotional process or journey. The first of the experiential antitheses underlying the intricate musical patterning has been established.

The second movement, by far the longest of the four, begins quietly meditative and moves into increasingly melancholy reflection. As the soloist in the company of flute, oboe and horn continues to muse we are very close to Bax's Celtic world of dreaming. But then comes a brightening which leads to some decisive insistencies, some calls to order from the piano. But at the end melancholy returns with the piano very dark. The third movement, the *Fuga Cromatica*, returns us to the coarseness of the public world with crude rhythms that remind us of the music hall and the bandstand. The piano interrupts this and takes over. It plays busily and becomes authoritative. As confidence grows, there develops a certain storminess that undermines steadiness. But the violence then eddies away into a cadenza which brings us to the finale. The vulgarities of the public world return to the sounds of a schmaltzy waltz. The piano steps in and deliberates. In the course of the movement it moves nimbly from the speculative to the confident and then, in another cadenza, slowly tails away ending in spaced out notes that confirm a quiet, confident, delicately noted state of acquiescence. With distinct hushed strings at the close we complete the process that has led to a coming to terms with the alarming percussive disturbance that began the concerto.

Ralph was pleased with the first public performance; he attended it with Fanny Farrer. He thanked the conductor Adrian Boult, telling him: 'I could not have imagined a better first performance'.[17] Boult himself was less pleased. Ten years later he wrote: 'It is surely common knowledge that Harriet Cohen's performance of the Vaughan Williams Pianoforte Concerto caused it to be completely dropped since it was first performed. The work (very stupidly as it was <u>written</u> for Harriet Cohen) was laid out for a pianist of the Busoni calibre, and though she made a very valiant effort, she could get nowhere near the spirit of it or even the notes in many passages.'

Harriet's lover Arnold Bax was greatly impressed by the concerto. His biographer reports that 'In a letter to the composer Herbert Howells from the late 1930s Bax wrote, 'Personally I love that work of Ralph's and like it indeed better than anything else of his I know. I don't think it is right formally at the end, for the last cadenza confuses the issue, but in my view that dynamo-like toccata is splendid and the *stretto* of the fugue one of the most stimulating bits of primitive violence in all music.'[18]

After the Second World War Ralph reworked the finale which had troubled Bax. Speaking of Howard Shelley's recording of the concerto in 1984 with Vernon Handley conducting, Simon Heffer has supplied a helpful and correctly unambiguous judgement of the work. 'It was not until many years after the composer's death, when it was at last brilliantly recorded in the original version but with the revised ending, that it quickly took its place as one of the most sublime works ever written for the piano by an English composer'.[19]

Whatever his views of the Piano Concerto in C major and the first soloist's performance, Boult was incorrect in saying that it was 'completely dropped'. The German conductor Hermann Scherchen included it in a programme for a concert in Strasbourg some months later. And in the following year, in August 1934, Harriet Cohen gave a repeat performance with, again, Ralph in the audience. Adeline listened to the concert on the wireless set at White Gates, reporting to her sister that 'Ralph's day in London was a complete success. He left at 8.30 am and returned at 10.30 pm and slept better than he has done for a long time. I listened in of course. 1st movement very craggy and the orch almost smothered. 2nd movement more flexible – Harriet more at ease throughout – last movement came out more clearly.'

Adeline also passed on Ralph's report that for the performance Harriet 'was in grey silk with a train'.

A fortnight after the premiere of the piano concerto, Ralph took the boat-train to Belfast where, on 17 February 1933, he conducted a concert dedicated to his work. While in Ulster he stayed with his cousin Mary Massingberd and her husband at their grand Ascendancy mansion, Blessingbourne, at Fivemiletown in County Tyrone. To their son, Peter Montgomery, Ralph wrote a long, carefully considered letter about the prospects for a young man contemplating a career in music. Back in London, Ralph in his 'Uncle Ralph' persona so frequently adopted when dealing with young women, was very pleased to congratulate his Irish student, Elizabeth Maconchy ('My Darling Betty') who had won a prize in the *Daily Telegraph* chamber music competition. Later the same year Harriet Cohen joined him in helping to promote a concerto that Elizabeth had written. With his characteristic solicitude for his students, past and present, Ralph also strove during this year to assist the career of the young Australian composer Alex Burnard who, years later, would be described by his compatriot Percy Grainger as 'exactly what the highest flight of Australian musical genius should be'.[20]

March 1933 was an historic month for the world. On 4 March, in the midst of a grim economic depression, Franklin Delano Roosevelt was inaugurated as President of the United States and his massive programme of public works known as the New Deal was begun. Less than three weeks later an Enabling Act in the German *Reichstag* granted Adolf Hitler the powers of a dictator. Nazi policies were rapidly introduced during the spring and the summer. In April, Julius Streicher, the editor of the Nazi newspaper *Der Stürmer* and publisher of anti-semitic books for children, organized a nation-wide boycott of Jewish businesses. The following month in just about every German city and university town the Nazis organized public burnings of thousands of books they considered decadent. But in Surrey, regular routines continued. In April, Ralph once more conducted at the Leith Hill Music Festival. The following month he and Adeline finally made up their minds to purchase White Gates. Adeline told her sister 'R went to see his lawyer yesterday – and now we really can say we bought White Gates – £3,200 is the price – and now we must build on or build a bungalow for R's mother.... More and more it comes out how uncomf [*sic*] her life is at L[eith] H[ill] P[lace].' The cowboy-built annexe they finally decided on, proved to be, in the account of one relative, 'a disaster'. In the middle of these difficulties and the ominous, disturbing news from Germany, Ralph suffered a personal setback. At midnight on 27 June he was walking to White Gates from the Dorking railway station after one of his almost daily trips to London and in the bright moonlight decided to take a short cut across a field in which a path ran by a stream. But clouds darkened the moon and Ralph stumbled and fell into the water. It was a two-foot drop and the 61-year-old Ralph broke his ankle, cracking the fibula in two places. He was ordered to bed for the next two weeks and then needed crutches to get about. Adeline reported: 'We have a nurse to come in every morning ... his great weight makes it such a problem'.[21]

The accident can only have added to the frustration and discontent that appear to have affected Ralph during these months and years, the ones that saw the writing of the Fourth Symphony. A first worry was that he might have difficulty attending the wedding of his young friend Gerald Finzi who was about to marry Joy Black, a beautiful, tall girl with whom Ralph greatly enjoyed playing tennis. Ralph explained his predicament to Finzi in six succinct sentences in a dictated letter:

- (a) I fell into the brook
- (b) I broke my ancle [*sic*]
- (c) I mayn't put my foot to the ground for a month.

But – (a) I have no pain
       (b) I am quite well
       (c) I was not drunk at the time

In the event Ralph was able to make it to the ceremony and the young couple's wedding reception was held at White Gates amidst furniture covered with dust sheets while builders worked on the ill-fated annexe. Ralph's recovery was sufficiently swift that he was able to fulfil his commitment to conduct his 'Pastoral Symphony' at the Proms on 31 August, though he needed assistance to climb up on to the podium and to get down. The builders' activities at White Gates now became sufficiently disruptive that Ralph and Adeline were compelled to move out for several weeks. After taking Ralph's mother for a short holiday at Eastbourne, they accepted the loan of the London flat owned by Hervey and Constance Vaughan Williams, Ralph's brother and sister-in-law. Based at 11 Roxburgh Mansions in Kensington Court, not far from Parry's old house that had meant so much to him, Ralph was again able to keep well up with London concerts. On 12 November Adeline noted a typical evening of this time: 'We have just had sup and now R has taken Fanny [Farrer] to Phil concert – all togged up and she in a noble black dress with glittering straps.'[22] The same day, Harriet Cohen sent the Vaughan Williamses flowers with a note announcing that she had made a piano arrangement of one of Ralph's forgotten works from the past, his Charterhouse Suite. Harriet would perform it towards Christmastime with the 28-year-old Constant Lambert conducting the orchestra.

The year of 1934 was to bring great losses to English music. In January, it was known that Edward Elgar was dying. Ralph had known him for about a quarter of a century. Early on, the relationship had been somewhat guarded, probably because of Elgar's sensitivity to published criticisms of him ('vulgarity' was a word used) by Ralph's long-standing friend, Edward J. Dent. Elgar was wary of what he perceived as a musical establishment centering upon Dent, Hugh Allen and Ralph, which he thought disrespectful of his work. But over the years Elgar and Ralph grew friendlier as they continued to encounter each other at the Three Choirs

Festival. In a BBC talk in 1957 Ralph recalled that Elgar was 'always gracious and friendly'. 'He wished us to be on Christian name terms, and even invited me to call him Teddy. This I could not do. He was at least ten years older than me and was already famous, so I compromised, agreeing to drop Sir and Dr'. Later on Elgar was a great admirer of *Sancta Civitas*. At one of their last meetings, in 1932, he also gave Ralph what proved to be a fruitful idea; he suggested that Ralph make a setting of 'Elinor Rumming', the bawdy characterization by the sixteenth-century poet John Skelton. Elgar's urging was an important impetus behind what proved to be one of Ralph's finest, most entertaining works, his Five Tudor Portraits. In February 1934 Ralph wrote the terminally ill Elgar an affectionate letter telling him of an imminent performance of *The Dream of Gerontius* that he was going to conduct at the Leith Hill Music Festival. 'Whether we shall do it well I do not know. But if enthusiasm and hard work can achieve anything be sure that it will not lack these.' With humility and tenderness Ralph concluded: 'And it will be one of the greatest moments of my life when I stand with trembling baton to conduct it – we have good soloists – Astra Desmond, Steuart Wilson and Harold Williams – and we shall think of you – please give us your blessing'.[23]

In the event Ralph's act of homage was extremely well received and widely admired. Typical of the responses were the words of Willie H. Reed, leader of the London Symphony Orchestra which performed that day. He wrote:

> I feel ... that I must congratulate you personally, if I may presume to do so, upon getting a sensitive and well balanced rendering and for imbuing it with that spirituality one always felt when Sir Edward himself conducted.
>
> I must say I was completely uplifted from beginning to end, and I felt that as long as his works are handled and given in the way that you and your splendid choir gave *The Dream*, so sure am I that these works will live.

Edward Elgar died on 22 February 1934. Almost exactly three months later Gustav Holst died. Shortly thereafter Sir Thomas Beecham announced in characteristically magisterial fashion that Ralph Vaughan Williams was now unquestionably England's greatest living composer. Few would have contested the statement. Ralph's pre-eminence was now a fact of national life. Ralph was devastated by the loss of Gustav Holst.

His old, dear friend had been taken ill during his visit to the United States in 1932 and he had continued unwell after his return to England. After a period in a nursing home he decided to pin his hopes on a major operation. But his heart proved to be insufficiently robust for the surgery and he died, peacefully, on 25 May. Ralph had lost his closest and most important male friend since the time of his closeness to Randolph Wedgwood some forty years before. That same day he immediately wrote to Holst's widow, Isobel, and his daughter Imogen, to offer consolation, his grief and distress disrupting his syntax. 'My only thought is now whichever way I turn what are we to do without him – everything seems to have turned back to him – what would Gustav think or advise or do.'[24] Gustav Holst's funeral service was in Chichester Cathedral on Midsummer Day. The choir he had founded, The Whitsuntide Singers, sang his music and also Ralph's and that of the Tudor composer Thomas Weelkes whom Holst had designated 'the true English artist', declaring 'No one in any age or country has expressed so many different ideas and moods in purely choral music'.[25] After the funeral Ralph spent a good deal of time and energy as chairman of the committee that organized a memorial for his friend which was the creation of a music room at Morley College. Ralph also worked hard to promote performances of Holst's music. Adeline worried about his numerous commitments, telling her sister on 13 February: 'R has many things on – I can't face his night journeys home'. But his efforts were suddenly hampered when he had yet another serious accident. Early that summer he went for a holiday on the Sussex coast. As he walked on the sands after a swim, he discovered that his foot was bleeding. The wound turned quickly into a poisoned abscess; it was on the same leg that he had gashed the previous year. Again he was confined to bed, this time for eight weeks. His personal discomfort, disappointment and frustration occurred at the same time as a further, dramatic and worrying deterioration in the political situation in the German-speaking countries. On 25 July the Nazis in Austria attempted a coup and assassinated Engelbert Dollfuss, the country's Chancellor. The Nazi takeover was thwarted on this occasion by the intervention of Mussolini, the leader of Fascist Italy. But in less than four years Hitler would march into Austria and, in the act of *Anschluss*, make it a part of the Third Reich. The uncertain days following the assassination in Vienna were another alarming time among the many turbulent events in Ralph's lifetime. As always he was very aware of current events. To Maud Karpeles he lamented, 'Poor Austria – I wonder what is going to happen

– this looks like the break up of everything with Mussolini thundering at the door.' He was also taken by the irony of the then theoretically pacifist Labour Party calling for Nazism to be contained. (Many of the Conservative Party were adopting an isolationist or, later, an appeasing policy towards the consolidation of Fascism on the continent.) Ralph noted the paradox: 'the funny thing is that it seems to be our pacifist party in England who are crying out for us to intervene.'[26]

A sad but inevitable miss for him during that summer of convalescence had been the Abinger Pageant for which his near neighbour E.M. Forster had written much of the script. Ralph himself had composed the music which included his 'O how Amiable' which was later published with a dedication to Fanny Farrer who, with other members of her family at Abinger Hall, was very much involved with the creation of the pageant. Perhaps to cheer themselves up, and also their young friend and ever willing chauffeur Honorine, Ralph and Adeline decided to treat themselves to a new car. For £45 they bought a Singer, a popular British car of the time. The new car made it possible for them to accept an invitation to what proved to be an historic occasion in the development of English musical life, the first opera festival organized by the wealthy landowner John Christie and his wife, the Canadian soprano Audrey Mildmay, on their estate at Glyndebourne in Sussex.

Ralph just made it to the Promenade Concert on 21 September where he had been booked to conduct his 'Sea Symphony'. The concert was an enormous success, the audience especially enjoying the dance beat of 'The Running Set', which was the first item on the programme. Ralph had to conduct sitting down, and he was carried on and off the podium. He wondered whether the tremendous ovation he received was due to the quality of his conducting or to the audience's appreciation of his sporting effort to go through with the performance. By November he had sufficiently recovered to have a 'season' in London with Adeline. As was their custom they stayed at the Evesleigh Court Hotel in Cromwell Road. During this visit the Viola Suite, which Ralph had agreed to write for the established violist Lionel Tertis, had its first performance on 12 November with the rakish Malcolm Sargent conducting the London Philharmonic Orchestra. Not one of Ralph's major works, it is nevertheless pleasantly listenable. There are eight movements, some of them, especially 'Carol', very beautiful. The instrumentation is, compared with much of Ralph's work, extremely delicate. That same month there was also a staging of *Job* at Sadlers Wells with a memorable performance in the role of Satan by the 25-year-old Australian dancer Robert Helpmann. Ralph was not particularly pleased by what he saw and heard. But others were, Adeline reporting a 'huge audience so enthusiastic that Satan had to say a few words'.[27]

Ralph was now making urgent efforts to reduce his excess weight. Three weeks later, five days before Christmas, Adeline told her sister 'R has lost 1 stone in eight weeks – he's very pleased and his breathing is much easier'. The various kinds of ill-health that contributed to Ralph's discomfort in the early 1930s were now being cured. In the first weeks of 1935 he was again staying in London, this time to assist Arnold Foster, Holst's old colleague at Morley College, in conducting the music at the English Folk Dance Festival at the Albert Hall. Three weeks later he again worked with Foster to stage the first memorial concert for Gustav Holst. Ralph conducted several other concerts at this time, one of them broadcast by the BBC. One listener, Benjamin Britten (who was ever prone to disparage Ralph's work), was appalled by his conducting. Britten wrote to his friend Grace Williams, a former pupil of Ralph's, declaring emphatically: 'R.V.W. I know is a nice man but he shouldn't conduct. It was hopeless. The concert came over quite well; it wasn't the wireless's fault. But, oh, the ragged entries, the half-hearted and doubtful playing – and the beastly tone…. I have never felt more depressed for English music than after that programme …'.[28] As Ralph became the leading figure in the musical Establishment, a younger generation, in which Britten's voice was one of the most audible, was ready to patronize or dismiss him.

During the same stay in London Ralph also attended a performance of a ballet *Great Agrippa or the Inky Boys* composed by his former pupil Elizabeth Maconchy. 'Uncle Ralph' gave this work very guarded praise and in his letter to her took the opportunity to pour heavy, abusive scorn on Stravinsky: 'I do feel that you are capable of so much finer thought than that Russian Monkey-brain and that you injure your real self by condescending to use any of his monkey tricks.'[29] Through these responses there appears to course an emotion that precludes objectivity or kindliness. Could Ralph have been jealous that Elizabeth was now drawing inspiration from a composer very different from himself?

Around this time preparations were beginning for the first performance of what many would regard as Ralph's finest Modernist work, the project that had been his principal endeavour over the last three years and more: his Fourth Symphony. Dedicated to Arnold Bax, it was played for the first time on 10 April in the Queen's Hall by the BBC Symphony

Orchestra, with Adrian Boult as conductor. The performance was one of the most important occasions in Ralph's career as a composer. Its lengthy gestation had been marked by a good deal of doubt, uncertainty and revision and it created a radically expanded range of mood and sound in his music. It provoked intense and conflicting responses at the time. And it has continued to do so ever since.

The process of composition began back in 1931 when Ralph spoke of writing a symphony in response to the music heard at what he described as the 'Freak Festivals' given at the meetings of the International Society for Contemporary Music. He was provoked by the Modernist idiom and in the Fourth Symphony it has clearly affected and infiltrated his composing. Probably to Ralph's discomfort Gustav Holst heard an early piano version and did not like it. But Ralph persevered with his strikingly innovative piece, though not with total confidence. Six months before the first performance he was writing urgently to its proposed conductor Adrian Boult: 'I want you to hear the Symph on 2 pianos soon because I want to get down to it and wash its face – Now have you any free dates?'[30] Perhaps it was at one of these meetings that he confided to Boult that some of the unhappiness that marks the symphony came from his learning that Adeline would never recover from her crippling illness.[31]

Ralph's former pupil, the composer Arthur Bliss, at one time a follower of the French Modernists *Les Six*, also helped him through the process of creating the symphony. Ralph, who had assisted Bliss with his Modernist *Colour Symphony* back in 1922, now wrote to him gratefully: 'thank you so much – I have my ups and downs – sometimes I hate it. I'm glad you like the slow movt best – you know that I owe two enormous last moment improvements to you'.[32] Even Ralph's closest, staunchest musical adviser Adeline had last minute doubts. Just two days before Adrian Boult premiered the piece she wrote to her sister 'Beloved Boo' about her changing attitude to the surprising work. 'The symph is emerging and now I couldn't bear you not to hear it. Last week I thought I couldn't bear anyone to hear it! It was wonderful to get the first movement going this morning – it's powerful – I ought to have had more faith.'[33]

Adeline's ambivalence is understandable. How taken aback those first listeners in April 1935, accustomed to Ralph's previous music, must have been! The symphony begins with what is still today a shocking explosion of violence and anger. Nothing of the kind had been heard in his work before. Is this a representation of a personal mood? Or of a social or political situation? Or all three? Ursula emphasized how closely it is related to the character of the man who wrote it. 'The towering furies of which he was capable, his fire, pride and strength are all revealed', adding, 'The Symphony has something in common with one of Rembrandt's self-portraits in middle age.'[34] Events in Ralph's story over the previous three years and more help to explain the opening anger. The remainder of the symphony can be heard as a series of attempts to come to terms with the shattering outburst that begins the piece.

The braying, percussive chords that open the work are succeeded by a second theme, a gentle, flowing meditative theme that occasionally sounds jagged and disrupted. At times sounding lost and lonely as it wanders on, this theme concludes with a subdued memory of the thunderous agitation at the start. There is then a falling away into quietness, all violence spent. The contrast between the beginning and the end of the movement is dramatic. Violent shock at the last is, at least temporarily, assimilated. The second movement, the *andante*, begins with a slow pondering that leads to a gently pulsing lyrical theme intimating revival and renewal. A first percussive climax shows some confidence achieved. But then follows a somewhat forlorn meandering with intricately patterned tensions and dissonant counterpoint. The wandering ends with another form of consoling, the melancholy compassionate lament of the flute that tapers off into another silence. The third movement, the *scherzo*, barges in, intrusively hearty; 'wake up, pull yourself together' music that joshes along, noisily jokey. There is just one pause, a moment of quiet thoughtfulness that is swiftly brushed aside by an 'oompah' bass and a march tune on woodwind. But the rending violence that is the premise and recurring subject of the symphony cannot be put aside by cheeriness and hearty humour. It sweeps up again at the beginning of the Finale and seethes. It may briefly decelerate to a mere bustling and even to some moments of meditation. But these are quickly ended and the violence, psychological or social, re-gathers and builds to an alarming knock-about climax. In the fugal epilogue it intensifies still further, reaches boiling point, and concludes in an explosion that is powerful and unanswerable. Listeners are left in shock and silence. The last bars of this powerful symphony are as violently destructive as those at the very beginning. Destructive turmoil has been experienced; it has been allowed its course, considered, and attempts have been made to contain it. But at the last it has triumphantly returned to dominate the concluding bars and to end the work with one final brutal detonation. The work is a presenting and a considering of destructiveness in life. It is the subject that T.S. Eliot was to address, memorably in his *Dry Salvages* published just six years after the first performance of the Fourth Symphony. At the end of the second movement of this 'quartet' Eliot writes of the ragged rock in the restless waters of life which:

> in the sombre season
> Or the sudden fury, is what it always was.

Ralph, as we know, was himself a man very capable of 'sudden fury' and he lived in a time and within a continent where such atavism disastrously affected human life. His Fourth Symphony is an attempt, powerful yet musically intricate, to confront this force. It was not, of course, a work of such conscious, explicit intention. As Ralph told his friend Robert Longman: 'I wrote it not as a definite picture of anything external e.g. the state of Europe – but simply because it occurred to me like this – I can't explain why – I didn't think that sitting down and thinking about great things ever produces a great work of art ... a thing just comes – or it doesn't – usually doesn't – I always live in hope, as all writers must, that one day I shall "ring the bell"....'[35]

Of the very many admiring letters Ralph received after the first performance of the Fourth Symphony, that from the composer Arthur Benjamin offered the most succinct, trenchant confirmation that such a day had come in Ralph's career.

> I write now to tell you how deeply moved I was with your new Symphony, how much I admired its sheer mastery, its vitality and beauty.... To me it is the crystallisation of all that contemporary composers have been <u>trying</u> to do and, as much as I admire Sibelius, I find him tentative in comparison to you. It was a joy to hear the public so spontaneously enthusiastic and so genuinely carried away.[36]

Another young composer, Edmund Rubbra, wrote to Ralph of the work's 'almost overwhelming power and beauty'. Maud Karpeles found the symphony 'tremendous' and sought to define 'what it conveyed to me – the feeling of some huge force driving us to fight and struggle, which may eventually shatter us to pieces. And yet we know in our hearts that there is something in life which withstands destruction and brings order out of disorder and the secret of it is to be found in music and particularly in your music....'[37]

EMINENCE

Chapter Fourteen

THE GATHERING STORM

On 17 May 1935, just over a month after the performance of the Fourth Symphony, Ralph received another memorable letter. It came from Buckingham Palace and announced George V's proposal to confer the Order of Merit on him. Created in 1902 by Edward VII, the order was constituted so as to contain no more than twenty-four of the most meritorious at one time. It was quickly recognized as a high honour. As a principled democrat, Ralph had long ago made up his mind to decline all honours awarded by the Crown. But this one had no particular connotations other than that of achievement, so Ralph, albeit with some misgivings, accepted. It was public confirmation, state confirmation, of his very considerable contributions to music. Adeline concurred in his long considered acceptance, telling her sister Boo, 'it is the only recognition I could bear for him'. Turning to the immediate, practical considerations she went on to say that they were about to approach a gents' clothes rental company for the attire required for the Court ceremony. 'July 9 is the "investiture" – evening dress coat – black breeches – silk stockings and court shoes. Let us hope Moss can provide.'[1]

Ralph went to Buckingham Palace on that summer day with his old friend, supporter and promoter, Hugh Allen, who was also to receive an honour on the occasion. Afterwards there was a party at the Farrers' house to celebrate the awards. When he received a telegram of congratulation from Imogen Holst, Ralph again revealed his uncertainty about accepting the royal honour. He wondered how her Socialist father would have responded to such an offer. 'I do hope Gustav would have thought me right not to refuse – I know he would have (probably did) refused himself – But it seemed right not to.'[2]

At this same time, Ralph was arranging to conclude his formal involvement with the music department at St Paul's School for Girls where he had filled in for Gustav since the time of his death. 'I hope I have been some use to you during this past year', he wrote to the High Mistress in July. Adding that 'though my official connection with the school will cease.... I hope I may still be allowed to remain a friend of the school where I have so many happy memories.'[3] As things turned out, Ralph was instrumental in negotiating the appointment of his young friend Herbert Howells to take over Holst's responsibilities at the school. Howells had been an enthusiastic admirer of Ralph's ever since 1910, when, at the age of seventeen, he had heard the composer conduct the first performance of his Fantasia on a Theme by Thomas Tallis in Gloucester Cathedral. In September 1935 Howells suffered a devastating blow when his 9-year-old son Michael contracted polio and died within a few days. From his profound grief Howells produced his large scale choral work *Hymnus Paradisi*. If the offer of the Order of Merit seems to have been a challenge to Ralph's commitment to democratic principles, the letter of condolence he had to write to his young friend at this terrible moment in his life was a difficult test for his commitment to agnosticism and to his uncertainty about a life hereafter. His words to Howells are reminiscent of those which he underlined in his copy of Plato's *Phaedo* and which were in his thoughts at the time of composing *Sancta Civitas*.

> ... I felt I must write just to tell you that one of your old friends is feeling for you. I have never had to suffer such a loss as this – but I sometimes try to imagine what it would be to lose one of those who are really one's own.
>
> One feels the futility of all things one usually sets value on when one is faced with reality.
>
> I don't think it is really any comfort – indeed 'comfort' would be just an impertinence – but I cannot help believing that a life once begun can never really stop – though it has stopped for us and that there may, after all, be a real joining some day.[4]

During the summer of 1935 Ralph was at work on another substantial composition, Five Tudor Portraits. Scored for baritone, contralto, chorus and orchestra, it is in marked contrast to the Fourth Symphony, being much lighter and more delicate. Ralph, at one stage of the writing referred to it as his 'Skelton Oratorio'. The sequence comprises settings of five pieces by John Skelton the sixteenth-century poet and satirist who had tutored the young Henry VIII, served as the parish priest at Diss in Norfolk, and was known for his 'ragged and rough' rhyming. The first portrait, a ballad, is of Elinor Rumming, a publican and brewer in Leatherhead in Surrey, with her:

skin loose and slack,
Grained like a sack;
With a crooked back,
Jawed like a jetty
A man would have pity ...

The heavy coarse beat of the music quickens to an *allegro* with the entrance of the other grotesque Brueghel-like characters who frequent the alehouse. One of these is gossiping Drunken Alice who speaks 'in her snout/Snivelling in her nose' and whose inebriated unsteadiness, burps and slurs are comically rendered by the piccolo, trumpet and horn.

The second portrait, 'Pretty Bess', a charming intermezzo, is a striking contrast to the coarse bawdiness that has gone before. A baritone with choral support sings a heartfelt love song to 'My proper Bess'. The lover's feeling for his beautiful but unresponsive lady is evoked, musically, by an exquisite lyricism. The third picture has for its subject John Jayberd of Diss, a fellow priest whom Skelton obviously loathed. In writing the man's epigraph Skelton describes him as 'A man renowned for malice,/ Double-hearted and double-tongued'. The music is a burlesca for male chorus with words in a mixture of church Latin and English. We are reminded of the coarseness in Carl Orff's *Carmina Burana* that appeared a few years later. The characterization ends nastily, unchristianly even, with an invitation to celebrate and drink on Jayberd's grave:

Drink your fill,
See he is buried
Under your feet,
A fool, an ass and a mule.

As we move on to the fourth portrait we encounter something that greatly contrasts with the hatred and cruelty that we have just observed in the late medieval church in the evocation of John Jayberd. The *romanza* 'Jane Scroop (her Lament for Philip Sparrow)' is both delicate and touching. It expresses the sadness of a convent child who, in pathetic innocence, grieves for the loss of her pet sparrow, Philip, killed by a cat. Very delicately the music ensures that the piece steers its way between parody and sentimentality. As Ralph wrote: 'There is no justification for describing these touching words as "Parody". Jane saw no reason, and I see no reason, why she should not pray for the peace of her sparrow's soul'. Genuine human feeling, we are reminded, can attach memorably, to even trivial things. The humour is finely done. After an opening cello solo, marked *lento doloroso*, comes little girl vehemence in her cry for vengeance against all cats. And after another extended lament comes another touch of mock epic in the allusion to the *Dies Irae* as the birds of the air are summoned to make their musical contributions to the internment. As Percy M. Young has observed:

> The obsequies are celebrated mock-pontifically in a parodial requiem which allows the two most familiar aspects of Vaughan Williams to contrast each other – the 'in church' and the 'out of doors'. The gentleness of the melodic outlines, the simplicity of the harmonic layout, the naive generation of effective birdsong, such as would have appealed to Handel, make a *tour de force* of tender observation.[5]

The concluding lines establish a genuine pathos and an adult sympathy with the child at this sad moment in her life. In the fifth and final portrait we turn to a far more boisterous figure, Jolly Rutterkin, the swaggering roisterer, with delusions of stylishness, who drinks:

> A stoop of beer at a pluck,
> Till his brain be as wise as a duck.

As the trumpets sound out over the horns and lower strings and the chorus enters with its rousing 'Hoyda, hoyda', this *scherzo* ends with a lively conviviality. As we complete our hearing of the last of these beautifully wrought specimens of Englishness at a particular moment in social history, the music returns us to the beginning at Elinor Rumming's pub.

Five Tudor Portraits was well received at its first performance in September 1936 at the Norwich Festival where it was followed by the young Benjamin Britten's *Our Hunting Fathers*. The reviewer from *The*

Times especially commended Astra Desmond for her performance in 'Elinor Rumming' in which she gave 'the most delicate picture of a drunken old hag at the famous brewing'. At one point during the performance Astra Desmond was disconcerted to see the elderly Countess of Albermarle, sitting on the front row, grow ever redder in the face. The contralto felt that the old lady might be about to have a heart attack. Astra Desmond prepared to lean down from the platform and offer smelling salts. But it turned out that it was outrage at Skelton's (and Ralph's) bawdy that was affecting the Countess. With an exclamation of 'Disgusting!' she upped and marched out of St Andrew's Hall. When Ralph learned of the incident he remarked that it was a compliment to the choir's diction, adding that it was a pity the Countess did not see the lines that he omitted in his setting.

Five Tudor Portraits was a finely entertaining work to lift the spirits in a year marked by calamity and loss. At the very beginning of the year, George V died. Ralph, at the instigation of his old annoyance Walford Davies, set 'Nothing Is Here For Tears', lines from John Milton's *Samson Agonistes*, as a choral song for mixed chorus and orchestra to commemorate the ending of a reign that had lasted for more than a quarter of a century. The work was broadcast on the BBC in the last week in January. Two months later Nazi Germany flagrantly defied the terms of the 1919 Treaty of Versailles by marching into the Rhineland and occupying it. The strengthening, ever more confident, Fascist impulse in Europe showed itself again in July 1936 – this time in Spain – when General Francisco Franco began his coup against the elected government of the Spanish Republic. So began the Spanish Civil War which would continue for the next three years and would be marked by appalling atrocities. Quickly it became a proxy war. Franco and his Fascists, the Falange, were supported by Hitler's Germany and Mussolini's Italy, the Rome–Berlin Axis, the alliance which would be formalized in October 1937. The Spanish Republic was supported by the 20-year-old Communist government of the Soviet Union. In this same year there came a great upheaval within the Soviet Union itself, as Stalin and his supporters purged the government and the Communist Party of those they considered subversive and counter-revolutionary. One cultural casualty of these turbulent times in Russia was the Fourth Symphony of the 30-year-old Dmitri Shostakovich. Earlier in that year, in January 1936, his opera *Lady Macbeth of Mtsensk* had been attacked in an article 'Muddle instead of Music', published in the official newspaper *Pravda* (reportedly on Stalin's orders). One consequence of this was that though Shostakovich finished his Fourth Symphony during the year and heard it in rehearsal, he nevertheless felt obliged to withdraw it. The work would not be heard in public for over a quarter of a century, long after Stalin's death.

In the context of such continent-wide turmoil Ralph produced his *Dona Nobis Pacem*. This cantata for soprano, baritone, mixed chorus and orchestra had been commissioned by the Huddersfield Choral Society and was given its first performance by them on 2 October 1936. The work very clearly has a cautionary intent; it is a reminder to its hearers of the horror, and also the pity, of war. It is very much a 1930's piece, sharing the apprehension of a coming war that was so very widespread at the time. For instance, less than a couple of years before, there had occurred the startling phenomenon of the Peace Pledge Union. Canon Dick Sheppard of St Paul's Cathedral in a letter to the then *Manchester Guardian* had invited men of military age to send him a postcard pledging never to support war. Within days he received 135,000 such cards. An important pressure group and organization were instantly created.

But for all its elements of admonition and propaganda *Dona Nobis Pacem* remains a powerful, often moving work of music. In method it is a pre-figuring of Benjamin Britten's *War Requiem* in that it is a setting of a selection of literary passages relating to peace and to war. After the opening *Agnus Dei*, in which an almost frenzied supplication from the choir accompanies the soprano's ethereal prayer, there comes a setting of Walt Whitman's 'Beat! Beat! Drums!' in which the many horrors of war are evoked in music dominated by trumpets and drums. The third movement, 'Reconciliation', switches to the quiet sadness with which Whitman and the composer contemplate the dead body of 'mine enemy, a man as divine as myself'. It is one of several passages in which, in the face of painful physical experience, we are given very raw and direct feeling. The central movement, the fourth, which is a setting of Whitman's 'Dirge for Two Veterans' was drafted before the First World War but dovetails into this 1930's work perfectly. The music delicately evokes the slow, solemn funeral rites for a father and son who were killed together. Womens' voices describe the rising of the moon and the whole chorus proclaims the arrival of the cortege at the double grave. As the dead march moves to a climax the onlooking speaker movingly cries out his feeling for these two victims of war.

In the fifth movement Ralph turns, in this time of an ascendant Adolf Hitler, to the words of another Victorian whose Liberal views had impressed him in his youth – the great orator and proponent of working-class suffrage, John Bright. In an age when the speech, like the sermon, was still recognized as a literary form, and was publishable as a genre of prose, Bright's orations were well known. He made an especially famous speech in the House of Commons in 1855 cautioning against the approaching Crimean War. One of its arresting and widely remembered sentences ran 'The Angel of Death has been abroad throughout the land; you may almost hear the beating of his wings.' In *Dona Nobis Pacem* the baritone declaims these eerie words so well known to Ralph's generation; the soprano and chorus respond with a desperate plea for peace culminating in the forlorn words from the prophet Jeremiah, 'Is there no balm in Gilead, is there no physician here?' But in the final movement in a glowing *passacaglia*-like passage come words of hope and optimism with the divine guarantee that 'Nation shall not lift up a sword against nation, neither shall they learn war any more'.

Given the hindsight we enjoy in regard to what was to happen in Europe at the end of the 1930s, these hopes seem sadly misplaced. And perhaps there is a rhetorical quality to the concluding optimism when, after the *passacaglia*, the orchestral part becomes urgently contrapuntal and 'peace and good will toward men' are proclaimed as the bells begin to ring. The 64-year-old Ralph appears, like Benjamin Britten's friend the 29-year-old poet W.H. Auden, to cling to what the latter in a famous poem about the 1930s called 'the clever hopes' of this doomed decade.

In 1936, the year in which the new king's love for the American divorcée, Mrs Wallis Simpson, steadily brought about a dramatic constitutional crisis, Ralph had his own domestic problems. His mother, who was now living at White Gates, seemed to be growing very weak and he and Adeline felt that they might soon lose her. In October Adeline fell and broke her left arm; her physical suffering was greatly increased. There was worse to come. Two months after Adeline's accident, Constance Vaughan Williams, the wife of Ralph's brother Hervey, stepped through the entrance gateway of Leith Hill Place and on to the main road. She was struck immediately, and very violently, by a passing cyclist and within hours Constance was dead. A distraught Hervey came to stay with his family at White Gates. To everyone's surprise his mother rallied strongly as she made efforts to support him. She even insisted on returning to Leith Hill Place to keep house for him there.

The year of 1937 began with a new king, the third within the last twelve months. In order to remain with Mrs Simpson Edward VIII had abdicated in December and his younger brother, the Duke of York, had taken over the throne as George VI. Ralph composed his Flourish for a Coronation, which was performed by the colourful Sir Thomas Beecham and the London Philharmonic Orchestra and Choir in early April. Six weeks later on the grand state occasion of the coronation in Westminster Abbey, Ralph's Festival Te Deum in F major was performed. It is a hearty, exultant work based on traditional themes and with no great thematic depth. The ceremony also included William Walton's more enduring Crown Imperial. Britain in this year still defined itself as a country with a great empire.

Ralph had more local concerns. Like his neighbour E.M. Forster he shared the poet John Betjeman's dislike of the ribbon development, the rows of roadside houses that were increasingly spoiling the visual quality of English towns during the 1930s. He willingly collaborated with Forster to create another pageant to support the campaigns of the Dorking and Leith Hill Preservation Society. He was also an invited guest at the coronation. He wore the court shoes he had bought for his Order of Merit investiture and his academic robes. He also sported a large velvet hat which had, as Adeline reported, 'a cunning pocket for sandwiches'. Ralph was pleased with his *Te Deum*; Adeline passed on his impression that 'it fitted in with the procession as the King and Queen came out during it – R was much too interested to feel hungry.'[6]

At the end of the coronation month Ralph took the train to Portsmouth to attend the naval review which was part of the national celebrations. He went with Honorine, who continued to be a prominent figure in the household of people who surrounded and tended Ralph and Adeline at White Gates. He and Honorine were the guests of Admiral Sir William Fisher, the victim of Virginia Woolf's hoax of years before, and now the Commander-in-Chief at Portsmouth. The two visitors greatly enjoyed themselves and Adeline took pleasure in passing on the news of the good time the two of them had during their day at sea. Unfortunately, the preparations for the large, complicated naval review had been a great strain on Adeline's brother. He became seriously ill and at the end of June he died. To Adeline this was another blow, another unhappiness adding to her increasing physical discomfort.

At this same time the alarming political situation in Europe suddenly impinged very directly and personally on Ralph. He received a letter from Hermann Fiedler, Professor of German at Oxford University, enquiring whether he would be prepared to accept the Shakespeare

Prize, a substantial financial award for conspicuous achievement in the arts, administered by the University of Hamburg and funded by Alfred Toepfer, a wealthy German businessman. Ralph acknowledged the honour that was being done him but was uneasy lest his acceptance might appear to condone the brutal regime which, among other acts of cultural vandalism, had instigated book burnings. In the same year (1937), Pablo Picasso showed his great painting *Guernica* – in part a protest against the bombing of a defenceless village in Spain – and in Munich the Nazis staged an exhibition entitled 'Degenerate Art'. This aimed to mock and vilify some of the leading Modernist artists. In his reply to Professor Fiedler Ralph wrote:

> ... I feel bound to explain that I am strongly opposed to the present system of government in Germany, especially with regard to its treatment of artists and scholars.
>
> I belong to more than one English society whose object is to combat all that the present German <u>regime</u> stands for.
>
> Therefore am I the kind of person to whom a German University would wish to offer a prize?[7]

As he pondered his decision Ralph consulted with friends. He also wrote to the eminent Classicist Gilbert Murray, whom he greatly respected, saying: 'I feel that for the sake of my profession I ought to accept such an unprecedented offer. But I want to be reasonably certain that I can do so with clean hands and not, thereby have my anti-Nazi teeth drawn.' In the event, Ralph decided to accept the prize on condition, as he told Fiedler, that he was free 'to hold and express any views on the general state of Germany which are allowable to a British citizen.'[8]

During 1937 Ralph appears to have become tired and depressed. In several letters he tells of his fear of never being able to compose again, of being 'dried up'. In November of that year his mother died. She was ninety-five years old and her passing was expected. Nevertheless, her death had a considerable impact on Ralph. He had always strongly rejected her rigorous, evangelical outlook. It made for a distance between them. But her death hit him unexpectedly hard. Adeline noted, 'I thought nothing more could hurt him but I was wrong.'[9]

At the time of his mother's funeral a despairing Ralph had entered, very casually, into a correspondence which would completely transform his life. In the late autumn, an unknown woman, Ursula Wood, had sent him a letter, care of the Royal College of Music, enclosing a scenario for a ballet she had created on the subject of Margaret and Clerk Saunders. This was one of the ancient ballads included in a very popular collection put together by Francis James Child at the end of the nineteenth century. The ballad tells of an ordained clerk who deceitfully prevails upon a young virgin to become his lover. In revenge, the youngest of her brothers murders him. Having considered the proposal Ralph wrote back, in a brief note beginning 'Dear Madam', that it seemed to him 'more suitable for miming to accompany a recitation or singing of the ballad'. But he added that he was sending on her scenario to Mr Douglas Kennedy of the English Folk Dance Society to 'see what he thinks'.[10]

Kennedy turned out to be interested and invited Ursula Wood to visit him at Cecil Sharp House near Regent's Park. When he told her that Ralph was disinclined to take on a story of seduction and murder, his visitor proposed Edmund Spenser's *Epithalamion* as an alternative. Kennedy duly passed on the idea to Ralph who was both interested and sceptical. In a manner typical of his low spirits at that time he wrote that although 'I should love to do a ballet with you … I warn you that I feel absolutely dried up at present and have the feeling that I shall never write another note of music'. Nevertheless, a triangular correspondence persisted during the last weeks of 1937 and the early ones of the following year. In March, at Ursula's urging, Kennedy suggested to Ralph that he invite her out to lunch so that they might discuss the project face to face.

Ralph agreed. A lunch date was arranged for 31 March 1938. It proved to be one of the most important days in Ralph's life. Within weeks he had entered into an enduring love affair.

Chapter Fifteen

A LOVE AFFAIR

The young woman whom Ralph went to meet on that spring day in 1938 had celebrated her twenty-seventh birthday just a fortnight earlier. She was close to forty years younger than he. She came from a well-to-do military family. Her birth certificate registered her as Joan Ursula Penton Lock (the 'Penton' being the surname of her maternal grandfather who had commanded the British army garrison on the Mediterranean island of Malta). Ursula was born in Valetta, the capital of the British colony where her father, Captain Robert Ferguson Lock, was her grandfather's aide-de-camp. Early in her childhood her grandfather was transferred back to England and the family took up residence amid the grandeur of Government House at Devonport.

Ursula gained a brother, John, when she was three and a sister, Rosemary, some four years later. But neither played an important role in her early life. She was for the most part a solitary child brought up by governesses; her greatest pleasure in life was reading. Among the many books she devoured she particularly enjoyed the Andrew Lang Coloured Fairy Books, 'full of stories of princes and princesses, talking beasts, adventures and magic from all over the world'.[1] She was also impressed by Anna Sewell's *Black Beauty* over which she cried a great deal, and J.W. Fortescue's *The Red Deer*, a very popular book of the time which made her, along with many others, a lifelong opponent of hunting. A French governess who Ursula remembered as 'Mademoiselle' introduced her to the French language and to the animal fables of La Fontaine and to the tragedies of Racine. But Ursula's greatest literary passion was for

English poetry. She became well read in it when still very young and shared the widespread enthusiasm of the time for the poetry of Robert Louis Stevenson. At her boarding schools she read Thomas Hardy's *Jude the Obscure* and *Tess of the D'Urbervilles* and more abstruse books such as Arthur Waley's *170 Chinese Poems* and the *Livre de Jade* by Judith Gautier, the French sinologist poet, feminist, and briefly in 1876, lover of Richard Wagner.

After the outbreak of the First World War in which Ursula's father was seriously wounded and lost an eye, the Lock family was moved about a good deal; to army camps at Ripon, Salisbury Plain, Camberley and Woolwich. Ursula still rarely made friends with children of her own age; her main relationships were with older people, her parents' friends and acquaintances. Following the war there was another posting to Malta and then in 1928, after another period at Woolwich, her father was appointed Commandant of the Chemical Warfare Experimental Station at Porton Down in Wiltshire. This army research unit had been established there in 1916 immediately after the introduction of poison gas as a weapon in the trench warfare in France. For her father the posting meant 'an absorbingly interesting job'.[2] But for Ursula there were scarcely any friends of her own age and little social life for a teenage girl. 'Three years isn't a long time, but those years in Porton seemed interminable,' she later wrote. Her class and her educational background did not allow her to look for work:

> there seemed nothing I could do to earn a living to escape from home … and I stuck around, a most unamiable, uneasy third adult at home. I must have been a great trial to my parents, for I sat about reading, changing books at [WH] Smith's as often as there was a shopping trip to Salisbury, and being as horrible as I could about hunting which they loved, and of course which I disapproved, refusing, whenever possible, to go to church where my father read the lessons'.[3]

There was some relief for her when her parents sent her to a finishing school in Brussels. This establishment with its somewhat faded splendour was presided over by Mademoiselle van Ove who reminisced about her times as governess to a succession of noble families in Russia. For the very first time Ursula enjoyed the long wished-for pleasures of a big city. She went to art galleries, to the opera, the ballet and to the theatre which became one of her greatest passions. But then came the return to what were for her the emptiness and boredom of life at Porton. 'The Downs were isolating and Salisbury, eight miles away, was not in those days a lively town'.[4] As daughter of the Commanding Officer of the military base she found little to do except to be ladylike. But she struggled to follow her own bent. She travelled down to Bournemouth to take drama lessons. With money from her grandmother she attended a summer school of drama in Bath where she played Pallas Athene in *The Trojan Women* of Euripides. At this school she first met Imogen, the daughter of Gustav Holst, who was in charge of the music for the play.

Ursula also began to write. She dedicated herself single-mindedly to poetry and when she was nineteen had the pleasure of seeing the first, of what proved to be a long succession, of her poems appear in print. Her first publication was in the little magazine established in 1924, *The Decachord*. Her poem appeared in an edition of 1930.

In that same year a young officer, Michael Wood, joined the personnel at Porton. Unlike most of the other officers there Michael shared Ursula's interest in the arts. He enjoyed drawing and painting and had aspirations to leave the army one day and devote himself to them. Michael had far more experience of the world than Ursula. He had had his setbacks. He had spent time in the army in India and got into trouble by contracting serious debts with local money lenders who assisted him in maintaining his polo ponies. The son of a doctor in Southport in Lancashire Michael appears to have been ill-prepared for the high living in the messes of British officers of the Raj. He was eleven years older than Ursula but the age gap never seems to have given her pause. All her life she was, and continued to be, comfortable in the company of people older than herself. During the early 1930s the couple drew closer, Michael often helping with the scenery painting for the amateur dramatics that Ursula enthusiastically helped to organize at Porton. They became engaged.

In the spring of 1932 Ursula auditioned for a student place at the Old Vic theatre school in London. She was successful. With the help of some more money from her grandmother she was able to take up the place. She found herself 'a tiny room in a hotel in Earl's Court' and in August began living the life of a single girl in London. She was now also close to the theatrical life of the capital, seeing some of the great actors of the day. She herself played a palace slave in an Old Vic production of George Bernard Shaw's *Caesar and Cleopatra*. Around this time the Old Vic merged with the Sadlers Wells Ballet to become the Vic–Wells Ballet. It was under the auspices of this new organization that there was a production of *Job, A Masque for Dancing*. Ursula attended one of the performances and was much impressed.

Perhaps Ursula was loath to end her theatre studies. But the customary elaborate family preparations for the wedding marched on inexorably. She and Michael Wood married in the last week of May 1933. Sharing the progressive taste of the young at the time Ursula determined that the wedding should not take place in a Victorian church such as her parents would have chosen. Her preference was for the newly fashionable English baroque and the couple were married in the Christopher Wren church of St Clement Danes in The Strand. The honeymoon was in Cornwall.

But then it was back to Porton Down. As the wife of a young captain Ursula no longer lived in the grand premises assigned to her father as commanding officer. She and Michael had very modest rooms at the Station Hotel. And so began her career as an itinerant army wife. But she also persevered with her writing and saw her poems published in *The* (then *Manchester*) *Guardian* and the *Spectator*. She also had theatrical hopes and ambitions. She worked on scripts and on choreography. In 1937 Michael was posted to the Isle of Wight and at around the same time Ursula's father took up a position at the Royal Military Academy at Woolwich. He and her mother now decided to base themselves in London and the couple took a large flat near Gloucester Road. This was where Ursula would stay when she was able to leave the Isle of Wight and visit London. And it was here that Ralph came to take her to lunch on that spring day in 1938.

When he appeared at the door Ursula was taken aback by the somewhat rakish appearance of a man who was old enough to be her grandfather. It was a time when men wore hats. But Ralph wasn't wearing the bowler that might be expected of a man of his age and class. Instead he wore a green pork-pie hat such as previously she had only seen on dashing cavalry subalterns. She was also taken by the debonair way he kept the taxi waiting while she prepared to leave. As the taxi moved east, Ursula quickly sensed that her companion's 'eyes, hands were somehow familiar, so that I felt that I was meeting again someone who I had known before'.[5] She later discovered that Ralph too had a similar sense of recognition. Ursula also noticed that his Burberry was well worn and hastened to assure him that an inexpensive restaurant, a Lyons, would be perfectly acceptable to her. But Ralph reassured her that something more costly would not lead him to starvation at the end of the month. Over lunch they talked of the projected masque and about poetry. Ursula told him of her ejection from her singing class as a consequence of her very poor performance of 'Linden Lea'. This amused him. Another bond was that she knew and admired other poems by the Dorset poet William Barnes, a favourite of his.

When the lunch came to an end, they did not part, as they had expected to do. They wandered through West End streets together and coming to a cinema where one of Walt Disney's short animation films in his 'Silly Symphonies' series was playing, they decided to go in and see it. When they came out, they were still not minded to go their separate ways. They strolled westwards and came into Hyde Park. They sat down beside the Serpentine and talked of madrigal poems and still more poets that each admired. Eventually Ralph hailed a cab and escorted Ursula back to her parents' flat. In the taxi, Ursula told an interviewer years later, Ralph took her in his arms and kissed her intensely. She gasped and said she was unaccustomed to such kisses. Ralph replied that she soon would be.[6]

Very shortly after their first meeting Ursula sent him some of her poems. He wrote back saying how he 'loved having them'. He was particularly taken by the three part poem *Variations*. The first part is on one level about mortality but on another can be seen to be about the impact, the sudden change and variation that the unexpected wrought in her consciousness. The last, trenchant, four syllable line in the following passage conveys the sudden and shocking apprehension of a hitherto loyal wife.

When I unplait my hair at night
I touch it as a stranger might
remembering well that I
of it, and all my body, have so slight
a regency.

So quickly does the spirit change,
one thought from custom can estrange,
and yet no sign be in the face
to show its depth or measure its far range
in such short space.

And when on windy hills I go
the dead leaves rise and fall and blow
between the stems from whence they fell,
so, soon, my thoughts will be like these and know
me infidel.[7]

In his letter of thanks for the poems Ralph mediates his own feelings through Keats's poem *La Belle Dame Sans Merci*. The opening greeting is a salute, in the superlative, to her beauty and also an acknowledgement of his susceptibility to her, *Bellissima Donna senza Misericordia*. He has 'thought a lot about you' he tells her and concludes declaring himself 'Yours in thrall'. Ralph also sent Ursula a gift of two volumes of Elizabethan lyrics and songs.

There were three more meetings in London before Ursula accompanied her husband to Portland where he had been posted for the summer. In May Ursula went up to see her soldier brother John who was on leave from India. She took advantage of her visit to have lunch again with Ralph. Afterwards they walked to the British Museum and found themselves studying the man-headed bulls in the Egyptian galleries. Ralph asked Ursula if she was a Christian and, as she later remembered, 'seemed relieved when I said that I was not'. In June Ursula had another opportunity to be in London when one of her women friends lent her a one-roomed flat in Lamb's Conduit Street in Bloomsbury. Ralph took her to dinner at Paganis, the grand restaurant with the striking Art Nouveau frontage, in Great Portland Street, opposite the Queen's Hall. Doubtless Ursula would have seen the fashionable restaurant's Artist Room with its walls covered with the signatures of leading figures in the arts world over the last half century, Puccini, Paderewski, Mascagni, Sarah Bernhardt. The couple then went to the Old Vic to see the Holland-based Ballet Jooss dance *The Green Table*, a ballet with music by Fritz Cohen, depicting the horrors of war and the fatuousness of diplomats and politicians in their efforts to halt it. Ralph met her at 5 p.m. after finishing his teaching at the Royal College of Music. He apologized that he would therefore be in his 'day clothes' rather than in evening dress. She had written to him asking him what he would like her to wear for the occasion. He replied, 'I believe I like you best as I first saw you in your short day frock – rather than in full evening – but perhaps that would dazzle me even more.'[8] Probably it was the morning after this night at the ballet that Ursula telephoned Ralph very early and invited him to come over and have breakfast. He set off instantly and arrived at the little flat with one side of his face still unshaven.[9]

They met one more time before Ursula went into isolation at Portland Bill where, she recalled 'there was nothing to do but go for walks'. Very occasionally she was able to go to London. On Midsummer Eve Ralph took her to a dance organized by the English Folk Dance and Song Society at Cecil Sharp House near Regent's Park. Ursula remembered 'It was a hot evening, so we left early and sat on Hampstead heath. The flowers were out and made a bower for us in the scented blue evening, with London lying below and St Paul's a black silhouette against the not quite dark sky.'[10]

Towards the end of her life Ursula recalled that she and Ralph had become lovers quite soon after first meeting each other.[11] They also quickly realized that their feelings for each other were 'too desirable for their circumstances'. They had an opportunity to stand back and consider the situation when the time came for Ralph to begin his visit to Germany during which he would accept the Shakespeare Prize in a formal ceremony. Early on the morning of Saturday 22 June he arrived at Liverpool Street Station, from where he was to travel to Harwich and thence to the Hook of Holland in the company of Professor Fiedler and his charming young daughter Herma, whose diary contains a very detailed account of the days they all spent together in Germany. She felt quick affection and admiration for the 65-year-old celebrity whom she and her father were to escort to the grand awards ceremony in Hitler's *Reich*. Herma found Ralph to be 'amazingly tolerant and modest'; like Ursula some time earlier she was much taken by his green pork-pie hat.

On their first morning in Hamburg they set off on a pilgrimage to the Brahms house. Later they were taken to the cinema to see Leni Riefenstahl's film of the Berlin Olympics of two years before. Like so many others then and since, Herma greatly admired the film, finding it 'beautifully photographed and artistically treated'. There was also a trip to the old Hanseatic city of Lübeck where Ralph was moved to see, inside the soaring brick-built Gothic *Marienkirche*, the organ once played by his great exemplar Johann Sebastian Bach and also by Bach's own exemplar, Dietrich Buxtehude. This made him realize again, very vividly, as Ursula later repeated: 'What musicians all over the world owed to Germany, the land of musical giants.'

At the ceremonial awarding of the Hanseatic Prize the Hamburg Philharmonic Orchestra was to play Ralph's Tallis Fantasia and 'A

London Symphony'. The conductor was Eugen Jochum who insisted that Hamburg was 'reasonably liberal'; he had refused to join the Nazi party and conducted works by Hindemith and Bartók, composers who were banned in concert halls elsewhere in the *Reich*. Herma remembered that Ralph was extremely co-operative at rehearsals and that the two men got on well. The concert and the ceremony passed off successfully, Ralph not disturbed to learn that he was forbidden to take his prize money out of Germany. (He wished to donate it to the Quakers but this too was not allowed. So he put it in a bank but could not access it until after the war when its value had greatly diminished.) During the concert Ralph was escorted by an impeccably uniformed member of the SS, complete with swastika armband. The young man was painfully bored by the music and Herma was amused and touched when Ralph, towards the end of the final movement of the symphony, murmured to him in carefully prepared German, 'It will soon be over now.'

More disturbing to Ralph was a visit that he and his companions paid to the Hamburg State Opera of which Eugen Jochum was also the musical director. They saw a production of a new opera by the American composer Vittorio Giannini based on the novel *The Scarlet Letter* by Nathaniel Hawthorne. The setting is the Puritan world of colonial New England at a time when a young wife, such as the heroine Hester Prynne, known to be unfaithful to her husband, could be compelled to wear the letter 'A' to identify and shame her as an adulteress. Herma commented that: 'The music was very luscious, typically Italian opera style and did not suit the bleak New England setting.' For Ralph at a delicate stage in his developing relationship with Ursula, this opera about adultery must have been a sobering, chilling experience. Commenting on it in a letter to Ursula from Germany he said it was 'All very gloomy'. He added, in what must clearly have been a considerable understatement: 'I feel that I do not thrill when young women are branded with "A"'[12]

But after this shocked paragraph the letter quickly switches to affection and on to suggestions of passionate feeling. He thanks her for the books she has sent him and says he is 'getting hold of Donne'. His 'ideal of love poetry' he tells her is the lines from the ballad:

I'd rather rest
on my true love's breast
than any other where.

He adds that he has been attentive to the project, the ballad of loving feeling, that they are sharing together. 'I copied out practically the whole of Epithalamium [*sic*] before I left England.' The letter ends with the short, very direct question: 'When do we meet again?' Some days after his return from Germany he sent another letter urging her to 'Write soon'. He also quotes some lines from George Meredith's poem 'The Woods of Westermain':

Enter these enchanted woods
You who dare.

In the context of their relationship these words would be a reminder to her both of the excitement and of danger. Ralph goes on to say 'I'm trying in vain to catch up with arrears of work owing to visits to Hamburg and evenings in woods (only 1!)'. The letter is lighthearted but it is uncertain whether the word 'woods' is intended as a pun and whether the evening refers to the recent visit to Hampstead Heath. But in any event the letter suggests a relationship both delicate and intense.[13] Later in the summer, on 17 August 1938, Ralph wrote again clearly anxious to arrange a meeting and making clear his availability, 'I am passing through London on the 26th – so that is good luck – are daylight meetings any good? If so, we will meet when and where you say.'[14]

Not until very late that year did Ursula have easy access to London. But in mid-December of 1938 Michael Wood, along with a team of fellow artillery officers, was posted to Jamaica where they were to undertake experiments in rocketry. The army was preparing for the new weaponry that would characterize the war that now seemed to everyone frighteningly inevitable. Ursula spent Christmas with Michael's mother Mabel and his brother in Brighton. But very soon afterwards she went to live in London where she had found herself a bed-sitting room in Guildford Place in Bloomsbury. From now on it would be easier to see Ralph again.

In the weeks that followed his return from Hamburg in the summer, Ralph had experienced what was clearly a major life crisis. In the second week of July he felt an overwhelming need to be on his own; 'to go into solitude', as Adeline put it in a letter. He took himself off to a remote country place in Wiltshire. Adeline wrote, appealing to him, 'only need a line to say how you are'. To her his difficulties seemed to derive from his ongoing fear that his creative energies as a composer had come to an end. In another of her anxious letters to him in Wiltshire she tried to reassure him that 'Even if compo.[sition] doesn't come the new scenes and the quiet will sow some seed'. But it seems very probable that he was also troubled by uncertainty and perhaps guilt about his developing relationship with Ursula. He secluded himself in the village of Stapleford near Salisbury where he rented accommodation from Mrs Simper in Rose Cottage. He wrote to Ursula: 'I am here in the Wiltshire Downs – and the hermitage is succeeding I think … I have been [for] wonderful walks on the downs – they were perfect – sun, high wind and wonderful July field flowers, the kind I like best.' For the first time in a letter to her he signs himself 'Love yrs'. But he has to confess that a new project 'has taken precedence over Epithal.' Apologetically he adds, 'You know I can't do things unless I think I ought to be doing something else.'[15] The new inspiration proved to be the origins of the Fifth Symphony. He had actually contributed some of its early passages, from the *scherzo* and prelude, to the music sequence at the Abinger Pageant in the middle of which Ralph, as his crisis struck, had abruptly departed. Amidst the personal turmoil in the summer of this year began one of Ralph's greatest and most popular symphonic works.

Adeline worried about him leaving home so abruptly. On 11 July she wrote again, appealing to him 'All well with us – only need 1 line to say how you are'. She also fretted that he had no toilet paper with him. Resorting to a genteel euphemism she apologizes, 'But how ashamed I was to have forgotten to put "de quoi" in your case.' She adds that Honorine 'has bought you a packet of Bromo'.[16] A few days later Honorine wrote, in her characteristically merry, high spirited fashion 'I hear that the Bromo wasn't necessary, after all we sent a packet rather than a roll in case we should leave a trail across the downs!!!' She also gave news of the Abinger Pageant, which, she reported 'went quite well yesterday … E.M. got a call at the end and made an inaudible speech'. Honorine concluded her rather breathless letter with some jokey comments about one of her fellow actresses in the Pageant. 'That little bitch Naomi got off with the nicest young man, I'll tear her eyes out when I see her, I feel quite void now my stage life is over, it was great fun'.[17]

A few days later a relieved Adeline told Rosamond Carr 'Tomorrow we go to Winchester to bring Ralph home. He is leaving Mrs Simpers today and spending a night in Salisbury after a walk. I am sure he has found his solitude completely satisfying'.[18] In the Close at Salisbury Ralph was the guest of the cathedral organist Walter Alcock, whom he remembered from his student days when the older man taught the organ at the

Royal College of Music. He found Sir Walter servicing the model railway which ran through his house and on which the choirboys were sometimes permitted to ride. After sunset he invited Ralph into the cathedral where, in the dark shadows of the great Gothic building, he played Bach for him.

After a week or two at home at White Gates, Ralph was again on the move. He went to Hereford to conduct a performance of *Dona Nobis Pacem*. The concluding prayer for peace must have sounded especially urgent, even desperate, to the audience, for this was a time when Britain was in a vibrant state of war jitters. It was the year of the 'Czech crisis'. Adolf Hitler was now threatening to invade the Sudetenland, the predominantly German-speaking area of Czechoslovakia, a nation state which had been created as a result of the Versailles Treaty at the end of the First World War. The British Prime Minister, Neville Chamberlain, and also the French premier, engaged in frantic diplomacy in order to appease him. Winston Churchill declared sombrely and unequivocally that war was inevitable. Amidst this national unease and the complexities of his new love, Ralph heard the premiere of a new work of his that exuded feelings of the utmost tranquillity and calm. This was his Serenade to Music, a setting for sixteen solo voices and orchestra of the lines beginning 'How sweetly sleeps the moonlight on the bank' from the final act of Shakespeare's *The Merchant of Venice*. It was composed for Sir Henry Wood the distinguished conductor, founder of the Promenade Concerts and Ralph's long-time associate, on the occasion of Sir Henry's golden jubilee as a conductor. Ralph dedicated the work to him 'in grateful recognition of his services to music'. A virtuoso piece with a specially composed passage for each of the star soloists who inaugurated the work, this exquisite piece is, as Michael Kennedy has put it, 'all silver and moonlight'. It was performed on 5 October 1938 with Sir Henry Wood himself conducting and an admiring Sergei Rachmaninov in the audience. It was the week in which Chamberlain returned from Munich declaring that as a result of negotiations with Hitler there would be 'Peace in our time'. The very day of the concert in which Ralph's ethereally beautiful music was first heard, German Jews were compelled to re-apply for their passports which henceforth were to be marked with a large capital 'J' identifying each of them as *Jude* ('Jew'). It was an important stage in implementing the policy of classing Jews as lesser citizens.

Exactly a week after the concert Ralph had his sixty-sixth birthday. Ursula sent him a letter of greeting and a poem. In his letter of thanks he returned the poem, 'rather too personal to show around, though I like it, (and your hair).' He asked her to 'forgive all my vagaries' and noted 'that you were the only one of my girlfriends who wrote to me on my birthday – it was sweet of you'.[19] The phrase 'one of my girlfriends', even if in context it does not suggest that she has become one of Ralph's many 'nieces', does nevertheless indicate a slowing of the relationship over the last two months during which they had little opportunity to meet. Later in life Ursula remembered that there were times early in their affair when Ralph's doubt, and also circumstances, led him to draw away from her. In December, for instance, he had a very busy schedule. In the first week, Adeline was seriously concerned when he came back from Newcastle with a heavy cold and exhausted. She worried: 'I felt in some agony at letting him go this morning for a long day's teaching at the R.C.M. then the night train to Edinburgh rehearsal for Sea Symph'.[20] He was standing in for Donald Tovey who was ill. Ralph was greatly excited by the performance of his first symphony of nearly thirty years before; he was exhilarated by the efforts of Tovey's provincial orchestra: 'Thursday night was <u>electrifying</u> – even if we'd had six rehearsals together it would have been very good – as it was it was <u>miraculous</u>'.

In very early January 1939 Ursula was established in her small flat in Bloomsbury. She and Ralph grew close again. Her diary records she had dinner with Ralph on 6 January and breakfast the following morning. About this time Ralph also helped Ursula in her efforts to find a job or at least something 'useful to do'. She had made a first attempt at voluntary work but it had proved unsatisfactory. So it was helpful to her when Ralph put her in touch with his old friend Maud Karpeles, Douglas Kennedy's sister-in-law, who was taking responsibility for children in an organization that assisted the rapidly increasing number of refugees from Germany and Austria. Ursula, very conscious of herself as a young, 27-year-old 'army wife', was rather nervous about meeting the well-known folklorist who was a generation older than herself. She was aware that Maud 'had been cross when Ralph had left her bedside when he'd visited her in hospital after a recent operation, rather too soon because he was going to take me out'.[21] In the event, after meeting Maud at her office in Bloomsbury House and then going on to lunch with her at a nearby Lyons Corner House, Ursula found that she and Maud got on very well together. They quickly became friends as well as colleagues. Ursula was now beginning to enter Ralph's social circle.

Through Maud Ursula also made some helpful literary contacts;

Ernest Rhys the elderly poet, who as a publisher, had founded the Everyman Library, and Henry Nevinson, the distinguished journalist and campaigner for progressive causes including women's suffrage. He was the husband of Evelyn Sharp, the sister of Ralph's old friend who had founded the English Folk Dance Society which in 1932 had merged with the English Folk Song Society. In the early weeks of 1939 Ralph sought to interest Ursula in folk song. At the English Folk Dance and Folk Song Festival at Cecil Sharp House in February he arranged for some of his personal favourites, such as 'Bushes and Briars' and 'Searching for Lambs', to be on the programme. Ursula also accompanied Ralph to the society's ball. Later they went to a concert at the Albert Hall and from there to a party for the performers. This was an occasion from which Ursula retained a vivid memory of Ralph as a social being, taking on his flirtatious avuncular persona: 'He was quickly settled into a huge sofa, with several beauties squashed in on each side of him and became "Uncle Ralph in tremendous form", telling stories and obviously feeling happy. It was apparent that everyone, men and women, loved him, and that imme-diately he arrived at a party it lit up and took on a glow because he was there enjoying himself.'

Ursula was both impressed and moved to see him the life and soul of the party. 'It was enchanting to feel this warmth and affection filling the room, emanating from him and surrounding him.'[22]

During the third week in January there was a pause in Ralph's meetings with Ursula because Adeline paid one of her infrequent visits to London. She and Ralph had lunch at the Eversleigh Hotel where, over the years, they had been regular guests. Then they attended the rehearsals and first performance of Ralph's Double Trio for Strings. It was played by the Menges Quartet and two other string players. Founded by the virtuoso violinist Isolde Menges, the quartet was one of the very first in that changing world of English music to include both male and female players. One of the later recruits to the ensemble, the viola player Jean Stewart, became a good friend of Ursula and consequently of Ralph. Composed in the Modernist idiom during the previous year the piece perhaps expresses some of the tumult and conflict of that time. Hearing it played, he was dissatisfied with it. He later made revisions but still found it 'dull and muddy'. As he later told Jean Stewart, 'I've tried all my life for clarity and never achieved it – I always put too many ingredients into the pudding'.

A work for which Ralph had an unquestionable affection was his Five

Tudor Portraits and was happy at the end of March to travel to Tyneside to conduct the Newcastle and Gateshead Choral Union in a performance of it. During his stay in the North East, as in other journeyings to conduct, he wrote to Ursula expressing his worries about their relationship, his suitability as an older lover and his jealousy of possible rivals. Less than three weeks after having dinner with her he wrote from Newcastle: 'We never seem to meet now – lost love. I have to be in [Newcastle] and now College term is over and I shall not be going to London except casually – so I suppose you will get tired of me and replace me by ...'[23]

There then follows a list of three younger suitors. But his anxieties seem to have been unnecessary; within a week or so they were seeing each other again in London. They were also continuing to work on *Epithalamion*. By April Ralph had completed the score and on 27 April he organized a play through at Cecil Sharp House. Jean Stewart was one of the instrumentalists and Maud Karpeles came to advise on matters to do with dance. The music worked well and Ralph took them all off to lunch at Paganis where Toscanini and some companions happened to be at a nearby table. In the afternoon Ralph and Ursula went shopping together in the West End. Perhaps they looked for things for Ursula's new flat. She had given up her tiny place in Bloomsbury and taken a larger flat at 7½ Thayer Street in Marylebone. It was on the top storey of a large apartment building that was demolished and replaced in the 1960s. Jean Stewart was later to have a flat in the same building. Ursula moved in on 19 April and here she was able to entertain Ralph regularly during the coming months.

Around this time they resolved to put their relationship on a new footing. They decided to arrange a foursome bringing them together with Adeline and Michael who had recently returned from his posting in the West Indies. The four met on 13 May at Sadlers Wells Theatre to see a double bill made up of *Job* and *Hugh the Drover*. The occasion seems to have been created so that the two lovers could appear as colleagues and friends before their spouses. Michael must surely have been pleased, perhaps honoured, to meet the famous, older man who was helping along his wife's literary career. Adeline was, of course, accustomed to seeing her husband in the company of a succession of attractive younger women. Here was just one more. Adeline was in a happy mood on that May evening. Just two days earlier she and Ralph had returned from a most enjoyable stay in the Cotswold area. 'We had 5 most enjoyable days and 3 nights at Cheltenham and 2 nights at Oxford – felt quite drunk with the spring beauty and Cotswold country'.[24]

A couple of weeks later Ralph was off to receive yet another academic honour. This time it was an honorary degree from Trinity College, Dublin. It was a tribute to the power of Ralph's reputedly very English music that such an award came from a nation, which under the leadership of Eamonn de Valera, was continuing to distance itself from Britain and preparing to declare its neutrality in Britain's looming war with Germany. In Dublin Ralph stayed in the suburban home of Professor George Hewson, the organist of Trinity College. He also managed to travel down into nearby County Wicklow to visit Ina Boyle, a former student of his whose work he had long tried to support and promote. She had recently emulated her teacher by composing a 'masque for dancing'. It was titled *The Dance of Death* and was based on a series of woodcuts by Hans Holbein. When Ralph went to see her she was composing another work in the same genre, a dance setting of the tenth book of Plato's *Republic*. She lived alone in Bushey Park, a large, somewhat run down, Ascendancy mansion close to the Wicklow Mountains. Due to her isolation her music was not greatly promoted in her lifetime. But since her death her importance in the history of music in Ireland has come to be better recognized.

Another former student at the Royal College of Music was Alan Bush who was now also one of Ralph's young teaching colleagues there. A Marxist and a Communist and, during his Berlin student days, a friend of Kurt Weill, Bertholt Brecht and Hans Eisler, Alan Bush twice during this year solicited Ralph's support for the left-wing Festival of Music for the People. Ralph declined on the grounds that he could not possibly meet the February deadline. But he also disputed Alan Bush's right to claim to speak for 'the people'. The same argument was renewed when, in July, Bush asked Ralph to give a guarantee of one hundred pounds to cover any overdraft incurred by the Workers' Music Association of which Bush was a leading member. Again Ralph distanced himself from Bush and his fellow Communist sympathisers who were extremely active in these years of political turmoil. He replied, 'I do not care about mixing propaganda and art and I do not quite see that the people who hold particular views should arrogate to themselves and none others the title of "Workers".'[25] Yet Ralph also hinted at some sympathy for the political views of his younger colleague: 'it seems to me ... bad to advertise through music any particular brand of political opinion, even if those opinions are to my mind admirable.'[26] And since music was Alan Bush's ultimate concern, Ralph concluded by agreeing to write to his bank and to supply the requested financial guarantee.

That same July Ralph and Honorine went to Glyndebourne together to see Mozart's *Don Giovanni*. Earlier in the year Ralph had volunteered to conduct a rehearsal of the Lewes Festival in the same country house venue. In the little opera house that had recently been rigged up inside, Ralph found himself conducting in what Adeline described as 'a most flimsy little hen roost'. To his complaint, the squirearchical founder of the opera, John Christie retorted stoutly, challengingly, 'it was used by the Queen of the Night'.[27]

Ralph's collaboration with Ursula on *Epithalamion* was continuing to advance. A production at the Royal College of Music was planned. Rehearsal dates were established and costumes settled. But then, suddenly, it all fell through. Douglas Kennedy who was in charge of the choreography decided that, like many at this moment of imminent war, he might be going to the United States. Ralph clearly felt the disappointment most intensely because of the setback it meant for Ursula. At the end of July he wrote to her, 'I thought the only thing to do when I got Douglas's letter was definitely to cry off ... so I wrote to all my people and told them so. I could not keep them shilly-shallying any longer.... My dear, I feel so sorry about it – not so much for my music, which if it is good can wait its time and if it is bad had better not be heard, but for you and the whole thing. You know I think I wrote it because I'm fond of you....'[28] It would be another fourteen years before *Epithalamion* was performed. It was presented on BBC Television in the first week of June 1953. Neither the writer nor the composer were very satisfied by the production of the work around which their lifelong love had begun.

A few weeks before the abandonment of the masque, Ralph's composition for harp and strings Five Variants of Dives and Lazarus had its first performance, conducted by Adrian Boult, at the New York World's Fair. A very stirring series of meditations on an ancient folk melody, long known to Ralph, it must have sounded to its first listeners like an elegy for that period, later popularly referred to as 'peace time', that was in the inexorable process of slipping away.

Having gained his ends in Czechoslovakia, Hitler was now threatening Poland. His hand was greatly strengthened on 23 August when his foreign minister, Joachim von Ribbentrop, signed a treaty of non-aggression with his Soviet Russian counterpart Vyacheslav Molotov. Just over a week later German troops entered Poland. A British ultimatum requiring Germany to halt the invasion was ignored. Accordingly, on 3 September,

Britain, together with France, declared war on Germany. It was the beginning of nearly six years of warfare during which the lives of many millions, including those of Ralph, Adeline and Ursula would undergo a then unimaginable transformation.

The weeks following Neville Chamberlain's announcement of a state of war with Germany were anti-climactic; militarily little happened and this period became known as 'the phoney war'. But in all walks of civilian life arrangements were being put in place to allow for worse to come. The Royal College of Music informed Ralph that his services would no longer be required; only teachers resident in London would be employed. His confinement to Dorking made him restless. But with characteristic public spiritedness he set about doing all he could to assist the 'war effort'. He joined the Save for Victory programme, which meant that he had to traipse round his area of Dorking selling National Savings stamps. He also became something of a rag and bone man, going about collecting bottles, rags, scrap metal and any other materials that might be of use in the war effort. He continued his work with the Dorking Refugee Committee, which assisted those who had fled the Nazis and wished either to stay in Britain or to move on to North America. He was less enthusiastic about contributing a broadcast to a BBC series about 'making music at home', organized as part of the war effort by Walford Davies. Adeline was scathing about the series of programmes which 'Walfy introduced last evening with more than Walfy's usual silliness. R simply doesn't know what he is supposed to say but must use up 15 minutes somehow.'

Writing was an activity to which Ralph now turned his considerable energy and talent. He contributed articles on music to a local newspaper *The Abinger Chronicle*, which also printed contributions from E.M. Forster, Robert Trevelyan and Ralph's Charterhouse contemporary, Max Beerbohm who, after years of expatriation in Italy, had recently returned to England. At this time Ralph also wrote a very fine, insightful essay on Beethoven. He had been preparing to conduct the Ninth Symphony at the Leith Hill Music Festival the following spring. But with that occasion now very much in doubt he decided to write down his conclusions, at times tentative, about the work which he had studied intensely in the course of preparing a performance. The result was 'Some Thoughts on Beethoven's Choral Symphony'. It is a substantial essay of some forty-five pages and ranks with the analyses written by Donald Tovey, George Grove and Richard Wagner as a reading of this great artefact of western culture.

It is a detailed, comprehensive musical analysis of the four movements of the work but it also stands very much in the literary tradition of the essay form. It has a certain tentativeness. Ralph's prose ponders, attempts understanding, essays, offers judgements, makes corrections and then comments further. Here is a characteristic uncertainty: 'I daresay I have laid too much stress on these minutiae which trouble me, but one is especially keenly alive to the faults of what is otherwise supreme.'[29] He is again unsure in comparing Beethoven with Bach. The music of Beethoven's first two movements, he writes, 'is like no other music, either before or since. It seems to have come straight from the eternal source of truth without human intervention'.[30] He goes on somewhat regretfully 'Standing on this ground, Beethoven, I have to admit, is in a different space from my beloved Bach'. But Ralph's background as a history graduate is apparent throughout the essay and makes it much more than a work of musicology. His background assists him with this problematical comparison. He explains: 'Beethoven lived in a time of greater intellectual expansion than Bach, whose theology was purely anthropomorphic, and whose music does not look for the Supreme Being beyond the stars, the Great King, the Bridegroom. Beethoven, when he looks into eternity sees clearer and further than Bach; but Bach when he thinks of his very human deity has the richer and warmer consciousness.'

Ralph sees Beethoven and his symphony in much more than a compositional and musical context. He supplies, for instance, an extensive literary framework to his analysis. He refers to Shakespeare, Milton, Shelley, Schiller, Tolstoy and to modern writers, for instance his distinguished neighbour and friend E.M. Forster. Ralph is very aware that the meaning of music cannot be translated into physical or material terms. But, he concedes, 'like all writers on music, I find it a convenient way, occasionally, of putting into words the scheme of the music'.[31] And the words he finds most apposite for characterising the experience afforded by the joyous climax of Beethoven's final symphony came from the poet Ralph had read and admired throughout his life, Walt Whitman. The vast range of feelings in Beethoven's last movement are those of someone who can declare as Whitman did in 'Song of Myself':

> I am of old and young,
> of the foolish as much as the wise,
> Regardless of others, ever regardful of others,
> Maternal as well as paternal,

a child as well as a man,
Stuffed with stuff that is coarse
and stuffed with the stuff that is fine.

To evoke the earthiness that accompanies the metaphysical in Beethoven's 'final unrestrained jubilation' Ralph, with a jokey, echoing allusion to 'Macnamara's Band', turns to another poet who urged:

Pour out the wine without restraint or stay,
Pour nor by cups but by the belly full,
Pour out to all that will.

The poet is Edmund Spenser and the lines come from *Epithalamion*, the poem which was the basis for the masque which Ralph and Ursula had recently been working on. This final quotation in the essay is an indication of how much this collaboration must have been in his mind at the time. His absence from London did not allow many meetings with her during the first months of the war. But on 23 October he managed to have lunch and tea with her and on 11 November, her diary records that they went to the ballet together. At this time she was assisting him as he again turned to work on his *Pilgrim's Progress*. She typed the libretto and made suggestions about the content. Writing to thank her for her efforts he signed himself, more warmly than usual, 'With all my love'. He agreed to her suggestion that he write to his cousin-in-law Virginia Woolf to enquire whether the Hogarth Press, which Woolf helped to direct, might be interested in bringing out a volume of Ursula's poems. There came a friendly reply after years of silence between them but no publication ensued. Ursula also proposed approaching the highly successful novelist and playwright J.B. Priestley. Ralph commented, 'If your "Dear Sir" to Priestley progresses as a certain former one did, I shall get jealous. So there'.

On Boxing Day 1939 he told Ursula that he was working on what was entitled, when it was first performed in a BBC broadcast almost exactly a year later, 'Six Choral Songs To Be Sung In Time Of War'. He asked Ursula to search Shelley for more passages to add to those he was setting. He was also delighted with 'the lovely poetry book' she had sent him for Christmas and curious to learn more about the American poet Emily Dickinson whom she had recommended. Literature continued to be an important bond between them.

In mid-January 1940 Ralph went to Oxford to help celebrate the seventieth birthday of Hugh Allen, the Cambridge friend of nigh on half a century who had continued to be a great supporter of his career. Food rationing, which was introduced that month and which was to become ever more stringent as the war progressed, did not unduly affect the quality and quantity of the festive meal. A few weeks after Ralph's return home there came a wrench in the White Gates household when the high-spirited daughterly Honorine left to get married. Her husband was Bernard Brown, a trumpeter who, after leaving Cambridge, had recently begun a career as a professional musician. Ralph and Adeline were both sad to see her leave but happy that she could put her great energies and abilities into creating a home of her own. Ralph was also pleased to learn that that year's Leith Hill Music Festival would go ahead after all, albeit on a reduced scale. Fanny Farrer had felt obliged to resign as secretary because of her ever increasing responsibilities in her full-time job at the Federation of Women's Institutes. Her successor, Margery Cullen, was immediately confronted with a daunting situation. The Meat Marketing Board had commandeered the Dorking Halls for use in the war effort. The Board, after a period of refusing her, finally were persuaded to allow her to remove the meat-packing machinery temporarily and stage the concerts. There was just one condition. If called upon, she and her committee members were to re-install the machinery within twenty-four hours. Margery Cullen accepted these responsibilities and the concerts went ahead. Stirring music was performed: *Elijah* and Handel's *Judas Maccabeus*.[32]

On 19 March – the day after Mussolini, on meeting Hitler at the Brenner Pass, had threatened to join Germany in the war against Britain and France – Ralph was in London to conduct his *Mass in G Minor* in St Paul's Cathedral. Ursula went with him. She long remembered the choir, surmounted by the great spaces of the baroque cathedral, singing in the dusk with little lights at their desks. The Dean and Chapter had thought it appropriate for Ralph to wear a cassock when he conducted the Mass. His girth was such, Ursula remembered, that the 'cassock did not meet although it was the largest they could find for him in the vestry'. Shortly afterwards he and Ursula agreed on a further and important development in their relationship. Ursula would be invited down to tea at White Gates with Ralph, Adeline and other guests. For the first time Ursula would be presented to his wife and acquaintances as more than a fleeting member of his entourage. The tea-party passed off well. The other guests were Ralph's school contemporary Max Beerbohm and his wife Florence. The 29-year-old Ursula listened politely to her companions, all in their late sixties, as they chatted away. Adeline talked with Lady Florence about the Beerbohms' abandoning of their many books and *objets d'art* in their home in Rapallo when they had felt compelled to leave Mussolini's Italy. Ralph and Max talked about Charterhouse as they both remembered it in Victorian times. Ralph did imitations of their headmaster and then the two of them sang music-hall songs, Max in a rather cracked tenor voice, Ralph in a lumbering bass. Adeline was kindly towards Ursula. The tea-party began a friendship that was steadily to deepen; Ursula was soon taking over a part of the role formerly performed by Honorine at White Gates.

Ralph was eager for more such meetings. He was full of love and admiration. He wrote: 'do you know the old saying that women should be divided into the high-heeled and the high-souled – You are both my dear.'[33] On another occasion, with a characteristic lack of punctuation, he wrote to Ursula excitedly:

My Dear, how about coming down here for lunch (12.30) on Friday 31st It would be lovely to see you again I nearly forgot what you look like – except that you are very alluring – I know you will put on your prettiest frock to give me pleasure – though of course it's intellect I really appreciate (!!??) I hope it will be weather for silk stockings and high heeled shoes ... so come, my dear, and allure me on Friday'.[34]

Another letter of the time dwells again on her clothes, saying 'once more I am all agog about the new stockings'. Ralph goes on to ask her whether she remembers 'what Dr Johnson said to David Garrick when he took him behind the scenes at the theatre'. The answer to that question indicates clearly the earthiness of the relationship now existing between them. A recent biographer of Johnson relates how 'Garrick informed David Hume that Johnson ... "out of considerations of rigid virtue", decided that he had to put an end to his backstage visits: "No, David," said he, "I will never come back. For the white bubbies and the silk stockings of your actresses excite my genitals."'[35]

As the Ralph–Ursula relationship consolidated within a larger social context, the war began to intensify. Within a few months Britain was being heavily and relentlessly bombed and faced the prospect of imminent invasion by the Germans. The war quickened markedly in

April 1940 when Germany invaded Denmark and Norway. As a result of British inadequacies in assisting the Norwegians, Chamberlain resigned in May and was replaced as Prime Minister by Winston Churchill. That same month the Germans proceeded to invade The Netherlands, Belgium and Luxembourg. And then, dramatically, began the Blitzkrieg against France, a campaign which in its rapidity and unqualified success astonished the world. By the end of June 1940, France, one of the great powers of Europe, signed an ignominious peace treaty with Germany. The French army, which in 1919, just over twenty years before, had been the largest on the planet, had been utterly humiliated. Hitler now proceeded with plans to invade an England that was in a state of shock at the loss of its most important ally. First Germany needed to destroy Britain's air defences in order to ensure an unimpeded invasion from the sea, and the Battle of Britain, a contest between young fighter pilots, duly began. And so too, a little later, did the Blitz, the systematic bombing of London. The whole population was issued with gas masks. Ralph's arrived in Dorking in July. London, particularly the working-class area of the City, was bombed night after night, often with incendiary bombs. The Blitz brought a tragedy for Ralph and Adeline. On 2 September 1940 bombs fell on Chelsea and Honorine, who was living in a flat there, was killed. She had been married just six months.

Ralph was distraught at the death of this happy, charming, ener-getic young woman who had become a surrogate niece to him. Mary Bennett, Adeline's niece, recalled that Ralph: 'always read the epistle and the Gospel for the week to Adeline after breakfast – on the morning of Honorine's funeral he read the whole funeral service to her after breakfast…. At the funeral R and A stood alone and looking <u>infinitely</u> dignified and pathetic.' Subsequently Ralph was a regular visitor to Honorine's grave. 'Ralph went every day at first and then once a week to see the grave … when later on … he couldn't find it, he came back in such distress, almost sobbing'.[36]

Ralph's grief was long lasting. Seven weeks after Honorine's death he told Imogen Holst: 'we don't quite realise she has gone yet – one keeps thinking she will come in at any minute as of old – we old people would not mind going.' The depression to which he and Adeline now seemed susceptible must surely have been aggravated by the other deaths that year: Donald Tovey, their close friend Dorothy Longman, and Adeline's eminent, and very supportive, brother, H.A.L. Fisher. Ralph went on to tell Imogen that his only contribution to the war effort was 'organising quite low brow concerts for soldiers in Dorking'. In fact, he was doing a good deal more. He had been appointed Chairman of the Home Office Committee for the Release of Internal Alien Musicians. He devoted a good deal of time and trouble to helping them and one consequence was a new friendship, with Robert Muller-Hartmann. He was a German composer who, with his wife and daughter, came to live in Dorking with Yanya and Genia Hornstein, friends of the Vaughan Williamses. The gap in the White Gates' household caused by Honorine's death was to some extent helped by Adeline's sister Emmeline and her husband R.O. Morris, who came to live there at this time.

Like other owners of substantial homes in the country, Ralph and Adeline were requested to 'billet' or give lodgings to individuals who had fled the bombing in London. One of these was a young teacher Frances Chaplin. A quarter of a century later she recalled for Ursula that: 'As a grammar school mistress from London I was billeted at White Gates, as I was alleged to be "quiet and musical" and I spent the first year of the war there ... I knew Honorine and in fact still have her bicycle basket and also the alarm clock dear VW bought that I might be in time for those early breakfasts I shared with him. I also met Bernard Brown and liked him very much.'

Frances went on to recall the life that Ralph and Adeline lived with the Morrises and 'all the cats'. One special image remained in her mind: 'I recall particularly one evening when I came in late and found all four elderly people sitting round the hearth each reading a volume of Trollope. They found great comfort in this account of a more stable world.'

Frances Chaplin also strongly concurred with Ursula's description of Adeline at this time. Ursula has written in her biography of Ralph that Adeline was now:

> very thin, the cool beauty of her youth had changed to gaunt and austere age. Her back was straight, her head beautifully set on her shoulders, and her heavy eyelids in their deep sockets lifted to show pale blue eyes where amusement could flash or fury blaze, though she usually looked at the world with gentle irony. Pain had taught her stillness and she had a quality of heroic endurance that could be intimidating. Though she could melt into friendliness there were tremendous barriers of reserve that froze between her and people she did not like.

Frances Chaplin strongly commended the page in Ursula's book on which these words appeared. She wrote to Ursula: 'I very much appreciated the detail of your portrait of Mrs Vaughan Williams on p208 of your book; I met all those facets of her character.' For Frances, her assessment of Ralph involved no qualification. He was, she wrote, 'a man whom I felt to be truly generous and wise, and in the literal sense magnanimous'.[37]

By the autumn, Ursula had left London to be in Bude in Cornwall where her husband, Michael, was now stationed. There seems to have been a silence between her and Ralph. A letter to her at this time assures her that he has not 'taken umbrage; he admires her new poems and urges her to 'write a lot more beautiful poetry and keep your beauty – my goodness what wonderful things to possess – to have beauty and to be able to make beauty. The Nazis can't destroy that.'[38] A few weeks later he learned from her that due to her protracted absence from London she had been obliged to sublet the flat in Thayer Street. His reply contains a very pointed paragraph of just two sentences. The first expresses regret about the loss of the well-remembered flat; the second insists on hope for them for the future. He writes, 'How sad about the flat – what memories. But there must be another flat and more memories.'[39]

At times Ralph worried that Ursula might break up from her husband from whom she was growing more distant. As she contemplated a return to London instead of staying with Michael, Ralph wrote with perhaps an allusion to his own longevity, writing in the last phrase in Latin: 'My dear, I am sure you ought to go with Michael. If you separated now you might find it difficult to join up again. And that would be bad *sub specie aeternatis*.' But later that year he was happy when Ursula told him of a new posting for Michael: 'it will be exciting if Michael gets the job you mention – it will be in London I suppose.' The prospect of her return grew even more exciting as he imagined, flirtatiously, the clothes she might wear: 'As regards stockings – failing silk, I advise the ribbed kind – I noticed a young woman sitting down the other day and the ribbed effect very pleasurably accentuates the curve of the knee – but of course a transparent silk ... sure of no wrinkles is the thing.... This is a short letter but I thought it important to discuss the stocking problem again. P.S. I don't know about rib stretching to the touch – I've never had an opportunity of testing.'[40]

During 1940 and earlier, Ralph's political response to the coming of the war had been an energetic commitment to an organization called Federal Union. Its principles were those propounded in the book *Union*

Now by Clarence K. Streit, an American journalist and political activist who had been an ardent supporter of the now failed League of Nations. In an upbeat letter to the somewhat downhearted Iris Lemare of the old Macnaghten Concert Society Ralph gave his understanding of what Federal Union was about: 'I hope for a United States of Europe to which all nations (including Germany) who do not believe in force will belong. Not a league of sovereign nations but a Union to which all nations will give up part of their sovereignty – preserving their individuality and nationality for their own affairs.'[41]

Given Hitler's intentions, these hopes seem naively optimistic and indeed Federal Union was a soon forgotten political movement. But his commitment of time and money to the organization is another example of his lifelong social and political concern. Ralph's proposals recall his well-meaning but ultimately unworkable reading of the General Strike in 1926. But in early 1941 he was confronted by a political matter which he immediately understood and on which, formulating the issues clearly, he acted decisively. In the second week of March that year he read in *The Times* that performances of works by the Communist composer Alan Bush had been banned by the BBC. This was because Bush had signed the 'People's Convention', a declaration organized by a left-wing group, containing a critique of the Churchill government as one that catered to the privileged and the wealthy and demanded the greatest wartime sacrifices from the poor. Ralph, a Liberal from Victorian times, was appalled by such censorship by the BBC. He immediately wrote to the Corporation to protest. 'So far as I know Dr. Bush's political views I am strongly opposed to them. Nevertheless I wish to protest against this victimisation of private opinion in the only way possible to me.' The BBC had recently commissioned from him, and paid him, for a patriotic choral song 'England, My England', a setting of well-known words by the 1890s poet W.E. Henley. Ralph wrote straightaway to refuse the commission and return the fee.

This was not to be the last time Ralph would stand up for principle during the Second World War. Later on he would do his utmost to defend the rights of the young composer and uncompromising conscientious objector Michael Tippett.

The BBC was conciliatory and Ralph's choral setting of 'England, My England' was eventually broadcast on 16 November 1941. The words are a rush of patriotic rhetoric, much inferior to the highly crafted, inspirational speeches broadcast by Winston Churchill during this year of crisis for the nation. Henley's wordy lines did not inspire memorable music.

> What have I done for you,
>> England, my England?
> What is there I would not do
>> England, my own!
> With your glorious eyes austere
> As the lord were walking near
> Whispering terrible things and dear
>> As the song on your bugles blown
>> England
> Round the world on your bugles down.

Ralph's setting could do little to make a song of any distinction from these slipshod words.

Ralph worked hard to stage some semblance of the Leith Hill Music Festival in this difficult year in which at night there was the blackout in Dorking and in London and most other cities and towns. The winter was bitterly cold. The Meat Marketing Board now refused absolutely to allow the Dorking Halls to be used for the festival. However the vicar of St. Martin's in Dorking stepped in and made the parish church available. Ursula joined Ralph and Adeline for the performance of *The Messiah* on 26 April and then had tea with them before catching the train back to London. Some weeks before, in early March 1941, she had resumed occupancy of the flat on Thayer Street while her husband remained at his posting near Leicester. Michael moved on to Cosham in Hampshire, where he served as the officer in charge of the anti-aircraft defences of Portsmouth and Southampton. Ralph was in London more frequently these days and so he and Ursula were again able to meet. He was still working with the Refugee Committee organized by the Home Office and he was also beginning to attend meetings of the recently formed Committee for the Encouragement of Music and the Arts. This product of war in which the arts enjoyed increasing popularity finally and permanently consolidated itself as the Arts Council. On his increasing number of visits to London Ralph would have his lunch with Ursula at the 'MM', a small dining club for musicians. It was located down in a basement near Oxford Circus tube station and run by the cellist Mary Mukle who, with her sister Ann, a pianist, had given the first performance of Ralph's 'Six Studies in English Folk Song' fifteen years before.

Ursula was now doing voluntary work for the Marylebone Citizens

268

Advice Bureau. On 3 May 1941, just a week after her visit to Dorking for the performance of *The Messiah* she underwent medical tests in London. As a consequence, on 7 May, as she noted in her diary, she had an operation in a facility in Harley Street. Much later in life, Ursula revealed to family members that there had been the termination of a pregnancy.[42] But the evidence from the time is not sufficient to suggest any implication this might have had for her developing relationship with Ralph. Her diary records that after the operation, which took place in the week generally considered to be the climax of the Blitz, she spent two days in bed in the Thayer Street flat and then went to Somerset for a week. She returned to London on 17 May and on the following day went with Ralph to a Mahler concert.

The following day German paratroopers landed on the island of Crete. This was a stepping stone in Hitler's assault on Europe. With his failure to bomb Britain into submission the main fighting in the war had moved eastward into the Balkans and Greece. Ralph, who followed the course of the war closely, was very much opposed to the British decision to send troops to help the Greeks. When the magazine *Civil Liberty* reported British failure in protecting civil freedom in Greece, Ralph wrote to the editor angrily, proposing that: 'the British troops be withdrawn and leave the Greeks to the tender mercies of the Germans – they will then probably learn what "civil liberty" means.' Ralph was entirely opposed to the ultimately unsuccessful British involvement in Greece and Crete; 'we ... risked losing the war in early days by sending to the aid of Greece troops which were badly needed in Africa.'[43] The keen social and political observer had now become a military observer. The world war had by now moved on to a second continent, Africa. Fighting was taking place between Britain and Italy in and around their colonies in Eastern Africa. Soon Hitler would have to come to the aid of his Italian ally in Libya and the protracted North African war would begin. On 21 June 1941 Hitler took another dramatic initiative, one which for many historians was the mistake that led to his ultimate defeat. Dishonouring the treaty of non-aggression with the Soviets, he launched a massive attack on Russia. Five days later when Ralph and Ursula had lunch together, the frightening prospect of an imminent German invasion of Britain was receding.

Around this time Ralph had been visited in Dorking by Muir Mathieson, a young Scot who had been a student at the RCM a decade earlier. Mathieson had gone on to have a rapidly successful career as a composer of film music. Alexander Korda, the great impresario in British film in the thirties and the founder of London Films, had made him the musical director of a major picture, *Catherine the Great*, when he was only twenty-three-years-old. Mathieson was now director of music for the Ministry of Information and currently beginning work on a major film with propaganda intent; it was entitled *49th Parallel*. He came to see Ralph to see if he would be prepared to write the music for the film. His visit was timely. He found Ralph 'strangely depressed at his inability to play a further part in the war'. Mathieson recounted to him the anti-Nazi story told in the film and tried to show 'how the cinema could help to achieve those very objects for which he was striving'. Ralph was convinced and set to work straightaway. The result was a powerful work of film music which marked the beginning of Ralph's near fifteen-year career in this new, twentieth-century musical form. The sound track of *49th Parallel* begins with a grand, heartening prelude with phrases that he later re-used in his second string quartet. Later in the score there is music with a jazz beat that looks forward to the *scherzo* of his Sixth Symphony. It all moves along compellingly. Ralph enjoyed working at the Denham film studios, telling his old RCM contemporary Fritz Hart, 'Writing in seconds to the stop watch is rather fun and composing and <u>scoring</u> extra bars during the rehearsal interval (5 minutes).'[44] To his publisher Hubert Foss at Oxford University Press he wrote happily: 'I thoroughly enjoyed my days at Denham and am quite prepared to do another film provided (1) I like the subject (2) I get good money (3) I have a say as to when and how the music should come in.'[45] Such commissions followed on swiftly. One was for a film about the RAF, *Coastal Command*, and another, *The People's Land*, a patriotic work on behalf of the wartime National Trust. Ralph very much enjoyed being among film people and made a number of new friends including the producer Michel Balcon, the director Anthony Asquith, and Ernest Irving, a fellow composer of film music who wrote the score for the classic Ealing comedy *Kind Hearts and Coronets*.

As he was drawn ever more into writing music for the cinema Ralph did not give up work on what was to be his major enterprise of the war years, his Fifth Symphony. In the third week of December he organized a playthrough on two pianos, by Hubert Foss and a friend, of the score as it then stood. The performance took place at Trinity College of Music, then in Mandeville Place, Marylebone, close to Ursula's flat. Ralph invited along two young colleagues whom he liked and respected, Herbert Howells and Gerald Finzi. He told the latter that the playthrough would be the basis of an important decision. It was 'to see if I like it well enough to go on with it. Your criticism would be much valued.'[46] Ralph was sufficiently pleased and reassured by what he heard that he quickly resumed work on this large, ambitious piece.

Just before this decisive playthrough, the war had taken a new turn. The Japanese had attacked the American naval base at Pearl Harbor in Hawaii. The war was now truly global. The British would soon lose Singapore to the Japanese and then continue to fight a lengthy campaign against them in Burma in which Ursula's brother was a serving officer. The bombing of London had lessened but was still a threat. Ursula was a firewatcher in her block of flats. Her friend, Jean Stewart, a violist who lived in a flat on the ground floor, shared the responsibility with her. The two young women often pooled their rations of food. Sometimes they entertained Ralph together for lunch or tea; he would take them to Henekeys, the local pub, and buy them expensive drinks which they enjoyed. He also charmed the barmaid who developed a keen interest in his music.

In April 1942, on one of his trips to the capital, Ralph visited the London offices of Oxford University Press, based in Soho Square. He had business to do with Norman Peterkin, who had taken over responsibility for publishing Ralph's work following the recent, surprising resignation of Hubert Foss. Peterkin found his visitor from rural Surrey 'looking more like an ancient Briton than ever, but perceptibly aged since I met him last'. Ralph handed over to his new editor a number of manuscripts for safe-keeping. These included an as yet unperformed concerto for oboe and strings, the Double Trio for Strings and the music for *Epithalamion*, the masque on which he had worked with Ursula early on in their relationship.

During his meeting with Peterkin, the 40-year-old William Walton arrived, bouncing and unexpected, in the front office where the current publications were on show. 'The Show Room girls told him I was engaged with VW and reported later that Walton remarked "I suppose the old buffer is going to monopolise him all morning." Peterkin subsequently escorted Ralph from his office and 'when VW learned that Walton had been waiting to see me apologised to him for keeping me engaged. According to the girls, VW was far nicer to W. than W. was to him, and W. is not considered to be a gentleman I gather!'[47] Walton then offered Peterkin an assessment of Ralph that surprised the publisher. 'Walton came into my room remarking "well, the old pussy cat has gone at last".

I supposed I must have shown some astonishment for he went on to say that, "of course V.W. was a really big pussy with very sharp claws" and "was the biggest intriguer of the lot"; that it was astonishing that nobody realised it (except W.W. apparently) and how he managed to get away with it as a result.' A somewhat puzzled Norman Peterkin concluded: 'I simply cannot comment on this for it runs completely counter to my conception of V.W. But I have seen little of him.'[48]

Ralph will almost certainly have seen Ursula on this visit to London. Earlier in the year, on Valentine's Day, she had sent him a poem that proposed a meeting. Every year since the early 1940s she had composed a poem for him for 14 February; this year's was also very much an invitation.

> Bring me a golden heart
> I have a silver key
> That will unlock the treasures
> Lying like all winter-hidden flowers,
> In secrecy.
> Bring me a day for pleasure
> And fully crowned with vine;
> Loose time among his hours ...
> I ask ... to answer this in your part,
> Dear Valentine.

Ursula was now growing further and further apart from her husband. She wrote in her autobiography 'So often during the last year we had felt like strangers. In London I was having a much more congenial life than I had ever had before, he a lonely and overworked time of responsibility.' She was glad they were not 'burdened with young children', 'a fate we had been diligent to avoid as we both hated family life.'[49] Just after Easter 1942 Ursula went down to Cosham near Southampton where Michael was stationed, 'another day when we seemed far apart, barely acquaintances.'[50]

Two months later the marriage concluded shockingly. On Friday 5 June Michael came up to London to spend the weekend with Ursula in the Thayer Street flat. They had a relaxed time together, ordering a Chinese meal to have at home on the first night and dining out on the other two evenings. They discussed a possible holiday together later in the month when Michael would have ten days leave. Ursula saw him off from Waterloo Station on the Sunday evening.

Early the following morning she was shocked and astounded to receive a telephone call informing her that Michael had suffered a heart attack. Her distress intensified when her phone went out of order. Ralph was due to come for lunch. He arrived and was 'a comforting presence'. Then Jean Stewart appeared at the door bearing a telegram for Ursula which had been delivered downstairs. It was from the War Office. Ursula was stunned by 'the unspeakable crudeness' of the message. It informed her that her husband had died at 10 a.m. and continued: 'body will be sent to London or one first class warrant issued for your attendance at funeral Southampton.' Ursula was in a state of utter shock. 'I couldn't focus, couldn't believe that while I'd been telephoning Michael was already dead, and how could he be dead when I'd seen him yesterday.'[51]

Ralph acted decisively. 'Ralph said at once "You must come home with me." En route to Dorking he contacted Adeline and let her know what had happened. When they arrived at White Gates Ursula found that 'a bed for me had been made up in the big galleried living-room they called the hall. "We wanted you near us", Adeline said. She was very quiet and kind....'

A new mode of life would now begin for Ursula, Adeline and Ralph.

Chapter Sixteen

A THREESOME

Following the brief but moving funeral service for Michael in a little hut that served as an army church near Southampton, Ursula returned to White Gates. Ralph took her over to Leith Hill Place to have tea with his brother Hervey, himself recently a widower. Ursula was touched and amused to see Ralph in the role of younger brother asking Hervey's permission to borrow the key to the garden so that he might show it to her. She felt she had a glimpse of Ralph's early life. 'The kitchen garden was a delight, surrounded by high walls on which grew old fashioned roses and espaliered fruit.'[1] The large garden was four acres square and tilted southwards to the downs. Ralph remembered the days when the great house with its cows, pigs and hens was entirely self-sufficient. Now, in wartime, the cattle were under the control of the Milk Marketing Board.

When the time came that she felt able to return to London to deal with the sad practicalities of bereavement, Ursula found that her many friends there were zealous in seeking to provide her with diversions. But then came a setback. She awoke one morning with an agonizing pain in her toe. A Harley Street orthopaedic surgeon told her that she had a fracture and for the then considerable sum of five pounds strapped it up for her. Ralph wrote anxiously 'I could not bear to think of your pretty foot all swollen and was afraid it might develop into something worse. But what a hard time you've had – Yes we will meet soon and down our cares in beer.'[2] Hobbling awkwardly she accompanied Ralph to the first performance of his motet 'Valiant For Truth' on 29 June in the Wren

274

church of St Michael's Cornhill, which miraculously stood untouched among the smouldering ruins of the City of London. Ralph's new piece, setting words from Bunyan, was part of a programme containing Tudor motets, Haydn's *Te Deum*, and new works by Ralph's friend and colleague of long standing Harold Darke, who had organized the concert. Ralph and Ursula had dinner together afterwards.

Disconcertingly, Ursula's foot was not healing. She consulted another doctor who discovered that there was no fracture at all. Rather a fine needle had pierced her toe and was affecting a nerve. Ralph's reaction to this was that of one of his generation and class: 'When I told this news both Ralph and his brother-in-law R.O. Morris who lived at White Gates, wanted to go and horsewhip the orthopaedic surgeon. Adeline said it would be better to get my five pounds back, but I rather favoured the horsewhipping. It was delightful to have such an eighteenth century revenge proposed.'[3]

Ursula now started to recover but the process was slow. She found it difficult to take care of herself in London so: 'finally at Adeline's invitation, I went back to Dorking for a month, with utmost thankfulness'.[4]

R.O. Morris, the husband of Adeline's recently deceased sister Emmeline, was extremely kind to Ursula during these weeks. He taught her to play backgammon and, as her foot got better, took her for walks in the Surrey countryside. Ralph also went out of his way to make Ursula feel part of the household. He invited her to bring her work into his study, making a space for her at one of his work tables. She would sometimes sit in the window seat watching him dashing to and fro from table to piano, sometimes stopping abruptly to ask her about her writing. 'It was a curiously successful arrangement, for we were easily silent together, or when one of us had something to ask, we did so without it disturbing each other.' The summer brought a growing together of this complex trio in which Ursula was to Adeline a daughter and friend, and to Ralph a daughter in Dorking, and in London, a lover. As Ursula later remembered, 'These mornings spent together were a consolidation of affection, a comfort and a pleasure to each of us. I think this shared retreat rather amused Adeline. It gave me the reassuring feeling of being wanted, missed when I wasn't there, which helped me enormously.'[5]

But the time came when Ursula felt the need to return to London to find work to eke out her widow's pension. She took a job as secretary-receptionist to Dr Paul Nathan, a refugee who, having fled from the Nazis, had set up a medical practice in Welbeck Street, close to Ursula's flat. Ursula made one stipulation: that there would be no appointments for patients between 12.30 and 3 p.m. so that she would be free to attend the lunchtime concerts at the National Gallery. These were an important part of cultural life in London during the war with the pianist Myra Hess very much a star performer. Ursula was able, therefore, to attend the concert which was given on Ralph's seventieth birthday in October 1942 and made up entirely of his compositions. Gerald Finzi's settings of Shakespeare's songs 'Let Us Garlands Bring', one of his finest works, was presented to Ralph as a birthday gift. After the concert Gerald and Joy Finzi invited Ursula to join them and Ralph for his birthday lunch. It turned out that they were admirers of her book of poems, which had recently been published by Basil Blackwell. From that occasion dated a long-lasting friendship. The Finzis would visit Thayer Street and Ursula would stay at their grand house in Berkshire. Ursula's first volume was *No Other Choice*. She suggested that the title referred to a poet's calling. But the love poems it contains suggest that it may also refer to the utter irresistibility of her socially difficult love for Ralph.

Certainly in these early months of her widowhood Ralph's physical feelings for her were intense. His many letters to her at this time often refer to their love-making. One of them characteristically refers to his pleasure in her silk stockings: 'I love writing the word "pair". It brings up lovely memories.' On another occasion as he lists possible trains from Dorking up to Waterloo he predicts ruefully that an appointment may reduce their time alone together. 'Saturday. I've got a man coming to see me at 10.00. I may catch the 11.18 (Wloo 12.3) But it may have to be 11.51 Wloo 12.43. But in any case, it will be a quick lunch and no time for any "funny stuff".'[6]

His seventieth birthday brought in a torrent of cards and letters of congratulation from all over the world. The BBC organized a Vaughan Williams week in its programming and had elaborate plans to present and promote him as an icon of Englishness. In this fourth, wearying year of war, with the sense of the need for patriotic invigoration the corporation started to build up that image of Ralph that still endures, to the detriment of the multifacetedness of his achievement as a composer. The branding process began with the BBC's carefully angled preparation for the birthday. An executive in the BBC Music Department K.A. Wright, wrote in an internal memorandum: 'I suggest that we think of Vaughan Williams not so much as a composer … but rather as a great personality in believing in and helping to develop the music of the people, whether in his work for folk music, festivals, or writing music for homely choirs and bands. This is an angle that would have wide appeal in the Dominions.'[7] After all the excitements of the birthday celebrations Ralph had one of his acute phases of doubt about his abilities as a composer. A number of his letters written in the autumn of 1943 contain expressions of self-depreci-ation. Following the moment of widespread recognition he would write, 'What I want to do now is to wipe the slate clean and try to learn how to compose music', and, a week later, 'I think I get more and more incom-petent as a composer.'[8] Yet in this mood he nevertheless returned, as the year drew towards its close, to his very substantial, ongoing project, his Fifth Symphony. On the last day of January 1943, his Leith Hill Music Festival colleagues, Ivy Herbert and Margery Cullen, played it through for him on two pianos in the village hall in Abinger. Adeline was well enough to be driven over from Dorking and to sit with Ursula in the small group of listeners. On the return to White Gates Adeline stumbled, sprained her foot, and was confined to bed for some days.

Ralph continued to work on the finalizing of the symphony. At one stage he placed a quotation from Bunyan at the head of the slow movement. It read 'Upon this place stood a cross, and a little sepulchre. Then he said: "he hath given me rest by his sorrow, and life by his death".' The words offer a means of coming to terms with Ralph's many losses in recent times, perhaps most particular, poignant and painful, that of Honorine. Perhaps in the renewal and resurrection that are also envis-aged in the symphony, the gracious coming of Ursula may also be heard. Ralph dedicated the work to the contemporary symphonist whom he most admired: 'Without permission and with the sincerest flattery to Jean Sibelius, whose great example is worthy of imitation'.

The Fifth Symphony had its first orchestral play-through at the Maida Vale studios of the BBC on 25 May, with Adrian Boult conducting. Ralph invited fifteen guests to come and hear it. The list is a roll call of those close to Ralph at this time in his life. It includes Ursula and her friend Jean Stewart, Adeline's sister Cordelia, Muir Mathieson, Gerald Finzi, Herbert Howells and Gordon Jacob, Ralph's frequent assistant with orchestration. Maud Karpeles was there and so were Ralph's old colleagues from the Leith Hill Music Festival, Fanny Farrer, Ivy Herbert and Margery Cullen. Bernard Brown, the widower of Honorine, was also invited.

The first public performance took place at a Promenade concert in the Albert Hall on 24 June 1943. Since Sir Henry Wood was ill, Ralph took his place as conductor. He was pleased with the occasion, writing to tell Sir Henry: 'The orchestra were splendid – and as I made no serious mistakes we had a very fine performance.'[9] It was a great success with those that heard it that summer night, clearly speaking with power to an audience bereaved, damaged and wearied by the ongoing war. The first movement begins with horn calls in D major that have an ominous, ghostly sound which for those first listeners in London must surely have brought to mind the air-raid sirens. Then comes reassurance, a quietly lyrical theme expressing sympathy, regret, gentle consolation. Meditation follows. A throb of feeling enters into it and, gathering in intensity builds to a grand swoop of sound. And then a great crescendo! After all the guardedness and reservations in the meditation music the crescendo sounds out what is fine and indeed noble in life. There follows a modest triumphing and the music quietens into reflection. It fades away and there is a return of the disturbing horns. The movement's ending is a reminder of the blitzed London in T.S. Eliot's *Little Gidding* whose ghostly visitor and mentor 'faded on the blowing of the horn'.

The second movement, the *scherzo*, is the shortest; it offers a suggestion of high spirits. But enduringly in the background there is melancholy. In the theme for oboe and cor anglais there is also malice. Some listeners have been reminded of Bunyan's 'hobgoblin and foul fiend'. There is a chirpy woodwind sound but it does not last long. Cheeriness in this movement is ambiguous, brief and perfunctory. It ends suddenly. The third movement, the longest of the four, is a *romanza* that begins with a lament on the solo cor anglais. There follows a sad meditation that is taken over redemptively by a swelling music that moves along in slow stately fashion. It climaxes in a sweep of rapturous sound that is a compensation for all the darkness and uncertainty that has gone before. The music of redemption is then pondered in a music of compassion and reassurance. Passages in this movement are from Ralph's proposed opera about Bunyan's pilgrim. The *romanza* is essentially a restatement of the first movement with the delicately qualified and understated positives given more extent and power.

The fourth and final movement, the *passacaglia*, opens slowly then quickens to a near bounce beat. A triumphant pealing of bells is suggested. We have moved on to, in several senses of the word, celebration. The essentially religious procedure informing the design of the symphony is made clear as the last few minutes take on the character of a benedictus and recessional. The symphony concludes in a silent composure that contrasts markedly with the unnerving opening bars with which the symphony begins. Adrian Boult, hearing the symphony on the radio, wrote to Ralph to congratulate him and to try to express what the music meant at that difficult moment in the war. He concluded: 'that its serene loveliness is completely satisfying in these times and shows, as only music can, what we must work for when this madness is over.'[10] Ursula, a member of the audience at that first performance, remembers how: 'in this radiant performance, fears and despairs were cancelled, beauty and serenity were all. It was still light, the evening of midsummer day, when we came out of the Albert Hall. There was a party of us, who I can't remember; Adeline's sister Cordelia and one of her nieces, but who else? We all walked down to Chelsea to the river. The day ended for me dining quietly with Ralph, the music still in the air.'[11]

Ralph's great aesthetic contribution to the war effort was accompanied by more practical ones. Some of them involved what were for him matters of high principle. That same summer he did his utmost to support a conscientious objector, Michael Tippett, a fellow composer who was much younger than he. Tippett had studied counterpoint with R.O. Morris and was now very much a part of Morley College, which had been such an important institution in the career of Gustav Holst and, to a lesser extent, in that of Ralph himself. Tippett had created an orchestra of unemployed musicians and given well-attended concerts all over the London area as well as at the National Gallery, Wigmore Hall and the Holst room at Morley College. When, as a conscientious objector, he was directed to do agricultural work, he refused. He was then summoned to attend a tribunal at the Police Court at Oxted in Surrey. Ralph spent a whole day travelling there cross-country on inconvenient buses in order to give evidence on Tippett's behalf. He told the Tribunal: 'I think Tippett's views are entirely wrong, but I respect him very much for holding them so firmly. I think his compositions are very remarkable and form a distinct national asset and will increase the prestige of this country in the world. His teaching work at Morley College is distinctly work of national importance to create a musical atmosphere at the College and elsewhere.'[12]

Neither Ralph's testimony nor that of other senior figures from the world of music convinced the tribunal, and Tippett was sentenced to three months' imprisonment in Wormwood Scrubs.

In the month in which the Allies, after their victory in North Africa, had accepted the surrender of Italy, Ralph found time to give his support in a more arcane controversy that was important in the musical culture of the church in which as an organist in South London he had begun his career. The Dean and Chapter of Ripon Cathedral, in an attempt to make worship more popular, had proposed the omission of settings of the canticles on Sundays. The idea was strongly opposed by Charles Moody, the cathedral organist, composer of anthems such as 'Before the Ending of the Day' and also a graduate of the same alma mater as Ralph, the Royal College of Organists. An agnostic, and yet a cultural Anglican and a great devotee of English church music, Ralph readily joined the resistance to what he called 'this ecclesiastical totalitarianism'. In a letter which he made publicly available he maintained that: '... the people should have a share in the service, but there is no more reason why they should join in the anthem and canticles than in the Absolution or the "comfortable words". And further I think the idea of choir service is a noble one, where the people come only to listen and meditate.'[13]

The last two phrases are a succinct expression of Ralph's humanist view of the function of religious observance.

The war was turning in the Allies' favour but air-raids were still a strong possibility. Ralph was a member of a Dorking fire-watching team and at White Gates kept his equipment (his tin helmet, torch, bucket and pump) close at hand. He and Adeline slept in a small bedroom that was sandbagged against bomb blasts. A succession of people shared the house with them. Cordelia's son Adam Curle, brought his wife and baby daughter to stay. And other nephews and nieces of Adeline were short- or long-term residents. Ralph's Leith Hill Music Festival colleague Ivy Herbert and her friend Molly Potto moved into the two rooms which Ralph and Adeline had had built. And R.O. Morris still working as a music scholar and composer much admired by Ralph continued to live there after his wife's death. He and his several cats shared the largest bedroom in the house. He compiled crossword puzzles for *The Times* and shared the fire-watching duties. Ursula was by now a regular visitor, often staying overnight. If she were there on a Sunday she would muck out the hen house. She also worked regularly with Ralph in the garden and did shopping. Adeline 'was by then almost immobilised, moving from her indoor chair to one that could be wheeled into the garden, and dependent on her maid, but she wrote and spoke as if she shopped herself.' Ursula's special pleasure was 'the Sunday lunches at the local pub, to save rations and to give the cook a half-day. I usually cooked the Sunday supper....'[14]

One of the wartime Valentines written by Ursula for Ralph conveys the domestic and horticultural character their relationship had by now assumed.

> What's to say, dear Valentine,
> that's not been said before?
> I draw two hearts that intertwine
> And write 'for-ever-more....
>
> But what has that to do with us
> Who dig a field together?
> More properly we should discuss
> The fittest sowing weather.
>
> You turn the turf with mighty spade,
> I'll follow with a fork,
> and so on, till such tilth is made
> that we can stop for talk.
>
> And then let us improve the spring
> with liquinure and lime,
> not heed the silly birds who sing
> the joys of kissing time,
>
> Nor heed the yellow celandine
> that opens to the sun ...
> but will you be my Valentine
> when all the digging's done?[15]

Ralph was uneasy about leaving his house as long as the air raids lasted. But he felt that certain journeys had to be made, even though train travel was becoming difficult. Very early in 1944 he went to Oxford to conduct the London Philharmonic Orchestra in a performance of the Fifth Symphony. In February he was up in London to hear his Double Trio played at the National Gallery. In Dorking he worked hard rehearsing the performance of Bach's St Matthew Passion at the Leith Hill Music Festival, which again had to be held in the parish church. The war continued to bring deaths. At the beginning of April Ursula learned that her brother John had died, heroically, in the campaign in Burma. He was just twenty-nine years old. On the day the heartbreaking news came, Ursula went to the National

Gallery to hear the Griller Quartet play Haydn's *Seven Last Words*. She commented that she could 'never hear that music without the desolation of that day returning'.[16] Some weeks later Ralph lost his closest living relative: his brother Hervey died at Leith Hill Place where he had lived alone since their mother had died just over six years before. Ralph had not wished to inherit the great house but Hervey had insisted on bequeathing it to him. Ralph went over and spent a day wandering over his childhood home and pondering what to do. He was reminded what a big concern it was. There was the large house itself, the cottages, the farm, the large kitchen garden and the orchards and the meadows where the bluebells and azaleas were then in flower. He had to make up his mind whether to live there. He decided not to. He told Ursula: 'If I had to decide what trees were to be cut, what vegetables planted, what cows sold, I should lose all pleasure in the place – and if I ran the place properly I shouldn't have any time for my own work.' Instead, he offered the property to the National Trust in whose ownership it remains to this day.

Ralph and Adeline spent some days at the house sorting out family possessions. He decided to leave the Reynolds and Gainsborough portraits of his great ancestor Josiah Wedgwood and his wife in the house together with works by Stubbs and Romney. They took back just a few things to White Gates including Ralph's father's bookcase, a Queen Anne secretaire and some black Wedgwood vases. If this clearing out made Ralph acutely aware of his family's past, the next stage in the history of Leith Hill Place brought back, astonishingly and delightfully, a figure from his own personal history. For the very first tenants whom the National Trust installed in the house were Ralph's old, very close Cambridge friend Randolph Wedgwood and his wife Iris. He had had a distinguished career with the London North Eastern Railway and had been made a baronet some two years before. A locomotive named for him was destroyed by a direct hit during the bombing but the company then gave his name to another of their large engines. The two undergraduate friends had been in touch very rarely during recent decades, but now it was a joy to both of them to be near neighbours.

The new occupants soon gave a party at the house to which Ralph took Ursula. She remembered the new perspective on him which this occasion gave.

> He took me with him to the tenant's party they gave at Christmas, their son and daughter-in-law were there with five children, and the

entertainer was a conjuror, Ralph's favourite party treat. It was pleasant to hear the Leith Hill people calling him 'Mr Ralph'. And he, in turn, was delighted when he was told that the locals once again referred to the house, as they had in his grandfather's time, as 'Wedgwoods'.

This was at the end of the year in which the war came to look definitely winnable. The Allies had invaded continental Europe on D-Day in June when their troops captured the Normandy beaches and then advanced steadily into France. But in that same month the Germans introduced a new mode of assault on Britain. They attacked the south-eastern counties with armed rockets, flying bombs that were popularly known as 'doodle-bugs' or 'buzzbombs'.

The attacks lasted some five months during 1944 until in the late autumn the Allies captured the sites from which they were launched on the French and Dutch coasts. At their height the rocket attacks had numbered a hundred a day.

White Gates was in a very vulnerable area. Sleeping arrangements in the house were reorganized. Adeline's personal maid, referred to as 'Salter', put her mattress in the passage outside the sandbagged bedroom in which Adeline and Ralph slept and which Ursula now shared with them. It was Adeline's decision, she reported, that she should bring her mattress into their room: 'Adeline insisted that I should put mine on the floor between her bed and Ralph's.'[17] One memorable night their worst fears seemed about to be justified. 'One buzzbomb fell very close, we heard it cut out and were all expecting to die. I remember that my skin felt like a tight dress, and was glad to be able to reach out a hand to Adeline and to hold Ralph's hand the other side.'[18] These were terrifying moments of suspense; 'the crash shook the house and the explosion was a quarter of a mile away, half masked by the clatter of glass as the study window blew inwards.'[19] At the place of impact people had been killed. 'We discovered next day that the bomb had fallen on a cottage far from any other house. People from London had come down for the night to get away from the raids; one man and a baby survived.'

For the Promenade Concerts that year Ralph had composed an oboe concerto, the soloist to be the highly regarded Léon Goosens. The threat of the flying bombs led to the first performance being relocated to Liverpool, where it was played on 30 September, with Malcolm Sargent conducting the Liverpool Philharmonic Orchestra. The piece originated in a rejected idea for the *scherzo* of the Fifth Symphony and much of it is in the idiom of that much larger work. The concerto can be both sprightly and poignant, and though not one of Ralph's profound works, it is highly entertaining and deservedly continues to be performed. It gives the greatest possible opportunity for display to a solo instrument which does not possess an extensive repertoire, the orchestra being reduced by Ralph to just eleven players.

Less than two weeks after the Liverpool concert another new work by Ralph had its premiere. This was his Second String Quartet and was part of a concert given on Ralph's seventy-second birthday at the National Gallery by the Menges Quartet. The violist in this ensemble was Jean Stewart, the close friend of Ursula and now of Ralph. He wrote it for her, as with previous female performers, for an exorbitant number of kisses. When he sent her the score, she was ecstatic: 'Without exaggeration this Quartet is the most lovely thing that has happened to me in my life, and it will continue to be a joy to me as long as I live.' It certainly is a fine piece for the instrument. From the outset the viola is at the centre of the music. It drives the swirling passion of the first movement, an *allegro apassionato*. For a moment there is a quieting with a sense of something strange, even eerie behind the tumbling emotions. The second movement, a *largo*, is entitled 'Romance' but is hardly that. It is slow, meditative with the deliberating sound of a Jacobean viol consort. There is a brief brightening with a key change to C major but the viola leads the movement back to a concluding, quiet, sorrowing. The *scherzo* introduces a theme taken from Ralph's music for the *49th Parallel* depicting escaping Nazis; the movement is one of tension, of storm and stress. Ralph apparently did not read T.S. Eliot but the viola here makes sounds that recall the lament of the 'disconsolate chimera' in the *Four Quartets*. The final movement, an *andante*, is subtitled from 'Joan to Jean'. This was because the chief theme had been intended to represent the character of Joan of Arc in a projected film of George Bernard Shaw's *St Joan* which was not made. The difficulties attendant upon passion that were explored in the two inner movements are put aside as the viola leads into a music that is reassuringly and uncomplicatedly melodic. The final bars recall the gradual-like calm at the end of the Fifth Symphony.

The last dark months of 1944 were a period of great anxiety at White Gates. Adeline, now seventy-four, developed a heavy cold which led to pleurisy and pneumonia and for several days it seemed that she might not live. In the midst of this anxiety there occurred a weird eerie intrusion. In the middle of the night the garden of White Gates was invaded by stampeding cows that trampled about noisily. In a state of shock, Ursula and Ralph got up, threw on some clothes and spent a good deal of time out in the bitter cold, struggling to drive the panicky beasts out of the garden. Adeline worried greatly about what was going on outside. But Ursula dated Adeline's recovery from the moment Ralph returned safely into the bungalow. 'Adeline was so relieved when Ralph returned triumphantly from this adventure that she seemed to start getting better, and in a few weeks she was fairly well again.'[20]

At Christmas-time 1944 Ralph and Ursula were at Cecil Sharp House for a carol concert which Ralph conducted enthusiastically. In the New Year he was immediately very busy. Foreseeing the outcome of the war the BBC requested him to write a 'Thanksgiving for Victory', later renamed *A Song of Thanksgiving*. He was also writing the music for a new film *Stricken Peninsula*. And around this time he also began work on his next symphony. Despite frequent colds his energy was strong. On the way to Oxford to conduct a performance of his Oboe Concerto with Léon Goosens, he stopped in London and with Ursula saw the new Laurence Olivier film, the highly patriotic *Henry V*, with a fine soundtrack score composed by William Walton.

After seeing Shakespeare's version of Agincourt, they followed the unfolding of another momentous victory played out in actuality in the early months of this historic year. In January Russian troops entered Germany from the east and shortly afterwards the western Allies were across the Rhine. On 30 April 1945 Adolf Hitler committed suicide as the Russian army took control of Berlin. Seven days later Germany formally surrendered and the following day, 8 May 1945, Victory in Europe (VE) Day was declared and wildly celebrated in the Allied countries. The war against Japan continued. On the evening of VE day Ursula gave a supper party at Thayer Street. She remembered that 'at some time late during the evening some of us went out to walk through London; windows were open with lights shining as they had not done for nearly six years; people were strolling, some dancing, some sitting exhausted on the pavement outside pubs which had long since run out of beer.... It was a strange lightheaded evening on which it was necessary to be with friends.'[21] It was a time for joy and also for remembering the many who had died in the war. As night started to fall on that eventful day, Bernard Brown, the young widower of Honorine, came to see Ursula and Jean Stewart. On the darkening roof garden of their block of flats he played the long, lamenting trumpet solo from Ralph's 'Pastoral Symphony'.

Exactly a month later, on 7 June, came an important event in the history of British music when Benjamin Britten's *Peter Grimes* was given its first and highly successful performance at Sadlers Wells. Ralph and Ursula were together in the audience. Another month later, in this year of changes, came a turning point in the political history of Britain. In the General Election of that July the Labour Party won a substantial majority over all other parties combined. For the first time Labour did not need a coalition partner in order to form a government.

The following month, August, brought about an event that marked a turning point not just in the world war but in the history of the planet. The United States attacked the Japanese city of Hiroshima with an atomic device. When this horrific bombing failed to elicit a Japanese surrender, a similarly devastating bomb was dropped in Nagasaki three days later. This produced a Japanese capitulation. On 15 August 1945, the day George VI presided over the state opening of the new British parliament, Victory over Japan (VJ) Day was proclaimed. Like many, Ursula was horrified by the way in which it had come:

> Hiroshima was an immense shock. Till then war had been horrible enough but there had been a certain traditional element for most of us, feeling ourselves on the side of freedom, of dragon slayers, however dreadful the means and terrors. This black celebration of man's power.... changed everything. All the old horrors of poison gas which had dismayed me at Porton came back, and the door had clearly opened on degradations of power that were intolerable.[22]

During that historic summer Ralph went off to visit his old acquaintance Bruce Richmond. The former editor of the *Times Literary Supplement*, now in his retirement, lived in a country house at Netherhampton in Wiltshire which had formerly belonged to the patriotic poet, Sir Henry Newbolt. (Ralph will surely have remembered the setting of his 'Songs of the Fleet' by his old teacher Charles Villiers Stanford.) The house had a fine garden to which Bruce Richmond was devoted. Ralph greatly enjoyed talking with him about the growing of fruit and vegetables. Such gardening, stimulated by his efforts to 'dig for victory' during the war, had now become for Ralph a lasting enthusiasm. The vegetables at Netherhampton were fertilized with a rare guano which, Adeline reported, Ralph was desperately keen to obtain for his own garden. But his gardening passions had to be subordinated to the claims of music. Two weeks before the Japanese surrender Ralph was in London to conduct at the Promenade Concerts. With the London Symphony Orchestra he performed the suite of seven movements which he had created from his music for the film *Story of a Flemish Farm*, a wartime drama set in Nazi-occupied Europe. He also conducted his Fifth Symphony and Five Tudor Portraits. In October he was again in London for some National Gallery concerts. At one of these he admired a quartet performed by one of the leading Modernists Béla Bartók. Ralph was accompanied by Ursula and Jean Stewart and they later dined with some other young people including Michael Tippett. It seems to have been a merry occasion, Ralph launching into a succession of stories in French. Along with Arnold Bax, now living at the White Horse Hotel in Storrington in Sussex, he had to dash to make the train.

Early in 1946 Ralph was back at Morley College which held so many happy memories for him, especially of Gustav Holst. One of Ralph's former pupils, the Cornish composer Inglis Gundry, asked for his assistance. Having served in the Royal Navy during the war and survived the torpedoing of his ship (more than a hundred and fifty of his shipmates had perished), Inglis Gundry was now on the staff of the college and he approached Ralph to help out with the teaching of a hundred or so young men and women of the Royal Navy. Ralph with his customary generosity to young musicians readily agreed. Ursula, who along with Maud Karpeles, accompanied Ralph to the college was much impressed by his power and effectiveness as a teacher: 'It was an illuminating and exciting morning'; the young audience 'listened with serious intentness'.[23] He also encouraged Inglis Gundry by attending his opera *The Partisans*, which dealt with the Yugoslav guerrilla forces, one of the more colourful groups in the alliance against Hitler. The recent outstanding success of *Peter Grimes* had prompted several young composers to attempt operas.

In this first year after the war, Ursula, though based in London, spent a good deal of time with Ralph and Adeline in Dorking, especially at weekends. The married couple were increasingly alone in the large house, various tenants and visitors having moved on and R.O. Morris and all his cats having left permanently for London to share a house with Hugo Anson, Registrar at the RCM. There seems to have been a lack of sympathy between Ursula and Adeline's sister Cordelia, 'the person she [Adeline] loved most'.[24] According to Cordelia's son Adam Curle, his mother, at least once, referred to Ursula as 'an adventuress'. But Ursula decided 'that she could spend time there even if ... Cordelia was staying in the house'. In Cordelia's absence Ursula seems to have been very close to Adeline who was becoming steadily more infirm:

> Adeline's life was restricted, by now she was practically immobile. Her chair had wheels and could be moved from the bedroom to the hall, and very occasionally she would choose to have her garden chair taken into the shade near the house. Otherwise she was indoors from week's end to week's end, reading, writing letters for Ralph or at his dictation, in a clear, rounded script, extraordinary when one looked at the crumpled and disfigured hands of the writer.[25]

Materially life continued to be difficult for people in Britain in that first year of peacetime and in the years that immediately followed. Rationing continued and at times became even more stringent than during the war. An American visitor to White Gates that year was the 35-year-old Bernard Herrmann, a successful conductor and composer who was later to achieve still greater and more popular acclaim as a composer of cinema scores such as those for *Citizen Kane* and *Taxi Driver* and for films such as *The Man Who Knew Too Much*, *Vertigo*, *North By Northwest* and *Psycho*. In 1946 he toured Britain conducting the leading orchestras and visiting the country's composers. He wrote an account of these travels for the *New York Herald Tribune*. Of his visit to Ralph he commented: 'If Benjamin Britten is the white-haired boy of British music, Vaughan Williams is still its saint. I had a twilight visit with him at his home in Surrey and found him at seventy-four intensely interested in contemporary music. He was full of praise for the music of Samuel Barber. He is now completing his Sixth Symphony.'

Bernard Herrmann also reported on an instance of Ralph's attitude to the current shortages in Britain. It showed both Ralph's stoicism and his generosity: 'When he told me that he was having difficulty finding music paper, I suggested that I might send him some from America. "That would be fine," he said, "but do not send me too much of it. There must be enough left for the other composers – the young ones. They need it more and have their work to do". For such fellow feeling he is much beloved by all British musicians.'[26]

Bernard Herrmann's young wife was deeply affected by the sight of Adeline on that visit. She later described:

> the living tragedy which instantly met your eyes – a very, very old

lady in a red shawl propped up in a kind of high chair arrangement, with her legs spread out before her on another high stool – these covered too with another crocheted grey shawl, so that she resembled an effigy upon a sarcophagus. She seemed preternaturally old – her face reddened and terribly dry and wrinkled, her spare white hair straight and cut short, parted in the middle and combed as though by an ignorant servant in the simplest, crudest style.[27]

The ongoing work on the Sixth Symphony was by no means Ralph's only musical project during that year. In March there was the first perfor-mance of his Introduction and Fugue for Two Pianos played by Cyril Smith and Phyllis Sellick, a husband and wife partnership, well known in the music world of the time. Ralph dedicated the piece to them. It is a work that clearly refers to Bach's Preludes and Fugues and has a certain energy and drive but is otherwise not especially memorable. He was also working hard on the music for the film *The Loves of Joanna Godden*, a dramatic love story produced by Ralph's Ealing friend Michael Balcon. The film was shown the following year. Ralph's music on the soundtrack was conducted by Ernest Irving, a long-term composer for Ealing Films to whom Ralph was also drawing close. A man of Ralph's generation, sharing his sense of humour, and highly experienced in film music and film-making, Ernest Irving was greatly impressed by Ralph's score and so too were Irving's colleagues in the production team. 'We have now received the score and have played it through from the sketch. It is the best music we have ever had here, and all the members of our little arcana were excited and delighted.'

In July 1946 Ralph, as was his custom, organized a play through of the latest draft of what was his chief creative concern at the time, his new symphony. He invited Michael Mullinar, an expert pianist, composer and teacher, whom he had known for some years, down to the White Gates for the weekend. And in the summer dusk before an audience of some twenty people the latest version of the symphony was played. Ursula remembered the occasion vividly: 'we sat in green twilight, for he had drawn the curtains of the gallery window against the late afternoon sunshine'. The occasion grew still more atmospheric. 'Sometime while we had been listening there had been rain, and by now the evening was brilliant with evening light and the colour of everything in the room was intensified. Adeline's crimson shawl, her face, the music paper on the piano were luminous points in the dusk.'[28] Later Michael Mullinar played a composition of his own, a setting of Edmund Waller's 'Old Age' with Ralph singing the words. Then, after Ralph had read more poems, by Waller and Andrew Marvell, Michael played the symphony again. He performed the work, Ursula noted, 'with unflagging excitement and inspiration', the memorable quiet 'last movement leading out into space'. 'Because of that day,' she reported, 'Ralph dedicated the symphony to him.'

A little later in the summer Ralph and Ursula went over to Glyndebourne for the day to see Benjamin Britten's new opera *The Rape of Lucretia*. They regretted that the cast they heard was not the one which included 'the impressive Kathleen Ferrier' and Mabel Ritchie whom Ralph had first admired twenty years before as Debussy's Melisande. Adeline reported to Cordelia, 'Ralph and Ursula were home from Glyndebourne by 11. R was disappointed that he didn't see the other cast as he missed Ferrier – Pollak and Ritchie – he admired a great deal of it....'[29] Shortly after this occasion Ursula and Jean Stewart and two friends took the opportunity to have a continental holiday, something that had not been possible for some seven years. To have a break from British rationing and general austerity they set off for Paris, then on to Switzerland for a couple of weeks. Adeline kept Ursula up to date with the news from White Gates; 'We have had a quiet week – when haven't we....' The customary reading aloud continued. Adeline and Ralph finished Hardy's *Jude the Obscure* and proceeded to another Victorian favourite, Thackeray's *The Four Georges*.

On her return from holiday Ursula met Ralph in London and watched him conduct rehearsals for the coming Hereford Festival. Afterwards they went to see the first part of what proved to be a two-part classic film, Sergei Eisenstein's *Ivan the Terrible*. It had recently opened in London, after being released in the Soviet Union two years before. Ralph, with his new interest in the medium of film, was much impressed by the beauty of the photography.

In the autumn Ralph had concerts to conduct in London and at the Dome in Brighton. He and Ursula spent the morning of the latter concert sitting on the beach together. In the afternoon there were rehearsals followed by the concert, which was not well attended. Worse still, as Ralph told Adeline, 'there was not a pretty girl in sight'. Ralph, now in his mid-seventies in the company of the 34-year-old Ursula, was also taken aback to overhear a policeman remark 'He's a fine old chap.' On 6 November Ralph again conducted, this time his 'London Symphony' at a gala concert at the Royal Albert Hall. Starring among the performers was the venerable 71-year-old Portuguese cellist Guilhermina Suggia, a colourful platform presence who was the lover of Pablo Casals and had been a trio partner to Ralph's old friend Jelly d'Aranyi. The concert was put on by a newspaper, *The Daily News*, which also organized a lavish dinner party at the Dorchester Hotel. It was attended by Queen Mary and the young Princess Margaret whom afterwards Ralph described as 'a pet'. Ursula remembered that there were a lot of cocktails before the food was served. The meal was then accompanied with a steady flow of champagne. By the time cigars were passed round, Ralph was unable to control his properly. Unluckily he dropped it and it fell under the full skirt of Lady Errington, a pretty girl who, as was often the case, was sitting beside him. 'What am I to do?' he asked. 'Let her burn alive, or dive under her petticoats?' Fortunately a waiter was able to stamp out the danger. As they left the Dorchester they all felt quite high. As Ursula put it 'we floated out; luckily everyone else was walking about three inches from the ground too, so our levitation was unnoticed.'[30]

Ralph spent the remainder of the year mainly at White Gates, with Ursula a continuing visitor. He read aloud Thomas Hardy's *The Woodlanders* to them. At Christmas they listened to the radio broadcast of the Festival of Nine Lessons and Carols from King's College, Cambridge, which had been relayed by the BBC every year for the last eighteen years and become, as it remains, a much loved institution in British musical culture. But in 1946 Ralph was appalled by the paucity of English carols in the programme. He wrote sternly to Boris Ord, the organist and choirmaster at King's: 'I deplore the almost entire absence of English carols in your King's College service. I think every English carol service ought to start with God Rest you merry and end with 1st Noel....'[31] Less than two years after the great moment of victory Ralph shared the intense and unceasing national pride of the time. In the midst of one of the coldest winters on record a new Britain was being created. On New Year's Day 1947 the country's railways were formally taken into public ownership; it was one of the steps in the Labour government's programme of controlling major industries and utilities for the well-being of the people. The policy was accompanied in matters of health, education and social services by the creation of a welfare state.

The aspiration and idealism that supported these radical changes in British life were also present in a new composition which Ralph took up in 1947. The score for *The Loves Of Joanna Godden* having been received by Ealing studios in December 1946, Ernest Irving then quickly broached the idea that Ralph might write the music for an important new film that was being planned at Ealing, one dealing with Captain Robert Falcon Scott's ill-fated expedition to the South Pole. With his many other commitments, above all the new symphony, Ralph was slow to accept the commission; in July he was still hesitating, even though he had come up with some 'very definite ideas'. But Irving was persuasive and Ralph agreed to a contract. He was soon intensely fascinated by the heroic and tragic story. He read books about Antarctica and photographs of the Scott expedition were propped up on the furniture around White Gates. A contract was finalized on 9 October 1947. Ralph was paid £750 for half-an-hour's music and £25 for each additional minute. These were exactly the same terms he had accepted for the much lesser film and score *The Loves of Joanna Godden*. Ralph began composing with just the script to go on. But to the great surprise of Ernest Irving, a very experienced film-maker, much of the score meshed perfectly with what was subsequently filmed. Some three years later he told Ralph: 'I have often recounted my amazement on finding that the Main Titles Music, written out of the blue, exactly fitted the glacier climb.'[32]

Ralph was extremely busy in this year in which his seventy-fifth birthday approached. In January he was hard at work on the new symphony. He looked for an assistant who could produce legible copies of his scoring and hand writing and also identify any problems in orchestration. Norman Peterkin, Ralph's new editor at Oxford University Press, recommended the 40-year-old Roy Douglas, a former member of the London Symphony Orchestra, who had assisted Richard Addinsell and William Walton. In February Ralph wrote to him urgently: 'I have been foolish enough to write another symphony. Could you undertake to vet and then copy the score. If in the course of this you have any improvements to suggest I will receive them with becoming gratitude.'[33] The two got on well and Roy Douglas continued as his assistant to the end of Ralph's life.

February 1947 was a bitterly cold month; rationing and austerity seemed endless. However the Valentine convention that had gone on between Ursula, Adeline and Ralph continued. Ursula would send one for Adeline and Ralph to share and another for Ralph to read privately. In this freezing month Ralph's poem offered him a prospect of an Ursula more lightly dressed in the warmth of Maytime. For the keen reader of *Vogue* magazine and connoisseur of lingerie, Ursula composed a poem decked out with the brand names of stockings: Aristoc, Bear Brand, Dimsheen, Morley, Silk Crepe. Flirtatiously she wrote:

> See, the shocking
> Thick stocking
> Flung away.
> I anticipate
> late coming state
> of May
> & fling my winter clouts away
> and also thrift,
> Getting myself the best shift
> Obtainable.
> Unrestrainable,
> because I do not think he comes to see
> me,
> but what I am wearing.
> If that has a bearing
> on the saint
> we celebrate
> on this date
> & in whose quaint
> honour,
> as she must go,
> (in spite of snow,
> or such irrelevances)
> out in what her swain fancies
> the best and thinnest things upon her.
> Hoping he will remember to say, BE MINE
> or at least, to send her a valentine.

In that same February Ralph was off to London to assist at rehearsals of *Shepherds of the Delectable Mountains* which had been scheduled by Sadlers Wells. He, Ursula and Adeline were now sufficient of a domestic threesome for Adeline to arrange his dates with Ursula on such visits to London. Typically, a postcard from her dated 7 February 1947 announces that 'R is coming up by car. How about a quick cup of coffee when he arrives at 10? (not too hot).'[34] The day after the first proper performance of the Bunyan work he was back in Surrey to conduct a performance

293

of Bach's St John Passion, which he had financed himself out of sheer admiration and enthusiasm. A week or two later, in March, he was hard at work rehearsing for performances of sections of Bach's Mass in B minor for which he had made an English translation. It was the month in which the Cold War may be said to have begun in earnest. For in March 1947 the American President formulated the Truman Doctrine, a set of policies calculated to halt Soviet control of Eastern Europe and to support the western democracies. The world was now dominated unmistakeably by the Soviet Union and the United States. The British imperial global order in which Ralph had grown up, and which he had taken for granted, was fast disappearing. In August 1947 the jewel in the British imperial crown was entirely re-set when the Indian subcontinent became independent in the form of two new republics, Pakistan and India.

In this context of world upheaval Ralph continued work on his great symphony. In March he organized another playthrough by Michael Mullinar at the Royal College of Music. But Adeline became seriously ill again and it had to be postponed. It eventually took place on 5 June 1947. The listeners were impressed. One of them, R.O. Morris, reported in a letter to Adeline: 'the sustained vigour and originality of the musical idea is most imposing – truly astonishing to one who knows how incessantly Ralph has been labouring in one way and another since the war started.'[35] Two days after the playthrough, Ursula's friend Jean Stewart was to marry her fiancé, George Hadley, a doctor and an accomplished cellist whom Ralph had quickly recruited for the Leith Hill Music Festival orchestra. Ursula and Ralph went to Oxford together to attend the ceremony after which Ralph made a kindly, well- received speech proposing the health of the couple. When Jean told him she would hurry back immediately after the honeymoon to play in *Flos Campi*, Ralph's work of love music, but feared that her playing might not be at its best, Ralph reassured her, 'My dear, you'll play it with half the technique and ten times the passion.'[36]

Immediately after their return to Dorking, Ralph and Ursula went over to Leith Hill Place to attend a large party given by Randolph and Iris Wedgwood to celebrate the centennial of Wedgwood residence in the house. It had been in 1847, when Britain had had a Whig government and Emily Brontë's *Wuthering Heights* was first published that Josiah ('Joe' Wedgwood III, the grandson of the great potter) had left Staffordshire and bought the mansion. Ralph was surprised and pleased to see how much brighter Iris had made his old home. The furniture and paintings that he and Adeline had decided to leave had been most effectively repositioned.

But after these social occasions it was back to work and to the customary demanding schedule. That summer for their end of term production the students at the Royal College of Music put on *The Poisoned Kiss* and Ralph spent a good deal of time helping at rehearsals. In August he prepared to conduct at the Promenade Concerts and immediately afterwards began rehearsals for the Three Choirs Festival at Gloucester. He stayed with two of his many old friends in the musical community, the cathedral organist Herbert Sumsion and his American wife Alice. While in Gloucester, Ralph heard a performance of *Dies Natalis*, by Sumsion's close friend Gerald Finzi. Ralph's *Magnificat* was also performed and he conducted his own Fifth Symphony for a BBC transmission. In September Ralph was back in London to preside with Maud Karpeles over a conference designed to establish an International Folk Music Council. His energy seemed endless.

October brought two important anniversaries in Ralph's life. On 9 October he and Adeline celebrated their golden wedding; three days later, he had his seventy-fifth birthday. As an anniversary gift for his wife, Ralph, with Ursula's help, purchased a small gold locket which was, as Ursula put it, 'plain enough he hoped for her to care to wear.' In the event Adeline was delighted with the gift, sending Ursula a postcard of thanks, exclaiming 'Wonderful to have the locket, an exquisite fit – and what infinite trouble you must have taken over it.'[37] For Ralph's big birthday there was an immense response: gifts, letters, cards from family, friends, colleagues and acquaintances, many of them from a distance in time as well as in space. Particularly pleasing to him was the congratulatory telegram from Sibelius. On 12 October there was a large party at the Dorking Halls with, as Ralph's special treat, a conjuror. The previous day at the same venue there had been a celebration concert given by the London Symphony Orchestra with Ralph's long-time associates Astra Desmond and Roy Henderson as soloists. The BBC broadcast several celebration concerts which included *Flos Campi*, *Sancta Civitas* and *Four Hymns* of over thirty years earlier. Ralph's position as the major figure in English public life was confirmed yet again.

With the festivities behind him Ralph returned energetically to work. On St Cecilia's Day in November, he conducted the first performance of his motet *The Voice Out of the Whirlwind* at St Sepulchre's Church, Holborn, long known through its association with Sir Henry Wood as The Musicians' Church. The anthem was an adaptation for voices of the 'Pavane of the Sons of the Morning' from *Job*. Just over three weeks later came a far more important occasion in Ralph's long career as a composer. On 16 December at the BBC's Maida Vale Studios there was held the first orchestral playthrough of the Sixth Symphony. Then Ralph took over for a second run-through. Adrian Boult resumed with a third performance with Ralph marking the score where he thought changes were necessary. Then, after this demanding morning, he went into the West End for a substantial lunch and then on to Millbank to see the Van Gogh exhibition at the Tate Gallery.

The following year the Tate Gallery mounted a retrospective exhibition of the Surrealist painter Paul Nash, whose *Totes Meer* (Dead Sea) remains one of the most memorable paintings from the Second World War. Ralph and Ursula went to see the exhibition on the morning of 21 April 1948, the day on which in the evening the Sixth Symphony had its first public performance. As usual Ralph had very serious last minute doubts. But on the night, and later, the new symphony elicited intense admiration. Richard Capell, a music critic who had admired Ralph's work for going on forty years, wrote in *The Daily Telegraph*:

> Only the greatly superior artists have so tirelessly renewed the adventure of the spirit.... The Sixth Symphony in E takes a new direction. It will challenge every hearer. The adventurous energy is terrific; and whatever words may be resorted to as a clue, the sheer musical means are compelling and engrossing.... The music says that the soul of man can endure pain and face the thought of a remoteness beyond the outermost of the planets.[38]

Critics of the younger generation also recognized the immense intellectual ambitiousness and achievement of the work. Desmond Shawe-Taylor, some forty years younger than Ralph and music critic of *The Sunday Times*, wrote in *The New Statesman* that the symphony represented:

> an extraordinary and unpredictable burst of creative activity for a man of 75, in which he seems to have effected a kind of synthesis of the two preceding symphonies, indeed to have summed up the whole of his lifework, but at the same time to have directed a serene and courageous glance into the future, to have meditated on first and last things with a grasp and profundity worthy of Beethoven.[39]

The work was also enthusiastically received in the United States.

When it had its first performance there at the New York Philharmonic Symphony Society less than a year after its London debut, the eminent conductor Leopold Stokowski wrote in a programme note, 'This is music that will take its place with the greatest creations of the masters'. And Olin Downes, the music critic of *The New York Times* also saw the achievement represented by the symphony as historic: 'This is one of the most powerful and deeply felt symphonic writings to have appeared since the turn of the century. The sincerity of the expression blazes in every page.'[40]

Accompanying the chorus of admiration were repeated questions and suggestions about what the symphony 'meant'. Explanations to do with social and political history and biography can only be gestural, and never precise. The symphony means what it sounds. And sounds mean beyond and other than, what words mean. Michael Kennedy has offered a very concise definition of the meaning of the symphony in strictly musical terms: 'First of all it means a closely and logically pursued musical argument on the conflict of major and minor thirds, and the interval of the augmented fourth which sets off more conflicts in keys separated by that interval.'[41]

But as Kennedy himself goes on to say, Ralph himself allowed that there was also a programmatic aspect to the work, referring to Prospero's well-known speech at the end of *The Tempest*. And certainly right from the opening bars, full of thunder and violence, the listener is involved with powerful emotions and strongly felt experience. There follows over the four movements, if not a narrative, then certainly a collocating of aural experiences and attempts to reach conclusions from them.

The symphony begins in tumult. Peter Maxwell Davies has commented: 'The extraordinary polyrhythms at the beginning of the Sixth Symphony; they're as "advanced" as anything in *The Rite of Spring*. They get into your physical system like very little music that I've conducted.'[42]

The music then steadies into a swinging melody. It brings to mind the jazz music that was one of the great innovations of the twentieth century and that became increasingly prevalent in British life when a vast American army came over to be ready for the great D-Day invasion of continental Europe. With a touch of nostalgia, the idiom of English folk music is recalled briefly, but the charming memory of such pastoral is swept away never to return. Other sound worlds have to be confronted. The movement returns to the turmoil of the beginning which was the most enduring, determining sound of Ralph's lifetime. This opening *allegro* concludes with a dull rumble that is ominous.

The second movement, marked *moderato*, quickly recalls one of the famous musical precipitates of the Second World War, the aggression motif in Shostakovich's Seventh Symphony, very much associated with the epic siege of St Petersburg (then known as Leningrad). A relentlessly repeated, bellicose phrase endures for some time before giving way to heart-rending moments of wistfulness and hopelessness. These, we will later realize, are a prefiguring of the reflections in the famously subdued, slow epilogue of this symphony. But now the discordances recur. Advance strongly. Then retreat a little. Reason, compassion, humanity are hung on to by a tremulous solo from the cor anglais. But it grows weak and fades into the background of distant, thudding explosions.

And then the third movement, the *scherzo* crashes in. Its high spirits are ambiguous. The music is cheery but sardonic, spirited but also near demented. The popular ditty of the trio transforms itself into a heavy goose-stepping march. Also, as Byron Adams has suggested, the 'saxophone theme sounds suspiciously like a grotesque jazz improvisation on Stephen Foster's "Swanee River" which under the title "Old Folks at Home" Vaughan Williams had earlier arranged for male chorus.... The overall effect ... is to heighten the jazzy and diabolical aspects of this passage....'[43]

There is also a suggestion of the blues; all of them sounds of the recent times. But even at its most humane this double-edged music is no salvation from the cataclysmic shock that has been alluded to earlier. It comes over as more of an amplification.

Then after the blaring *allegro vivace* comes an arresting contrast, the suddenly subdued, quiet, slow epilogue. This was the movement which more than any other in all of Ralph's symphonies provoked amongst its first listeners, and later ones, a search for a meaning. Various programmatic allusions have been ascribed to it. It has been suggested, for instance, that this movement evokes a world of post-atomic devastation. Very audibly it is a music of meditation. Quietly it wanders, muses and sometimes keens. At times it sounds of quiet desperation as it turns and turns about, obsessively seeking progression. Ralph is unlikely to have known Jean Paul Sartre's *Huis Clos* but the tormented movement in the music has at times the desperate psychological claustrophobia of that play, a product of the war first produced in 1944 some four years before the symphony. Slow clock chimes announce that time is being called on the desperate endeavour. The music becomes ghostly and runs out into silence. Then comes the surprising aftermath to the symphony; the listener is left not depressed but wondering.

Wilfrid Mellers, who has given a thorough, strenuously musicological account of Ralph's career, found it appropriate to describe this final movement programmatically. He writes:

> the epilogue is perhaps the ultimate auralisation of agnosticism, telling us that The Unknown Region which the hopeful young Vaughan Williams had set out to explore, is not a metaphysical 'other world', but is unknown, and always will be, simply because it is unknowable. The epilogue discovers that in the unknown region there must be nowhere: a fact offering occasion for neither hope nor regret. The difficult faith of the Fifth Symphony is relinquished; man is alone, in the dark cold and empty desolation. Acceptance brings to this strange music a serene insecurity; a courageous testament of our frightful century....[44]

Certainly this great, extremely subtle work of music can be seen as an attempt, very soon after the events, to render, obliquely, the reverberations of the horrific war that produced the Holocaust and Hiroshima and to come to a conclusion about them. Part of its understated power surely comes from Ralph's closeness to both the great wars of the century. But like all great works of art it transcends the specifics of its time. Ralph himself pointed, as Mellers reminds us, to Prospero's summation of the circumscription of human lives:

> We are such stuff
> As dreams are made on, and our little life
> Is rounded with a sleep.

But the work is more than just a philosophical statement; it stays close to acutely felt experience. Simon Heffer has seen 'the way the jazz saxophone in the *scherzo* is first brutalised and then snuffed out' as suggesting 'something more than just a Shakespearean vision'.[45] He points to the account of the work's origins given by Sir Malcolm Sargent, a devoted and regular conductor of the symphony. Sir Malcolm, presumably as a result of conversations with Ralph, pointed to the occasion in March 1941 when a bomb fell on the Cafe de Paris in the West End of London, killing the bandleader, Ken 'snakehips' Johnson and members of his West Indian Dance Orchestra as well as many of the patrons of the cafe.

The symphony certainly alludes to such memories and profoundly felt experiences. The moment in the *scherzo* is not the only one. But the work as a whole is also a quest for intelligibility in difficult experience.

The Sixth Symphony relates an enduring story, a journey into uncertainty, or, put more specifically and positively, into what John Keats, in a completely different time and generation, phrased as 'negative capability'. This occurs, he famously went on to say to his brothers, 'when a man is capable of being in uncertainties, mysteries, doubts, without any irritable reaching after fact and reason ...'. The rich and deep complexity of certain passages in Ralph's art needs to be better recognized. Here, in the concluding movement of the Sixth Symphony, is one of the finest examples.

Chapter Seventeen

IN THE COLD WAR

The year of the Sixth Symphony was one in which the Cold War intensified dramatically. The Soviet Union and its ally East Germany denied the three western allies, Britain, France and America, access to Berlin over which the four victorious powers exercised joint control. So began the Berlin Airlift. Both the United States and the Soviet Union grew increasingly defensive and inward-looking. In America the House Un-American Activities Committee strenuously pursued alleged Communists. A famous prosecution involved Alger Hiss, an official of the Federal Government in whose melodramatic prosecution the young Republican lawyer, Richard Nixon was fiercely energetic. Five months before Ralph's symphony was performed, the 'Hollywood Ten' (a group of film artistes) was blacklisted by the controllers of the American film industry, for refusing to testify before HUAC. A composer who fell foul of the committee was Hanns Eisler who, after fleeing Nazi Germany in the 1930s, was in 1948 forced by HUAC to leave the United States. There was political paranoia in the Soviet Union. This was the year of the Zhdanov Decree, which denounced artists guilty of western formalism. One victim of this policy was Dmitri Shostakovich, who was dismissed from the Conservatoire and plunged into professional disgrace and financial hardship. Reportedly, for a period he feared a night-time knock on the door and deportation to one of the gulags, the Stalinist detention centres.

It was the year George Orwell was completing work on his bleak, horrified vision of a totalitarian state in his highly successful novel *Nineteen Eighty-Four*. But there were also other and more creative visions

appearing in Britain. This was the year in which against relentless opposition the Labour Government finally enacted the legislation to establish
the National Health Service (NHS). The Aldeburgh Festival was begun
and the first post-war Olympics were held in London. The ss *Windrush*
docked at Tilbury to be seen later as a marker for the beginning of the
multicultural Britain that Ralph was never to know.

For him it was a year of great achievement which confirmed him still
more as a national treasure. A month before the immense success of the
provocative Sixth Symphony, his Partita for Double String Orchestra
had been broadcast on the BBC, with Adrian Boult conducting. A
second reworking of the Double Trio for Strings of 1938, the piece is
another instance of Ralph composing in a Modernist idiom. The Prelude
has cross-rhythms and syncopations segueing into a lively *scherzo* and
thence to an *intermezzo* entitled 'Homage to Henry Hall', the dance
band conductor who, with his signature theme 'Here's to the next Time',
enjoyed widespread radio popularity. Ralph himself went on to give the
first concert performance of his Partita at the end of July.

That spring there was also a successful revival of *Job* at Covent
Garden. Ralph was disappointed by the new sets that had been designed
by the painter John Piper, who also did stage designs for Benjamin
Britten's operas at Aldeburgh. Along with the dark scenery Ralph was
also displeased by the director's ignoring of the numerous fine details in
the stage directions. Nevertheless, the orchestra pit was of a size to allow
Ralph's full orchestral score to be heard in a staging for the first time.
This and the excellent choreography left him reasonably content with the
production. During this year he was also working very hard to complete
another major, theatrical project. This was his setting of an opera, or, as
he himself termed it, a 'morality', of John Bunyan's *The Pilgrim's Progress*.
The subject had engaged him for a very long time, ever since he had
written incidental music for the few scenes given at Reigate Priory over
forty years before. Since that time he had set several other episodes. As
he was working at it now, he was also, Adeline recalled, 'reading me the
Acts of the Apostles of which I was most ignorant.'[1] By the second week
of August he was able to send a copy of the vocal score and libretto to
his long-standing friend Steuart Wilson who, after a long distinguished
career as a tenor, had been appointed Director of Music at the BBC.
Wilson appears not to have proposed taking the project further, perhaps
agreeing with Ralph's concession in his accompanying letter that 'Of
course the obvious criticism is that it is not "dramatic".' He immediately

tried to deal with that objection by going on 'but then it is not meant to be. Whether this is a good excuse I do not know. It is more of a ceremony really than a drama.' Unavailingly, he also sought to reassure Steuart Wilson about the size of the orchestra and the doubling, or even the quadrupling of the many parts. But the struggle to get the *Pilgrim* staged would continue.

That same summer the Three Choirs Festival was at Worcester. Adeline suggested that Ursula, who had never attended the festival, should accompany Ralph there. The poignancy of Adeline's situation is caught succinctly and touchingly in a couple of sentences in a letter she wrote to friends abroad: '... I have a faithful maid who helps me – I am rather an infirm person and am looked after to an extent that makes me ashamed – My husband is full of energy....'

At Worcester Ralph stayed with old friends, Canon and Mrs Briggs, and Ursula had a room in a house on the Green. Ralph conducted a performance of *Job* which, in the great stone cathedral, sounded very different to what they had recently heard in London. The following day the two of them made an excursion into A.E. Housman country. They went to Wenlock Edge, which Ralph had never seen before, and then on to the impressive castles at Stokesay and Ludlow. Back at Worcester there was a tea-party for them at the Briggs and afterwards, at the house of the Headmaster of Kings School, a sherry party that developed into a madrigal party with Ralph singing for at least an hour. Gerald and Joy Finzi were there and on the following morning they helped Ursula scour the antique shops for a gift to take back to Adeline. In the afternoon Ralph and Ursula drove back to Surrey through Gloucester and the Cotswolds. They made a small detour to Down Ampney so that Ralph might show Ursula the vicarage in which he had been born but barely remembered.

His creativity continued irrepressibly. *Scott of the Antarctic* had its first public screening at the Odeon, Leicester Square, on 29 November 1948, with Ralph's soundtrack music played by the Philharmonia Orchestra conducted by Ernest Irving. This music, for the best film with which he was ever associated, immediately provided an inspiration for his next symphony. Just over two weeks after the premiere he mentioned to Irving, 'writing an Antarctic Symphony using the same themes, which I have slowly revolving in my mind'.[2]

During the first weeks of the New Year Ralph was suffering from rheumatic aches but he agreed nevertheless to go to London to sit for a portrait bust by Jacob Epstein, the pre-eminent sculptor of the day in

Britain. His heads of leading public figures of the day remain an important part of British art history in that period. Ralph was put in touch with
the sculptor through Ursula, whose friend, Sheila Doniach, an emigrée
Russian pianist, was also a friend of Epstein. Ralph enjoyed the sculptor's
company and liked doing impressions of him. The bronze bust, for which
Epstein charged two hundred guineas, shows a strong weathered face
with a highly intelligent piercing look. It is now in the National Portrait
Gallery in London. Epstein remarked of his sitter, 'he reminded me in
appearance of some eighteenth-century admiral whose word was law.'
Epstein was also impressed by 'the logic and acuteness of everything he
discoursed upon.'

Another new acquaintance was a local masseur, a Mr Collins, who
came twice a week to help Ralph with his winter aches and pains. As
Epstein had discovered, Ralph was a great teller and receiver of stories, a
taste which Mr Collins shared. They had many entertaining exchanges.
They were both of the 'Have you heard the one about ...' school of
humour. They also enjoyed listening together to the evensongs broadcast by the BBC. A visitor to White Gates remembered calling on Ralph
and Adeline after one of the visits from Mr Collins and waiting for the
composer in 'a large unkempt sitting room furnished with a concert
grand and worn armchairs. Everywhere a litter of books and papers; and
the gallery running round the room looking like a gallery in a library, full
of music bound in black serviceable bindings in negligent bookcases....
An enormous tiger-like cat is asleep under the tea-table. VW comes in
in slippers and a grey cardigan ... and no collar because the masseur has
just left.'

When Adeline was then brought into the room in her chair the visitor
was impressed by her 'strong frail face ... very intelligent and with the
quality of serenity that only seems to come after prolonged suffering. She
is almost completely helpless with arthritis and her hands so fantastically
crippled that they are no longer hands and you feel neither surprise nor
revulsion'. Ralph, the visitor went on, 'is rather deaf.... I don't raise my
voice enough and he misses some of the conversation.' However, the
overall effect left on the writer by the visit was far from dispiriting. 'But
I haven't given you any impression of the vitality in both of them, and
their sense of fun, and a simple charm as though they were nobody and
their infirmities were nothing.'[3]

Ralph's aches and pains and deafness certainly did not slow down his
musical activities. In the last week in February he conducted his 'London

Symphony' at the Albert Hall and two days later, on 24 February, he was in the recording studio to conduct his Sixth Symphony. In the first week in March, Ralph and Ursula went off to Birmingham together to stay, as she remembered, at a 'comfortable hotel with huge bedroom fires – a luxury long forgotten in the south....'[4] They were there at the invitation of Tom Harrison who had produced the Abinger Pageant before the war, and was now working in Birmingham where he was mounting a production of *Sir John in Love* at the Midland Institute.

Driven up from Dorking by his chauffeur Beagley, Ralph met Ursula at Paddington Station with numerous provisions to safeguard his health. Adeline wrote ahead to tell her that 'he will have chocolate, lozenges and petit-beurre and aspirin – hot bottle and rug. R likes Famel Syrup and he does cough more easily....'[5] Sustained by his two ladies, Ralph was also very pleased and invigorated by the quality of Tom Harrison's production performed by the Clarion Singers, a highly idealistic, innovative choir directed by Katharine Thompson. Ralph wrote excitedly to thank her after 'Mrs Wood and I got home safely after a really thrilling day on Sunday'. He enthused about the Clarion Singers: 'I thought, for a company mostly young and all, I believe amateur, without stage, scenery, property, costumes or orchestra, to hold our attention riveted for the whole afternoon was astonishing.'[6] When he returned to White Gates Adeline was greatly impressed by the improvement in his health, commenting 'Birmingham is the place to recover in!'

Shortly afterwards Ursula went to Paris for a few days, spending time with her pianist friend Katharine Long. In the summer she spent two weeks in Cornwall taking part in a film with Joy Finzi, her two sons and some Oxford students. The director was John Schlesinger, an undergraduate from Balliol College who was later to make films such as *Midnight Cowboy, Far From the Madding Crowd* and *A Kind of Loving*. His mother played in the Newbury String Players, an ensemble created and directed by Gerald Finzi. The film-making in Cornwall was full of near disasters and the result, Ursula commented, 'was not exactly a masterpiece'.[7] At the same time Ralph went off to Cambridge where he and Rosamond Carr were the guests of his former student, Patrick Hadley. They all attended a performance of Purcell's *King Arthur*. Provocatively, Ralph reported to Ursula that the highlight of the show was Carr's friend Anne Keynes who 'ravished my heart in a filmy quite transparent tunic with sleeves attached to the wrists. When she lifted her arms it was most alluring – she also by the way sang charmingly.'[8]

That summer he worked on a subject that he first had in mind many years before. This was a setting of two poems by Matthew Arnold: *The Scholar Gypsy* and *Thyrsis*. The work was given the title 'An Oxford Elegy' and was first performed with the Fantasia on the Old 104th Psalm Tune at a private concert that Ralph organized at White Gates on 20 November 1949. The mixed chorus was the Tudor Singers, Steuart Wilson was the speaker, and Michael Mullinar the pianist. The strings were the Schwiller Quartet, the group which forty years before had given the first performance of Ralph's first string quartet. An Oxford Elegy is a work of enduring idealistic belief, but also one sounding of autumnal regret, bringing to mind the melancholy of some of Ralph's early song settings. Individuals from the past were very much in his thoughts at this time. During that year he wrote a kindly birthday letter to his fellow student John Ireland, and another to the Staffordshire composer Havergal Brian to whom he reported, in August: 'The very day [your letter] arrived I was occupied in making a latin version of 'Sancta Civitas'. Perhaps you do not remember that in very early days you helped me a lot with the score, for which I am grateful.'[9] For another old friend, Robert Trevelyan, Ralph worked hard but unavailingly, to gain some public recognition in the form of an honorary degree.

This was the third year of the Edinburgh Festival which Ralph disparaged as the 'Snobopolis Festival'. But it was here that the film in which he had most recently been involved had its first screening. This was *The Dim Little Island*, a short, ten-minute film commissioned by the Central Office of Information and produced and directed by Humphrey Jennings. It was a propagandist piece intended to boost British morale in that post-war, post-imperial time of ongoing austerity. Ralph is one of four speakers in the film, the others being Ralph's fellow Carthusian, the architectural critic and highly popular cartoonist Osbert Lancaster, the naturalist and radio personality James Fisher, and John Ormiston, an industrialist with a distinguished military record in the recent war. Ralph is here given his place among the great and the good of contemporary British life. He speaks in praise of the musical culture of the country, commending its base which is 'the great mass of musical amateurs who make music for the love of it'. Part of his Five Variants of Dives and Lazarus is played stirringly on the soundtrack. The image of Vaughan Williams as an emblem of Englishness, one that has obscured the full range of his great achievement, is here yet again strongly confirmed.

At this time he was also honoured for his work in another film. From Ealing Studios Ernest Irving wrote to tell him that he had received an honour in the Soviet Union, a diploma and a statuette for his score to *Scott of the Antarctic*. In his suavely humorous way Irving continued: 'There being no British representative present it was accepted on your behalf by the correspondent of *The Daily Worker*. As you are, of all men, a daily worker, I suppose you won't mind this.' By return Ralph retorted testily, 'I do not want the horrid little thing ... the whole thing was so obviously a political ramp.'[10]

As the New Year of 1950 began, the daily worker continued to be extremely busy. So much so that he had to write to his good friend and colleague Margery Cullen, Honorary Secretary of the Leith Hill Music Festival, declining to write a new work for performance in Surrey as part of the Festival of Britain that was being planned for the following year. As spring approached he was back in the West Midlands. This time in Wolverhampton where, in March 1950, he and Ursula were the guests of Dr Percy M. Young, who was in charge of music at the Wolverhampton and Staffordshire Technical College. The energetic, ebullient, football-loving Dr Young was an enthusiastic but discriminating admirer of Ralph's compositions, and was in the process of writing a book about him. At the Civic Hall in the then county borough there were performances, which Ralph admired, of two of his best, but neglected works, his Mass and his *Riders to the Sea*. He was also honoured with a civic reception at which his increasing deafness caused a momentary difficulty. When the mayor made a speech praising his achievement, Ralph, sitting with his old friend the singer Clive Carey, readily joined in the applause. Ursula had quickly to lean across the Mayoress to restrain him. The day ended happily with an enjoyable dinner party given by Dr Young.

Another admirer of Ralph's music was completing a book about him. This was Hubert Foss, Ralph's former publisher at Oxford University Press. Some three months after the visit to Wolverhampton Ralph received a copy of Foss's *Ralph Vaughan Williams: A Study*. He was much affected by the qualities, the high idealism and nobility which the book attributed to him. Thanking Foss, he wrote: 'I am quite overpowered by the affection and thought in your book. I feel hopelessly unable to live up to it. Indeed I owe you rather a grudge because I hoped for the rest of my life, to be able to live comfortably following my lower instincts, without ideals.... But alas ... I shall have to try and live up to my (or rather your) ideals.'[11]

But as books about him began to appear, Ralph's career was far from ending. In fact it was burgeoning. During 1950 he worked intensely on his opera *The Pilgrim's Progress* with Roy Douglas assisting. In November of that year his Concerto Grosso for Strings was played at the Albert Hall by the massed orchestra of the Royal Music Schools Association with Adrian Boult as conductor. A five-part work lasting some twenty minutes, the piece is full of melody and good spirits. It was another instance of Ralph's concern to be involved in, and to contribute to the larger musical culture. And at its grassroots. He wrote parts for young people with elementary and middling skills as well as for professional players. Two of the young performers that day turned out to be the son and daughter of Mrs Machray with whom some thirty-five years before Ralph had been billeted at Bishop's Stortford during the Great War. So there was for him a happy reunion in what was a joyous, excited occasion. After the concert Ralph and Ursula were at Covent Garden for a performance of *Tosca*.

Less than a month after this, in every sense of the word, popular occasion, Ralph found himself having to defend his democratic credentials in a postal altercation with his long-time friend and fellow composer, Rutland Boughton. For the most part neglected today, Rutland Boughton, some five years younger than Ralph, was a well-known figure in British musical life in the first half of the twentieth century. A friend of George Bernard Shaw he had attempted to create a British Bayreuth at Glastonbury and had composed several operas on Arthurian themes. The opening of Boughton's foundation, supported by Thomas Beecham, Ethel Smyth, Gustav Holst and John Galsworthy, was halted by the outbreak of the First World War. But in the 1920s Boughton was to have spectacular success in London with his opera *The Immortal Hour*. In 1926 he was a strongly outspoken supporter of the miners' strike and in the following years became increasingly left-wing. At a meeting of the Composers' Guild he presented Ralph with a peace manifesto and asked him to sign it. This was the time of the war between North Korea and United Nations forces. The Communist countries were active in promoting a peace campaign. Himself now a member of the French Communist Party, Pablo Picasso created a powerful painting imaging the conflict, and also devised a famous dove as an icon for the Communist cause. He was also one of those who came to Britain to promote the cause in a conference in Sheffield which the British Government, under intense pressure from the United States decided, at the last minute, to suppress. Ralph refused to sign the declamation which Rutland Boughton put to him. He later felt it necessary to defend himself at some length against the blame and criticism in a letter Boughton sent to him. Employing the idiom of the Cold War, Ralph declared that: 'this bogus Russian "peace" manifesto.... was simply a means to sow dissension and want of will among the Western countries.' He insisted that 'this so-called 'peace' manifesto was designed to weaken the resistance to their infamous designs of tyranny [sic] and imperialist aggression.'

At this time Ralph also had conservative attitudes to cultural issues. When Robert Trevelyan's wife Elizabeth wrote to him about the proposed abolition of the Third Programme on the BBC, he saw no need to defend it. He told her: 'I feel myself that their programmes must improve a lot before we make serious efforts to retain them.' He was quite content with the more popular wavelengths. 'I find there is almost as much music as I want to listen to on the Home Service and even occasionally on the Light, as there is on the Third.' He goes on to show himself as a man of musical tastes belonging to a world prior to that of the post-war period revival of interest in the baroque. 'The Third Programme People are much too fond of dreary 17th and 18th Century music which may be very interesting to the antiquarian and musicologist but has no real artistic value.' Ralph also thought that those giving talks on the Third needed to take lessons in 'the elements of English elocution'.[12]

As the New Year, 1951, approached and the date for the first performance of *The Pilgrim's Progress* drew closer, work on the opera became ever more intense and demanding. There were rehearsals at White Gates. In a letter, Adeline described a visit from: 'the producer, such a friendly cultivated man, I wish you could have seen him, illustrating Apollyon with Ursula as the Pilgrim thrusting at his heart – it was to measure the timing of the thrusts to the music – Ursula was in her glory! And did it all very well.'[13] Ursula recalled that: 'it was a hectic spring, with Pilgrim rehearsals and performances, satisfaction and dissatisfaction about the production.... It was a comfort to have Beagley and the car to take Ralph from Dorking to Covent Garden and back, and I spent much time making picnic meals to be shared on those journeys between one rehearsal and another.'[14]

As he approached his eightieth year Ralph coped with a demanding schedule. Ursula wrote that 'Ralph is managing well, though this week has been rather too much of a good thing – leaving the house at 8.40 – Rehearsals 10–13.30, sandwiches in the car, conducting rehearsals from 2.45–5.30, and then an evening concert'.[15] But there was also time for partying in Ursula's Marylebone top-floor flat. On one occasion there was so much singing and dancing that she trembled for the floor. An increasingly frequent member of Ursula and Ralph's extensive social circle in London was Sir Gilmour Jenkins, a very senior civil servant at the Ministry of Transport. A suave, elegant man, a generation younger than Ralph, he was very interested in classical music and would subsequently sing the role of Pilate for Ralph at the Leith Hill Music Festival. Sir Gilmour had figured prominently in Ursula's diary for some years. He was often her companion when Ralph was away from London.

During the rehearsal period for *The Pilgrim's Progress* the Opera House was staging Janáček's *Katya Kabanova* in the evenings. To have a break and a diversion Ralph and Ursula stayed behind for one of the performances. It was the first Janáček opera Ralph had seen since his time in Prague many years before and he greatly enjoyed it. Yet this was but a brief respite. Tensions continued to intensify during the concluding rehearsals and climaxed on the first night. Ursula recalled: 'Ralph was terribly nervous before the performance – his tie would not tie, his sleeve links were recalcitrant, and he blazed with rage at a photographer who tried to intercept him in the Opera House on his way to his seat. Cordelia, Mary Wilson, Gil Jenkins, and I had to surround and protect him, and there were very few of his friends he wanted to see until it was over.' The tension finally eased at the end of the fourth and final act with the sounds of the hymn tune 'York' which had introduced Bunyan's dream at the beginning of the work. Ralph went up and took a curtain call, enthusiastically grasping the hand of the singer, the Maori bass-baritone Inia te Wiata, who was the first Pilgrim. After the final curtain there was champagne in the old crush bar. Eventually, he and Ursula left and were driven home. In the car, she remembered, Ralph said: 'They won't like it, they don't want an opera with no heroine and no love duets – and I don't care; it's what I meant, and there it is.'[16]

This first gala night of *The Pilgrim's Progress* was 26 April 1951. Nevill Coghill was the director and the young Leonard Hancock was the conductor. It was Covent Garden's main contribution to the Festival of Britain organized by the government to commemorate the anniversary of the Great Exhibition in Hyde Park promoted by Prince Albert exactly a century before. The response to that opening night was, as Ralph had foreseen, not entirely positive. It was generally agreed by reviewers that the costumes were a disaster and that the lighting was crude. But the music was, as it continues to be, much admired. Whether the piece worked as an opera was a more contentious question. Writing in *The Daily Telegraph* on the morning after the first night, Richard Capel, who was an admirer of Ralph's music, wrote that: 'Only genius could have saved, at Covent Garden, a production so wanting in the dramatic element – so anti-theatrical.... In a word, the Pilgrim's ordeal is not realised.'[17] Writing a little later in *Music and Letters*, Herbert Murrill saw the issue less negatively. He argued that Vaughan Williams:

> positively disregards theatrical and operatic convention; throws to one side the nice delineation of character, the careful balance and adjustment of climax points, the pointed underlining of the dramatic situation; and with a sort of humble self-confidence writes a loose-knit and contemplative score that succeeds by its integrity and becomes a unity by its single-mindedness. So I say that if *Pilgrim's Progress* achieves greatness – as I think it does – it achieves it through its disregard of stage conventions, and not in spite of this....'[18]

But not all the critics placed the opera in such a favourable light. Cecil Smith reviewing the performance for *Opera* was unequivocal. 'It is hard to imagine a job worse done. Mr Coghill taught ... the Pilgrim the gestures of a country vicar or perhaps of a provincial Elijah.... The delineation of lust and frivolity in the Vanity Fair scene was enough to send one to the nearest convent in the hope of a gayer time.'[19] In a revival of nearly sixty years later, in 2013, this particular tableau in the Pilgrim's journey again proved hard to stage. There was in the costumes and staging an overstated reaching for earthiness and sensuality as if to compensate for their faintness in the music. In some of the other tableaux in the piece the music is much more convincing and affecting: the early scenes hymning 'The House Beautiful', the Pilgrim's long monologue in prison and the indicating of the Delectable Mountain by the woodcutter's boy.

The many beauties of the work have not ensured it a rich performance history. After the scheduled second group of performances in the 1951–2 season the work was deleted from the Covent Garden repertoire. There was a single performance in Leeds in July and the opera was revived for a brief period in Cambridge in 1954. Otherwise the work was not staged at a major venue until the London revival of 2013 supported by the Vaughan Williams Trust. Its lack of success was the greatest disappointment in Ralph's long career as a composer. Later in the 1950s, when Michael Kennedy mentioned the opera to him, there was a quick change of subject. 'I remember mentioning the opera while lunching with RVW in the Grand Hotel, Manchester. "The *Pilgrim* is dead, and that's that", he said curtly, in a manner which allowed of no contradiction and manifestly concealed a bitter disappointment.'[20]

In the weeks leading up to the first night of *The Pilgrim's Progress*, Adeline became unwell. She ran extremely high temperatures which the doctors were at a loss to explain. Ursula recalled, 'All through these weeks Adeline was very ill. Ralph, torn between musical anxieties and home despairs, between total involvement in performance and total hopeless worry in between, was getting more and more exhausted.'[21] After the first night Adeline recovered somewhat and was able to listen to a BBC relay of the opera. On 6 May, ten days after the first night, Ralph was again in London for the first performance of his Sons of Light, a cantata for children's choir, setting poems written by Ursula. Ralph had been requested to supply such a piece by the viola player Bernard Shore, who also served as Staff Inspector of Schools in Music at the Ministry of Education. Ursula based her text on a Jewish legend told her by her friend the novelist Elias Canetti that the angels of creation were the letters of the alphabet. Bright, lively music with a succession of rousing fanfares, the piece celebrates creation and concludes with a commending of humanity's power through language, man's ability to name.

> Man shall awake and speak their names aloud
> and set a name on fire and wind and cloud
> from whence all living creatures take delight.
> Rejoice, man stands among the sons of light.

The cantata was sung by a choir of over a thousand young people conducted by Adrian Boult. There was a joyous mood in the hall that suited that festival year. Ursula remembered 'a sense of surprised unreality when Ralph and I took a call together on the stage of the Albert Hall, with Adrian Boult joining our hands, just in the place where, between a rehearsal and a performance of the 'London Symphony' a few years earlier, Ralph had fully declared his affection.'[22] Four days after this occasion, on 10 May, Ralph was again in the capital. Students at the University of London were preparing to perform Toward the Unknown Region and he was most interested to hear again this work of more than forty years before, so he and Ursula attended one of the rehearsals. Afterwards Ralph had tea with Ursula at her flat and then returned to

Dorking. Ursula had dinner with her close friend Gilmour Jenkins and the Danish Icelandic singer Engel Lund. As they were finishing their coffee, the telephone rang. It was Ralph. He told her that Adeline had died in her sleep that afternoon. He asked her if she would come. Cordelia had also come to be with him. Ursula set off immediately.

Ralph's marriage that had lasted more than fifty-three years was now over. Ursula was moved when she realized that Adeline's life had come to its end while the students in London were singing the words of Toward the Unknown Region. On the following day Ursula went into the garden at White Gates to find flowers to place in Adeline's room. She found that: 'she looked as fragile as the body of a small bird. Her early beauty, her lively mind, her austere discipline, her tenderness and edged wit had dissolved and left no trace on the wrecked face that lay between hyacinths and jonquils on the pillow.'[23]

Chapter Eighteen

THE WIDOWER

Adeline was buried beside her parents in the hillside graveyard of the parish church of her childhood at Brockenhurst, Hampshire. Ralph returned home to what Ursula described as 'a frenzy of activity'. He threw away masses of photographs and tore up a great number of letters. He cleared out cupboards and desks and, taking Cordelia's advice, sent off Adeline's jewellery and clothes to various nieces. The wheelchairs and crutches were quickly assembled for removal by the Red Cross. He asked Ursula to come and take over the running of White Gates for him. But she decided that it would be best if she kept her base in London and stayed at Dorking just at weekends. He decided not to cancel any of his many engagements saying, 'it's no good looking back, no good at all'. But his determined activity was sometimes interrupted by a feeling of desolation. To his friends Victor and Mary Shepherd in South Africa he wrote in one simple, brief sentence: 'My wife died about a month ago, so now I'm all alone.'[1]

Exactly a week after Adeline's passing he went to hear the posthumous first performance by the Kantrovich Quartet of Robert Müller-Hartmann's string quartet, insisting to Genia Hornstein on that occasion, 'I'm not going to be a hermit'. Four days later he was at the Festival of Britain concert at the Dorking Halls to hear the Surrey Federation of Women's Institutes sing his often rollicking 'Folk Songs of the Four Seasons'. A few days later he was in London to attend the opening by Princess Margaret of the rebuilt Cecil Sharp House in Camden. He also went to the premiere of Benjamin Britten's Spring

314

Symphony. On 23 June 1951 came the first performance, in the newly opened Royal Festival Hall, of a beautiful gem-like work of his own, his 'Three Shakespeare Songs'. It was conducted by his pupil of years before, Armstrong Gibbs, at whose request he had composed the piece. A setting of three interrelating Shakespearian texts to do with transcendence, 'Full fathom five' and 'The cloud-capped towers' from *The Tempest* and 'Over hill, over dale' from *A Midsummer Night's Dream*, the piece which lasts about seven minutes is a shimmering triptych. It sounds hauntingly of a shifting place between this world and a world beyond, one known only to Puck and to Oberon.

In July Ursula persuaded Ralph to have a holiday while White Gates was being redecorated. They went to Hythe in Kent and also to Dungeness and saw the area where Ralph had spent some time at the gunnery school during the First World War. Perhaps his interest in the place was fired by his involvement some years before with *The Loves of Joanna Godden,* which is a film very much about that locality. For their favourite pastime of reading aloud to each other they now chose Ralph's lifelong favourite *Lavengro,* George Borrow's picaresque account of rural England just before the coming of the railway. Ursula enjoyed their days on Romney Marsh describing it as 'a magical garden of wild flowers, bugloss and poppies, daisies, camomile, campion and horned poppies, while over the marsh lay the hazy bloom of flowering grasses.'[2] In a letter to Gerald Finzi Ralph spoke belittlingly of the place 'where Ursula has conducted me for a holiday. A real lower middle class existence with ice-creams on the beach in the morning and a trip in a motor boat.' Ursula, to whom the letter was dictated, protested she had wanted to go to France; Hythe was Ralph's preference. On an outing to Rye he had something of a triumph. Nearing his eightieth year he climbed the steps and then the ladders that led up to the roof of the church tower. At the top he posed nonchalantly with a foot resting on the low parapet while he surveyed the view.

They returned to White Gates to find the main room painted fresh, clean white and the old ragged linoleum replaced. But there was still a good deal that needed to be done in the view of Ursula, who was taking increasing responsibility for the upkeep of the house. In the first week in August she complained to her mother that:

> My big difficulty is that the house is in the most fearful state – walls
> peeling, paint round the windows rusty, all the linen in rags, and

so forth. It's quite understandable that it was so as Mrs VW didn't really <u>see</u> such things, and didn't mind about them much if she did. I can't bear it to be like that, and I'm gradually tidying up. It's very difficult for though Ralph is an angel about it all, I have to do it in such a way that it's not implicit criticism of her and her ways, and even more particularly with her sister, do I have to go carefully as you can guess. However I got the staff to do quite a lot of papering and colour washing'. Ursula still resisted the idea of living in the house full time. 'I feel a bit weighed down with the responsibility sometimes as it's easy enough if one is <u>in</u> the house all the time, but I'm sure it's right not to be and so ... I divide the best I can.'

Ralph now began to remunerate Ursula for her services. In the same letter she announced that 'Ralph has suddenly given me an allowance or a present of £200 a year. It's marvellous and does make life easy.'³ She bought a Sheraton commode for five guineas and a fur cape for twenty pounds.

Ursula also began hunting for a larger flat in London. She found one eventually in Bloomsbury. It was in Gordon Mansions, Torrington Place, just a few steps east of Heals on Tottenham Court Road. The red-brick building was in the Queen Anne style of the late nineteenth century and had a very pleasant pub, The Marlborough Arms, on the ground floor. Ursula's new flat was large enough for Ralph to have a room of his own. There was also a room set aside for Gilmour Jenkins, who by now had become a very close friend to both of them. The Permanent Secretary at the Ministry of Transport, Sir Gilmour was also a close friend of Gerald Finzi to whom he had given a government job at the beginning of the Second World War. Finzi's biographer relates that:

> he interviewed Gerald and clearly rooted for him. He was the arche-typal civil servant with immaculate taste who sings in or runs a choir or excels in some other branch of the arts.... Jenkins struck up an affectionate friendship with Finzi, later remarking on 'a real bond of sympathy from our very first meeting at my round table'. He was deeply grateful to Gerald for getting him out of the official rut and interested once more in real things and meeting people with real interests outside Government and transport circles.⁴

At the end of the summer Ralph and Ursula were off to Worcester again for that year's Three Choirs Festival. The night before their departure, after she had gone with Gilmour Jenkins to see the festival fireworks at Battersea Gardens, Ursula gave a sherry party. Among the guests were the young composer Tony Scott, the Finzis, Gil Jenkins, Ralph and Elias Canetti. A future winner of the Nobel Prize for Literature, Canetti was the author of *Auto da Fe*, which had been translated into English by one of his numerous lovers, Randolph Wedgwood's daughter Veronica, who was developing what proved to be a distinguished career as a historian. Like Veronica, Ursula was a great admirer of Elias Canetti for 'his tremendous knowledge of literature, philosophy and history'. She was also a close friend of Canetti's wife Veza who 'was a passionately faithful supporter of all he did'. Ursula 'spent a lot of time with them both, though it was difficult to persuade her to come out; the usual pattern was for me to visit her, and for Canetti to come to my parties.'[5]

Coming to know Ralph through Ursula, Canetti admired him greatly, describing him as 'great-hearted, independent, with no notion of aristocracy, submissive, but without acute rebellion, a man who one would like to cover pages and pages about'. Canetti also left a glimpse into the 'menage à trois' which, he reported, Ursula set up with Ralph and Gilmour Jenkins in the flat at Torrington Place and later in the house in Hanover Terrace. Canetti presented Jenkins as a highly sexed Falstaffian figure and he saw Ursula as belonging to a generation of English, upper-middle class women for whom affairs were 'no longer against the prevailing morality, if anything the opposite'. He added that 'the ones who were that way indeed were vehemently so.' He cites Ursula as an example:

> one woman, whom I knew well though I didn't love her, had fixed herself up in the following way (following a cold and unhappy marriage to an officer, who died during the war): she lived under one roof with two old men, one of whom, a senior civil servant, was a veritable satyr, and the other, much older, the most wonderful pure man, Ralph Vaughan Williams, the composer and pride of the nation.

Later in his book Canetti suggested that the arrangement had elements both of comedy and of the kind of ethical and emotional delicacy that one might find in a Henry James novel. 'I can't possibly tell the wonderful and hilarious story of his Ursula and her Falstaff, who was, so to speak, part of the furniture of this marriage, who lived in the house of this wonderful man.... But how charming it would be to think the noble old man <u>knew</u> it all, and had the greatness of heart to approve it, or at least tolerate it, for her sake, because he didn't want to be without her in his old years.'[6]

After her sherry party on that August evening in 1951 Ursula did the packing for Gilmour Jenkins for an official visit he was to make to Scandinavia. Then she went with Ralph to Dorking to help him get ready for the visit to Worcester. The next day they set off driving through Dorchester-on-Thames and Tewkesbury stopping off to see the ancient abbeys in both places. High points in the festival were performances of Ralph's Fifth Symphony and *Sancta Civitas* which, in the galleried cathedral, had a resonance that greatly pleased Ralph. There were excursions to Malvern, Symonds Yat and Tintern. They came home via Stratford-upon-Avon where the Clarion Singers, whom Ralph had so much admired on his visit to Birmingham, gave a highly entertaining, light-hearted performance of *Sir John in Love*. Afterwards Ralph and Ursula were entertained by the Director of the Shakespeare Memorial Theatre, the prominent actor Anthony Quayle. He also gave them tickets for *Henry IV Part I* for the following evening. This, Ursula remembered, had long-term consequences for them. After the performance she and Ralph disagreed strongly about the character of Hotspur, so Ralph suggested that they both re-read the play. When they returned to Dorking he went on to suggest that they read all of Shakespeare's plays – which they did ... reading from an early nineteenth-century edition comprising ten volumes which Ralph had long owned. They read every single play and the project lasted over a year. It is yet one more indication of the seriousness of Ralph's interest in literature.

He had a quiet birthday that year. In the same October of 1951 there was a General Election. With some misgivings Ralph voted Labour, but was on the losing side. The Conservative Party now formed the government and would continue in power until long after the end of Ralph's life. Winston Churchill now returned as Prime Minister. Ralph encountered him on 14 December, after a foggy journey to Bristol where the university, of which Churchill was Chancellor, conferred on him their first ever honorary doctorate of music. A buoyant, cherubic Churchill, in resplendent black and gold academic attire, grandly saluted Ralph as 'our greatest English composer, and great musical ambassador'. A banquet followed the ceremony. Bristol Cream sherry was abundantly available and Ralph, who greatly enjoyed sweet wines, treated himself to a good deal of it. In the afternoon he and Ursula visited Arnold Barter, an employee of the Wills Tobacco Company and conductor of the Bristol Philharmonic Society and Chorus, who had admired and promoted Ralph's work for some forty years. In the Barter house there was a bright fire against the winter day, a copious tea and many interesting memories. On the evening train back to Paddington Ralph slept soundly and, on waking, informed Ursula that he would order a store of Bristol Cream sherry immediately.

In the first week of the New Year Roy Douglas came to White Gates to help with the emerging symphony. Ralph was also working on his short Romance in D flat which had been commissioned by the American harmonica virtuoso, Larry Adler, after the two had entered into discussion following a concert at the Wigmore Hall. When performed at a Promenade Concert the piece provoked such an enthusiastic response that it had to be repeated. Early in January 1952 Ralph was in London and attended performances of two important works of Modernist music. To an old friend he wrote: 'I went to *Billy Budd* twice and also listened to it, and am still unmoved by it, though I recognise its great skill.'[7] He was also present at the opening of Alban Berg's *Wozzeck* at Covent Garden. To Hubert Foss he wrote: 'I am up chiefly for the first night of *Wozzeck* – up to the present Berg has merely bored me – but I went to a bit of a rehearsal the other day and I was so intrigued by the stage that I did not bother to listen to the music: which perhaps is the best way of listening to it, and what the composer meant.'[8]

And yet in the last line of the letter he also described the tenor role of the Captain as 'a fine comedy part'. Back in Dorking Ralph completed the score of what he entitled *Sinfonia Antartica*, which he dedicated to his good friend from the film world, Ernest Irving.

In the first week of February 1952 King George VI died. His elder daughter was proclaimed Queen Elizabeth II and so began the sixth reign of Ralph's lifetime. In the afterglow of the Festival of Britain the accession was hailed as the start of a second Elizabethan age, a heartening phrase which some believe only to have lost its currency some four years later at the time of Britain's political and military debacle at Suez. The country's financial situation in 1952 was such that currency allowances for foreign travel had dwindled to £25 per person. But Ursula gradually persuaded Ralph that a holiday in France would be good for them. They went first to Paris where they stayed in a hotel with windows overlooking the courtyard and gardens of the Palais Royal. Ralph was keen to show Ursula the nearby Hotel du Portugal et de l'Univers and his other haunts from the time he had taken lessons from Maurice Ravel well over forty years before. They went on to Chartres and then to St Malo which again held many memories for Ralph (this time of his holiday there with Aunt Sophy, his mother, Hervey and Meggie when he was ten years old). They then took the bus to Dol where, in an old-fashioned Norman hotel they ate a hearty dinner with Ralph drinking a quart of the local cider and ending the day with a nightcap of that other apple drink of the locality, Calvados. By the time they reached Rouen their ration of money was running problematically short. Their last meal before boarding the boat train for England was just two apples and a bar of chocolate. But despite the financial shortages this was a very happy holiday, the first of a succession which punctuated their years together.

In this, his eightieth year, the Royal College of Music resolved to commission a painting of Ralph and selected as artist the leading Establishment portraitist, Sir Gerald Kelly, the President of the Royal Academy and the regular choice of the royal family. Sir George Dyson, the current Director of the Royal College escorted Sir Gerald, a hearty clubman of very conservative tastes, down to Dorking with a view to arranging some sittings in Sir Gerald's studio. After some initial grousing, Ralph went there but on each occasion fell asleep while Sir Gerald painted and offered his many lordly reminiscences. The painter was invariably vexed by Ralph's choice of tie. Later that June came an outing that was more to Ralph's taste. This was to the King's Lynn Festival at which, at the invitation of his former student Patrick Hadley, Ralph was to lecture on East Anglian Folk Songs. He and Ursula were chauffeured by Beagley to Hadley's house in the Norfolk village of Heacham, known for its production of lavender. Ursula remembered how the air was highly scented 'and the fields were dusky blue with flowers'.[9] Patrick Hadley, who as a very young officer had lost a leg in the last days of the First World War, was now a Fellow of Gonville and Caius College and pursuing a highly successful academic career in music at Cambridge. At Heacham he had an excellent cook and wine cellar and gave them a fine dinner in his beautiful garden with a good deal of Moselle wine, 'while hundreds of shooting stars fell out of the sky'. The following afternoon the lecture with illustrations supplied by expert singers was a great success. It was attended by two guests from nearby Sandringham, the Queen Mother and Princess Margaret. Ralph was again presented. The day concluded with an impressive performance of his Fifth Symphony conducted by Sir John Barbirolli in the grand church of St Nicholas with its fine roof decorated with medieval angel carvings.

Continuing to be popular, the Fifth Symphony was also played at the Proms that year, at the same concert at which the Romance written for Larry Adler was performed and so well received. The night before, Ralph and Ursula had gone to the Little Mermaid Theatre which the enterprising actor and director Bernard Miles had created in his garden in St John's Wood. It would later move to Puddle Dock in the City of London. Bernard Miles figured early in that revitalization of English theatre which was such a feature of the 1950s. As in the case of other young talents, Ralph was quick to help him. Miles recalled that 'he was one of the first to spring forward with financial sustenance for the birth and founding of our tiny theatre in St John's Wood ... he continued that help over the succeeding years.'[10] That summer night in the tiny venue Ralph and Ursula heard Kirsten Flagstad sing the title role in Purcell's *Dido and Aeneas* in which, more than half a century before, Ralph himself had sung in a performance at the Lyceum Theatre. A little later in the year when he and Ursula went to the Three Choirs Festival at Hereford, he made a point of visiting a place that he also remembered vividly from the past, the ruined Augustinian Priory at Llanthony in the Black Mountains in an area where he had collected folk songs at the end of the Edwardian decade. But Ralph was no longer keen to climb those hills as once he had been. As Ursula remembered: 'This time it had to be by car, a large old-fashioned Rolls Royce, far too wide for the lanes, but we were lucky and did not meet any traffic.... When we got to Llanthony the country was dark, overcast by rain clouds with sudden streaks of silvery light, sinister and unfriendly but very beautiful.'[11] Back in London they attended the commemoration service in Westminster Abbey on 30 September for the centennial of the birth of Ralph's old teacher, Sir Charles Villiers Stanford. Ralph walked in a procession of choir and clergy to lay a wreath on the memorial stone. Six years later, Ursula was to watch as a stone for Ralph himself was placed beside it.

His eightieth birthday in October brought a torrent of cards, letters, gifts, parties and celebration concerts. As Ursula noted: 'White Gates was full of celebration, tissue paper, greetings, telegrams and champagne.'[12] On Monday 6 October the incorporated Society of Musicians gave a dinner in Ralph's honour at which Herbert Howells spoke at length about Ralph's achievement as a composer, the enthusiastic applause that followed causing some embarrassment to the guest of honour. Then came a concert at Dorking given by the Leith Hill Music Festival Choir with

Adrian Boult and William Cole sharing the conducting. The programme included 'Five Mystical Songs', *Benedicite,* 'The Hundredth Psalm' and 'An Oxford Elegy'. Sadly, Ralph's long-time friend Steuart Wilson was in hospital and unable to repeat the role of speaker in the last work; his role was taken by a new friend, the poet Cecil Day Lewis, the husband of Michael Balcon's daughter, Jill. Another celebration concert was arranged by the London County Council and given in the fashionable new venue of the Royal Festival Hall. Ralph was invited to choose from his works for the programme and he selected the Fifth Symphony, Thanksgiving for Victory (now re-titled 'A Song of Thanksgiving'), *Flos Campi* and, his recent collaboration with Ursula, The *Sons of Light.* The performance ended with a great surge of applause from the audience. When he made his way up on to the podium he seemed a little bemused by the warmth and protractedness of the greeting. Then came a grand party upstairs with a huge birthday cake and a host of well-wishers, known and unknown.

One of Ralph's oldest and dearest friends Randolph Wedgwood was greatly touched to witness the happiness and youthfulness which Ralph, with Ursula beside him, exuded on these occasions. He wrote: 'It must have moved your heart to be so surrounded by love and enthusiasm. I know it moved me, and I felt proud to be there and to contribute my share to the good wishes and to the enthusiasm. You looked young and happy – and emotions like that bring you youth and happiness all through.'[13]

As life calmed down a little, Ralph and Ursula went to Manchester to be present when John Barbirolli conducted the preliminary rehearsals of the new symphony, The *Antartica.* Ralph's friendship with Barbirolli was a recent one dating from an occasion in Oxford when the dynamic conductor had directed a performance of Ralph's Sixth Symphony. Barbirolli's biographer relates:

> For a while after its premier Vaughan Williams felt uncertain about the *Scherzo* movement. While pleasing everyone else it did not quite come off for him. At the Sheldonian Theatre, Oxford, he heard Barbirolli conduct the Sixth Symphony twice in one day, first at a rehearsal, then in public. On his own initiative Barbirolli took the *Scherzo* at a slightly slower tempo than the one marked in the score. At once the *Scherzo* made full sense to the man who had written it. Vaughan Williams thanked him for his elucidation and altered his metronome mark accordingly; a considerable compliment, as Barbirolli rightly claimed.[14]

Ralph and Ursula were also joined there by their other new young friends Michael Kennedy and his wife Eslyn, with whom they were developing a close, affectionate relationship. Roy Douglas was also present and helped to make adjustments to the score. Ralph and Ursula returned south and over the Christmas period gave a large party at which they used up the very large amount of champagne that Ralph had amassed at the time of his birthday. Invited by the *Sunday Times* to contribute to their 'Books of the Year' spread Ralph chose, along with a work of history and a book about the River Thames, the Penguin selection of the poems of C. Day Lewis and *Period Piece* by his relative Gwen Raverat. This family memoir interested him greatly and brought back many recollections of his boyhood.

The first month of the New Year, 1953, was one of the most eventful of Ralph's long life. The Seventh Symphony was to receive its first public performance on 14 January, with John Barbirolli conducting the Hallé Orchestra and Choir. Margaret Ritchie was the singer of the wordless soprano part. Some days before this concert, Barbirolli was in London conducting Wagner's *Tristan and Isolde* at Covent Garden. Ralph and Ursula were at one of the performances the night before they were to return to Manchester. After hearing the great opera of love Ralph asked Ursula to be his wife. As Ursula wrote in her autobiography: 'After sharing that music our half-and-half life seemed to reach its natural conclusion and marriage was what we both wanted.'[15] The following morning they were off to Manchester again to join John Barbirolli for the run up to the launch of the new symphony. Ursula continued, 'We caught the breakfast train in a state of dazzled glory, though we didn't immediately tell John what he had brought about.'

With a hectic rehearsal schedule it proved difficult to find time for the wedding ceremony. But eventually they arranged for it to take place on 7 February, a week before Valentine's day 1953. It was also a week before the premiere of *Sinfonia Antartica*. Exactly a year later a very happy Ursula wrote a pre-Valentine poem explaining:

We could not wait, St. Valentine,
to marry on your day,
'A week,' we said 'before we wed–
a wasted week to stay–'
We could not do it, Valentine,
But hasted us away, to church, and feast, and bed.

And now a year, St Valentine,
has almost passed away,
A happy year, spent with my dear,
A yearlong month of may,
  I could not wish a Valentine
more sweet, more kind, more gay
at church, and feast and bed.

The ceremony took place in the vestry chapel of St Pancras Church, the grand Regency building with portico, pediment and columns on the corner of Upper Woburn Place and the busy Euston Road. The church, which in 1952 was only recently restored following bomb damage in the war, was close to Ursula's flat in Torrington Place. Ralph was surprised when Ursula, very much a non-believer, expressed a strong preference for a church wedding. She explained that she wanted only the very best English words to be used in their ceremony. The ceremony was a quiet one. The wedding party was small. It included: Ursula's parents, Jean Stewart and a couple of other friends. Ralph's best man was Sir Gilmour Jenkins.

The news got out very quickly and the press, who had learned of the secret wedding, were at the door by the following day. While the snow fell unceasingly, Ralph and Ursula spent the day sending formal cards to inform friends of their wedding, fending off reporters and answering the many letters about *Sinfonia Antartica*.

Chapter Nineteen

10 HANOVER TERRACE

Ralph had been nervous about the new symphony, having doubts about a symphony that had begun as film music. To Alan Frank, a successor of Hubert Foss at Oxford University Press, he once suggested that the publicity: 'should merely say that some of the themes are taken from the music which I wrote for *Scott of the Antarctic*. Otherwise people will think it is a mere bit of carpentry – which as a matter of fact, it largely is; but don't tell anybody this.'[1]

But Ralph's modesty notwithstanding, the *Sinfonia* (an Italian word recalling Corelli) is an impressive listening experience unmistakeably symphonic in force and in structure at every level. Ambitiously it ponders, in generally sombre tones, the relationship of human consciousness to the incalculable vastness of the cosmos which surrounds it. Starting with the words of its title *Sinfonia Antartica*, the seventh symphony is the most explicitly programmatic of Ralph's symphonies. Each of the five movements is prefaced with a literary quotation. (In some of the early performances these were spoken by an actor.) The music has immediate, direct references to extra-musical entities. The first quotation from Shelley, defining and saluting the ultimate human capacity to endure and prevail against the very worst trials, confirms the heavy, dogged persistence that is sounded in the opening minutes of the first movement. It is a perseverance that finally must withstand the unnerving wailing of choir, soprano and orchestra conveying the great inhuman wastes of this planet and of the universe beyond.

The one moment of light relief in the symphony comes in the second movement, the *scherzo*. For the superscription Ralph took some words from Psalm 104 beginning with the words 'There go the ships and there goes that Leviathan'. The disjunction between the great beast at home in the deep and the frail human constructs devised to sail on it is developed with some humour in the course of the movement. There are comic sounds of frisking, galumphing creatures and musical onomatopoeias, suggesting their sounds, cries and movements. There are also occasional, disturbing interruptions; these are ominous sounds that bring to mind the danger, the vulnerability, the tenuousness of those setting out on unknown seas. After the marine creatures move off and away and into silence there comes the third and longest of the five movements. It is entitled 'Landscape', and thus refers to yet one more art form other than music. The literary reference is to Coleridge's rapt awe at the prospect of the creation of the glaciers in his 'Hymn Before Sunrise in the Vale of Chamouni'. The movement is a powerful evocation of a vast terrain, inhospitable to human beings. Aided by organ and wind machine the orchestra conveys disturbingly the grinding of ice upon ice, its cracking and melting into the waters. The block chords confirm the high drama of the process, horns and flutes suggesting the frozen immobility of the background. There comes a lashing cutting wind that finally abates only to leave the listener with intimations of nothingness similar to, but not as dramatically powerful as that of the Sixth Symphony.

But this suggestion is by no means the last word in *Sinfonia Antartica*. In the next movement, the *intermezzo*, a lyrical piping from the oboe, brightly reminds us of the persistence of the human spirit. Ralph refers to two lines from a lyric poem by John Donne asserting the endurance of love. As it moves towards its conclusion the movement allows hints of a funeral march but the ending, though elegiac, reiterates in delicate harp chords something worthy of commemoration.

The fifth and final movement, the epilogue, is a resolving of the dialectic that has run through the symphony. The desolate blasts, the keening winds and tempests are back again. But there is also a music of briskness and of stoical commonsense that echoes the spirit of the words from Captain Scott's diary that head the movement. The opening brings sounds of purposeful, busy activity. Then comes determined marching. But this is lost in the sounds of immeasurably larger forces. The composer – we sense his voice – ends the symphony with a compassionate, quiet, resigned lament as all music fades and we are with the inhuman wind-machine conveying the sounds of blown snow. The final bars also invite us perhaps to remember the previous symphony and also that of the *Pastoral*. The later symphonies more than once recall their predecessors and so intimate a larger musical narrative.

On that first night in Manchester, there had been, understandably, a protracted silence before the applause began. But when it started, it went on and on. Ralph left his seat to join John Barbirolli on the stage and the applause surged wildly, the audience rising to its feet. The new work had successfully begun its career.

After all the doubt, hard work and nervousness preceding the performance, the grand dinner party that the Barbirollis gave afterwards had come as a massive relief. A great deal was drunk and there was inebriation. Ursula was glad that the dinner was held at the Grand Hotel where they were staying; it was, she remembered: 'nice not to have to do more than totter to the lift'.

After another performance of the symphony on the following day, Ralph and Ursula had returned to London for its first performance in the capital at the Royal Festival Hall. In the days between these two symphonic concerts the octogenarian Ralph found time to give a lecture on Gustav Holst at Morley College and to conduct a rehearsal of the St Matthew Passion in Dorking. In London, *Sinfonia Antartica* was again enthusiastically received. The dedicatee, Ernest Irving, sat proudly in his wheelchair to listen to his music. The concert was followed by another supper party given for Ralph and Ursula by Robert Longman and his second wife, Lisette. It was more sedate than the one in Manchester; the guests included Steuart Wilson and the Day Lewises. The following morning Robert wrote to Ralph with characteristic affection reminding him that almost exactly forty years before he had given a supper for him following the first London performance of the 'London Symphony'.

Around this time Ralph received a letter from another old friend Adrian Boult, who clearly felt disappointed that Ralph had entrusted the new symphony to John Barbirolli rather than to himself. He expressed the hope that Ralph would remember him when launching future orchestral compositions. Caught up in the new and intense friendship with John Barbirolli and his wife, the oboist Evelyn Rothwell, Ralph responded to his old promoter: 'I should, of course, love you to give a first performance of something of mine and if I ever write anything more for orchestra, we will consider it....' He added: 'I asked John to do this last one because the year before he had done all my Symphonies at his concerts and I felt I owed him something.'[2]

In the spring came some respite from all the activity surrounding *Sinfonia Antartica* and Ralph and Ursula had a delayed honeymoon. They went to Venice. On the journey out they stopped at Bergamo, Desenzano and Sirmione on the southern shore of Lake Garda. After a couple of days in Verona they reached Venice where they established themselves in the annexe of a *pensione* on the Zattere. It was right next door to where John Ruskin had lived. They could look across the choppy waters to the long island of the Giudecca where, immediately opposite, stands the fine Palladio church of Il Redentore. Ralph immediately took upon himself the organization of their sight-seeing, checking guide books, opening times and ticket costs. The latter was important because British passport holders were still allowed to take only small sums of money out of the country. The newly-weds visited the usual tourist destinations. They explored the Doge's Palace and St Mark's and went up the Campanile to enjoy the grand view. They crossed the lagoon to the island of Torcello. There was one specially magic day when the noisy vaporettos went out of service and there were only gondolas on the canals. So the visitors had the rare opportunity to experience the unique city as travellers had seen it and described it in the times before the coming of the internal combustion engine. The day had a memorability to it such as marked many of their experiences together and made theirs such a happy marriage.

After a stop-over in Milan where they saw the paintings in the Brera, the couple returned to Britain. They decided that they would sell White Gates and look for a house in London. In their house-hunting they were helped by Mary Carter, a violinist who had performed with Ralph at Dorking. She drew their attention to 10 Hanover Terrace, a vacant property next door to where she herself lived. A very grand house in white stucco, it is a part of one of the palatial terraces built beside Regent's Park by John Nash in the early 1820s. The terraces are a section of his grand redesign of London that extended south, via Portland Place and Regent Street, all the way to the Mall. At the north-western edge of Regent's Park, close to where the London Central Mosque now stands, the long white frontage of Hanover Terrace has a Doric pavilion at each end and one in the middle topped by a pediment surrounded by statues of Classical figures. The front doors of the twenty houses (and Ralph's blue plaque) are inside a loggia which runs the length of the building. Each house has a basement, three storeys and a breadth of three windows. Number 10 had views over the park and its lake; immediately in front there were red may trees and an early flowering chestnut. Ralph and

Ursula were to live their marriage at a fine address indeed.

On 8 April 1953 they made an offer to the Commissioners of Crown Lands for a lease on the property. On their return from Italy they learned that their offer of £4,000 had been accepted. The lease was for a period of twenty-one years. Ralph, presumably with Ursula's future in mind, commented that this seemed rather short and wanted it to be extendable. They were unable to move in immediately as the damage caused by wartime bombing was still being repaired, so it was midsummer before the Vaughan Williamses formally took possession, and September before Ursula had completed the installation of Ralph, his books and papers and the Steinway specially chosen for him by her friend the pianist, Kathleen Long. There were rooms on the top floor for Gilmour Jenkins. Another friend, Frank Hollins, moved into the mews house at the rear of number 10.

In London that spring, Ralph and Ursula were immediately caught up in the rehearsals at Sadlers Wells for revivals of his first opera, *Hugh the Drover* and his finest and profoundest work for the theatre, *Riders to the Sea*. They were also involved in the increasingly hectic preparation for the coronation of the young queen in early June. Ten British composers had each been invited by the Arts Council to team up with a poet to produce 'A Garland for the Queen' which would serve as an equivalent to 'The Triumphs of Oriana', the song sequence created for the first Queen Elizabeth some four centuries earlier. Among the partnerships now created were those between Herbert Howells and Walter de la Mare, Gerald Finzi and Edmund Blunden and Michael Tippett and the highly successful fifties writer of poetic drama, Christopher Fry. Ralph asked Ursula to be his collaborator in the commission. Together they completed a part song 'Silence and Music'. It is a solemn piece, very traditional in sound compared, for example, with the work supplied by another partnership, the Canzonet by Alan Rawsthorne, setting words by W.H. Auden's erstwhile collaborator Louis MacNeice.

Ralph made other musical contributions to the coronation. William McKie, the Australian who was Organist and Master of the Choristers at Westminster Abbey invited him to compose a brief anthem to be heard in that part of the service in which the Queen received Holy Communion. This was 'O Taste and See', a motet for unaccompanied choir with an organ introduction. He also made an arrangement of his setting of the hymn the 'Old Hundredth', to be sung by the congregation. In the course of the negotiations about these musical contributions Ralph, Ursula and William McKie and his wife drew close to each other and the large range of Vaughan Williams's friendships was further extended. For the actual day of the coronation Ralph wrote to ask his new friend whether he and Ursula might watch the grand ceremony from the organ loft as Ralph had done at the last coronation in 1937. He wrote to McKie: 'is there any chance you could squeeze my wife (formerly Ursula Wood) and me on to the organ screen at the ceremony? I will slim for the purpose if necessary.' McKie replied that all the places in the organ loft were already promised. He arranged for Ralph and Ursula to have places in the musicians' section of the north transept.

One of Ursula's most vivid memories of being at the coronation was the singing of Ralph's arrangement of 'The Old Hundredth': 'Ralph's direction in the score – "all available trumpets" – was fully honoured and, and, they blazed triumphantly the introduction to the tune. Everyone was singing … three trumpets carried Ralph's descant tune magically through the great building over the unaccompanied voices of the choir.'[3]

It was a moment remembered by many others who gathered and huddled around their black and white television sets or their wirelesses to experience the historic occasion. When the ceremony ended there was a great hubbub outside the abbey as the eight thousand guests who had been packed inside prepared to disperse: 'peers, their robes hooked over their arms, were searching for peeresses and gossiping with each other.' To Ursula: 'it looked as if an enormous cast was assembling for *Iolanthe*.' She and Ralph moved on to the reception at Westminster Hall where most of the buns were gone and they had to make do with a shared brioche and a glass of wine until their car came to take them back to Dorking.

The following day they were back in London, this time for the rehearsals of *Epithalamion*, now retitled *The Bridal Day*. Fifteen years earlier this was the work that had brought Ralph and Ursula together. And now, at long last, as part of the coronation festivities it was to be performed. The first idea had been to stage it at Hampton Court but then it was decided to make a television programme out of it. At the rehearsal Ursula and Ralph were pleased with the orchestral playing, the singing and the performance of Cecil Day Lewis as the narrator. But they found the overall television production entirely unsatisfactory. It looked to them congested, muddled and disjointed from the music. They decided that the piece, which was so special for them, belonged on the stage.

That same week another composer had a major disappointment.

Gloriana, the opera which Benjamin Britten had written for the coronation, had only a lukewarm reception from both audience and reviewers.
Ralph, who, with Ursula, was in the Royal Opera House for that gala
first night felt it necessary to show solidarity with a fellow composer and
with the profession of music. They sat in the orchestra stalls with Arthur
Bliss, Arnold Bax, Malcolm Sargent and William Walton, every one of
them a knight. Ralph was very much at the centre of Britain's musical
establishment. But he felt uncomfortable with the negative response of
the audience and decided that it was necessary to comment publicly on
the unfortunate occasion. He wrote to *The Times* and without offering
any appraisal of Britten's opera, stressed one major point, 'The important
thing to my mind, at the moment, is that, so far as I know, for the first
time in history the Sovereign has commanded an opera from a composer
from these islands for a great occasion. Those who cavil at the public
expense should realise what such a gesture means to the prestige of our
music.'[4]

During the following weeks of summer (the last one at White Gates)
life quieted a little and Ralph was again able to devote time and his
considerable energy to composition. One expedition was to Bournemouth
to conduct his 'London Symphony' at the Winter Gardens there. On their
way to the concert he and Ursula stopped off at the Balmer Lawn Hotel,
close to Brockenhurst where Adeline lay buried. They visited the Fisher
family grave where she had been interred and studied the recent inscrip-
tion of her name. Ralph spoke to the sexton and confirmed arrangements
for the upkeep of the grave. As he and Ursula turned to leave the country
churchyard, Ralph mused that Adeline had returned to the place and the
people who meant most to her. He and Ursula walked away thoughtfully
amidst the old trees, the birds and the sound of bells.

During the last days in Dorking, Ralph completed his new work.
This was his Christmas cantata *Hodie.* He and Ursula completed the
libretto – a sequence of poems dealing with the Nativity. It is a large scale
choral work, with some solo items, in which the style of the individual
song-settings varies a great deal. It ranges from the joyousness of '*Hodie
Christus natus est*' to the tenderly delicate lyricism of the setting of
Thomas Hardy's 'The Oxen'. Throughout the sequence there is a melodic
pleasingness that will surely guarantee a long-term performability at
Christmas-time.

Hodie had its first playthrough among friends and colleagues at
the RCM on 3 September 1953. In that same month the removal to 10

Hanover Square was completed. A new mode of life was quickly established in the grand house. Each month, for instance, there was a 'Singery', a madrigal party to which a dozen to two dozen people were invited. For at least two hours they would sing Gibbons and Weelkes, Bennet and Mundy, Morley and Pilkington, Wilbye and Byrd. There would be twelve to fourteen madrigals on each occasion, with a brief interval midway for refreshments. But Ralph, ever the serious musician, insisted that the break be brief: 'You can gossip any time; you are here to sing.'

This strict rule did not apply to their first Christmas in their new home. Gerald Finzi's son Christopher was one of the guests and flamboyantly assisted with the making of the punch. They departed from the recipe by quadrupling the brandy and omitting the soda water. There followed a very lively festive occasion. This Christmas cheer was a helpful break from a gruelling December in which, day after day, Ralph and Ursula had gone down to Kingsway Hall where Decca were recording all seven of the symphonies that Ralph had composed up to that time. Ralph worked closely and intensely with Adrian Boult and the London Philharmonic Orchestra. For Ursula, sitting among the murky, greenish-blue tipped seats and hearing the rumble of the trains passing under the hall, the experience was 'a lesson, in musical structure, as well as in professional concentration, to watch composer, conductor and players listening critically to every detail of their work as it came back from the machine while the live sound was fresh in their ears.'[5]

For Ursula, there came a break from these recording sessions when, at Ralph's insistence, she sat for her portrait to be painted. It seems likely that she did not like the result very much. In his will Ralph bequeathed the portrait to Elias Canetti.

The New Year 1954 brought a prospect that Ralph regarded with a special sense of anticipation and hope. *The Pilgrim's Progress* was to be revived; this time at Cambridge by the University Musical Society. The work, which always remained particularly important to him, now had the chance of being rehabilitated after its lack of success in London in 1951. Ralph went up to a cold wintry Cambridge for the rehearsals. These were mainly in Boris Ord's large sitting room in the Gibbs Building in Kings College. They were sometimes disheartening for Ralph. But the actual performances were, by common consent, a great, and for many a memorable success. A young physicist John Noble, who played the Pilgrim, was especially admired both for his singing and for his quiet dignity in the role. George Trevelyan's son Humphry, a Goethe scholar and a Fellow of

King's who took the role of Lord Hate-Good, wrote to tell Ursula of 'the immense success *The Pilgrim's Progress* has been. People in the university began to realise about Thursday that something great was going on in the Guildhall and they started flocking and going twice and three times and trying to go again and not being able to get in.' He continued: 'It was wonderful to hear how it was spoken of by everyone who had seen it – with a sort of quiet yet exalted enthusiasm; and it was wonderful to feel, as one of the cast, that one was taking part in a great and spiritual event, such as comes only rarely.'[6]

Ralph's happy feelings of vindication by these performances were accompanied by the pleasure of meeting so many old Cambridge friends. He and Ursula saw G.E. Moore and his wife, various Trevelyans and Patrick Hadley at Gonville and Caius College. They also saw Gwen Raverat and Frances Cornford, both distant relatives of Ralph.

A few weeks later he was in his old haunts conducting the St John Passion at Dorking. A year earlier he had retired from his position as conductor of the Leith Hill Music Festival but he still made himself available as a guest conductor. But his long-time veto on performance of his own works was no longer in force and the organizers immediately took the opportunity to perform his Toward the Unknown Region, the Oboe Concerto, (with John Barbirolli's wife Evelyn Rothwell as soloist), and Five Tudor Portraits with the now 60-year-old Astra Desmond as the contralto.

The weather continued to be extremely cold and Ralph and Ursula were glad, a few days after the festival, to set off again to Italy and sunshine. They took the boat-train to France and travelled overnight to Pisa, which was warm and radiant. They proceeded to Florence, where they feasted on the many art treasures. For Ralph it was a great joy to revisit the Medici Chapel and to see again the work that had, over many years, remained so vivid in his memory, Michelangelo's *Night and Day*. They travelled on to Siena by road. Another creaky bus took them to San Gimignano where Ralph searched for the Pinturicchio and Ghirlandaio frescoes, which he also clearly remembered. From Siena Ursula reported that 'Ralph walks miles and drinks heartily'. Perhaps he rested a good deal too for she seems to have had time to write extremely lengthy travelogue letters back to Gil Jenkins in London. Ralph was full of energy and excitement about their travels. Ursula recalls that: 'in Rome Ralph throve on long walks and chianti, on tiny sips of strong coffee and lemon water ices.... His ankles hardly ever ached, he could dash about all day and sit up half the night watching the city's life, sleep at siesta time, and be up early.'[7]

On the Spanish Steps they accidentally met Meredith Davies, a young advocate of Ralph's music who was studying conducting at the nearby Accademia di Santa Cecilia; he would go on to make the first recordings of *Riders to the Sea* and *Sir John in Love*. They met him again at a dinner party given for them by the British Council. A fellow guest was Jaques Ibert, the French composer who was about to take over as the director of the Paris Opera. He and Ralph found a great deal to talk about. Ralph had hoped to hear Roman choirs sing Palestrina but they were all busy with rehearsals for the canonization of a saint. So he and Ursula had to make do with a performance of *La Traviata*. They were back in Britain by the end of May.

They greatly enjoyed entertaining in their fashionable new house in Regent's Park. But not all their invitations were accepted. Fanny Farrer who, years before had often made up a foursome with Ralph and the Longmans on walking holidays, was one who declined to come. Fanny, who had served for years as Secretary of the Leith Hill Music Festival, sent Ralph a one sentence refusal, 'Darling Conductor – I think I will not come to London to dine with you, though you know I remain always your loving Sec.'[8]

During the summer Ralph began to sketch out a new symphony. He also put the finishing touches to his Bass Tuba Concerto in F minor, written for Philip Catelinet, a performer in Salvation Army bands and principal tubist of the London Symphony Orchestra with whom, under John Barbirolli, the work had its first performance on 13 June. At the time the piece was considered to be an amusing eccentricity on Ralph's part. But it has continued over the years to hold its own in the concert hall and Michael Kennedy was surely right to single out, 'the splendid middle movement', commenting that it is 'a token of the composer's prodigality that he was able to expend so beautiful, fresh and shapely a tune ... on a work which he must have known would have limited hearings.'[9] During this period the ever-energetic Ralph also completed his violin sonata which he had written for the Canadian violinist Frederick Grinke whose performance of The Lark Ascending had greatly impressed him. He had begun composing the sonata in 1952 in the disturbed period between the death of Adeline and his marriage to Ursula. It dates from the time in which the new living arrangements with Gilmour Jenkins were being debated and confirmed. The work has a Modernist sound to it as it registers feelings of feverish malaise and uncertainty. It suggests a composer who is still familiar with the emotional turbulence expressed in the Fourth Symphony of some twenty years earlier. Perhaps Ralph may have remembered William Walton's violin sonata of a couple of years before. This work covers a similar wide range of deep and complex emotions. The first movement of Ralph's violin sonata begins with a violent outpouring but the violin takes over with a soothing, singing melody that sounds very much Vaughan Williams. But it does not last. The two instruments are soon harshly conflicted. The painful interior dialogue continues until the piano turns to calming. The violin meanders and seems lost. But then after another upsurge of conflict and quarrel, shrillness returns. There is a struggle for repose. The violin settles for melancholy and the piano authoritatively controls and ends the movement with a succession of three assured notes.

Turmoil is the principal subject of the second movement, the *scherzo*. After a cheery start the conversation becomes agitated and then frenetic. The violin approaches delirium as it climaxes. Then it subsides wearily into exhaustion. The third movement, a set of variations, begins by proposing a more measured approach. The gong-like piano sounds hint at the contemplative music of China. There is a theme that comes from the piano quintet of more than half a century before. The work ponders a lifetime. There is the possibility of a romantic duet but the violin loses its way and goes wandering. But there comes resolve from the piano and the violin starts to sing more confidently. For a brief while there is the suggestion of the assurance of a cadenza. The music now recalls The Lark Ascending and a time in Ralph's life when he and his music came to a moment of transcendence. There is a gentle tailing away as the two instruments quietly share the music. Sickeningly vertiginous emotions are contained.

The first public performance of this troubled work of musical meditation took place in a BBC broadcast on 12 October 1954. Michael Mullinar was Frederick Grinke's piano accompanist. The two had rehearsed the piece with the composer at Hanover Terrace. But Ralph was not in England to hear the radio performance. He was in Ithaca, in upstate New York, where he was Visiting Professor of Music at Cornell University for the autumn term of 1954. The appointment had been arranged for him by Keith Falkner, an associate professor in the Department. Ralph had known Falkner, a pupil of his friend Hugh Allen, since long before the Second World War when Falkner, a baritone, began a highly successful singing career. When Ralph and Ursula arrived in New York, Falkner was on the dockside to welcome them. He was accompanied by his senior colleague Donald Grout, a distinguished music scholar, author of *A History of Western Music* and president of the American Musicological Society. They escorted the two visitors to their luxurious hotel in Manhattan and later accompanied them to the top of the Empire State Building. As Ursula recalled: 'we watched the sunset colours fading over the water and all the city light coming out in chains and garlands along the streets and in the towering buildings. From there we could see that New York is almost as much a water city as Venice.'

Ralph felt as he had on his last visit. He said: 'I think this is the most beautiful city in the world.'[10]

The following day the four of them drove north to Ithaca. Here they were lodged in a country club. They had two rooms, each with a bath and one fitted up with a piano and table as Ralph's work room. Ursula was delighted with the arrangements 'because it gave us an experience we might have had if we had lived together as young people sharing a bed-sit'. Faculty wives took her to supermarkets which at that time were unknown in England. The day after their arrival, 28 September, a somewhat nervous Ralph gave his first lecture. During that same week he gave two more, becoming increasingly relaxed. After the final one on 5 October, Ursula reported excitedly to her parents 'R's lectures are a terrific success', adding that 'he is terrifically well and bouncy'.[11] Under the title 'The Making of Music' they are reprinted in *National Music and Other Essays* which, with a preface by Ursula, was published in 1963. They are in many respects a restatement of the views presented in the lectures he gave at Bryn Mawr College on his last visit to the United States in 1932. He offers down-to-earth, commonsensical answers to four questions: What is music? How and when do we make music? And finally, what are the social foundations of music? Some of the many incidental remarks are of interest for showing Ralph's view in relation to his times. There is some gentle mockery of the then just emerging period instrument movement. It would mean, he remarks, that we should have to 'make use of that atrocious bubble-and-squeak monstrosity, the so-called baroque organ. Our oboes would have to bray like bagpipes and our horns bellow like bulls.... I cannot imagine anyone wanting to substitute the coarse tone and asthmatic phrasing of Bach's oboe for the exquisite cantabile of one of our fine symphonic players in the great watching song from the Matthew Passion.'[12]

At the same time Ralph is more positive about Stravinsky than he had often been in the past. He recognizes that 'when Stravinsky writes his Symphony of Psalms, one can feel that he is dealing with something fundamental, almost primitive.'[13] He also offers a robust concise defence of his lifelong concern for folk music now seen by some young critics as part of his datedness and conservatism. Ralph's polemical tone quickens as he writes, 'About fifty years ago Cecil Sharp made his epoch-making discovery of English folk song. We young musicians were intoxicated by these tunes.... And we proceeded to pour out Overtures and Rhapsodies and Ballad Operas to show the world that we were no longer a land without music. We had our critics, who took the curious line that, though it was perfectly right and proper for a Russian or a Norwegian to build up his style on his own national memories, if an Englishman tried to do so, he was being what they described by that appalling word "folky".'

After he had given these lectures at Cornell, Ralph and Ursula set off on a North-American wide tour which Keith Falkner had carefully arranged for them. Donald Grout, a seasoned expert in American cock-tails, gave them a thorough course on how to drink their way across the continent. He then drove them to Toronto where Boyd Neel was now Dean of the Music Department at the university there. A former naval officer and then a doctor Boyd Neel had, some years before, become a student of Ralph's at the RCM and gone on to form his own string orchestra which had made the first recording of Ralph's Fantasia on a Theme by Thomas Tallis. At Toronto, Arthur Benjamin's opera *A Tale of Two Cities* was being rehearsed. Ralph immediately determined to go and listen and was much impressed by what he heard. They returned briefly to Cornell via Niagara Falls, then took the train to Detroit and Ann Arbor, and thence to Chicago and St Louis, where they began the three-day long train journey to Los Angeles. Here there was an espe-cially warm welcome from both students and their professors. After all the travelling and the lecturing at each of their stops Ralph and Ursula began to feel weary and decided to have a break. They had a week beside the sea at Santa Barbara and enjoyed the pelicans, the hibiscus and the humming birds. At the university there was another pleasant surprise. Music and drama students were preparing to stage *Riders to the Sea*, first as a play then as an opera. Ralph was much taken with these two, very sparse, productions.

It was now time to turn for home. They set off back east on the legendary train known as the 'Santa Fe' and stopped off at the Grand

Canyon. Ralph did not make the descent. He decided that the mule that was offered to him was 'not up to my weight'. So he contented himself with walking on the rim, marvelling at the grandeur of the two sunsets and the one dawn they were there to experience. Then it was back to Cornell for a few weeks more activity in the university music community. There were concerts of Ralph's music and he himself conducted his 'London Symphony' with the Buffalo Symphony Orchestra.

At Thanksgiving Donald Grout and his wife gave a lavish farewell dinner party. After coffee Donald, at Ralph's request, played Bach to the company. The next day Ralph and Ursula left for New York where they were entertained by Rudolph Bing, the Director of the Metropolitan Opera at a performance of *Die Meistersinger*. Around this time Ralph gave Keith Falkner a parting gift, the song 'Menelaus on the Beach at Pharos', a setting of a poem by Ursula. We now know the piece as one of the 'Four Last Songs', all of which have words by Ursula. Keith, accompanied on the piano by his wife Christabel, gave its first performance on 14 November. The Vaughan Williamses were off next to New Haven, where Ralph was to be awarded the prestigious Howland prize for 'distinguished achievement' in the arts. Previous recipients had been Gustav Holst and Paul Hindemith. After Ralph came Aaron Copland and Virgil Thomson. The honour brought a medal and one thousand dollars. With this and all the other money Ralph had made from his trans-American lectures they felt able to indulge themselves. Ursula remembered, 'Ralph whisked me off clothes shopping, we lived in taxis, and had little suppers about 1 a.m. every night.'[14]

Then it was time to board the *Queen Mary* for the voyage home.

HAPPILY EVER AFTER

Chapter Twenty

EXCURSIONS

The Atlantic was extremely rough but Ralph enjoyed the violent winter storms. A warm welcome awaited them when they arrived back in England. Gil Jenkins and Ursula's parents were at the dockside in Southampton. At Waterloo Station Adrian Boult and his wife were on the platform. And when they finally drove up to Hanover Terrace there stood a beaming Genia Hornstein. Ralph and Ursula had had an immensely enjoyable time in America but they were happy to be back. After their many thousands of miles of travels it was good to settle for a while and to enjoy their new home.

They were back in good time to organize a Christmas carol party for their many friends. Ralph was happy and relieved to be able to devote himself to composition again. The five years together in the house in Hanover Terrace were as Ursula said, and many friends and onlookers have confirmed, 'the happiest years of our life'. 'He was full of invention and new works were achieved in spite of the beguilements of London which he enjoyed as much as I did now that he had returned to live in town once more, from what he had recognised, in the early years at Dorking, as exile.'[1] In that December of 1954 he immediately resumed work on the Eighth Symphony and was able, as Ursula recalled, to play through the first version to her by the middle of January. Soon after, Roy Douglas came to help with its further development. Ralph also now completed a work which, presumably through the good offices of his friend, the tuba player Philip Catalinet, he had written for the Salvation Army Staff Band. This was his Prelude on Three Welsh Hymn Tunes which the band premiered at their headquarters in Judd Street in Bloomsbury. Ralph and Ursula attended the occasion and were delighted with the performance and the reception that followed. Ralph always admired and supported the brass band tradition as an important part of English musical culture. A year later, in 1956, he would be guest of honour and present the prizes at the National Brass Band Championships. And for the competition a year after that he would write a test piece made up of a theme and eleven variations.

In the first weeks of the New Year 1955 he and Ursula revelled in the various entertainments London had to offer. They went to a succession of plays, concerts and foreign films. They attended Michael Tippett's *The Midsummer Marriage*, and on 19 January heard Malcolm Sargent conduct the first London performance of *Hodie*. In the spring they had a holiday in Cornwall. They were in Padstow for May Day and the ancient town rite of the Hobby Horse. They were impressed and moved. Ursula remembered: 'The conjunction of the hobby horse, the strange tune of death and resurrection, dancers in the street, flowers in the men's hats, and the unselfconscious air of celebration, the music reaching back into centuries past and the dance perhaps even further, gave us a day of unforgettable spring ceremony.'[2] Their great pleasure in this occasion helped to confirm their belief in ritual drama, a belief which had been strengthened not long before, by a performance of their own *The Bridal Day* mounted, unexpectedly, by students at the Chelsea College of Physical Education. This had been far more successful than the television version of two years before.

After their enjoyable Cornish break, they returned to Regent's Park to deal with their finances. Ralph was becoming increasingly concerned to ensure that his royalties would pass to Ursula after his death. He wrote to communicate his concerns to the Performing Rights Society Ltd, which acted for him in these matters. In the first week in June they replied confirming that: 'your performing fees will automatically pass to your wife on your death after Probate of your will has been granted, if, as you state, you bequeath your Estate, apart from a few legacies to her.'[3] Large sums of money were involved. In a statement of earnings for the year ending on 31 March 1955 Ralph declared that his performance fees for his many compositions amounted to £15,341 and 18s and 11d. Royalties from publishers brought in £5,828 and 3s, and his conducting fees were £132 and 11s and 6d. His total income for the year was £21,302 and 13s and 5d. In today's money that would be well over three hundred and ninety thousand pounds.

In a letter of 9 June to his accountant, Albert Sturgess, Ralph noted that he had 'recently made over to my wife about 30 thousand pounds,' (or, in today's money, well over half a million pounds). His motive was in part, that 'after five years ... this will, I understand, be free of estate duty.'[4] This transfer of assets appears to have involved shares. A document in the British Library records Ursula now owning shares in Benskins Watford Brewery, Beechams, British Transport, Reckitt and Colman, and the Westminster Bank. At the time of her marriage she said, she 'had precisely twenty-five pounds in the bank and my widow's pension had ceased. So Ralph really had endowed me with worldly goods, as well as a very beautiful seventeenth century cameo ring.'[5] Ralph's remaining portfolio included investments in: Burmah Oil, BP, Imperial Tobacco, J. Lyons, and Wedgwoods. He also received income from the English Hymnal Company Ltd. His three Ordinary shares and his four Founder shares brought in £365 each year. The concerns over financial planning for the long term would continue over the coming months and eventually be resolved by the creation of the Vaughan Williams Trust.

In July they had some respite from these complicated issues when they went to stay in Cheltenham for the festival. Here they ran into a very old friend, George Hannam Clark, an actor whom Ralph had first known over half a century before when they had both worked in Sir Frank Benson's theatre company at Stratford. In the evenings in the bar after festival events there was a pleasant opportunity for them to recall jokes, scandals and escapades. For the benefit of Michael and Eslyn Kennedy and Herbert and Alice Sumsion and other younger people who were also attending the festival, the two veteran performers also duetted music hall songs, particularly numbers from the *Ziegfeld Follies*. A week or two later Ralph again sought to revisit an important part of the world of his youth, that of the gypsies.

Recently, from out of the blue, he had received a letter in large, sloping handwriting. It began:

> I have for long hesitated to write to you, as I am a complete stranger and you a great man.... I am a Gypsy sir, and I know nothing of Music, but through you I have found Faith, and am able to under-stand a little more about Life.... You must be one of the few people, dear sir, who have no need to fear what is to come, as you have already glimpsed a little of what lies on the other side.

343

Ralph's gypsy correspondent was Juanita Berlin; she went on to tell him that she knew a version of 'Raggle Taggle Gypsies' and some other songs. Ralph immediately wrote back expressing interest and just as quickly received an invitation to visit her and her husband in their field at Brick Kiln Farm in Minstead near Lyndhurst in the New Forest. Juanita explained that she sang 'only when I have a few beers'. She continued: 'I can dance like a peacock but I like some port to get started on. I hope you will not be a Teetotaller as I would not wish you to think I am always after the drink, but it helps you to remember things gone deep.' She also enclosed a photograph of herself which 'someone took of me this year, I am 29 but am becoming fat so I don't suppose I shall dance much more.'

Ralph duly set off for Hampshire with Ursula. They were driven down by Frank Hollins, a civil service colleague of Sir Gilmour Jenkins, and their close neighbour living in the mews house attached to 10 Hanover Terrace. The journey was the last in the long list of Ralph's forays in quest of folk songs. Ursula remembered arriving at 'a little strip of field in which an old fashioned gypsy caravan stood with a wooden shack beside it. A splendid horse looked over a gate, gold and silver bantams perched in the hazels bordering the grass and a huge yellow dog followed our hostess to meet us.'[6] Juanita had already outlined her plans for the evening in a letter to Ralph. 'If you could come here to our field at about six o'clock on Saturday we will show you a nice pub. It may not be a very special one to look at, but we want one where we can sing and dance, and not everyone will take in travellers. They are all right really but some beat their wives when in the liquor.'

Ursula remembered that a great number of travelling people soon turned up at the pub and Ralph found himself buying a great deal of brown ale for the men and port for the women. He was surprised to find that the attractive Juanita's husband Sven was not a gypsy but an artist who had lived and worked among the St Ives group in Cornwall. He was acquainted with Barbara Hepworth and Ben Nicholson and had written a book on the Cornish primitive painter Alfred Wallis. Ralph and Frank Hollins struggled to write down the songs that were sung for them. But individual voices were soon drowned by group singing and jostling dancers. Ursula felt harassed by 'a very sinister and rakish figure ... hissing into my ear.'[7] In the tightly packed room the noise grew ever louder and at last Juanita herself entered the dancing. 'Alas! she had barely started when the landlord came in and said we were too noisy and disreputable a crowd, and we must leave. We were bundled out into the night.' But for the three visitors from Hanover Terrace, the night never-theless ended with a touch of gypsy picturesque. Ursula remembered that after the travelling people had gradually dispersed from the pub near the Rufus Stone, Frank, Ralph and I picknicked on the heather by moonlight about 11 p.m.'[8]

Marriage to Ursula brought a great geographical broadening of Ralph's life. Shortly after this very last excursion into Romany Rye they set off on a visit to Greece. This fulfilled a long held ambition for Ralph. He had been at Salonika for a period during the First World War but had otherwise seen little of that historic country. They set off on 3 September for a three-week tour in an organized party of some thirty people led by the Reader in Classical Archaeology at Cambridge University, R.M. Cook, who was assisted by his wife. On the first day Ralph experienced a violent toothache and had to have an emergency extraction which, given his celebrity status, was quickly arranged by the British Council in Athens. Doubts about his ability to go on were removed by his recourse to a good deal of Scotch. The group moved on to visit Mycenae, Corinth and Olympia. At the different stops Ralph did a good deal of swimming; he was much motivated by the new swimming outfit that Ursula had bought him, his first for decades. At Delphi he was taken up the hill by donkey while the rest of the party made the climb on foot. They crossed the sea to Crete; Ralph greatly enjoyed the museum of Heraklion. At Delos, Ralph bought a conch shell and, first to the consternation and then the amuse-ment of other members of the party, set about teaching himself to play it. The realm of sound was an enduring fascination to him. They returned to Athens and then made for Venice where Frank Hollins awaited them with his car. They drove home together through France, first following the left bank of the Rhone then going along the Loire and visiting some of its chateaux. They stayed in Tours and made a point of visiting the house in which one of their favourite poets, Ronsard, had spent his last years. Ursula was also an admirer of Eleanor of Aquitaine and made sure they went to Fontrevault to see her tomb and effigy which was as splendid as she expected: 'Eleanor, lying holding an open book, more likely love songs than psalms'. They visited too the Abbey of Solesmes in which Ralph was keen to hear the plainsong.

After their return home Ralph was immediately back at work. On 11 October he was in Birmingham to conduct his *Serenade to Music* prior to a performance of his strongly contrasting work the violent Fourth Symphony under the baton of Rudolf Schwarz. Then came a sequence of occasions on which he set off to help honour figures who had been important to him in time past. First of all, in the middle of October, he and Ursula were off to Ireland where, at the University of Cork, he was to deliver the first Arnold Bax Memorial Lecture. Harriet Cohen, Bax's long-time lover, had asked Ralph to become Vice-President of the Arnold Bax Society founded shortly after Bax's death some two years earlier. Ralph, who had dedicated his Fourth Symphony to Bax, readily agreed. In a heavy fog he and Ursula flew to Dublin where they found themselves delayed. It required the intervention of their housemate Sir Gilmour Jenkins, Permanent Secretary to the Ministry of Transport, to ensure their safe arrival in Cork after the comfort of a specially arranged lunch and a bottle of wine. Ralph gave a lively lecture that provoked the citizens of the new Irish Republic which was then only seven years old. Eruditely he explained the similarities between songs generally considered to be unquestionably Irish and certain English ones. He presented them all as 'individual flowers on a common stem'.

Ralph also took an aggressive line when, on 22 October in the church of St Mary le Tower in Ipswich, he delivered an address at a ceremony honouring Martin Shaw on his eightieth birthday. The relationship with this fine musician, who had pursued a successful career in both the church and the theatre, was one of Ralph's oldest friendships dating back to the time of the compiling of *The English Hymnal* in Edwardian times. Speaking forcefully from the chancel steps in the church Ralph began by praising Martin Shaw as 'a fine organist, pianist and composer', one who 'comes of professional stock, to whom art is something serious and means thoroughness and hard work'. Very much in polemical mood Ralph paused to dismiss 'the movement on foot to dethrone the language of our English Bible and to substitute for it something in the style of the popular press'. Then he launched into what was virtually an attack on his listeners as he urged the case for music of quality in church services. Rhetorically, evangelically he concluded: 'It is easier to languish sentimentally in some of our worst popular tunes. It is up to you, guided by your priest and choirmaster, to establish a good tradition. Here is Martin Shaw ready to advise and help you – but without your cooperation he can do nothing.'[9]

Next in the succession of lectures he delivered at this time was one given at the Composer's Concourse organized by the Marxist composer Alan Bush, who had been one of Ralph's colleagues at the Royal College of Music. Bush, whose opera *Wat Tyler* would be produced in London in late 1956, invited Ralph to give his memories of Parry and Stanford as teachers. On this occasion Ralph's tone was more measured as he sought to assess the two men who had helped to launch his career. His loving admiration for Parry was as strong as ever, but now his estimation of Stanford concluded far more positively than on some occasions in the past. 'With Stanford I felt I was in the presence of a lovable, powerful and enthralling mind; this helped me more than any amount of technical instruction.'[10]

As he drafted these lectures Ralph continued energetically to compose. At this time he agreed to write the music for a new film *The England of Elizabeth*. This was being produced by the British Transport Commission with which Gilmour Jenkins was closely involved. The music is generally melodic but not Vaughan Williams at his most sophisticated. One of the best passages is 'Tintern', a compelling sequence just for strings. An anthology of the music from this film was compiled by Muir Mathieson and published in 1964, after Ralph's death, as 'Three Portraits'. But Ralph's most urgent musical concern in the final months of 1955 was the completing of his Eighth Symphony. Early in February of the following year he and Ursula went up to Manchester for rehearsals for its premiere. He also rehearsed the Hallé Choir for a performance of the St Matthew Passion. On the day he had a heavy cold and was running a temperature, but with his characteristic toughness and determination he very successfully completed the performance. A few weeks later he was back in Manchester to attend the premiere of the new symphony on 2 May.

The occasion was a triumph. When the jokey second movement, the *scherzo*, was played, laughter rang out in the Free Trade Hall. He and Ursula were surrounded and pursued by reporters when they left. Twelve days later when the symphony was heard for the first time in London at the Royal Festival Hall, the reception was again extremely warm. Ralph appeared on the stage beside Sir John Barbirolli and the entire audience rose to applaud and to cheer him. Quickly the success of the symphony was widespread. The work was played at venues throughout Europe. In the United States in October, Eugene Ormandy and the Philadelphia Orchestra gave the first American performance, in New York. Ormandy wrote warmly to Ralph to tell him of its enthusiastic reception: 'every performance was greeted with shouts of bravo and prolonged applause, something we rarely hear after a first performance of a new work these days.'[11] The New York Music Critics' Circle voted it the best symphonic work of 1956.

The Eighth Symphony contrasts markedly with its predecessors which address, for the most part sombrely, the bleakness of experience. The brightest and shortest of Ralph's nine symphonies, the Eighth charms from the outset. Humorously, the first movement 'Fantasia' is subtitled *Variazoni senza Tema* or, perhaps we may infer, variations in search of a theme. The music begins lightly with a lifting, piping melody and later in the Fantasia this pleasing, gently flowing lyricism will recur. But the movement is more than merely charming. There is conspicuously intricate thematic development. On occasion there comes a scurrying, raucous percussion and an urgent building up to heavy dramatic insistences. The music of this composer, we are reminded, is not unaware of violent conflicts. But here in this symphony of light relief it is but a filtered memory, a suggestion. At the end of the movement we are brought back to the gentle piping as the music trails slowly and quietly away.

The *scherzo*, which so amused that very first audience in Manchester, is a perky piece and unfailingly cheerful. The composer is determined to entertain; he concludes the movement with a jolly pastoral dance and a twiddle of a finish. The third movement, the *Cavatina*, played entirely by the strings, asks us to be more serious. The bouncy rhythms of the preceding *scherzo* performed by wind instruments alone are replaced by long, flowing Elgarian lines. We are taken back to the gentle melancholy characteristic of many of Vaughan Williams's earlier works. The opening, lyrical melody has a touch of sadness which becomes increasingly textured as the strings pulse ever more strongly. Then the emotion abates as a solo violin reminds us of, in a subdued fashion, the ascending lark of yesteryear. And indeed in its reappearance in the much more recent violin sonata. The *Cavatina* ends mooningly and in the closing becomes serene.

But at the beginning of the last movement, *Toccata*, the composer sounds the gong resoundingly. We are summoned to a festival of instruments. In his note to the symphony Ralph suggested that the opening is a 'rather sinister exordium' and though this note may lead us to wonder what subversives might be present at the party, it does not spoil our fiesta. All is joyous and celebratory. The music moves along merrily; climactically the bells ring out and we end with a grand emphatic finale. Hospitably the composer bids us farewell with the gift of a profound gaiety such as W.B. Yeats at the end of his life imagined in his poem *Lapis Lazuli*.

The day after the first performance of the Eighth Symphony was Cup

Final day at Wembley. Manchester City with their very popular German goalkeeper Bert Trautmann were to play Birmingham City. Ralph and Ursula decided not to travel on one of the heavily crowded trains from Manchester to London. Instead they hired a car and drove home. Genia Hornstein, now a close friend of Ursula, accompanied them. A good part of their journey in that time just before the coming of the motorways was down the long north–south road through Staffordshire, the county that had been so important in Ralph's ancestry. They broke their journey in the historic city of Lichfield in south-eastern Staffordshire, a place well known to Ralph's Wedgwood and Darwin forebears. They visited the medieval cathedral with its beautiful Renaissance stained glass, and went on to Dr Samuel Johnson's house in the cobbled market square. Ralph was unable to climb the stairs in the high eighteenth-century house, but Ursula did. She was greatly intrigued to come across a portrait of Erasmus Darwin, the doctor, poet and scientist (and grandfather of the author of *On The Origin of Species*), who had lived in Lichfield for many years during Georgian times. Ursula was very much taken by the facial resemblance between Ralph and one of his many distinguished ancestors.

Back in London, Ralph was touched to find that he had been sent a present, an etching by Walter Sickert portraying a fiddle player. It had been sent to him by Simona Pakenham who had also recently sent him the manuscript of a book she had written about him which would be published in 1957 with the title *Ralph Vaughan Williams: A Discovery of his Music*. Ralph wrote to invite her to the Singery at his home on 7 May. Very soon Simona Pakenham was a member of his inner circle. Just forty that year, Simona, a close friend of Jill Day Lewis, was also a beautiful, elegant woman. She had a career as an actress and had also been a BBC announcer. As Ursula observed, Ralph quickly became 'devoted' to her. 'He loved to have pretty women about, and good looks added to intelligence absolutely won his heart.'[12]

Some time later Simona told Ursula that she 'had never seen so much kissing in my life as that first Singery'. Less than a week later, there came a more sombre occasion. This was the performance of another new work, arrestingly titled 'A Vision of Aeroplanes'. It was performed at St Michael's Church, Cornhill, in the City of London as part of the commemoration of the forty years which Ralph's old colleague Harold Darke had served there as organist and choirmaster. Herbert Howells and George Dyson also contributed compositions. 'A Vision of Aeroplanes' sets words from the first chapter of the Book of Ezekiel in which the prophet has a vision of terrifying creatures decked in apparatus that enables them to fly. Comprising three parts, Ralph's motet for mixed choirs has a demanding part for organ which at times sounds like violent destructive thunder. At other times the voices swoop and swirl menacingly. The music sounds of the cataclysm and catastrophe which Ralph remembered from the recent war and which, in the current Cold War, campaigners in the burgeoning Campaign for Nuclear Disarmament believed, could come still more devastatingly, again.

Just over a week after this work was first heard Ralph was stricken with phlebitis in the leg. He was immobilized for a period and had to spend as much time as possible with his foot up. This meant that he could not make a return visit to the Cheltenham Festival which he had so much enjoyed on his last visit. But he was recovered sufficiently to be able to attend the Three Choirs Festival at Gloucester where, forty-six years after his first performance there, he conducted The Lark Ascending. Ralph and Ursula had accommodation in the school house of the cathedral. So also did the Finzi family, David Willcocks (the conductor from Hereford), and young Irish composer Howard Ferguson. This house-party, Ursula remembered 'felt as if it was an end of term spree at a very lively co-ed school'.[13] With the Finzis, Ralph and Ursula went to see Rutland Boughton and his wife Kathleen who lived not far away. They all spent a happy morning together. Ursula was impressed when the old Marxist, whose compositions no longer enjoyed the acclaim they once had, expressed total contentment with his life. His satisfaction was to be shattered by the political shock that disrupted the world that very year.

On their return to London the Vaughan Williamses started to prepare for the holiday they had decided to have in Majorca. Three days before they were due to fly came the news that Ralph's old, and once closest friend, Randolph Wedgwood, had died. George Trevelyan, another member of that Cambridge group of friends wrote sadly to share with Ralph their loss. The sometime Master of Trinity College, Cambridge, commented: 'I feel a mere shadow now-what days we have all had since 1893.'

In a rather subdued mood Ralph and Ursula arrived in Palma. Leaving a rainy England they and their fellow passengers carried umbrellas and raincoats which greatly amused the Spanish airport officials. But they quickly adapted. Within hours of arriving at their hotel on a rocky shore at Bedinet they were bathing in the warm ocean and beginning what was to be another restorative holiday. At the hotel they received a phone call from Peggy Glanville Hicks who had once been Ralph's composition student. She invited them to lunch. An ebullient Australian who often dressed as a man, Peggy was working for the *New York Herald Tribune* as a critic and feature writer. On Majorca she was collaborating with Robert Graves on the libretto for her opera *Nausica*, which was based on Graves's novel *Homer's Daughter*. Ralph was pleased to meet the writer, a fellow Carthusian, albeit a generation younger, and the foursome met up in a cafe and enjoyed a good deal of wine. Neither man had been particularly happy at Charterhouse but now, as they drank along, they remembered it with some nostalgia and launched into a boisterous duetting of the school song. Their singing was abruptly halted by an extremely violent thunderstorm.

Each morning and evening Ralph worked at his new symphony – his ninth. Otherwise he and Ursula had a quiet, leisurely holiday. There was just one excursion, to Valdemossa where Chopin had spent a winter with his lover, George Sand, at the end of the 1830s. They visited the rooms described in Sand's *A Winter in Majorca*, enjoyed the fine views from them and inspected Chopin's piano. They went to a nearby cafe to watch local folk dancers perform a fertility dance reminiscent of the Morris. Ralph was greatly interested and spent several hours drinking wine with them and studying the elaborately attired man-woman who led the dance. Before their return to England came distressing news. They received a letter forwarded by Gil Jenkins, who, as the senior civil servant at the Ministry of Transport had the power to expedite airmail. The letter came from Joy Finzi and told them of the death on 27 September of Gerald Finzi.

It had been known for some time that he suffered from Hodgkin's disease and had not long to live. But his death nevertheless came as a great shock and loss. The two couples had seen a good deal of each other in recent years. They had, as Ursula said, 'a delightful arrangement: We were their town house, they our country estate'. Less than a week after Gerald's passing, Ralph wrote for *The Times* an assessment of his achievement. He commended his compositions and singled out his extraordinary affinity with the poetry of Robert Bridges and Thomas Hardy. He went on to point out Finzi's achievement as a musicologist and the importance of his championing of eighteenth century music. He also noted his friend's social responsibilities as an artist which led him to found the Newbury String Players which 'bring good music to the small villages of the neighbourhood which otherwise would have been without any such artistic experience'. There was a personal touch as Ralph remembered that, 'visiting the Finzi's house, with its wonderful view of the distant Downs, was a happy experience.'[14] In his obituary for the *Journal of the English Folk Dance and Song Society* Ralph remembered how Gerald 'an enthusiastic country dancer' would, with his wife, 'organise summer country dance parties', which were one of his enduring happy memories of the Finzi country home at Ashmansworth in Berkshire.

In the same month that he wrote these recollections, Ralph prepared a memorandum designed to organize his own legacy. On his initiative the Ralph Vaughan Williams Trust had now been established. The members included Sir Eric Edwards, Michael Tippett, Edric Cundell, Bernard Shore, Robert Armstrong, Bernard Brown (Honorine's widower), Albert Sturgess (Ralph's accountant), Gilmour Jenkins and Ursula. The secretary was Frank Thistleton, who had amassed a good deal of experience as Secretary of the Musicians' Benevolent Fund. In his memorandum of 29 October to this newly created committee, comprising both musicians and lay members, Ralph compiled a list of organizations and individuals that he wished to be supported after his death. The largest sums were assigned to the International Council of Folk Music, the Butterworth Trust and the Purcell Society. Among other groups Ralph wished to assist were: Finzi's Newbury String Players, The Dorking Bach Choir, the Royal Music Society, the Morley College Music Department and his old friends in the then named Macnaghten New Music Group. Two individuals he named were Martin Shaw and the widow of Gustav Holst.

As October came to an end and Ralph continued to work on his symphony, the precarious peace in the world was suddenly in jeopardy. Britain and France landed troops in Egypt to recover the Suez Canal, the international waterway which had recently been nationalized by the Egyptian government of President Nasser. There were highly suspenseful days prior to a United Nations resolution requiring Britain and France to proceed no further. This was more than a diplomatic humiliation. It was a concluding moment of the imperial power which Britain had exercised throughout Ralph's long lifetime. At this very same moment the Soviet empire was confronted by a serious challenge. Rebellion broke out on the streets of Budapest against the government of Hungary that deferred to the Kremlin. Brutally, the Russian government sent in tanks to crush the revolt in the Hungarian capital. The onlooking world wondered what the western response might be. There was nothing of any significance.

Despite much diplomatic negotiation, the Hungarian rebellion was snuffed out. Many idealistic Communists were finally disillusioned with Soviet Russia as the champion of their beliefs. Commitments of a lifetime shattered, believers felt betrayed, duped, even foolish. One of them was Ralph's long-standing friend Rutland Boughton, who had been their host just a couple of months before. He wrote to Ralph at some length about his resignation from the Communist Party and his pain at the loss of the assumptions on which he had based his life. Ralph replied in early December expressing understanding, and in no way implying 'I told you so'. He could see that a commitment to Communism might be motivated by a zeal for the common good, something he himself all his life had believed in and actively promoted. He wrote: 'It seems to me that all right-minded people are Communists, as far as that means that everything should be done eventually for the common good.' He added: 'I see no reason why the Russian atrocities should prevent you remaining a communist in the ideal sense of the word. The Russians are a strange mixture of artistic ideals and barbarism, and the barbarians seem to come out top, whether they call themselves Czarists, Karentskiists or Stalinists.'[15]

A few days later, at Christmas-time, Ralph and Ursula had a carol party. In a letter to Michael Kennedy with whom at this time he was in regular correspondence he reported, 'We had a very nice carol party here the other night – we sang all REAL carols, no Wencelasses, or silent nights: we started at half past eight, had half an hour's break about ten and finished up with the first Nowell about 12.30 then more drinks.' The drinks, as on other occasions at Hanover Terrace, were a 'very potent cup'.[16]

Early in the New Year 1957, perhaps with his biography in mind, Michael Kennedy wrote asking Ralph a number of questions, including his view on who was the greatest figure in his lifetime. 'I don't think Churchill,' replied Ralph. The answer came at a time when people were keen to remember the decisiveness and fortitude of the war leader which contrasted strikingly with the vacillations of his successor during the very recent Suez crisis. Two of the names that Ralph suggested – Whitman and Brahms – were to be expected. Both had been central to Ralph's intellectual and musical history since his youth. But the third suggestion, General William Booth, is at first sight surprising. The charismatic evangelist who founded and led the Salvation Army unquestionably had a worldwide influence for human good, though not on those sections of society with which Ralph was most closely associated. Yet throughout his composing career snatches of Salvation Army bands can be heard in his music. Through his teaching at Morley College he did have some knowledge of the poor and the disadvantaged. And very recently he had greatly enjoyed working with the Salvation Army Staff Band and particularly with its tuba player, Philip Catalinet. Perhaps this brought him to a greater understanding of Salvationism. Above all it must have been the sheer evangelical and spiritual power associated with William Booth and his Army that impressed him. Ralph himself was also, in the field of music, both a spiritual warrior and a practical missionary.

In the same letter Ralph invited the Kennedys down to Dorking where, on 23 February, he was to conduct the St John Passion yet one more time. Five days before that there was the signing and witnessing of his will. The three executors were his solicitor Edward Franck, his accountant Albert Sturgess and Ursula. The first sentence ran: 'I desire that my body be cremated.' Then followed a list of monetary bequests. All his performing rights were left to The RVW Trust. A sum of five hundred pounds was left to each of the following: Michael Mullinar; Cordelia; Cordelia's son, Adam Curle; Gilmour Jenkins; Holst's widow Isobel; Adeline's nephew, Robert de Ropp. Imogen Holst and Bernard Brown were left twice that sum as was the Butterworth Trust. Two hundred and fifty pounds was bequeathed to the National Society for the Abolition of Blood Sports.

Bernard Brown and Cordelia were invited to take what they wished from Ralph's books and personal belongings; the remainder was left to Morley College. Particular personal possessions were bequeathed to individuals. Ursula's sister Rosemary was to have Ralph's two volumes of *Bewick's British Birds and Animals*. Edward Rubbra was given Beethoven's tuning fork which Ralph had been given by Gustav Holst (who himself had received it from an admirer). Michael Kennedy was left a John Nash landscape painting. Ralph bequeathed the portrait of his wife, painted five years before, to Elias Canetti.

That spring, after Ursula had recovered from a bout of Asian flu (which Ralph managed to avoid), they went down to Brighton for a brief holiday. They took the opportunity of visiting Ralph's old prep school at nearby Rottingdean. The headmaster gave them a tour of the buildings which Ralph found little changed after well over seventy years. Back in Brighton he and Ursula went and sat on the beach together as they had done at an earlier stage in their relationship when Ralph had conducted a concert at the Dome. Perhaps they remembered the comments by a passing policeman about the difference between their ages. Ralph now gave Ursula very vivid, detailed memories of his schooldays at Rottingdean to be used later in her biography. Some weeks later they were off to north-eastern Scotland, to a music festival organized by the Marchioness of Aberdeen at Haddo House, the grand eighteenth-century mansion which was the ancestral home of the Gordon family. Many of their fellow house guests were musicians whom they knew well. Ralph's 'A Sea Symphony' was performed in a manner that greatly pleased him and he himself conducted Parry's Blest Pair of Sirens to enthusiastic acclaim. This stay in rural Aberdeenshire amidst such congenial company was another of the memorably happy occasions in Ralph and Ursula's final year of marriage.

He continued to tinker, as he had done for many years, with his opera *A Poisoned Kiss,* the libretto rights of which he had become the owner. Ursula helped him to make the lyrics more stage worthy and he was pleased with the performance given at the Royal Academy of Music in July. Ursula also collaborated with Ralph's former pupil Elizabeth Maconchy on a one act opera. It was about a young and very active rake who was punished by being turned into a sofa and condemned to remain until the act of love was performed on him. The collaboration brought Elizabeth and her husband William le Fanu into the lives of the Vaughan Williamses and work on the comic opera caused a great deal of laughter in the house in Hanover Terrace.

As the summer approached Ralph was feeling weary and run down. For a restorative they decided on a holiday in Austria. But it did not achieve the desired end. In their years of marriage they had a number of happy holidays but this one was, as Ursula put it, 'our least successful abroading'. Perhaps because of Ralph's continuing fatigue they did not respond to the paintings which they saw in Munich or to the Mozart places in Salzburg. The most important memory came when they went for a trip in a silent, electric boat on the Königssee. In the middle of the lake, the captain stopped, produced a flugelhorn, and played a few notes which came echoing back from the surrounding mountainside. Ralph was impressed by the demonstration, 'a good sound' he commented, 'I shall put it into the symphony'.[17]

They were glad to be at home again but still Ralph felt weak. His doctor diagnosed acute anaemia and prescribed a range of medication. He recovered somewhat. Nevertheless Dr Ray Rowntree concluded that he should enter the Middlesex Hospital for tests. While he was there,

Ursula's father was also taken into hospital for a major operation and she had to go away for several days to help tend him. The procedure failed to save his life. During the days between his death and funeral a distraught Ursula travelled back to Hanover Terrace to be with her ailing husband. The doctors now decided that he too needed major surgery; he had developed a prostate condition. Ralph strongly resisted any interruption of his calendar of engagements and they managed to fit in several occasions to which he felt particularly committed. They attended a performance of the *Sinfonia Antartica* at the Proms and they also went to the New Opera Company's production of Arthur Benjamin's *A Tale of Two Cities*, an opera which Ralph had long admired and sought to promote.

Then came the inevitable day for his admission to hospital. He insisted on taking the manuscript of the current symphony with him. Ursula stayed as long as possible after his admission and finally returned home in a very anxious state. The following day she hurried back to the Middlesex to find him, after the operation, 'doped and rather cross'. When she was next allowed to visit, she found him 'in such a filthy temper that I began to feel reassured'. The following day a bright and breezy Ralph telephoned her to announce proudly that he had lived up to his reputation by kissing the night nurse. Apparently, he did not manage to respond successfully to a dare from one of his male visitors to kiss the Matron of the Middlesex. Ursula came for him to be discharged and took him immediately to the Finzi house for convalescence. Very quickly he was back to work on his symphony.

Chapter Twenty-One

THE FINAL YEAR

Not long after came Ralph's eighty-fifth birthday and a long succession of occasions which various organizations had planned in order to honour him. The Royal Philharmonic Society invited him to choose a programme of his own works to be performed at a celebration concert on 9 October in the Royal Festival Hall. He selected 'The Pastoral Symphony', *Job* and an orchestral version of On Wenlock Edge which John Barbirolli had revived with great success some months before. Ernest Benn, the General Manager of the Festival Hall, had an extended tribute to Ralph printed on the front page of the programme; he also requested Cecil Day Lewis to write a birthday poem to be spoken at the concert by Jill Balcon. When Ralph entered the Ceremonial Box at the Royal Festival Hall, the entire audience stood up to applaud him. Afterwards there was a grand party with a large number of friends and colleagues gathering to congratulate him. Two days later the Macnaghten Concerts Society, with whom Ralph had enjoyed a friendly relationship for more than a quarter of a century, also presented him with a concert, this one made up of works written as birthday presents for Ralph by friends and ex-pupils. It ended however with some very traditional music, a sequence of the madrigals that Ralph so greatly enjoyed. The following day he and Ursula were off to Dorking for a party and a gift from members of the Leith Hill Music Festival. The present was a landscape painting by John Nash, the second which Ralph owned by this artist. Six days later there was another large party, this time at the home of Guy Warrack, the President of the Composers' Guild. Here

Ralph was given two more presents: the score of the Thomas Tallis forty part motet *Spem in Alium*, and a facsimile score of the Bach B minor Mass. This latter gift was a special delight to him; he was most anxious to get home to examine it. The blots and burns and corrections on it gave him a precious sense of closeness to the composer whom he admired more than all others. A more lighthearted gift that greatly entertained him was a cartoon birthday card drawn by Bernard Stone and his wife. There was a sketch of the front of 10 Hanover Terrace with an official notice ordering 'Queue Here For Birthday Kisses. Open 9 A.M. – 9 P.M. (Crown Estates)'. Four young female figures, seemingly topless, recline expectantly in the road in front of the house.

Birthday celebrations continued. On 27 October in the Royal Albert Hall he was treated to a concert of music far less ethereal than that associated with Bach. Twenty-one brass bands competed in playing his Variations, the theme with eleven variations which he had composed for them. The bands played with zest and Ralph was greatly entertained. The following day he and Ursula travelled to Manchester to be present at another concert given in his honour by the Hallé Orchestra and made up, again, entirely of his own compositions. For the orchestra's opening of this, its centennial year, Ralph had composed for John Barbirolli his Flourish for Glorious John. And now, after Ralph had been summoned to the stage to receive the enthusiastic, affectionate greeting of the audience, a chair was produced to enable him to sit while the Hallé played the Flourish to and for him.

Despite these many, often time consuming distractions Ralph kept his mind insistently focused on the completing of the symphony. Early in November Roy Douglas came to Hanover Terrace to help make improvements to the score. At 5.30 p.m. that afternoon the usual 'Committee' that Ralph created to offer advice and judgement assembled in the house. It comprised the musicians: Arthur Bliss, Herbert Howells, Scott Goddard, Alan Frank and Myers Foggin of the Royal Philharmonic Society to which Ralph would go on to dedicate the work. Sir Gilmour Jenkins, Frank Howes and Ursula were also there. Much discussion followed the playing through of the piano version. Ralph decided against any major alterations until he had heard an orchestral run-through.

He now began to suffer from a resurgence of phlebitis in his leg and had again to spend days resting in bed, using a tilting table which Gil Jenkins had found for him and which allowed him to write and compose whilst propped up on the pillows. Among his many visitors during this time of enforced rest were his cousin, the actress Rachel Kempson, and her attractive daughter Vanessa Redgrave. He, of course, greatly enjoyed such female company. He and Ursula were delighted when the whole Redgrave family, including Rachel's husband, the distinguished actor Michael Redgrave, attended their carol concert which was their Christmas Singery, Michael adding a fine tenor voice to their ensemble.

At this Christmas-time – Ralph's last – he was approached by a film company who were producing a film to commemorate the William Blake centenary. Ralph was invited to make settings of some of Blake's poems for inclusion in the soundtrack. At first he was reluctant because he had always preferred Blake's art to his poetry. He particularly disliked 'That beastly little lamb'. Nevertheless he finally consented and set ten poems for tenor voice and oboe. The settings came in a rush of creativity between 30 December 1957 and 5 January 1958. Ursula remembered that 'the tune for "Little Lamb", which he had firmly said he would never set, woke him in the night.'[1] The ten songs are Ralph's final response to Blake and in their simplicity and spareness form a great contrast with *Job*. Within the somewhat tense musical idiom there lies a great range of very elemental human feeling ranging from the tenderness of 'The Shepherd' to the compassion of 'Ah, Sunflower' to the agony of 'Cruelty' which is reminiscent of Benjamin Britten's recent style in song-setting. The conjunction of oboe and tenor voice makes for a music that is limpid, and like Blake's words, very much an understatement of the profound issues addressed. The alternation of accompanied and unaccompanied settings underscores the contrast between the radical innocence and the destructive evil which Blake's texts present. Ten Blake Settings is a fine, economical work from Ralph's last year, treating profound subjects with delicate musical allusiveness.

In the early days of the New Year of 1958, Ralph who had barely recovered from his bout of phlebitis began intensive rehearsals for the St John Passion at Dorking. It was performed there, very successfully in February. Some time later he also conducted the St Matthew Passion. Christopher Finzi and Noel Taylor, using newly available technology, set up tape recorders to capture the occasion. Ralph was very pleased to have this very first recording of one of his live Surrey performances. And a most successful one.

Conducting such concerts was beginning to exhaust him. One of his favourite relaxations continued to be visits to the cinema, theatre and opera. In these months he and Ursula saw Visconti's widely admired production of *Don Carlos*, Rossini's *William Tell*, Poulenc's *Carmelites*, which Ralph disliked, and Bartók's *Bluebeard's Castle* which he found exciting and beautiful. Of all the proponents of the Modernist idiom in the music of the first half of the twentieth century, Bartók was the composer to whom Ralph was most, and continually, sympathetic. Perhaps in this last twelve months of his five-year marriage to Ursula, Ralph was newly attuned to the resonances between a man and a woman such as Bartók's music probes. Many onlookers were impressed by the changes and the sheer happiness that Ursula brought into his life. Rutland Boughton sent her 'an extra hug ... for 200% plus she has made of her man'. The South African composer Priaulx Rainier wrote to her from her loft studio in St Ives of 'the beauty and richness you brought into the latter life of one of England's greatest men'. She added: 'only those of us who know you personally can be aware of your sensitivity towards the art of living and what that must have meant in the life of another artist'. Veronica Wedgwood told her: 'the whole world owes so much to you for having made Ralph so serenely happy, so gloriously able to go on with his grand and beautiful work right to the end.'

On 14 February 1957 Ursula gave Ralph what was to prove to be her final Valentine.

Since thirty-eight or thirty-nine –
You have been my Valentine
Each time I gave my heart away,
I bring my heart again today.
Take it Love, and keep it safe
Green and gay and loving Ralph,
bless it too, Saint Valentine,
and make me his and make him mine
so that our hearts always intertwine.

Seven weeks later the first orchestral play through of the Ninth Symphony took place, on 21 March 1958 in St Pancras Town Hall. Ralph himself had to pay for it. He received a rather curt letter from the management of the Royal Philharmonic Orchestra informing him that 'The total cost of this rehearsal, including instrument transport and hire of hall will be £255.17.6d.' Ralph and Roy Douglas sat close to the conductor and a large number of friends and colleagues looked on from the balcony while the orchestra played the work through twice. Twelve days later on 12 April

1958 Sir Malcolm Sargent gave the first public performance with the Royal Philharmonic Orchestra. The critical reception was by no means as warm as that which had greeted the preceding symphony. One reviewer spoke of 'composing for the sake of composing'. Another declared that the themes 'plainly resemble the themes of his other works'. The second movement was said to be 'silly'; even 'asinine'. Disappointed, Ralph felt that he had outlived his time. The next morning a friend (presumably Michael Kennedy) called and asked Ralph what he thought of the notices. 'I don't think they can quite forgive me for still being able to do it at my age,'[2] was the reply.

Unfortunately, Ralph was not to live to see the appreciation and understanding of the work that commentators have shown in more recent years. The Ninth Symphony is manifestly a work of great thematic richness that shows a delicate, subtle probing of both music and experience. Ralph once connected the ending of his 'London Symphony' with the concluding paragraphs of *Tono-Bungay* by H.G. Wells; his final symphony sounds very much informed by the stoical, compassionate pessimism expressed in the concluding lines of Thomas Hardy's *Tess of the D'Urbervilles* as the author contemplates and comments on Tess as a tragic figure tossed about like a plaything by the President of the Immortals. Ralph had admired this novel throughout his life and, as Alain Frogley demonstrates in his illuminating and exhaustive study of the work *Vaughan Williams's Ninth Symphony*,[3] it was very much in his mind as he composed his final symphony.

A stoical melancholy pervades the work right from the doleful chords with which the first movement begins. A bright lyrical theme intrudes on this continuing insistence but, as later in the movement, is swiftly swept aside by heavy pounding forces. And then we are in a world of eerie desolation with the flugelhorn darkly pondering. In his very detailed reading of the symphony Wilfrid Mellers wonders, interestingly, whether Ralph 'might have taken a hint from Miles Davis's haunting use of the flugelhorn in his recordings during the fifties'.[4] Sadness and Ralph's version of the blues build to unhappy climaxes before the music falls away mournfully. The second movement, the *andante sostenuto*, begins with another attempt at song from the flugelhorn but this is set aside by a heavy repetitive beat that is sinister and threatening. To offset this there comes a swaying, dancing passage, another attempt at joyous movement. There is a slow gathering of feeling but then the ominous returns more heavily and crushingly than before. More is heard of lyrical melancholy that moons along, lost and forlorn, before, as at the end of the first movement, it fades to a silent conclusion.

The jokiness of the third movement, the *scherzo*, with the crude beat of the marching band and the music hall routines, seem coarsely irrelevant. They jig away in the background without obscuring the ongoing haunted refrain suggesting vulnerability. There is a painful feeling of isolation. The final movement is wistful, persistently elegiac throughout the highly complex contrapuntal interweaving. Melancholy lingers, wanders, turns about showing changing colours. But then large Hardyesque forces return to intervene. Tension builds and heightens. And then come the great hammer blows that speak of mortality and the unavoidable conclusion of human life. First one, then a second and then the third, all of them destructive and decisive. All that is left after the great apocalyptic blows are the fading harp glissandos that are the rippling of their aftermath.

After all the hard work and tension preceding the launch of this intricate symphony, Ralph and Ursula felt the need for a rest. On 14 April they flew to Naples. They spent three days sightseeing in the city with rain falling for much of the time. They then crossed over to the island of Ischia where they had booked a stay in the Villa Christabella, one of the several houses owned there by William Walton and his wife. They had a fine view but the weather continued stormy and they were compelled to spend a good deal of time indoors. They passed much of their time reading, returning to Ralph's all-time favourite, George Borrow's *Lavengro*. They also took the opportunity to work on an opera that they had decided to write together with Ursula supplying the libretto. It was called *Thomas the Rhymer* and was based on two ancient ballad stories. Roy Douglas, who happened to be holidaying in Italy, popped over to the island and played over the first scene for them. Ursula wrote to tell Michael Kennedy, 'I am very pleased and the music is exactly what I hoped for. It's great fun trying to think dramatically in terms of duet, trio and chorus, and generally of ensemble. I'm enjoying it enormously, Ralph is not over-tyrannical – all things considered. Roy feels it is a pity that there will be no correspondence to publish between the exacerbated composer and outraged librettist'.[5]

Towards their last week the weather improved and grew hot. As Ursula remembered, 'The white flowery cistus that covered the ridge behind the house burst into flower and the fireflies arrived'.[6] Lady Walton took them on tours of the island and they also had a day on Capri. On their way back to Britain they made a point of being driven up the steep hill of Capo di Monte and seeing the impressive collection of Titians in the gallery there. The visit was made to fulfil a promise exacted by Sir Gerald Kelly who, after attending the orchestral rehearsal of Ralph's symphony, had also insisted on painting another portrait of him, declaring 'he is much more beautiful than he was'.

Two days after their return flight to Britain they were in Nottingham where, on 16 May, Ralph received an honorary degree from the university. Greatly invigorated by the holiday in Italy Ralph was in the mood for one in England. He suggested Lincolnshire. So on a bright morning in June they took the train to the county town where they visited the imposing, hilltop cathedral with its many impressive medieval carvings. They hired a car and meandered across flat countryside to Gunby Hall where Ralph's cousin, Diana Montgomery-Massingberd, received them warmly and excitedly. She and Ralph shared memories that went back to the long lost world of the 1890s and especially to that occasion when a group of young musical house guests had performed Ralph's very early composition 'Happy Day at Gunby'. To Ursula's astonishment Ralph could remember all the players and their names and precisely where each of them had stood for the performance in the elegant music room. In this last year of his musical career Ralph was vividly in touch with its beginnings.

After Gunby he and Ursula drove on to Boston, Spalding and Crowland, stopping to look at their characterful churches and arriving in Peterborough in time to spend half an hour in the cathedral before it closed. Later in the evening there was a folk dance occasion in the close and Ralph was pleased when some of the dancers recognized him and came to talk to him. Back in London he was very happy to receive a visit from another figure from the distant past, Percy Grainger, who was over from America with his wife, Ella. There were also congenial visits at this time from Eugene Goosens, Lionel Tertis and another friend whom Ralph had first met more than sixty years before in 1892, when they were fellow students, George McCleary.

A more recent friend was William McKie, the organist of Westminster Abbey with whom Ralph had first had dealings at the time of the coronation. One evening, Ralph and Ursula were invited to have dinner with William and his wife at their house in Little Cloister beside the abbey. After the meal, William led the way into the quiet empty abbey, switched on a few lights and left his guests to experience the soaring, shadowy Gothic architecture while he went up into the organ loft and began to play Bach. For the visitors it was an impressive, memorable experience. Over half a century before when he had lived in nearby North Street and Barton Street, Ralph, very much an outsider, had often walked past the great building that was at the centre of the nation's dynastic and musical history. Now, in his last months of life he was an insider, very much an intimate of the great building.

They went to this year's Cheltenham Festival where Ralph, once again, greatly enjoyed himself, the Barbirollis giving a very sociable dinner party in a hotel on Cleeve Hill on an evening with a spectacular sunset. Ralph had also hoped to go to Norfolk again to hear Lionel Tertis play *Flos Campi*, but a second recurrence of phlebitis kept him in Hanover Terrace. He and Ursula continued to work on *Thomas the Rhymer*. Ralph also agreed to take on another project. Simona Pakenham was preparing a script for a Christmas piece, *The First Nowell*, based on medieval mystery plays and she came over to ask Ralph to supply carol tunes, choruses and incidental music. He readily agreed. What he composed, supplemented by additions from Roy Douglas, was heard at a concert at St Martin's in the Fields at the Christmas after his death.

In the later summer, Ralph and Ursula went to stay with Joy Finzi. The holiday was intended to help Ralph recover from another operation, a minor one, which he had undergone in the Middlesex Hospital in mid-July. They used Joy's home as a start for a touring holiday in Dorset. Travelling in her van they explored the area around Bridport having bed and breakfast at the tiny thatched pub in the quiet village of Loders. As a homage to the poet who wrote the words of 'Linden Lea' they visited the village of Winterbourne Came where William Barnes had served as vicar. Ralph bought postcards of the conspicuously phallic Cerne Giant, wrote ribald comments on the back and sent them to male friends: Michael Kennedy, Frank Hollins, Paddy Hadley and Gilmour Jenkins. They visited Old Sarum and Stonehenge which had been so much in Ralph's thoughts as he completed his final symphony. They made a point of going on to Salisbury, Ralph's favourite provincial city. They were greatly moved by the floodlighting recently introduced outside the Cathedral. Ursula remembered 'the cathedral transformed to gold, and details that one had not noticed standing out, so that the design was even more noble than in daylight. A dazzled owl flapped in and out of the lights gilding the spire and, as the evening got darker, both the blue night sky and the golden building intensified in brilliance'.[7] It was Ralph's last sight of a building that for him, as for his great admiration Thomas Hardy, had

had lifetime significance. The journey home from Dorset was also his last sight of his beloved countryside.

In the last month of his life Ralph continued to make every effort to encourage music at the grassroots level. He was pleased that Swaffham Primary School in Norfolk was to name one of its houses after him. He sent a message to be read out to the children in which he stated his belief that 'music will enable you to see past facts to the very essence of things in a way in which science cannot do'. He was also excitedly grateful to learn that the choir at the ancient Grammar School in Wolverhampton, a city where he had long had enthusiastic supporters, was to perform his Sons of Light. This work was of special significance to Ralph because it was a collaboration with Ursula. To the music master at Wolverhampton School, the zealous Frank Rust, Ralph wrote by return of post and in his own handwriting, 'I am delighted that you are resurrecting the Sons of Light. I thought they were quite dead'. When he received a photograph of the schoolboys poised to perform his cantata Ralph again replied immediately and most appreciatively, 'You are evidently doing a good and stimulating work among your pupils – your orchestra and chorus look so delightful in the photograph'.[8]

At the beginning of the last week of Ralph's life a young American composer came to visit him at Hanover Terrace and wrote a lengthy description, now in the British Library, of the time he spent with him. He noted that the large bookcase in the sitting room contained volumes by Dylan Thomas and W.H. Auden, Modernist poets not usually associated with the otherwise wide-ranging literary tastes of Ralph and Ursula. Ralph spoke of Sibelius as 'the most original composer of our time' and expressed admiration for his visitor's compatriot Samuel Barber. Asked about the then much argued issue of 'tonality versus non-tonality' Ralph commented that it was 'a difficult hypothetical question'. Ralph wondered if his visitor had 'come under the spell' of the Parisian music teacher Nadia Boulanger, of whom Aaron Copland, one of her many distinguished students observed, she 'knew everything there was to know about music'. Ralph seemed mildly in opposition to her teaching, though allowed that she was a tremendous musician and 'a most charming lady'. He strongly urged his young visitor to obtain the score and a recording of Gustav Holst's Hymn of Jesus. Ursula commented, 'It's cold and frosty music but in its own way beautiful beyond belief'.[9]

The visitor's overall impression was that 'Vaughan Williams looked elderly, although not particularly tired in appearance. His legs were failing him somewhat and he was hard of hearing. His speech was slightly hesitant but could be vigorous and witty … his eyes keen with the quality of seeming to search everything very deeply'.

The conversation ended as Ralph made a movement to escort the young man from the house. 'Vaughan Williams' last words to me after I assisted him from his chair and we walked to the door were 'I do hope to hear your music some day young man. You'll have to excuse me now … I must get back to my work'.

Some of the compositions currently occupying his mind were 'The Four Last Songs', *The First Nowell* and *Thomas the Rhymer*. He was also preparing for, and very much looking forward to attending, the recording sessions in Walthamstow Town Hall in which Sir Adrian Boult was to conduct the Ninth Symphony. They were due to take place on 26 August. But Ralph was not to be there. In the early hours of that day he was sleepless and increasingly unwell. Ursula summoned Gilmour Jenkins from upstairs and he immediately phoned Dr Ray Rowntree who came over. Ralph died of coronary thrombosis shortly afterwards. Ursula described his passing: 'he slipped away, with his head on my shoulder, and his hand in mine. I opened our window to the dawn, and after a time I played his pastoral symphony – and the music flowed quietly and serenely out into the still morning.'[10]

Chapter Twenty-Two

IN MEMORIAM

On 28 August 1958, William McKie played the organ at a private cremation at Golders Green attended by Ursula and a few close friends. Very shortly after Ralph's death it had been established by the Dean of Westminster that Ralph's ashes would be laid in the North Choir Aisle of the Abbey next to Stanford and Purcell. The grand ceremony began half an hour before noon on Friday 19 September.

The abbey was full as the service opened with a playing of the stirring Five Variants of Dives and Lazarus. This choice of a melody which Ralph had so loved, created, as one present that sombre morning was to recall, 'a mood of remembrance which will haunt those who experienced it to the end of their days'. Bach's D minor Concerto was then played by David Martin and Frederick Grinke. There followed the Pavane, Galliard and Epilogue from *Job*. Three English items had been selected by Ralph himself for the actual funeral service. These were *The Sentences* from William Croft's Burial Service, Lord Mornington's chant for Psalm 104 and Maurice Greene's anthem 'Lord, let me know my end'. While the bronze casket was being carried to its resting place, the hymn 'Come down, O Love Divine' was sung by the whole congregation. The hymn tune 'Down Ampney', now sung at the termination of Ralph's story, was named for the Cotswold village in which it had begun.

The party which proceeded to the graveside interment included Ursula, Cordelia, Maud Karpeles, Steuart Wilson and Christopher Finzi. Sir Gilmour Jenkins represented The RVW Trust. Robert Armstrong, later to be knighted and named Secretary to the Cabinet, who had for several years attended the 'singeries' carried the insignia of Ralph's Order of Merit. After the interment, as the choir sang Ralph's coronation piece 'O Taste and See' bright sunshine suddenly burst into the dark abbey. Trumpeters from Kneller Hall sounded out rousingly the fanfare 'Sing to the Lord with cheerful voice', the notes of hope and triumph mitigating the sadness and sense of loss. After the Blessing came Bach's St Anne Fugue, also chosen by Ralph. Then, as the large congregation started to leave, the bells of the abbey rang out with a half-muffled peal.

The Queen was represented by Sir Arthur Bliss, Master of the Queen's Music. There were scores of other dignitaries. Many representatives of the Diplomatic Corps and the Commonwealth came to honour Ralph as one of Britain's great men. There were numerous figures from the world of music. Some, such as Paul Robeson and Aaron Copland, were not close to Ralph. Others were representatives of successive stages in his career: Imogen Holst, Rutland Boughton, Martin Shaw, Jelly d'Aranyi, Astra Desmond, Mr and Mrs Cyril Smith, Myra Hess, Larry Adler.

Members of the congregation were impressed by Ursula as she led the mourning on that great occasion. Dame Veronica Wedgwood, the daughter of Ralph's dear and lifelong friend Randolph, wrote to her to express something of what many others had felt. 'You looked most lovely – as he would have wished. Were you carrying myrtle or bay? I was not sure but only felt that the exquisite living green leaves in your hands were most beautifully right: not a dead wreath but living fronds shining like immortality. This must have been a terrible ordeal for you, but the rare grace that you brought to it was something that no one who saw you will forget'.

Ursula herself wrote, modestly, but briefly and incisively about the death of the great Englishman who had been her husband. From Balmoral she had received a message telling her that 'the Queen was so much distressed to learn of the death of Doctor Vaughan Williams', and that she sent 'her heartfelt sympathy'. In her letter of thanks Ursula wrote, 'My husband died peacefully in the hour before the dawn, after a very usual day of work and seeing people. It is the greatest comfort that he died at the height of his powers, still full of invention and inspiration, yet with so much work completed.'[1]

Endnotes

Chapter One *Childhood and Schooldays*

1   Shakespeare, *Richard II*, Act II, sc. 2, 11–29
2   Frances Cornford quoted in Ursula Vaughan Williams, *RVW: A Biography of Ralph Vaughan Williams* (Oxford University Press, 1988), p.215
3   Ibid, p.10
4   *National Music and Other Essays* (Oxford University Press, 1963),p.6
5   Vaughan Williams (1988), p.14
6   Ibid, p.20
7   Ibid, p.18
8   Ibid, p.18
9   Ibid, p.18
10 *The RCM Magazine*, Vol. 55, No.1, p.24
11 *National Music and Other Essays* (1963), p.179
12 *The RCM Magazine*, Vol. 55, No.1, p.21
13 Vaughan Williams (1988), p.17
14 *The RCM Magazine*, Vol. 55, No.1, p.24
15 *National Music and Other Essays* (1963), pp.177–8
16 Vaughan Williams (1988), p.21
17 Ibid, p.24
18 Ibid, p.22
19 Ibid, p.24
20 Ibid, p.24
21 Michael Kennedy, *The Works of Ralph Vaughan Williams* (Oxford University Press, 1964), pp.11–12
22 *National Music and Other Essays* (1963), p.178
23 Vaughan Williams (1988), p.22
24 *National Music and Other Essays* (1963), p.179
25 Vaughan Williams (1988), p.23
26 Ibid, p.27
27 Ibid, p.27
28 *The Carthusian* (1952)
29 British Library 1714/1/19/46
30 Vaughan Williams (1988), p.27
31 *The Carthusian* (1952)
32 Vaughan Williams (1988), p.29
33 *National Music and Other Essays* (1963), p.30
34 Gwen Raverat, *Period Piece – A Cambridge Childhood* (Faber and Faber, 1962), p.273
35 Ibid, p.273
36 *National Music and Other Essays* (1963), p.178

Chapter Two *Kensington*

1   J. Ellis Cook in *The RCM Magazine*, Vol. 55, No. 1
2   *National Music and Other Essays* (1963), p.182

3   Ibid, p.183
4   Ibid, p.181
5   David Manning (ed.), *Vaughan Williams on Music* (Oxford University Press: New York, 2008), p.295
6   Dan H. Laurence (ed.), *Shaw's Music, 1893–1950* (Bodley Head, 1981), Vol. III, p.168
7   *Ralph Vaughan Williams Society Journal*, 55, October 2012, p.21
8   *The Teaching of Parry and Stanford*, BBC Third programme (broadcast 1 January 1956)
9   Manning (2008), p.317
10 Ibid, p.318
11 *Ralph Vaughan Williams Society Journal*, No. 55, October 2012, p20
12 *National Music and Other Essays* (1963), p.179
13 *Musical Times*, Vol. 46, No. 753, 1 November 1905, p.726
14 *National Music and Other Essays* (1963), p.180

Chapter Three *Cambridge*

1   Gwen Raverat, *Period Piece – A Cambridge Childhood* (Faber and Faber, 1962), pp.185–6
2   Ibid, pp.185–6
3   Hugh Cobbe (ed.), *Letters of Ralph Vaughan Williams 1895–1958* (Oxford University Press, 2008), p.620
4   George Moore, *Principia Ethica* (Cambridge Unversity Press, 1903), p.189
5   Paul Levy, *G.E. Moore and the Cambridge Apostles* (Weidenfeld and Nicolson, 1979), p139
6   Cobbe (2008), p.279
7   Vaughan Williams (1988), p.39
8   David Cannadine, *G.M. Trevelyan. A Life in History* (HarperCollins, 1992), p.111
9   Cannandine (1992), p.235
10 British Library 1714/1/19/46
11 Raverat (1962), p.233
12 The incident was mentioned in a letter from Bertrand Russell to Michael Kennedy – see Kennedy (1964), p.42
13 British Library 1714/1/1/81
14 *National Music and Other Essays* (1963), p.183
15 Vaughan Williams (1988), pp.41–2
16 *National Music and Other Essays* (1963), p.183
17 Vaughan Williams (1988), p.37
18 *National Music and Other Essays* (1963), p.185
19 Ibid, p.184
20 British Library 1714/1/1. The bushy bearded Sedley Taylor scorned as a 'manikin' by Karl Marx was an economist, not a physicist. Around the time of Ralph's birth he had been a member of a committee that brought about the funding of Girton College, Cambridge.
21 Vaughan Williams (1988), p.38
22 George Frederick McCleary. British Library 1714/1/1

Chapter Four *London, Love and Marriage 1895–7*

1   *National Music and Other Essays* (1963), pp.197–8
2   Ibid, p.196
3   Ibid, p.185
4   Ursula Vaughan Williams, *RVW: A Biography of Ralph Vaughan Williams* (Oxford University Press, 1988), p.85
5   Ursula Vaughan Williams and Imogen Holst (eds), *Heirs and Rebels: Letters between Vaughan Williams and Holst* (Oxford University Press, 1959), p.3
6   Hugh Cobbe, *Letters of Ralph Vaughan Williams 1895–1958* (Oxford University Press, 2008), p.15
7   Paul Levy, *G.E. Moore and the Cambridge Apostles* (Weidenfeld and Nicolson, 1979), p.186
8   David Manning, *Gustav Holst. A Great Composer* (Oxford University Press, 2007), p.314
9   'Gustav Holst: An Essay and a Note', *National Music*, p.135
10 Ibid, p.152
11 Manning (2007), p.312
12 Gustav Holst: 'An Essay and a Note', *National Music*, pp.152–3
13 *National Music and Other Essays* (1963), p.193
14 Mary Bennett, *The RCM Magazine*, Vol. 55, No. 1, p.19
15 Vaughan Williams (1988), p.48
16 H.A.L. Fisher, *An Unfinished Autobiography* (Oxford University Press, 1940), pp.32–3

17   British Library 1714/4/1/45
18   Mary Bennett, *The RCM Magazine*, Vol. 55, No. 1, p.19

Chapter Five *Berlin and After*

1   Mary Bennett, *The RCM Magazine*, Vol. 55, No. 1, p.19
2   Michael Kennedy, *The Works of Ralph Vaughan Williams* (Oxford University Press, 1964), p. 43
3   Hugh Cobbe (ed.), *Letters of Ralph Vaughan Williams 1895–1958* (Oxford University Press, 2008), p.22
4   Ursula Vaughan Williams, *RVW: A Biography of Ralph Vaughan Williams* (Oxford University Press, 1988), p. 53
5   Cobbe (2008), p.27
6   Ibid, p.32
7   Ibid, p.28
8   Ibid, p.29
9   Ibid, p.36
10 Ibid, p.36
11 Vaughan Williams (1988), p.56
12 Ibid, p.57
13 British Library 1714/1/2/63
14 Vaughan Williams (1988), p.57
15 Ibid, p.57

Chapter Six *Barton Street, Westminster*

1   Ursula Vaughan Williams, *RVW: A Biography of Ralph Vaughan Williams* (Oxford University Press, 1988), p.58
2   Imogen Holst, *Gustav Holst. A Biography* (Faber and Faber, 2012), p.10
3   British Library 1714/1/1/51
4   Cited in Lewis Foreman's notes to *Ralph Vaughan Williams: Early and Late Works*, World Premiere Recordings, Dutton Epoch Records, p.5
5   British Library 1714/1/2
6   Arnold Bax, *Farewell my Youth* (Longmans Green, 1945), p.82
7   'Collecting Folk Songs' in Celia Newbury (ed.), *Vaughan Williams in Dorking* (The Local History Group of the Dorking and Leith Hill Preservation Society, 1979), p.4
8   David Manning, *Vaughan Williams on Music* (Oxford University Press, 2007), p.117

Chapter Seven *Cheyne Walk, Chelsea*

1   David Manning, *Vaughan Williams on Music* (Oxford University Press, 2007), p.116
2   Wilfred Mellers. *Vaughan Williams and the Vision Of Albion*, second edition (Barrie and Jenkins, 1991), p.50
3   Percy M. Young, *Vaughan Williams* (Dennis Dobson, 1953), p.62
4   Charles Edward McGuire, 'An Englishman and a Democrat: Vaughan Williams, large choral works and the British festival tradition' in Alain Frogley and Aidan J. Thomson (eds), *The Cambridge Companion to Vaughan Williams* (Cambridge University Press, 2013), p.124
5   *National Music and Other Essays* (1963), p191
6   Ibid, p.191
7   Ibid, p.191
8   Edwin Evans, 'English Song and 'On Wenlock Edge' in *The Musical Times*, June 1918, pp.247–8
9   Em Marshall, *Music in the Landscape. How the British Countryside Inspired our Greatest Composers* (Robert Hale, 2011), p.78
10 Manning (2007), p.227
11 Ibid, pp.227–8
12 Ursula Vaughan Williams, *RVW: A Biography of Ralph Vaughan Williams* (Oxford University Press, 1988), pp.83–4
13 Michael Kennedy, *The Works of Ralph Vaughan Williams* (Oxford University Press, 1964), p.92

Chapter Eight *The First Two Symphonies, 1910–14*

1   Hugh Cobbe (ed.), *Letters of Ralph Vaughan Williams 1895–1958* (Oxford University Press, 2008), p.67
2   Ibid, p.69

3 Ursula Vaughan Williams, *RVW: A Biography of Ralph Vaughan Williams* (Oxford University Press, 1988), p.400
4 Ibid, p.402
5 Ibid, p.71
6 British Library MS Music 1714/1/4/35
7 British Library MS Music 1714/1/4/59
8 Alain Frogley, 'History and Geography: The early orchestral works and the first three symphonies', in Alain Frogley and Aidan J. Thomson (eds), *The Cambridge Companion to Vaughan Williams* (Cambridge University Press, 2013), p.93
9 Michael Kennedy, *The Works of Ralph Vaughan Williams* (Oxford University Press, 1964), p.133
10 British Library MS Music 1714/1/4/74
11 Vaughan Williams (1988), p.94
12 Ibid, p.95
13 Ibid, p.103
14 Kennedy (1964), p.101
15 Ibid, p.103
16 British Library MS Music 1714/1/4/90
17 Cobbe (2008), p.91
18 Christopher Hassall, *Edward Marsh: Patron of the Arts* (Longmans, 1959), p.231
19 Cobbe (2008), p.95
20 Arnold Bax, *Farewell my Youth* (Longmans, 1943), p.93
21 Ibid, p.93
22 Vaughan Williams (1988), p.111
23 Cobbe (2008), p.94
24 Quoted in Lewis Foreman, *Bax: A Composer and his Times* (Scolar Press, 1983), p.116
25 British Library MS Music 1714/1/5/23
26 Vaughan Williams (1988), p.113

Chapter Nine *World War One*

1 Ursula Vaughan Williams, *RVW: A Biography of Ralph Vaughan Williams* (Oxford University Press, 1988), p.119
2 Harry Steggles in *The RCM Magazine*, Easter Term 1959
3 Hugh Cobbe (ed.), *Letters of Ralph Vaughan Williams 1895–1958* (Oxford University Press, 2008), p.109
4 Vaughan Williams (1988), p.121
5 Cobbe (2008), p.124
6 J.Ellis Cook, *The RCM Magazine*, Vol. 55, No. 1, p.24
7 Vaughan Williams (1988), p.127
8 Cobbe (2008), p.119
9 Ibid, p.122
10 Ibid, pp.122–3
11 Vaughan Williams (1988), p.129
12 Ibid, p.129
13 Ibid, pp.131–2

Chapter Ten *In Lodgings*

1 'The Letter and the Spirit' in *National Music*, p.127
2 Hugh Cobbe (ed.), *Letters of Ralph Vaughan Williams 1895–1958* (Oxford University Press, 2008), p.127
3 Michael Kennedy, *The Works of Ralph Vaughan Williams* (Oxford University Press, 1964), p.147
4 Cobbe (2008), p.265
5 Ursula Vaughan Williams, *RVW: A Biography of Ralph Vaughan Williams* (Oxford University Press, 1988), p.140
6 British Library MS Music 1714/1/6/42
7 British Library MS Music 1714/1/5/211
8 Hervey Fisher, *A Romantic Man and Other Tales* (Martin Secker, 1920), p.152
9 Cobbe (2008), pp.132–3
10 Vaughan Williams (1988), p.144
11 British Library MS Music 1714/1/6/66
12 Cobbe (2008), p.135

Chapter Eleven *A Career Re-established*

1   British Library MS Music 1714/1/6/80
2   British Library MS Music 1714/1/6/ 92
3   British Library MS Music 1714/1/6/89
4   British Library MS Music 1714/1/6/114
5   Michael Kennedy, *The Works of Ralph Vaughan Williams* (Oxford University Press, 1964), p.216
6   Hugh Cobbe (ed.), *Letters of Ralph Vaughan Williams 1895-1958* (Oxford University Press, 2008), pp.145-6
7   Ursula Vaughan Williams, *RVW: A Biography of Ralph Vaughan Williams* (Oxford University Press, 1988), p.156
8   British Library MS Music 1714/1/6/158
9   Kennedy (1964), p.213
10 Charles Reid, *Malcolm Sargent: A Biography* (Hamish Hamilton, 1968), pp.125-6
11 Cobbe (2008), p.151
12 Ursula Vaughan Williams and Imogen Holst (eds), *Heirs and Rebels: Letters between Vaughan Williams and Holst* (Oxford University Press, 1959), p.62
13 Wilfred Mellers, *Vaughan Williams and the Vision of Albion*, second edition (Barrie and Jenkins, 1991), p.195
14 Vaughan Williams (1988), p.161

Chapter Twelve *Pondering Apocalypse*

1   Michael Kennedy, *The Works of Ralph Vaughan Williams* (Oxford University Press, 1964), p.215
2   John Bridcut talks about 'Passions', *Ralph Vaughan Williams Society Journal*, No._50, February 2011, p.9
3   Jennifer Doctor, 'Working for her own salvation: Vaughan Williams as teacher of Elizabeth Maconchy, Grace Williams and Ina Boyle', in Lewis Foreman (ed.), *Vaughan Williams in Perspective* (Albion Music, 1998), p.181
4   Michael Mullinar, 'Dr Vaughan Williams as a Teacher' in *The Midland Musician*, January 1926, pp.8-9
5   Doctor (1998), p.190
6   Kennedy (1964), p.203
7   Ibid, p.202

Chapter Thirteen *White Gates*

1   Ursula Vaughan Williams, *RVW: A Biography of Ralph Vaughan Williams* (Oxford University Press, 1988), p.185
2   Ibid, p.185
3   Ibid, p.179
4   Quoted in Michael Kennedy, *Adrian Boult* (Hamish Hamilton, 1981), p.126
5   British Library MS Music 1714/1/8/44
6   British Library MS Music 1714/1/8/45
7   Hugh Cobbe (ed.), *Letters of Ralph Vaughan Williams 1895-1958* (Oxford University Press, 2008), p.199
8   British Library MS Music 1714/1/8/106
9   Cobbe (2008), p.204
10 Ibid, p.206
11 *National Music and Other Essays* (1963), p.42
12 Ibid, p.29
13 Ibid, p.39
14 Ibid, p.71
15 Cobbe (2008), p.188
16 Ibid, p.207
17 Ibid, p.211
18 Lewis, Foreman, *Bax: A Composer and his Times* (Scolar Press, 1983), p.249
19 Simon Heffer, *Vaughan Williams* (Faber, 2008), p.80
20 Letter in the Burnard papers, Special Collections, Library of The University of Newcastle, Australia
21 British Library MS Music 1714/1/8/51
22 British Library MS Music 1714/1/8/58
23 Cobbe (2008), p.224
24 Ibid, p.227
25 Ursula Vaughan Williams and Imogen Holst (eds), *Heirs and Rebels: Letters between Vaughan Williams and Holst* (Oxford University Press, 1959), p.52
26 Vaughan Williams (1988), p.201

27 British Library MS Music 1714/1/8/72
28 Quoted in Paul Kildea, *Benjamin Britten, A Life in the Twentieth Century* (Allen Lane, 2013), p.98
29 Cobbe (2008), p.235
30 Ibid, p.231
31 British Library MS Music 1714/1/9/150. Adrian Boult recalled this at the age of ninety in a conversation with a journalist.
32 Cobbe (2008), p.235
33 British Library MS Music 1714/1/9/98
34 Vaughan Williams, p.190
35 Cobbe (2008), p.254
36 British Library MS Music 1714/1/9/ 113. Letter from Arthur Benjamin, dated 21 April 1935.
37 British Library MS Music 1714/1/9/126

Chapter Fourteen *The Gathering Storm*

1 British Library MS Music 1714/1/9/102
2 Hugh Cobbe (ed.), *Letters of Ralph Vaughan Williams 1895–1958* (Oxford University Press, 2008), p.238
3 Ibid, p.239
4 Ibid, p.240
5 Percy M. Young, *Vaughan Williams* (Dennis Dobson, 1953), p.74
6 Ursula Vaughan Williams, *RVW: A Biography of Ralph Vaughan Williams* (Oxford University Press, 1988), p.214
7 Hugh Cobbe (ed.), *Letters of Ralph Vaughan Williams 1895–1958* (Oxford University Press, 2008), p.249
8 Ibid, p.251
9 British Library MS Music 1714/1/10/72
10 Cobbe (2008), p.253

Chapter Fifteen *A Love Affair*

1 Ursula Vaughan Williams, *Paradise Remembered* (Albion Music Ltd, 2002), p.11
2 Ibid, p.33
3 Ibid, p.39
4 Ibid, p.33
5 Ibid, p.82
6 John Bridcut, 'Sonata for Three', *Mail Online* (20 May 2008)
7 Ursula Wood, *No Other Choice* (Basil Blackwell, 1941), p.14
8 British Library MS Music 1714/1/11/11
9 Bridcut (2008)
10 Vaughan Williams (2002), p.83
11 Oliver Neighbour, 'Ralph, Adeline and Ursula Vaughan Williams. Some Facts and Speculations (with a note about Tippett)' in *Music and Letters*, Vol. 89 Issue 3, pp.337–45
12 Hugh Cobbe (ed.), *Letters of Ralph Vaughan Williams 1895–1958* (Oxford University Press, 2008), p.260
13 British Library MS Music 1714/1/11/16
14 British Library MS Music 1714/1/11/17
15 Letters, p.263
16 British Library MS Music 1714/1/11/38
17 British Library MS Music 1714/1/11/45
18 British Library MS Music 1714/1/11/64
19 British Library MS Music 1714/1/11/25
20 British Library MS Music 1714/1/11/68
21 Vaughan Williams (2002), p.88
22 Ursula Vaughan Williams, *RVW: A Biography of Ralph Vaughan Williams* (Oxford University Press, 1988), pp.224–5
23 British Library MS Music 1714/1/12/12
24 British Library MS Music 1714/1/12/93
25 Cobbe (2008), p.276
26 Ibid, p.278
27 British Library MS Music 1714/1/12/91
28 Cobbe (2008), p.278
29 *National Music*, p.87
30 Ibid, p.90
31 Ibid, p.115

32 Vaughan Williams (1988), p.233
33 British Library MS Music 1714/1/13/23
34 British Library MS Music 1714/1/13
35 Peter Martin, *Samuel Johnson: A Biography* (Phoenix, 2009), p.214
36 British Library MS Music 1714/1/9/80
37 British Library MS Music 1714/3/1/147
38 Cobbe (2008), p.306
39 Ibid, p.311
40 British Library MS Music 1714/1/13/37
41 Cobbe (2008), p.307
42 Bridcut (2008)
43 Cobbe (2008), p.332
44 Ibid, p.323
45 Ibid, pp.322–3
46 Ibid, pp.328–9
47 Ibid, p.338
48 Ibid, p.339
49 Vaughan Williams (2002), p.114
50 Ibid, p.112
51 Ibid, p.115

Chapter Sixteen *A Threesome*

1   Ursula Vaughan Williams, *Paradise Remembered* (Albion Music Ltd, 2002), p.117
2   Hugh Cobbe (ed.), *Letters of Ralph Vaughan Williams 1895–1958* (Oxford University Press, 2008), p.342
3   Vaughan Williams (2002), p.119
4   Ibid, p.120
5   Ibid, p.120
6   British Library MS Music 1714/2/1
7   Cobbe (2008), p.341
8   Ibid, p.351
9   Ibid, p.359
10 Ibid, p.360
11 Vaughan Williams (2002), p.128
12 Ursula Vaughan Williams, *RVW: A Biography of Ralph Vaughan Williams* (Oxford University Press, 1988), p.255
13 Cobbe (2008), p.363
14 Vaughan Williams (2002), p.135
15 British Library MS Music 1714/2/1/1
16 Vaughan Williams (2002), p.132
17 Ibid, p.133
18 Ibid, p.133
19 Ibid, p.133
20 Vaughan Williams (1988), p.262
21 Vaughan Williams (2002), p.143
22 Ibid, p.144
23 Vaughan Williams (2002), p.267
24 Vaughan Williams (2002), pp.145–6
25 Vaughan Williams (2002), p.146
26 Bernard Hermann, *New York Herald Tribune*, 22 December 1946
27 British Library MS Music 1714/1/16
28 Vaughan Williams (2002), p.268
29 Ibid, p.268
30 Ibid, p.271
31 Cobbe (2008), p.408
32 British Library MS Music 1714/1/19 No. 149
33 Cobbe (2008), pp.409–10
34 British Library MS Music 1714/1/18/31
35 Vaughan Williams (1988), p.276
36 Ibid, p.276
37 British Library MS Music 1714/1/17/42
38 Michael Kennedy, *The Works of Ralph Vaughan Williams* (Oxford University Press, 1964), p.301

39 Ibid, p.303
40 Ibid, p.302
41 Ibid, p.349
42 Peter Maxwell Davies quoted in Alain Frogley and Aidan J. Thomson (eds), *The Cambridge Companion to Vaughan Williams* (Cambridge University Press, 2013), p.302
43 Byron Adams, 'The Stages of Revision of Vaughan Williams's Sixth Symphony' in Byron Adams and Robin Wells (eds), *Vaughan Williams Essays* (Ashgate, 2003), p.12
44 Wilfred Mellers, *Vaughan Williams and the Vision of Albion*, second edition (Barrie and Jenkins, 1991), p.194
45 Simon, Heffer, *Vaughan Williams* (Faber & Faber, 2008), p.118

Chapter Seventeen *In the Cold War*

1   British Library MS Music 1714/1/17/38
2   British Library MS Music 1714/1/17/78
3   Unattributed memoir, British Library MS Music 1714/1/18/172
4   Ursula Vaughan Williams, *RVW: A Biography of Ralph Vaughan Williams* (Oxford University Press, 1988), p.289
5   Ibid, p.289
6   Hugh Cobbe (ed.), *Letters of Ralph Vaughan Williams 1895–1958* (Oxford University Press, 2008), p.443
7   Ursula Vaughan Williams, *Paradise Remembered* (Albion Music Ltd, 2002), p.153
8   Vaughan Williams (1988), p.292
9   British Library MS Music 1714/1/18/93
10 British Library MS Music 1714/1/18/120
11 Cobbe (2008), p.466
12 Ibid, p.488
13 British Library MS Music 1714/1/18/35
14 Vaughan Williams (2002), p.161
15 British Library MS Music 1714/1/19/80
16 Vaughan Williams (1988), p.308
17 Michael Kennedy, *The Works of Ralph Vaughan Williams* (Oxford University Press, 1964), p.311
18 Ibid, p.311
19 Ibid, p.314
20 Ibid, p.315
21 Vaughan Williams (2002), pp.161–2
22 Ibid, p.161
23 Vaughan Williams (1988), p.309

Chapter Eighteen *The Widower*

1   Ursula Vaughan Williams, *RVW: A Biography of Ralph Vaughan Williams* (Oxford University Press, 1988), p.310
2   Ursula Vaughan Williams, *Paradise Remembered* (Albion Music Ltd, 2002), p.163
3   British Library MS Music 1714/1/19/68
4   Stephen Banfield, *Gerald Finzi: An English Composer* (Faber & Faber, 1997), p.279
5   Vaughan Williams (2002), p.146
6   Elias Canetti, *Party in the Blitz: The English Years* (New Directions: New York, 2005), pp.177–8
7   British Library MS Music 1714/1/19/180
8   *Letters*, p.493
9   Vaughan Williams (2002), p.166
10 British Library MS Music 1714/1/24/119
11 Ursula Vaughan Williams, *RVW: A Biography of Ralph Vaughan Williams* (Oxford University Press, 1988), p.325
12 Ibid, p.326
13 Ibid, p.327
14 Charles Reid, *John Barbirolli: A Biography* (Hamish Hamilton, 1971), p.291
15 Vaughan Williams (2002), p.169

Chapter Nineteen *10 Hanover Terrace*

1   Hugh Cobbe (ed.), *Letters of Ralph Vaughan Williams 1895–1958* (Oxford University Press, 2008), p.499

2   British Library MS Music 1714/1/20/3
3   Ursula Vaughan Williams, *Paradise Remembered* (Albion Music Ltd, 2002), p.334
4   Cobbe (2008), p.524
5   Vaughan Williams (2002), p.341
6   Ibid, p.344
7   Ibid, p.345
8   British Library MS Music 1714/1/21/79
9   Michael Kennedy, *The Works of Ralph Vaughan Williams* (Oxford University Press, 1964), p.363
10 Ursula Vaughan Williams, *RVW: A Biography of Ralph Vaughan Williams* (Oxford University Press, 1988), p.348
11 British Library MS Music 1714/1/21/74
12 *National Music*, p.225
13 Ibid, p.220
14 Ursula Vaughan Williams, *RVW: A Biography of Ralph Vaughan Williams* (Oxford University Press, 1988), p.357

Chapter Twenty *Excursions*

1   Ursula Vaughan Williams, *Paradise Remembered* (Albion Music Ltd, 2002), p.174
2   Vaughan Williams (1988), p.361
3   Ibid, p.185
4   Hugh Cobbe (ed.), *Letters of Ralph Vaughan Williams 1895–1958* (Oxford University Press, 2008), p.560
5   Vaughan Williams (2002), p.172
6   Vaughan Williams (1988), p.363
7   Ibid, p.363
8   British Library MS Music 1714/1/21/196
9   David Manning (ed.), *Vaughan Williams on Music* (Oxford University Press, 2007), pp.275–7
10 Ibid, p.321
11 British Library MS Music 1714/1/22/112
12 Vaughan Williams (1988), p.370
13 Vaughan Williams (2002), p.184
14 Manning, (2007), p.326
15 Cobbe (2008), pp.602–3
16 Ibid, p.604
17 Vaughan Williams (1988), p.381

Chapter Twenty-One *In The Final Year*

1   British Library MS Music 1714/1/23/102
2   Michael Kennedy, *The Works of Ralph Vaughan Williams* (Oxford University Press, 1964), p.343
3   Alain Frogley, *Vaughan Williams's Ninth Symphony* (Oxford University Press, 2001)
4   Wilfrid Mellers, *Vaughan Williams and the Vision Of Albion*, second edition (Barrie and Jenkins, 1991), p.236
5   Kennedy (1964), p.193
6   Ursula Vaughan Williams, *Paradise Remembered* (Albion Music Ltd, 2002), p.193
7   Ibid, p.399
8   British Library MS Music 1714/1/24/13
9   British Library MS Music 1714/1/23/170
10 Letters, p.644

Chapter Twenty-Two *In Memoriam*

1   British Library MS Music 1714/1/24/115

Select Bibliography

Books

Banfield, Stephen, *Gerald Finzi: An English Composer* (Faber, 1997)

Bax, Arnold, *Farewell my Youth* (Longmans Green, 1945)

Canetti, Elias, *Party in the Blitz: The English Years* (New Directions: New York, 2005)

Cannadine, David, *G.M. Trevelyan. A Life in History* (HarperCollins, 1992)

Newbury, Celia (ed.), *Vaughan Williams in Dorking* (The Local History Group of the Dorking and Leith Hill Preservation Society, 1979)

Cobbe, Hugh (ed.), *Letters of Ralph Vaughan Williams 1895–1958* (Oxford University Press, 2008)

Fisher, H.A.L., *An Unfinished Autobiography* (Oxford University Press, 1940)

Fisher, Hervey, *A Romantic Man and Other Tales* (Martin Secker, 1920)

Foreman, Lewis, *Bax: A Composer and his Times* (Scolar Press, 1983)

Foreman, Lewis (ed.), *Vaughan Williams in Perspective* (Albion Music, 1998)

Frogley, Alain, *Vaughan Williams's Ninth Symphony* (Oxford University Press, 2001)

Frogley, Alain and Thomson, Aidan J. (eds), *The Cambridge Companion to Vaughan Williams* (Cambridge University Press, 2013)

Hassall, Christopher, *Edward Marsh: Patron of the Arts* (Longmans, 1959)

Heffer, Simon, *Vaughan Williams* (Faber, 2008)

Holst, Imogen, *Gustav Holst: A Biography* (Faber & Faber, 2012)

Kennedy, Michael, *The Works of Ralph Vaughan Williams* (Oxford University Press, 1964)

Kennedy, Michael, *Adrian Boult* (Hamish Hamilton, 1981)

Kildea, *Benjamin Britten, A Life in the Twentieth Century* (Allen Lane, 2013)

Laurence, Dan H. (ed.), *Shaw's Music, 1893–1950* (Bodley Head, 1981), Vol. III

Levy, Paul, *G.E. Moore and the Cambridge Apostles* (Weidenfeld and Nicolson, 1979)

Manning, David, *Gustav Holst: A Great Composer* (Oxford University Press, 2007)

Manning, David (ed.), *Vaughan Williams on Music* (Oxford University Press, 2007)

Marshall, Em, *Music in the Landscape: How the British Countryside Inspired our Greatest Composers* (Robert Hale, 2011)

Mellers, Wilfred, *Vaughan Williams and the Vision of Albion*, second edition (Barrie and Jenkins, 1991)

Moore, George, *Principia Ethica* (Cambridge Unversity Press, 1903)

Raverat, Gwen, *Period Piece – A Cambridge Childhood* (Faber and Faber, 1962)

Reid, Charles, *Malcolm Sargent: A Biography* (Hamish Hamilton, 1968)

Reid, Charles, *John Barbirolli: A Biography* (Hamish Hamilton, 1971)

Vaughan Williams, Ralph, *National Music and Other Essays* (Oxford University Press, 1963)

Vaughan Williams, Ursula, *RVW: A Biography of Ralph Vaughan Williams* (Oxford University Press, 1988)

Vaughan Williams, Ursula and Holst, Imogen (eds), *Heirs and Rebels: Letters between Vaughan Williams and Holst* (Oxford University Press, 1959)

Wood, Ursula, *No Other Choice* (Basil Blackwell, 1941)

Young, Percy M., *Vaughan Williams* (Dennis Dobson, 1953)

Newspapers, journals and periodicals

Hermann, Bernard, *New York Herald Tribune* (22 December 1946)

The Carthusian (1952)

Musical Times, Vol. 46, No. 753 (1 November 1905)

Musical Times (June 1918)

Ralph Vaughan Williams Society Journal, No. 50 (February 2011)

Ralph Vaughan Williams Society Journal, No. 55 (October 2012)

The RCM Magazine, Vol. 55, No. 1

The RCM Magazine (Easter Term, 1959)

Recordings and Broadcasts

Foreman, Lewis, notes to *Ralph Vaughan Williams: Early and Late Works*, World Premiere Recordings, Dutton Epoch Records

Vaughan Williams, Ralph, *The Teaching of Parry and Stanford*, BBC Third programme (broadcast 1 January 1956)

INDEX

Abinger Chronicle, 259
Abinger Pageant, 252, 305
Adams, Byron, 298
Addison, John, 116
Adler, Larry, 319, 321, 368
Aitken, Max (Lord Beaverbrook), 218–19
Alcock, Sir Walter, 252–3
Aldeburgh Festival, 302
Allen, Hugh Percy, 56, 173, 179, 223, 233, 262, 336
    support for RVW, 56, 62, 141, 124, 172, 174
Amos, Maurice Sheldon, 47, 53, 59, 66, 67
Ann Arbor, University of Michigan, 337
Aristophanes, 51, 125
Armstrong, Sir Robert, 352
Arnold, Matthew, 306
Arts Council, The, 268, 329
Asquith, Anthony, 270
Auden, W. H., 239, 329, 365

Bach, Johann Sebastian, 65, 83, 91, 174, 249, 253, 338, 364
    attitude of RVW to, 27, 38, 187, 212, 260, 337
    influence on work of RVW, 173, 187, 190, 289
    works by, 30, 176, 184, 281, 289, 294, 358, 367, 368
Bach Choir, 23, 171–2
    and RVW, 173–4, 184, 212
Bagot, Jane (Vaughan Williams, Lady), 15, 16, 79
Balcon, Jill, 357
Balcon, Sir Michael, 289, 322
Bantock, Granville, 95
Barber, Samuel, 288, 365
Barbirolli, Sir John, 320–1, 322, 323, 327–8, 333, 334, 347, 357, 358
    friendship with RVW, 322, 364
Barnes, William, 99, 247, 364
Barter, Arnold, 318
Bartók, Béla, 190, 219, 250, 287, 360
Bax, Arnold, 38, 99, 154–5, 156, 219, 220–1, 287, 331

friendship with RVW, 38, 227–8, 346
influence on work of RVW, 157, 218
Beagley, J., 305, 309, 320
Beckett, Samuel, 10
Beecham, Sir Thomas, 174, 188, 224, 240, 308
Beerbohm, Sir Max, 29, 31, 35, 259, 262, 263
Beethoven, Ludwig van, 31, 42, 47, 176, 261, 296, 354
    attitude of RVW to, 27, 38, 41, 80, 260
    influence on work of Ralph Vaughan Williams, 175
    work of, 41, 57, 85, 259–60
Benjamin, Arthur, 230, 337, 356
Benson, Sir Frank, 149, 201, 343
Berners, Lord, 191
Bernhardt, Sarah, 248
Betjeman, John, 240
Bing, Rudolf, 338
Blackwell, Basil, 276
Blake, William, 43, 206, 359
Bliss, Sir Arthur, 171, 179, 228, 331, 358, 368
Bomberg, David, 163
Borrow, George, 10, 126, 139, 200, 315, 362
Bosanquet, Vivian, 22, 23
Boughton, Rutland, 308, 309, 350, 353, 360, 368
Boult, Sir Adrian, 154, 167, 322, 341
    and the Bach Choir, 173, 212
    conducting works by RVW, 174, 219, 220, 221, 228, 258, 277, 296, 302, 308, 312, 327, 332, 366
    friendship with RVW, 167, 279, 327
Bournemouth Symphony Orchestra, 100
    founding of, 96
    performing works by RVW, 96, 105, 331
Boyle, Ina, 172, 193, 257
Brahms, Johannes, 56, 81, 83

attitude of RVW to, 38, 80, 249, 91, 353
death of, 80
influence on work of Ralph Vaughan Williams, 43, 102
works by, 23, 63, 83
Brecht, Bertholt, 257
Breitkopf and Hartel, 158, 161
Bridcut, John, 200
Bridges, Robert, 351
British Broadcasting Corporation (BBC), 181
British Council, The, 334, 345
Britten, Benjamin, 239, 302, 359
    and RVW, 184, 215, 227, 288
    works by, 238, 286, 290, 314–15, 331
Broadwood, Lucy, 101, 102, 105, 111, 117, 175
Brooke, Rupert, 54, 161
Brown, Bernard, 262, 265, 277, 285, 352, 354
    see also Honorine Brown
Brown, Honorine, 213, 214, 252, 258, 265
    death of, 264–5
    marriage of, 262
    role in household of RVW, 203, 226, 240, 263
    see also Bernard Brown
Bruch, Professor Max, 81, 85, 97
Bryn Mawr (Pennsylvania), 215, 217, 336
Bucks, Beds and Oxon Festival, 125
Bunyan, John, 117, 179, 302
Bush, Alan, 257, 267, 346–7
Busoni, Ferruccio, 137
Butterworth, George, 141, 146, 148, 151, 158
Buxtehude, Dietrich, 249
Byrd, William, 41, 43, 332

Calvocoressi, M.D., 121, 122
Camargo Society, 206, 207
Cambridge, University of, 55, 129, 320, 333
    RVW at, 34, 44, 45–60
Cameron, Mrs Julia, 72

Canetti, Elias, 312, 317, 332, 354
Careno, Madame, 93
Carl Rosa Opera Company, 106, 129
Carr, Rosamond, 211, 213
Carson, Edward, 152
Carter, Mary (Mrs Field Reid), 328
Cecil Sharp House, 242, 249, 255, 256, 285, 314
Chamberlain, Joseph, 94
Chamberlain, Neville, 253, 259
Chaplin, Charlie, 66
Chaplin, Frances, 265
Charterhouse School, 40, 100
    RVW at, 25, 28–35, 51, 191, 263, 351
Chaucer, Geoffrey, 45, 179
Cherubini, Liugi, 23
Child, Harold, 138, 139, 140
Christie, John, 226, 258
Churchill, Sir Winston, 41, 49, 196, 253, 264, 267, 318
Clarion Singers, 305, 318
Cohen, Harriet, 217, 218–19, 220, 221, 223, 346
Conrad, Joseph, 120, 155, 202
Cook, A.J., 196
Corelli, Marie, 118, 150
Cornford, Frances, 333
Covent Garden, see Royal Opera House
Craig, Gordon, 146, 148
Cullen, Margery, 262, 277, 307
Cunningham, William, 51
Curle, Adam, 280, 287, 354
Curle, Cordelia, 28, 76, 178, 179, 192, 277, 279, 287, 288, 290, 310, 354, 367
    attitude towards Ursula Lock, 287
    on death of Adeline Vaughan Williams, 313, 314
    son of, 180, 280, 354

Daily Mail, The, 99
Daily Worker, The, 307
D'Aranji, Jelly, 190, 191, 211, 291, 368
Darke, Dr Harold, 275, 349
Darwin, Charles, 17, 19, 20, 22, 35, 128
Darwin, Erasmus, 17, 18, 150, 349
Darwin, George, 45
Davies, Meredith, 334
Davies, Walford, 125, 237, 259
Davison, Emily, 152
Dearmer, Percy, 109, 110, 114, 125, 146, 191
Debussy, Claude, 122, 124, 129, 130, 153, 290
de la Mare, Walter, 329
Delius, Frederick, 121, 219
Dent, Edward Joseph, 161, 187
Desmond, Astra, 218, 224, 237, 295, 333, 368

de Valois, Dame Ninette, 206, 207
Diaghilev, Sergei, 99, 121, 128, 136, 185,
    and RVW, 148, 206–7
D'Indy, Vincent, 121
Disraeli, Benjamin, 21
Dolin, Anton, 207
Doniach. Sheila, 304
Dorking Bach Choir, 352
Dorking Refugee Committee, 259
Douglas, Roy, 360, 362
    assistant to RVW, 292, 308, 319, 323, 341, 358, 364
Down Ampney, 15, 16, 19, 115, 303, 367
Duckworth, Stella, 74, 75
Duncan, Isadora, 110, 146, 148, 216
Duncan, Raymond, 147
Dvořák, Antonín, 89, 97, 116

Ecoivres, 162, 163, 168, 175
Edward VII:
    coronation of, 98, 99,
    death of, 135
    as Prince of Wales, 70, 130, 233
Edward VIII, 239–40
Eisler, Hanns, 301
Elder, Sir Mark, 130
Elgar, Sir Edward, 142, 170–1
    death of, 223, 224
    Dream of Gerontius, The, 137, 141
    'Enigma' Variations, 95, 100
    influence on work of RVW, 96, 224, 348
    and RVW, 43, 95, 145, 223–4
Eliot, T.S., 91, 145, 164, 174, 190, 229–30, 284
    Dry Salvages, 230
    Little Gidding, 278
    music for work of, 110
    Wasteland, The, 174, 175, 198
Elizabeth I, 329
Elizabeth II, 55, 319
    coronation of, 329–30
Elizabeth, The Queen Mother, 320
English Folk Dance and Song Society, 214, 249
    Journal of the, 352
English Hymnal, The, 110, 114, 115, 116, 125, 142, 192, 343, 346
Epstein, Jacob, 303, 304
Evans, Edwin, 99, 121, 125, 206

Fachiri, Adila, 190, 211
Falkner, Keith, 336, 337, 338
Farrer, Lady Evangeline, 38
Farrer, The Hon. Dame Frances (Fanny), 277, 334
    Leith Hill Festival, 200, 262
    and RVW, 200, 211, 213, 220, 223, 226
Fauré, Gabriel, 122, 129
Federal Union, 266, 267

Ferguson, Howard, 350
Ferrier, Kathleen, 290
Festival of Britain, 307, 310, 314, 319
Fiedler, Herma, 249
Fiedler, Professor Hermann, 240, 241, 249
Field House School, 24, 25, 26, 27
Finzi, Gerald, 215, 270–1, 276, 277, 295, 303, 305, 315, 317, 329, 350–1
    death of, 325
    and Sir Gilmour Jenkins, 316
    marriage, 222–3
    son of, 332, 359, 367
Finzi, Joy, 276, 303, 305, 352, 364
Fisher, Adeline, see Adeline Vaughan Williams
Fisher, Charles, 165
Fisher, Cordelia, see Cordelia Curle
Fisher, Edwin, 99
Fisher, Emmeline, see Emmie Morris
Fisher, Florence, see Florence Maitland
Fisher, H.A.L., 197, 216, 264
Fisher, Herbert, 70, 71, 76, 77, 150, 166
Fisher, Hervey, 71, 103, 113, 120, 177
Fisher, Jack, 97
Fisher, Admiral Sir William, 151, 240
Fletcher, Dorothy, see Mrs Robert Longman
Fontane, Theodor, 82
Foreman, Lewis, 96
Forster, E.M., 203, 226, 240, 259, 260
Foss, Hubert, 192, 270, 271, 307, 319, 325
Frogley, Alain, 143, 361
Fuller-Maitland, J.A., 100, 101, 105, 106

Gardiner, Balfour, 154
Garibaldi, Giuseppe, 49
Garnett, David, 202
Garnett, Edward, 202
Garrick, David, 263
Gatty, Ivor, 83, 204
Gatty, Margot, see Hugo Parrington
Gatty, Nicholas, 46, 93, 98, 110, 195
Gatty, Rene, 83, 85, 89, 91, 92
George V, 136, 179
George VI, 319
Gibbs, Armstrong, 187, 315
Girdleston, Duck, 31, 33
Gladstone, Dr F.E., 39
Gladstone, William, 21, 50
Glanville-Hicks, Peggy, 351
Glyndebourne, 226, 258, 290
Godfrey, Sir Dan, 96, 100, 105
Grainger, Percy, 154, 155, 176, 222, 363

Graves, Robert, 164, 351
Gray, Alan, 55
Grinke, Frederick, 335–6, 367
Grout, Professor Donald, 336, 337, 338
Grove, Sir George, 36, 41, 259
Grove's Dictionary of Music and Musicians, 106
Gunby Hall, 30, 102, 363
Gundry, Inglis, 287
Gurney, Ivor, 164, 172

Hadley, Mrs George Hadley, see Jean Stewart
Hadley, Patrick, 172, 305, 320, 333
Haig-Brown, Dr William, 32, 33
Hallé Orchestra, 107, 323, 358
Hamilton, H.V., 31, 32
Hammond, Basil Edward, 50, 51
Handel, G.F., 27, 31, 111, 137, 170, 174, 236, 262
Hardy, Thomas, 74, 91, 103, 107, 200
    attitude of RVW to, 64, 103, 200, 364–5
    influence on work of RVW, 64, 332, 362
    works by, 63–4, 244, 290, 291, 361
Hart, Fritz, 63, 270
Harty, Hamilton, 107
Haydn, Joseph, 27, 33, 81, 126, 275
Heffer, Simon, 221, 299
Hepworth, Barbara, 344
Herbert, George, 16,145
Hermann, Bernard, 288
Herzogenberg, Heinrich von, 81
Heseltine, Philip, see Peter Warlock
Hess, Dame Myra, 276, 368
Hewitt, James, 24
Hewitt, William, 27
Hickox, Richard, 156
Hindemith, Paul, 219, 250, 338
Hitler, Adolf, 238
    Anschluss, RVW on the, 225–6
    death of, 285
    Germany under, 249–50
    in the lead-up to the Second World War, 253, 258, 262
    and the Second World War, 237, 253, 264, 267, 269, 287
    and the Spanish Civil War, 237
Hollins, Frank, 329, 344, 345, 364
Holst, Gustav, 39, 89, 92, 96, 103, 105, 128, 129, 146, 157, 163, 167, 178, 184, 201, 202, 215, 338
    collaboration with RVW, 110–11, 115, 125, 214–15
    death of, 224–5
    early life of, 67, 68
    friendship with RVW, 62–3, 67, 69–70, 114, 118, 181, 182–3, 192–3, 287, 354, 233–4
    influence on work of RVW, 70, 206, 228

view of RVW on work of, 192–3
    works by, 96–7, 99, 114, 151, 172, 194, 211, 225, 365
Holst, Imogen, 92, 172, 233, 264, 354, 368
Hornstein, Genia, 265, 314, 341, 349
Hornstein, Yanya, 265,
Housman, A.E., 10, 124, 129, 199, 303
Howells, Herbert, 191, 220, 234, 270, 277, 321, 329, 349, 358,
Howes, Frank, 358
Howland Prize (University of Yale), 338
Hudson, W.H., 200

International Society for Contemporary Music, 187, 192, 228
Ireland, John, 86, 98, 115, 219, 306
Irving, Ernest, 270, 289, 292, 303, 307, 319, 327
Ives, Charles, 117, 179

James Allen's Girls' School, 105
Janáček, Leoš, 49, 192, 310
Jenkins, Sir Gilmour (Gil), 310, 313, 316, 317–18, 324, 327, 329, 334, 335, 341, 346, 347, 354, 358, 364
    and the Ralph Vaughan Williams Trust, 352, 367
Jochum, Eugen, 250
Johnson, Dr Samuel, 18, 349
Jones, David, 164, 174
Jonson, Ben, 110
Joseph, Jane, 181, 182

Karpeles, Helen, see Helen Kennedy
Karpeles, Maud, 148, 225, 230, 254, 256, 277, 287, 295, 367
Kelly, Sir Gerald, 320, 363
Kempson, Rachel, 359
Kennedy, Douglas, 148, 151, 242, 254, 258
Kennedy, Helen, 151
Kennedy, Michael, 151, 155, 323, 343, 354, 361, 362, 364
    on work of RVW, 108, 115, 142, 187, 199, 253, 297, 311–12, 334
Keynes, Sir Geoffrey, 206
Keynes, Maynard, 47, 54, 126, 206
Kneller Hall (Royal Military School of Music), 185, 368
Korda, Alexander, 269–70
Kreisler, Fritz, 145

Lambert, Constant, 207, 223
Lasker, Vally, 184, 215, 219
Lavengro, 126, 140, 315, 362
Lawrence, D.H., 136, 189, 198, 202, 218

Lawrence, T.E., 202
Lear, Edward, 29, 84
Leather, Ella, 126, 127
Leeds Festival, 62, 120, 192
Leith Hill Musical Festival, 111, 184, 200, 212, 310, 321–2, 358
    founding of, 38, 101, 111
    and RVW, 128, 130, 169, 176, 185, 204, 222, 224, 259, 277, 281, 294, 307, 333, 357
    during the Second World War, 262, 268, 277
Lenin, Vladimir Ilyich Ulyanov, 182
Lewin, Colonel, 33, 111
Listener, The, 143
Liverpool Philharmonic Society, 81
Llewellyn Davies, Crompton, 67, 88, 113, 176
Llewellyn Davies, Theodore, 65
Lloyd George, David, 77, 135, 136, 166, 176, 180, 197
Lock, Major-General Sir Robert, 243
Lock, Ursula, see Ursula Vaughan Williams
London Philharmonic Orchestra, 226, 240, 281, 332
London Symphony Orchestra (LSO), 116, 156, 224, 287, 292, 295
Longman, Dorothy, 189, 212, 264
Longman, Robert, 162, 230, 327

Macmillan, Harold, 161
MacDonald, Ramsay, 204, 210
McCleary, Dr George, 56, 57, 58, 363
McGuire, Charles Edward, 118, 119
Mackail, Clare, 145–6
McKie, Sir William, 329–30, 363, 367
Macnaghten Concerts Society, 267, 352, 357
Macnaghten New Music Group, see Macnaghten Concerts Society
Maconchy, Elizabeth, 172, 193, 204–5, 221, 227, 355
Maeterlinck, Maurice, 153
Mahler, Gustav, 80, 95, 130, 143, 145, 269
Maitland, Ermengard, 46, 73, 76, 118
Maitland, Florence, 46
Maitland, Fredegond, see Fredegond Shove
Maitland, Frederic, 46, 73, 85, 117, 118, 157
Manning, Frederic, 164
Marsh, Edward, 95, 153, 175
Massingberd, Stephen, 30, 32
Mathieson, Muir, 269, 277, 347
Maxwell Davies, Peter, 297
Mellers, Wilfrid, 116, 193, 299, 361
Menges Quartet, 255, 284

Michelangelo, 34, 333
Middlesex Hospital, 355–6, 365
Moeran, E. J., 191, 219
Montgomery-Massingberd, Diana, 21, 363
Moore, G.E., 47, 333
Morgan, J.P., 119
Morley College, 145–6, 227, 287, 354
  and Gustav Holst, 145, 181, 183, 225, 279, 327
  impact on career of RVW, 279
  RVW as teacher at, 161, 181
Morris, Emmeline, 105, 128, 170, 203, 211, 265, 275
Morris, R. O., 170, 203, 211, 265, 275, 279, 280, 287, 294
Morris, William, 68, 90, 186
Mozart, Wolfgang Amadeus, 23, 137, 184, 258, 355
  attitude of RVW to, 27, 81, 123, 178
Mukle, May, 268
Müller-Hartmann, Robert, 265, 314
Mullinar, Michael, 205, 289, 294, 306, 335–6, 354
Murray, Gilbert, 216, 241
Music and Letters, 170, 171, 311
Musical Times, 125
Mussolini, Benito, 225, 226, 237, 262, 263

Nash, John (architect), 328
Nash, John (painter), 163, 354, 357
Nash, Paul, 296
Nathan, Dr Paul, 275
National Gallery, concerts at the, 276, 279, 281, 284, 287
Neel, Boyd, 337
Nevinson, Evelyn, see Evelyn Sharp
Nevinson, Henry, 255
Newman, Ernest, 125, 216
Nixon, Richard, 301
Nottingham, University of, 189
Novello, Ivor, 203

Olivier, Sir Lawrence, 285
Ord, Boris, 291, 333
Owen, Wilfred, 164, 174
Oxford University Press (OUP), 192, 271, 292, 325
  see also Hubert Foss

Pakenham, Simona, 349, 364
Pankhurst, Emmeline, 152
Parnell, Charles Stewart, 37
Parratt, Sir Walter, 55, 111
Parrington, Hugo, 195
Parry, Sir Hubert, 32, 36, 40–1, 61, 80, 96, 129, 130, 172, 179, 355
  influence on work of RVW, 30, 41, 42
  tutor to RVW, 39–41, 42, 43–4, 51, 54, 62, 205, 215–16, 223, 347

Peterkin, Norman, 271, 272, 292
Piper, John, 302
Picasso, Pablo, 122, 129, 136, 190, 241, 308
Pottipher, Mr, 104, 105
Pound, Ezra, 174
Pountney, David, 130
Priestley, J.B., 261
Purcell, Henry, 145, 367
  attitude of RVW to, 41, 43, 63
  works by, 63, 126, 146, 302, 321
Purcell Society, 101, 105, 352

Quayle, Anthony, 318
Queen's College, Oxford, 39

Raff, Josef Joachim, 29
Ravel, Maurice, 99, 121, 122, 128, 320
Raverat, Gwen, 35, 51, 206, 323, 333
Rawsthorne, Alan, 329
Redgrave, Sir Michael, 359
Redgrave, Lady, see Kempson, Rachel
Rhys, Ernest, 254
Richmond, Sir Bruce, 138, 149, 166, 286
Riley, Athelstan, 110
Ritchie, Mabel, 290
Rosenberg, Isaac, 164
Rossetti, Christina, 100, 102, 105
Rossetti, D.G., 72, 73, 102, 107
Rothenstein, William, 170, 171
Royal Academy of Music, 355
Royal College of Music, 61, 87, 98, 172
  founding of, 36–7, 55
  RVW as student at, 35, 36–44, 55–6, 60, 63
Royal College of Organists, 37, 280
Royal Opera House, 54, 157, 165, 184, 308, 309, 319, 323, 331
  work of RVW performed at, 117, 179, 302, 310–11
Royal Philharmonic Society, 174, 191, 357, 358
Rubbra, Edmund, 230, 354
Rushton, Julian, 96
Ruskin, John, 23, 41, 43, 91, 186, 328
Russell, Bertrand, 52, 53

Sadler's Wells Ballet Company, 245
St Aubyns School, see Field House School
St Barnabas' Church, South Lambeth, 65, 66, 86
St Pancras Town Hall, 360
Salvation Army Staff Band, 341–2, 353–4
Sargent, Sir Malcolm, 188, 331
  and the work of RVW, 191, 226, 283, 299, 342, 361
Sassoon, Siegfried, 164

Sartre, Jean-Paul, 298
Scholes, Percy, 180
Scott, Captain Robert, 152, 326
Seeley, John, 50,
Sert, Misia, 149
Shakespeare, William, 16, 45, 91, 260, 285, 299, 318
  influence on RVW, 20–1
  music for plays, 118, 149–50, 151, 201, 253, 276, 315
Sharp, Cecil J., 141, 151, 202, 215–16, 337
  and folk songs, 104, 109
  see also English Folk Dance and Song Society
Sharp, Evelyn, 202, 206, 255
Shaw, George Bernard, 29, 40, 171, 218, 248, 284, 308
Shaw, Martin, 109, 110, 146, 191, 346, 352, 368
Shelley, 221, 260, 261, 325
Sheridan, Richard Brinsley, 68
Sheppard, Canon Dick, 238
Shore, Bernard, 312, 352
Shove, Fredegonde, 46, 73, 118
Shostakovich, Dmitri, 237, 238, 298, 301
Sibelius, Jean, 49, 178, 230, 277, 295, 365
Simpson, Mrs Wallis, 239–40
Songs of Praise (hymn book), 192, 213
Spencer, Herbert, 41
Spencer, Stanley, 164, 165, 174
Spenser, Edmund, 185, 242, 261
Spooner, The Rev. Canon W.J., 75
Stalin, Josef, 182, 237, 238
Stanford, Sir Charles Villiers, 36, 55, 61, 81, 184, 286, 321
Steggles, Harry, 162, 163, 164, 165
Stephen, Sir Leslie, 74, 105, 118, 126
Stevenson, R.L., 74, 107, 120, 244
Stewart, Jean (Mrs George Hadley), 255, 256, 271, 273, 277, 284, 285, 287, 290, 294, 324
Stinchcombe Festival, 176
Stoeckel, Carl, 177, 178
Stokowski, Leopold, 297
Strachey, Lytton, 47, 54
Strauss, Richard, 80, 130
Stravinsky, Igor, 10, 122, 136, 137, 158, 227, 237
Streicher, Julius, 222
Streit, Clarence K., 266
Stresemann, Gustav, 217
Sumsion, Herbert, 295, 343
Swaffham Primary School, 365
Synge, J.M., 193

Tallis, Thomas, 24, 41, 50, 112, 116, 131, 137, 141, 183, 234, 249, 358
Tchaikovsky, Pyotr Illyich, 106
Terry, Ellen, 110
Tertis, Lionel, 226, 363, 364

Thackeray, William Makepeace, 20, 59, 290
Thomas, Dylan, 365
Three Choirs Festival, 23, 27, 126, 130, 141, 145, 217, 295, 303, 316–17, 321, 350
Tippett, Michael, 267, 279, 287, 329, 342, 352
Toscanini, Arturo, 256
Tovey, Donald, 254, 259, 264
Trevelyan, George, 47, 48, 49, 50, 51, 59, 66, 67, 68, 214, 333
Trevelyan, Humphry, 333
Trevelyan, Robert, 214, 259, 306, 309
Trinity College, Cambridge, 15, 58, 350
see also University of Cambridge
Trinity College, Dublin, 257

Vaughan-Williams, Adeline, 26, 70–2, 75, 109
courtship, 70, 72–3
death, 109, 313
difficulties in marriage, 98, 127–8
illness, 128, 147–8, 186, 199, 201, 211, 215, 228, 239, 240, 277, 280, 284–5, 288–9, 294, 312
wedding, 75–6
relationship with Ursula Wood, 256, 262–3, 275, 283, 290, 292, 293, 295, 303
Vaughan-Williams, Rev. Arthur, 16
Vaughan-Williams, Constance (Mrs Hervey Vaughan-Williams), 223, 239
Vaughan-Williams, Sir Edward, 16
Vaughan-Williams, Hervey, 19, 21, 24, 28–9, 34, 138
Vaughan-Williams, Lady (Jane Bagot), 79
Vaughan-Williams, Margaret (née Wedgwood), 22, 23, 24
Vaughan-Williams, Margaret (Meggie), 19, 20, 21, 22, 34, 38, 101, 103, 111, 213, 220
Vaughan Williams, Ralph, 238
birth, 15
childhood, 19–24
collaborations with others, 109, 110, 125, 202–3, 228, 258, 261, 322, 329, 365
death, 111, 366, 367–8
and the First World War, 161–9, 174–6, 198, 199, 201
marriage to Adeline Fisher, 75–6
marriage to Ursula Wood, 323–4
and the Second World War, 221, 258–300
at school, 24–8, 28–35

at university, 44, 45–60
see also Adeline Vaughan Williams, Ursula Vaughan Williams, works by RVW
Vaughan-Williams, Sir Roland, 35, 70, 74, 75
Vaughan-Williams, Ursula:
birth, 243
collaborations with RVW, 258, 261, 271, 322, 329
first meeting with RVW, 242, 243, 246–7
as lover of RVW, 249, 250, 251, 252, 254, 256, 263, 266, 275, 276, 280–1, 287, 292–3
marriage to first husband, 245–6
marriage to RVW, 323–4, 325
pregnancy, 269
relationship with Adeline Vaughan Williams, 262–3, 265–6, 273, 275, 280, 283, 287–8, 293, 303
Verdi, Giuseppe, 38, 39, 49, 86, 201
Vocalist, The, 91, 101
Vogue, 72, 147
Vulliamy, Mrs Edward, 185, 186

Wallis, Alfred, 344
Wager, Sarah, 21, 22, 26
Wagner, Richard, 27, 34, 38, 41, 43, 61, 69, 80, 81, 82, 89, 95, 126, 137, 143, 217, 244, 259, 323
Waley, Arthur, 244
Waller, Edmund, 290
Walthew, Richard, 38, 39, 43
Walton, Sir William, 240, 271, 285, 292, 331, 335, 362
Warrack, Guy, 357
Weill, Kurt, 257
Warlock, Peter, 174
Wedgwood, Caroline, 19
Wedgwood, Iris, 294
Wedgwood, Josiah, 17, 18, 19, 150, 282
Wedgwood, Margaret, see Margaret (Meggie) Vaughan Williams
Wedgwood, Sir Ralph (Randolph), 47, 51, 52, 58, 59, 66, 67, 73, 84, 86, 87, 89, 91, 94, 103, 113, 114, 115, 120, 152, 188, 225, 282, 317, 322, 350
Wedgwood, Sophy, 19, 20, 22, 24, 34
Wedgwood, Veronica, 360, 368
Weelkes, Thomas, 225, 332
Whitman, Walt, 107, 118, 119, 143–4, 145, 147, 177, 216, 238, 260, 353
impact on work of RVW, 40, 53
Whitsuntide Singers, 183, 225
Wilde, Oscar, 64
Willcocks, David, 350
Williams, Grace, 172, 227

Williamson, Honorine, see Honorine Brown
Wilson, Sir Steuart, 218, 224, 302, 303, 306, 322, 327, 367
Wolverhampton Music Society, 182
Wood, Charles, 55, 129, 187
Wood, Sir Henry, 106, 116, 253, 277, 295
Wood, Michael, 245, 246, 251
Wood, Ursula, see Ursula Vaughan Williams
Woolf, Virginia, 47, 77, 126, 135, 136, 150, 240, 261
works by RVW, 91, 115, 137
chamber:
Double Trio, 255, 271, 281, 302
Introduction and Fugue for Two Pianos, 289
Phantasy Quintet, 154, 157
Quintet in C minor, 102
Second String Quartet in A minor, 284
Six Studies in English Folk Song, 199, 268
Two Pieces for Violin and Piano, 185
On Wenlock Edge, 124–5, 129, 149, 357
Violin Sonata, 335–6
choral/songs:
Along the Field, 199
Benedictus, 322
Dona Nobis Pacem, 238–9, 253
Eight Traditional English Carols, 172
'England, My England', 267–8
Epithalamion, 242, 256, 258, 261, 271
Fantasia on the Old 104th Psalm, 306
Festival Te Deum in F major, 240
'Five English Folk Songs', 156–7
'Five Mystical Songs', 145, 322
Five Tudor Portraits, 42, 224, 234–7, 255–6, 287, 333
Flourish for a Coronation, 240
'Folk Songs of the Four Seasons', 314
Four Hymns, 214, 295
Four Last Songs, 366
Hodie, 331–2, 342
The House of Life, 107
The Hundredth Psalm, 322
'Linden Lea', 99, 129, 151, 247, 364
Magnificat, 217–18, 295
Mass in G minor, 182–3, 187, 262, 307

Old Hundredth, 330
'An Oxford Elegy', 306, 322
Prayer to the Father of
  Heaven, 42
Sancta Civitas, 187, 193,
  197–9, 224, 234, 295, 306,
  318
Serenade to Music, 253
Silence and Music, 329
'A Song for Thanksgiving',
  285, 322
Songs of Travel, 107–9
'Rest', 100
Sons of Light, 312, 322, 365
'Sound Sleep', 102
Three Shakespeare Songs, 315
Ten Blake Songs, 359
Toward the Unknown
  Region, 118–20, 125, 142,
  144, 214, 312–13, 333
Valiant for Truth, 274–5
A Vision of Aeroplanes,
  349–50
The Voice out of the
  Whirlwind, 295
Willow Wood, 72–3, 102
'Words and Silence', 329
concerto:
  Concerto in F minor for Bass
    Tuba and Orchestra, 334
  Concerto in A minor for
    Oboe and Strings, 271,
    283–4, 285, 333
  Flos Campi, 189–91, 193, 294,
    322, 364
  The Lark Ascending, 112,
    172–3, 335, 350
  Piano Concerto in C major,
    217, 218–21
  Romance in D flat, 319
  Suite for Viola and Small
    Orchestra, 226
film:
  49th Parallel, 270, 284
  Coastal Command, 270
  The Dim Little Island, 306
  The England of Elizabeth, 347
  The Loves of Joanna Godden,
    289, 291–2, 315
  The People's Land, 270
  Scott of the Antarctic, 292,

303, 307, 325
  Story of a Flemish Farm, 287
hymnody:
  'Abinger', 213
  'Down Ampney', 115, 367
  'White Gates', 213
opera and other stage works,
  138–41
  Aristophanes's *The Wasps*,
    51, 125, 129–30, 186
  The Bridal Day (formerly
    Epithalamion), 330–1, 342
  The First Nowell, 366
  Hugh the Drover, 89, 112, 115,
    130, 149, 180, 187–9, 191,
    195, 256, 329
  Job, A Masque for Dancing,
    111, 206, 207–9, 210, 226–7,
    246, 256, 295, 302, 303, 357,
    360, 367
  The Merry Wives of Windsor,
    151, 201
  Old King Cole, 185–6
  The Pilgrim's Progress, 115,
    179, 302–3, 308, 309,
    310–12, 332–3
  The Poisoned Kiss, 202–3,
    206, 295, 355
  The Rape of Lucretia, 26
  Riders to the Sea, 193–4, 201,
    307, 329, 334, 338
  *The Shepherds of the
    Delectable Mountains*, 117,
    179, 192, 293
  Sir John in Love, 201–2, 305,
    318, 334
  Solemn Music for the Masque
    of *Charterhouse*, 223
  Thomas the Rhymer, 366
symphony:
  Symphony No. 1 ('Sea
    Symphony'), 103, 106, 112,
    115, 116, 120, 131, 142,
    143–5, 156, 171–2, 191,
    226, 355
  Symphony No. 2 ('London'),
    112, 148–9, 154–5, 157, 161,
    167, 250, 290–1, 304–5, 312,
    331, 338
  Symphony No. 3 ('Pastoral'),
    112, 174–6, 177–8, 178–9,

191, 192, 223, 285, 327, 357
Symphony No. 4, 210, 212,
  215, 222, 227–30, 233, 234,
  335, 346
Symphony No. 5, 252, 270–1,
  277–9, 281, 284, 287, 295,
  299, 318, 320–1, 322
Symphony No. 6, 270, 285,
  288, 289, 295–300, 301,
  302, 305
Symphony No. 7 (*Sinfonia
  Antartica*), 26, 319, 322,
  323, 325–8, 356
Symphony No. 8, 341, 347–9
Symphony No. 9, 103, 259,
  361–3
orchestra:
  Bucolic Suite, 96, 97
  Concerto Grosso for Strings,
    308
  English Folk Songs Suite, 185
  Fantasia on a Theme by
    Thomas Tallis, 112, 116,
    130–1, 137, 141, 183, 234,
    249, 337
  Five Variants of Dives and
    Lazarus, 258, 306, 367
  Flourish for Glorious John,
    358
  Heroic Elegy and Triumphal
    Epilogue, 97–9
  Norfolk Rhapsody Nos 1–3,
    116–17
  Partita for Double String
    Orchestra, 302
  Prelude on Three Welsh
    Hymn Tunes, 341–2
  Serenade in A minor, 96
  Serenade for Strings, 345
  'Solent', 103
  Symphonic Rhapsody, 105
  Variations, 358
Wright, Joseph (of Derby), 18
Wurm, Stanislas, 163
Wyndham Lewis, 177

Yale University, 177
Yeats, W.B., 72, 193, 217, 348
Yorkshire Post, The, 120
Young, Dr Percy, 207, 236